HIGHER EDUCATION'S RESPONSE TO THE COVID-19 PANDEMIC

Building a more sustainable and democratic future

Sjur Bergan, Tony Gallagher,
Ira Harkavy, Ronaldo Munck
and Hilligje van't Land (eds)

Council of Europe
Higher Education
Series No. 25

Council of Europe

The opinions expressed in this work are the responsibility of the authors and do not necessarily reflect the official policy of the Council of Europe.

All rights reserved. No part of this publication may be translated, reproduced or transmitted, in any form or by any means, electronic (CD-Rom, internet, etc.) or mechanical, including photocopying, recording or any information storage or retrieval system, without prior permission in writing from the Directorate of Communications (F-67075 Strasbourg Cedex or publishing@coe.int).

Cover design: Documents and Publications Production Department, Council of Europe
Cover photos: Shutterstock
Layout: Jouve, Paris

Council of Europe Publishing
F-67075 Strasbourg Cedex
http://book.coe.int

ISBN 978-92-871-8697-3
© Council of Europe, February 2021
Printed at the Council of Europe

Contents

PREFACE — 5

A WORD FROM THE EDITORS AND A CALL TO ACTION — 7
Sjur Bergan, Tony Gallagher, Ira Harkavy, Ronaldo Munck and Hilligje van't Land

PART I – CONTEXT — 19

Chapter 1 – Universities must help shape the post-Covid-19 world — 21
Ira Harkavy, Sjur Bergan, Tony Gallagher and Hilligje van't Land

Chapter 2 – Higher education, civic engagement, Covid-19 and the "new normal" — 31
Ronaldo Munck

Chapter 3 – The pre-Covid-19 world: race and inequity in higher education — 41
Henry Louis Taylor, Jr

PART II – CHALLENGES AND RESPONSES — 51

Chapter 4 – Some challenges facing higher education in Europe in view of the Covid-19 pandemic — 53
Ellen Hazelkorn

Chapter 5 – Challenges to US higher education in performing local missions during and after the Covid-19 pandemic — 67
David Maurrasse

Chapter 6 – Public responsibility for higher education in the time of Covid-19 — 79
Sjur Bergan

Chapter 7 – Past, present, future: re-thinking the social responsibility of US higher education in light of Covid-19 and Black Lives Matter — 87
Ira Harkavy and Rita A. Hodges

Chapter 8 – Beyond a "new normal": Covid-19, Black Lives Matter and the remaking of higher education — 97
Peter Englot and Nancy Cantor

Chapter 9 – University challenge – The role of research-intensive universities in crisis management — 107
Åse Gornitzka and Svein Stølen

Chapter 10 – Maireann na daoine ar scath a chéile: Dublin City University, Covid-19 and the creation of the "next normal" — 115
Daire Keogh

Chapter 11 – Public work and reclaiming the democratic impulse of higher education in these pandemic times — 121
Paul C. Pribbenow

Chapter 12 – Higher education should embrace this liminal moment because there will be no "new normal" — 129
James T. Harris and Nicholas R. Santilli

Chapter 13 – Covid-19 and "the crises in higher education" — 137
Liviu Matei

Chapter 14 – Resilience and resistance: the community college in a pandemic — 147
Brian Murphy

Chapter 15 – The University of Bologna during the Covid-19 pandemic: protect, provide and innovate – Responses from a resilient community   155
Elena Luppi, Elena Consolini, Alessandra Scagliarini, Mirko Degli Esposti and Francesco Ubertini

Chapter 16 – Re-thinking African higher education in the post-Covid-19 era   165
Barnabas Nawangwe

Chapter 17 – Leveraging the Covid-19 crisis to advance global sustainable universities: re-creation of valuable higher education   173
Kiyoshi Yamada and Koji Nakamura

Chapter 18 – Leadership and opportunities for sustainable higher education vis-à-vis the pandemic   181
Santiago Acosta

Chapter 19 – American higher education: rescuing democracy's purpose and policies   189
Martha J. Kanter and Carol Geary Schneider

Chapter 20 – Romanian higher education facing Covid-19: new challenges for the university–state partnership   203
Ligia Deca, Delia Gologan and Robert Santa

PART III – A DEMOCRATIC, SUSTAINABLE UNIVERSITY   213

Chapter 21 – Academic freedom and institutional autonomy: victims of the Covid-19 pandemic?   215
Sjur Bergan

Chapter 22 – The impact of Covid-19 on internationalisation and student mobility: an opportunity for innovation and inclusion?   225
Dorothy Kelly

Chapter 23 – Internationalisation of higher education in a post-Covid-19 world: overcoming challenges and maximising opportunities   233
Hans de Wit and Giorgio Marinoni

Chapter 24 – Recognition of foreign qualifications in the time of Covid-19   241
Stig Arne Skjerven

Chapter 25 – From fire-fighting to re-thinking external quality assurance: European quality assurance agencies' response to the challenges of the Covid-19 pandemic   249
Maria Kelo

Chapter 26 – Sustainable financing of higher education after the pandemic   257
Jamil Salmi

Chapter 27 – The challenges of the Covid-19 pandemic for higher education legislation in Europe   265
Dennis Farrington

Chapter 28 – The challenges of the Covid-19 crisis for students   275
Robert Napier

Chapter 29 – Addressing the challenges of the Covid-19 pandemic: a view from higher education staff   281
Rob Copeland

Chapter 30 – Universities as catalysts of post-Covid recovery and renewal in communities   293
John Gardner

Chapter 31 – The local university mission after Covid-19: two Irish case studies   303
Tony Gallagher and Ronaldo Munck

BIOGRAPHICAL NOTES   311

Preface

The Covid-19 pandemic affects all Council of Europe member states, most other countries in the world and all sectors of society. Public health is of immediate concern, but our education response is no less vital. I am therefore pleased that our Education sector responded very quickly and convincingly, with a first extraordinary online meeting of the Steering Committee for Education Policy and Practice (CDPPE) on 24 April and a second on 11-12 June 2020. The education response to Covid-19 will also be at the centre of the informal conference of Ministers of Education organised under the Greek Presidency of the Council of Europe's Committee of Ministers on 28-29 October 2020. At the time of writing, we hope this conference can be held in Athens, but we are prepared to move it online. This dilemma illustrates the much greater uncertainty with which the world of education has had to live since March 2020.

This book on the higher education response to the Covid-19 pandemic is particularly timely, given the high proportion of international students and staff in higher education. We do not yet know when and to what extent face-to-face teaching and international exchanges can resume.

We need to do everything in our power to ensure that the current health crisis does not turn into a deeper crisis of democracy, in spite of the warning signs we see in several countries. This book provides a broad overview of the higher education response to Covid-19, with an emphasis on higher education's democratic mission. We can effectively confront neither the medical nor the societal challenges of the pandemic without the commitment and contribution of higher education.

It is therefore appropriate that the book grows out of the Council of Europe's long-standing work on the democratic mission of higher education, in close co-operation with our US colleagues in the International Consortium for Higher Education, Civic Responsibility and Democracy, and more recently also with the International Association of Universities and other partners. All five editors have been engaged in this work for many years. I would like to thank them, as well as all the contributors who responded enthusiastically in spite of the short deadline they were given at a particularly busy time of the year. Not least, I would like to thank our editorial assistant, Irina Geantă, for pulling all the threads together.

This book represents a milestone: it is the 25th volume published in the Council of Europe's Higher Education Series, which was launched in December 2004. That this milestone volume focuses on the worst peacetime health crisis we have faced for a century, and that it also addresses a crisis of democracy, is of course a sad reflection of the current state of Europe and the world. It is, however, also a testimony to the ability of our Education Department and our Higher Education Series to react rapidly to societal developments and to do so on the basis of the Council of Europe's main values: democracy, human rights and the rule of law.

I hope this book will provide interesting reading and that it will also stimulate debate and action.

Snežana Samardžić-Marković
Director General for Democracy
Council of Europe

A word from the editors and a call to action

*Sjur Bergan, Tony Gallagher, Ira Harkavy,
Ronaldo Munck and Hilligje van't Land*

CONTEXT

The Covid-19 pandemic that started developing in China in autumn 2019 and rapidly spread to other parts of Asia, then to Europe and then to almost all countries of the world, is likely to be seen as a watershed in many different ways. Barely anyone alive in 2020 had been faced with a similar generalised health emergency in peacetime, even if many in Africa, Asia and elsewhere have had to face more localised epidemics. During the century that separates the Covid-19 pandemic from the disease commonly referred to as the Spanish flu, the world has changed profoundly. One of the ways in which it has changed is in improving cultural sensitivity and in being less prompt – at least in official terms[1] – to assign responsibility for pandemics to individual countries. The Spanish flu did not originate in Spain, nor was Spain particularly important to its propagation, but the name stuck.

Another important development over the past century is the vastly increased interconnectivity of almost all parts of the world. In the case of Covid-19, this meant the pandemic spread rapidly – indeed, it evolved from an epidemic to a pandemic[2] – and public authorities and societies everywhere had little time to prepare for an emergency of unprecedented scope.

Higher education had to react rapidly and take daunting decisions on how to reorganise teaching and learning, as well as research and other activities. In doing so, institutions needed to take account of the health and safety of students and staff as well as of the framework established by public authorities for addressing the sudden health crisis. While health was the immediate concern, institutions also needed to consider how they could best enable students to continue their studies and take their exams. If teaching and exams were to be suspended, postponed or cancelled, students would lose important time and substantial investment, and many might not have been able to return to higher education after a hiatus. The well-being and prospects of countless individuals as well as of entire societies therefore depended partly on how well and how rapidly the academic community and its leaders responded to the Covid-19 crisis.

---

1. The Trump Administration did seek to link the Covid-19 pandemic to China by fairly consistently referring to it as the "Chinese virus" (Viala-Gaudefroy and Lindaman 2020).
2. The World Health Organization defines a pandemic as a "worldwide spread of a new disease"; see www.who.int/csr/disease/swineflu/frequently_asked_questions/pandemic/en/, accessed 27 July 2020.

Like most sectors of society, the primary response of higher education focused on the immediate challenges posed by this unprecedented situation and this is reflected well in the contributions to this volume, as outlined below. In particular, the Covid-19 crisis has highlighted, even exacerbated, the persistent underlying inequities that have limited – for too many people, for too long – the opportunities to benefit from and experience higher education. As many contributions also indicate, this has served as a "wake-up call" warning that these inequities can no longer be addressed partly, or fitfully, but that a longer-term, strategic approach is needed. In this volume we contend that the roots of that response can be found in a growing movement aimed at enhancing the democratic mission of higher education and the building of sustainable democratic societies.

LEARNING FROM OUR RESPONSES

Even if the Covid-19 pandemic was in many ways unique, history has no shortage of examples of epidemics, pandemics and other emergencies. It would also be unwise to assume that the Covid-19 pandemic will be the last emergency of its kind and that there will be no need for future generations – or our own – to learn the lessons of spring and summer 2020, and beyond.[3]

Academics are used to analysing and reflecting on their own experience and that of others, so the thought of gathering essays from across the world of higher education came naturally to us. The response from potential authors was overwhelming, even if authors were contacted at a time of year when academics are busy with exams and other end-of-year activities and the deadline given was exceedingly short. The response was all the more overwhelming as no end-of-year activities were in a state we could call "normal" in June and July 2020. Rather than a normal, if busy, routine, higher education institutions, students, staff and public authorities had to re-think and reorganise teaching, learning, research and exams. They had to do so convincingly enough for the qualifications earned during the academic year 2019/20 to be considered as on par with those earned in any other year, and fast enough not to affect preparations for the next academic year – admission to study programmes and progression within them – or graduates' employment possibilities in a terribly bleak job market. This had to be done without knowing what the academic year 2020/21 would be like, how much teaching and learning could be done face to face (almost certainly not as much as most would have wanted) and how much would be conducted online (very likely considerably more than most would have foreseen even in mid-spring).

The eagerness of potential authors to contribute and their unfailing capacity to submit their contributions within the deadline given – or almost – testify to the need that most members of the academic community feel to draw lessons from the Covid-19 pandemic, to be better prepared for the next disaster, and to bear witness to the extraordinary efforts of faculty, staff and students.

---

3. A northern hemisphere bias: in March 2020 the southern hemisphere lessons are those of autumn and winter. Likewise, the reference to academic years, for example 2020/21, is that of the northern hemisphere.

The result of this reflection – which is for the most part a reflection on action – is the book you are about to read. It is of necessity incomplete. First of all, even if the book includes at least one chapter from every continent, most of its authors are based in, and write against the background of the experience in, Europe and North America. Within these two continents, the collective experience is highly diverse, but it does not claim to present anything like an overview of the Covid-19 response on a global scale.

Secondly, the topic of the book is something of a moving target. At the time of writing – mid-to late July 2020 – no continent has yet seen the end of the Covid-19 pandemic and some continents, Europe included, may well be heading for a second wave. The United States and Latin America are still grappling with the first Covid-19 wave, with no end in sight. We cannot know what the situation will be by the time the book is published or what will happen between now and then, but we do know that reality has a habit of upending predictions. Three months before the authors sat down to write, most of us had still not understood how serious the Covid-19 pandemic was or would be. Three or six months from the time of writing, the situation is likely to be different from our current predictions, to the extent we venture to make any.

Thirdly, most contributions address teaching and learning more than research and community outreach. All are integral parts of the mission of higher education, and the fight against the virus cannot succeed without a concerted research effort. The search for a vaccine (or treatment) aside, however, the task of organising teaching and learning seemed to most higher education decision makers the more urgent concern, the one for which firm deadlines had to be met, and this is reflected in the contributions.

DEMOCRACY IN THE TIME OF THE PANDEMIC

In spite of these uncertainties, there are things we definitely do know. We do know that pandemics can turn our world and our values upside down, revealing at times deep structural problems. We do not know how our societies will change, but we do know that we will need to work hard to make and keep our societies ones in which we would like to live. We do know that some governments have seen an opportunity to use the emergency for a broader attack on democracy, human rights and the rule of law, and we do know that some members of society are happy – or at least indifferent – to allow this to happen. And we do know that it is one of the missions of higher education to prevent this from happening and, phrased more positively, to help build and maintain the culture of democracy, without which democratic institutions, laws and elections will not function in practice. Furthermore, these institutions, laws and elections need to be strong enough to build the resilience of societies in face of the strong arms of autocrats, real or would-be. Gabriel García Márquez wrote about love in the time of cholera; we write about democracy in the time of Covid-19.

We do so on the basis of experience gathered over two decades of transatlantic co-operation in building the democratic mission of higher education (see Harkavy et al., Chapter 1 in this volume). From an initial bilateral co-operation between the Council of Europe[4] and the International Consortium for Higher Education, Civic Responsibility and Democracy,[5] the co-operation has expanded to include other partners, most notably the International Association of Universities[6] and the Organization of American States.[7] Individual institutions such as Queen's University Belfast[8] and Dublin City University[9] also play key roles.

It was this long-standing co-operation and the many academics involved in it that enabled us to identify authors quickly and, we believe, helped elicit quick and positive responses. This is not unimportant to the Covid-19 pandemic and its aftermath. The response to the crisis and its aftermath will be stronger if it can build on reflection undertaken before disaster hits. Successful improvisation requires careful preparation. That is not to say that the post-Covid-19 world, or the role of higher education in it, will copy the world we knew until spring 2020. However, it does mean that the values and principles on which we will build the post-Covid-19 world must reflect values and principles developed before the pandemic struck – values and principles developed, argued and embodied by the organisations and institutions we represent and that the many contributors to this volume represent.

OUTLINE OF THE BOOK

This book gives voice to leaders of higher education and public authorities, to students and staff, to those with responsibility for broad areas of higher education policy and practice and to those responsible for specific fields, such as legislation, internationalisation or the recognition of qualifications.

Part I – Context

We open with a number of chapters that set the overall context of the book in terms of the impact of the Covid-19 pandemic on the world of higher education and the urgent issues now emerging.

In Chapter 1 "Universities must help shape the post-Covid-19 world" Ira Harkavy, Sjur Bergan, Tony Gallagher and Hilligje van't Land set out the challenges posed as many of our accepted understandings are shaken by the crisis and its aftermath. Higher education has played an exemplary role in terms of mobilising its resources to meet the societal challenge faced. It now needs to reaffirm its commitment to the broad values of democracy, human rights and the rule of law to guide us in

---

4. For the Council of Europe's Education programme, see www.coe.int/en/web/education; for higher education specifically, see www.coe.int/en/web/higher-education-and-research/home, both accessed 27 July 2020.
5. See www.internationalconsortium.org/, accessed 27 July 2020.
6. See www.iau-aiu.net/, accessed 27 July 2020.
7. See www.oas.org/en/, accessed 7 August 2020.
8. See www.qub.ac.uk/, accessed 27 July 2020.
9. See www.dcu.ie/, accessed 27 July 2020.

the period to come. While powerful forces may seek to roll back the gains in these areas, higher education needs to be at the forefront of efforts that pledge their commitment to the public good.

Ronaldo Munck in Chapter 2 addresses the theme of "Higher education, civic engagement, Covid-19 and the 'new normal'", setting the challenges facing higher education in their broader context of global governance, and questions whether we can actually return to normal. As with other disasters Covid-19 may generate a strong social countermovement based on solidarity and common purpose. Out of the chaos caused by Covid-19 we may yet see a powerful revival of social engagement in our universities as they address the needs of their communities in partnership. Covid-19 has exposed and exacerbated stark divides in individual countries and globally: it is urgent that universities address these as part of their social responsibility.

In Chapter 3 Henry Louis Taylor, Jr turns to one of those stark divides in "The pre-Covid-19 world: race and inequity in higher education", which explains the background to the Black Lives Matter (BLM) movement in the United States and the impact it has had in higher education. US universities have often had a fraught relationship with the African American communities they are situated within. Community engagement needs to address these issues in an open way. The conversations now under way as a result of the BLM movement are posing the need for radical change, the reimagining of institutions, including higher education, and, above all, the centring of anti racism as a prerequisite for the achievement of democracy.

Part II – Challenges and responses

In the second section of the book we have a wide range of contributors, many of them leaders of higher education institutions, addressing the major challenges and responses that have emerged from the Covid-19 crisis.

Ellen Hazelkorn opens in Chapter 4 with a review of "Some challenges facing higher education in Europe in view of the Covid-19 pandemic", set in the context of the growing interconnectedness of the world even before the pandemic. The immediate response of the higher education institutions and staff has been nothing short of heroic but now questions are emerging as to the aftermath. Will this degree of commitment and sacrifice be taken as the new norm? Will higher education prioritise the newfound mood of co-operation, for example in the health research area, or will there be a brutal "survival of the fittest" ethos that sees many colleges fall by the wayside? Many of our contributors will also seek to answer these questions.

In Chapter 5 David Maurrasse addresses the "Challenges to US higher education in performing local missions during and after the Covid-19 pandemic" and stresses the variable impact on university relationships with the community. The challenge of Covid-19 has been to advance these local missions even further to address the conjoint health/economic crisis that many countries face. The inequities of "race" and ethnicity have been exacerbated as existing vulnerabilities deepen but so also has the societal rejection of these deep divides been intensified. While many higher education institutions themselves face a looming financial crisis, they are being called on to do more for and with their communities.

Sjur Bergan turns in Chapter 6 to the vital question of "Public responsibility for higher education in the time of Covid-19", which becomes ever-more important as the fragility of the social order and of higher education is exposed, even as its institutions are called on in terms of public responsibility. We have seen many states openly taking responsibility for the health crisis as adequate health care for all became a societal need. Public responsibility for higher education as we move beyond the immediate Covid crisis will become an immediate issue and it cannot be evaded. The weaknesses of both the health and education systems have been cruelly exposed and a strong public effort to redress these will be called for.

In Chapter 7 Ira Harkavy and Rita A. Hodges address "Past, present, future: re-thinking the social responsibility of US higher education in light of Covid-19 and Black Lives Matter". The founding purpose of most colleges and universities in the United States included a strong emphasis on social responsibility and yet that mission is still not realised. The Covid-19 pandemic and the murder of George Floyd have exposed persistent deprivation, poverty and racism across society. There is now a huge challenge for higher education to address its public responsibility in regard to such afflictions. This is a moral question as much as anything and demands us to ask bluntly: what does higher education contribute to the public good?

In Chapter 8, called "Beyond a 'new normal': Covid-19, Black Lives Matter and the remaking of higher education", Peter Englot and Nancy Cantor show the deadly convergence of the Covid-19 pandemic and systemic racism in the US and its impact on higher education. This is seen as a moment of truth when the raw power of facts speaks powerfully. A "new normal" that does not address these issues will be inadequate if higher education is to fulfil its social responsibility. What is needed now is not just well-intentioned statements but a genuine process of institutional transformation that can advance equity, both within higher education and in society at large.

Åse Gornitzka and Svein Stølen speak in Chapter 9 to "University challenge – the role of research-intensive universities in crisis management". Suddenly society, the media and the political order are interested in research, data and analysis as all grapple to understand and deal with the many facets of the Covid-19 crisis. In an extremely pressured situation, higher education institutions have been coupled to government's crisis-management efforts. Based on the experience of Norway, the authors offer general thoughts on the future of the research-intensive university in the light of these dramatic months in the first half of 2020. In particular, this chapter helps us think through the intimate, but sometimes conflictual relationships between knowledge and democracy.

In Chapter 10 Daire Keogh addresses the theme of *"Maireann na daoine ar scath a chéile* [people live in one another's shadow]: Dublin City University, Covid-19 and the creation of the 'next normal'" in a chapter that looks at how one public university in Ireland addressed the crisis while in a period of presidential transition. The crisis exposed stark divisions in Irish society but also brought to the fore great reserves of communal spirit and innovation. A broad commitment to the UN Sustainable Development Goals was matched by a strong commitment to social transformation in Ireland itself. Harnessing the knowledge and commitment of the university will be key in the period ahead as we move towards the "next normal".

In Chapter 11 on "Public work and reclaiming the democratic impulse of higher education in these pandemic times", Paul C. Pribbenow addresses the way one smaller private US higher education institution has addressed the triple crisis of Covid-19, the economic crisis and the crisis of racism. The health of the university depends on the health of its very diverse community. Each university acts in terms of its own path dependence, its history and its traditions but there is always a choice. There is now an urgent need to pivot the university to deal with the social impact of this triple crisis and to generate a powerful response based on its democratic commitments.

James T. Harris and Nicholas R. Santilli, in Chapter 12, turn our attention to how "Higher education should embrace this liminal moment because there will be no 'new normal'", based on the US experience. Given the prognosis for the virus, coupled with the political instability and contestation in the US, there will be no return to "normal" any time soon. Nor can higher education institutions committed to democratic values accept the status quo as normal in any way. The damage being done to democracy is deep and long-lasting. Higher education needs to lead in charting a new path forward that will lead to a more democratic and just society.

In Chapter 13 Liviu Matei addresses the question of "Covid-19 and 'the crises in higher education'" from a broad European perspective that sets up a reference framework to understand the current crisis in higher education. While its impact is not clear, as yet, we do know it is severe and that universities, along with other public institutions, are struggling to cope with the complex impacts of the crisis. It is important to bear in mind that the crisis is both external to the university – the public health emergency – but also internal insofar as many weaknesses have been exposed. It is also necessary to examine whether the crisis can also be an opportunity for decisive transformation.

Brian Murphy in Chapter 14 turns to "Resilience and resistance: the community college in a pandemic" from a US perspective. The public community colleges suffered the same fate of closures and the emergency shift to online teaching as their university neighbours. But they did so with far fewer resources to fall back on and with a student population that was already struggling to make ends meet. It is thus important to highlight the diversity of the higher education sector. We also learn, though, that in this community sector there was a great deal of resilience and the sector dealt with the pandemic in a collegial and civically engaged manner. We are, finally, driven to foreground the issue of equity both within the colleges themselves and in their immediate surrounds.

In Chapter 15, Elena Luppi, Elena Consolini, Alessandra Scagliarini, Mirko Degli Esposti and Francesco Ubertini discuss "The University of Bologna during the Covid-19 pandemic: protect, provide and innovate – responses from a resilient community". The university was mobilised across the research and online learning fronts as it sought to respond to the pandemic. In terms of its "third mission", cultural and communication initiatives have been developed for the university community and for citizens more widely. What was an undoubted period of challenge also allowed for self-assessment and reflection as the university prepared itself for a new period of innovation as its future mission was being rethought.

In Chapter 16, Barnabas Nawangwe engages in "Re-thinking African higher education in the post-Covid 19 era", showing the way the pandemic has left the continent exposed and its higher education systems facing grave challenges. Both public and private universities face a sharp decline in student fees that they depend on to survive. Nevertheless, African universities have shown a huge ability to innovate in facing the challenges posed by Covid-19, not least in moving education provision online and in the promotion of blended learning. The digital divide in society is, of course, outside the universities' control and will pose a large challenge in terms of social inclusion in the period ahead. Despite the serious dent to economic growth, the universities are well situated to contribute to human development in the future.

Kiyoshi Yamada and Koji Nakamura in Chapter 17 address the issue of "Leveraging the Covid-19 crisis to advance global sustainable universities: re-creation of valuable higher education", based on the case of Japan. There is a sense that there will be no going back to the past after the pandemic. Instead there is a growing commitment to push forward in a positive spirit in pursuit of the realisation of the sustainable university. The "new normal" will involve, as elsewhere, the digital transformation of the university in Japan, and also "learning security" as the means to maintain the quality of education for students.

In Chapter 18, Santiago Acosta directs us to the topic of "Leadership and opportunities for sustainable higher education vis-à-vis the pandemic" based on the experience of Ecuador, and Latin America more generally. In the midst of an unprecedented public health crisis, the weaknesses of the higher education system have come to light, including the poor image people have of online learning, which has simply tended to reproduce the old classroom methodology. The system itself, particularly the public sector, suffers from severe disjuncture. However, there are now new opportunities opening up through, for example, the increased prestige of research and the possibility of revalidating the role of the university in public opinion.

Martha Kanter and Carol Geary Schneider in Chapter 19 turn our attention to "American higher education: rescuing democracy's purpose and policies". They start from the premise that democracy is under siege everywhere and that higher education needs to rise to the challenge to ensure the vitality and integrity of democracy in the period ahead. In the US this means, above all, closing the historic race, class and income divides that cut across society. Higher education has its role to play to build a society where all are respected and have equal access to social and political power. This strategy will, of necessity, be co-created with our graduates and citizens.

Ligia Deca, Delia Gologan and Robert Santa in Chapter 20 address the issue of "Romanian higher education facing Covid-19: new challenges for the university–state partnership". Despite the many challenges that universities face, not least in terms of funding and autonomy, they have played an active role alongside the public authorities in dealing with the Covid-19 crisis. The state–university relationship will be a crucial one in the post-pandemic situation and the university will need to foreground its pivotal role in safeguarding democratic society. Universities showed themselves capable of quickly pivoting to the needs imposed by the public health crisis. They might now need to redefine the balance between institutional autonomy and public responsibility.

Part III – A democratic, sustainable university

In our final section, various contributors explore the view of key stakeholders such as staff and students, the pressing issue of internationalisation and the ever-present need to address the local mission of higher education. It closes with a reflection on the importance of a democratic university post-Covid-19.

Sjur Bergan examines in Chapter 21 how two fundamental values of higher education – "Academic freedom and institutional autonomy" – may be affected by the Covid-19 crisis. This can happen through political attacks by governments eager to take advantage of the crisis to reduce the scope for critical analysis and as a consequence of the broad emergency measures taken to deal with the immediate health crisis. This pressure may result in a broad reorientation of research as well as teaching and learning in the wake of the crisis. To determine the extent to which academic freedom and institutional autonomy are affected, we need to establish not only whether higher education has suffered restrictions during the crisis – it clearly has – but whether the restrictions are unreasonable or disproportionate.

In Chapter 22, Dorothy Kelly puts forward some reflections on "The impact of Covid-19 on internationalisation and student mobility: an opportunity for innovation and inclusion?" The Covid-19 pandemic has reminded us how interconnected the world is and the pressing need for more robust global governance mechanisms to address such crises. In a context where xenophobia will inevitably increase, Kelly argues that it befits us as educators of engaged critical citizens to continually address internationalisation in an open spirit and to find new ways to enhance international student mobility.

Hans de Wit and Giorgio Marinoni in Chapter 23 also address the question of "Internationalisation of higher education in a post-Covid-19 world: overcoming challenges and maximising opportunities". They also show how there has been an enormous disruption of higher education as a result of the Covid-19 pandemic that is particularly acute in the area of internationalisation. They address its impact in terms of student and staff mobility, international research practices and the impact of internationalisation on the local mission of the university. The authors point to the different ways we can overcome the challenges posed.

Also addressing international issues, Stig Arne Skjerven turns in Chapter 24 to the "Recognition of foreign qualifications in the time of Covid-19". The Covid-19 disruption to what we have taken to be normal academic mobility, in Europe and beyond, will create a challenge in the area of how foreign qualifications will be recognised. Recognition is a powerful tool to enhance mobility for the purpose of study, research and teaching. The chapter discusses whether recognition will now be challenged in its dual role of "door opener" (to enhanced mobility) and "gate keeper" (to maintain trust in the receiving country).

Maria Kelo takes us in Chapter 25 into the issue of quality assurance in a European context in "From fire-fighting to re-thinking external quality assurance: European quality assurance agencies' response to the challenges of the Covid-19 pandemic" by explaining the role of the European Association for Quality Assurance in Higher Education (ENQA), which represents over 50 quality assurance agencies across the European Higher Education Area (EHEA). These are designed to provide a common basis to build trust in the higher education system while being sufficiently flexible to accommodate different modalities. The Covid-19 crisis led to across-the-board closure of higher education institutions' on-site activities and thus posed serious issues for the accreditation process.

In Chapter 26 we turn to another crucial practical issue, with Jamil Salmi addressing the challenges to "Sustainable financing of higher education after the pandemic". Before the Covid-19 crisis, higher education did not, on the whole, have a sustainable financial strategy. That problem has now, for obvious reasons, been greatly exacerbated as a global health crisis turns into a global economic crisis. There are still some systems that are relatively well funded through a combination of public resources and substantial student fees. Both these contributions will now be threatened by the looming financial crisis and we can only expect more difficulties as we move out of the immediate Covid-19 crisis.

In Chapter 27, Dennis Farrington addresses the specific issue of "The challenges of the Covid-19 pandemic for higher education legislation in Europe". It was through public health legislation that most governments closed down many universities across the world. Likewise, it was through institutional autonomy enshrined in legislation that most universities were able to very quickly shift most of their educational effort online. The question that now arises and that we need to address is how higher education can continue to innovate and plan for future pandemics and what this might entail in terms of changes in higher education legislation.

We turn next to the views of university students and staff and how the Covid-19 crisis has affected them. In Chapter 28, Robert Napier addresses "The challenges of the Covid-19 crisis for students". Reduced student mobility, the issues related to the emergency turn to online learning, the mental health impact of the pandemic and reduced economic circumstances have affected students everywhere. The impact of the digital divide in society is now being felt acutely, as some students are able to cope with the new normal but others are not, due to economic circumstances. The strain of a return to campus will be felt acutely by students. International students are a particular concern. The democratic future of higher education depends on how we address these issues.

In Chapter 29, Rob Copeland turns our attention to "Addressing the challenges of the Covid-19 pandemic: a view from higher education staff". The Covid-19 crisis has had a huge impact on those who work in our universities; they have responded in a resilient way and implemented the shift to online delivery of teaching. But now they ask if public responsibility for higher education will continue and even be enhanced, as it necessarily must. After the emergency response to the pandemic, many staff wonder whether academic freedom will continue. Democracy and sustainability in higher education as we move beyond the immediate emergency will require the engagement of staff and their organisations.

John Gardner, in Chapter 30, shows how we might consider "Universities as catalysts of post-Covid recovery and renewal in communities". Universities globally will continue to be centres of excellence in terms of research, education and innovation and we can, indeed, expect their reputations to be enhanced by their dynamic role during the pandemic in so many ways. But we should be asking more from our universities, not least that they become even more embedded in their local communities that have suffered so much from the health and now economic crises. Above all, we should not allow arguments of financial stringency to provide cover for a retreat from the social responsibility role that the university carries.

Finally, in Chapter 31 Tony Gallagher and Ronaldo Munck turn back to an underlying theme of the whole volume, namely "The local university mission after Covid-19", with a case study of two Irish universities on different sides of the contested Irish border. Buffeted by the Brexit crisis, particularly in Northern Ireland, the whole island was then subject to the Covid-19 crisis. Our case studies show that universities can enhance their local mission in this context and can do it in a collaborative manner that cuts across political divisions and enhances social progress. The local mission of the university will be crucial to building a post-Covid democratic and sustainable future.

CONCLUSION

The book you are about to read looks at our immediate past and our present, but it does so with an eye on our future. It is our hope, as editors, that the book will inspire both action and debate. We hope it will help make the history of higher education in the Covid-19 pandemic one of lessons learned rather than lessons forgotten. We hope it will help convince both the higher education community itself and society at large that no crisis response in modern, complex societies can succeed unless it builds on the results of research and the competence of higher education graduates in a very broad range of academic disciplines. We hope it will demonstrate that academic competence and commitment to the public good must come together to build a future that will be marked by the experience of the Covid-19 pandemic but that will also surpass this experience – a future in which reflection and action reinforce rather than separate each other and contribute to a more sustainable and democratic future.

We would like to thank all those who responded enthusiastically and efficiently to our invitation to contribute to this exercise in learning and reflection. Above all, we would like to place on record our profound appreciation of the work of the person who combined reflection and action in practice and made both fit within the cover of this book: our editorial assistant Irina Geantă.

REFERENCES

Harkavy I., Bergan S., Gallagher T. and van't Land H. (2020), "Universities must help shape the post-Covid-19 world", Chapter 1 in this volume.

Viala-Gaudefroy F. and Lindaman D. (2020), "Donald Trump's 'Chinese virus': the politics of naming", *The Conversation* (21 April 2020), available at https://theconversation.com/donald-trumps-chinese-virus-the-politics-of-naming-136796, accessed 27 July 2020.

Part I

CONTEXT

Chapter 1

Universities must help shape the post-Covid-19 world

Ira Harkavy, Sjur Bergan, Tony Gallagher and Hilligje van't Land[10]

INTRODUCTION

"The world will never be the same again". This is perhaps the least hazardous prediction one can make about the consequences of the Covid-19 crisis. This crisis will surely change all societal institutions. The precise nature of that change is, at this time, unknowable.

The safe prediction that the world will change leaves open the form and direction this change will take. But it cannot and should not be left unguided, subject to the whims of those seeking to re-establish old systems of power, oppression and inequity. We contend that higher education must play a major role in helping to shape the post-Covid-19 world and must do so by reshaping higher education itself. In this chapter we highlight developments which provide a foundation for that task.

The post-Covid-19 world must be based on the values we cherish: democracy, human rights and the rule of law, as well as social justice, inclusion and equity. Higher education can add momentum by renewing our commitment to academic freedom, institutional autonomy and engagement by students, faculty and staff, and by re-emphasising the role of higher education institutions as societal actors for the public good.

SOCIAL SOLIDARITY

We witnessed elements of this as the Covid-19 crisis began to unfold. Higher education institutions, particularly academic medical centres, as well as individual staff and students, in many instances responded with extraordinary dedication and resolve, providing desperately needed health care and research, helping assure the safety of their students and staff, supporting local businesses, donating medical equipment, teaching their students and engaging with their communities remotely.

---

10. A first and considerably shorter version of this article was published in *University World News*, 19 April 2020; see www.universityworldnews.com/post.php?story=20200413152542750, accessed 29 July 2020.

Higher education's role in developing skilled and dedicated doctors, nurses, social workers, teachers and other professionals has never been more important. We have seen medical scientists rapidly repurpose their labs better to understand the virus and engineers repurpose design and production facilities to supply much-needed personal protective equipment. And we have seen almost unprecedented levels of collaboration and sharing of intelligence in a globally connected race to develop vaccines. In Europe, we have also seen efforts to make the best use of the talents and resources of refugees who could not fully document their qualifications, notably through the Council of Europe's European Qualifications Passport for Refugees and its use to enable refugees with health-related qualifications to work under the supervision of duly licensed health professionals (Council of Europe 2020). This civic spirit, this social solidarity, needs to extend beyond the Covid-19 crisis and become higher education's defining characteristic.

Echoing the Council of Europe, we contend that there are four purposes of higher education:

- preparation for sustainable employment;
- preparation for life as active citizens in democratic societies;
- personal development;
- the development and maintenance, through teaching, learning and research, of a broad, advanced knowledge base. (Council of Europe 2007: para. 5; see also Bergan 2005).

Current events, however, have led us to reconceptualise these purposes as part of a larger goal: developing and maintaining sustainable democratic communities and societies, characterised by participation, co-operation and a commitment to the public good. Specifically, this involves educating students for democratic citizenship, developing a culture of democracy (Council of Europe 2018) and creating knowledge to advance the human condition.

The need for democracy will be greater in the aftermath of the crisis. We already see attempts by some government leaders to use the crisis to gather more powers into their own hands, in some cases without time limits. We hear claims that authoritarian systems are better placed to deal with emergencies while forgetting that the tendencies of authoritarian leaders and regimes to hide inconvenient truths helped make Covid-19 a pandemic. We see concerns about rising nationalism and populism (Lichfield 2020), the risk of new forms of autarchy and challenges to international solidarity, as possible outcomes of the crisis, all of which risk casting our democracies as casualties.

SUSTAINING A CULTURE OF DEMOCRACY

Higher education can and must ensure we take a different course. As participants underlined at a Global Forum that we organised through an international partnership in June 2019:

> Education, including higher education, is responsible for advancing and disseminating knowledge and developing ethical and able citizens. It therefore plays an essential role in modern democratic societies. Education is key to

developing, maintaining and sustaining a culture of democracy without which democratic laws, institutions and elections cannot function in practice. (Global Forum 2019: paragraph 1)

Higher education institutions, particularly research universities, are among the pre-eminent institutions in societies throughout the world. They are sources of new ideas and discoveries, including technological advances, are hosts of cultural and artistic centres that foster creativity and are local, national and global economic engines. Most importantly, they teach the teachers and the teachers' teachers, across all subjects, thereby helping to shape the entire schooling and educational systems at all levels (Bok 1990; Harper 1905; Harkavy 2006).

Just as we see higher education as shaping the schooling and education systems, we see these systems as shaping the very nature of society itself. We recall the words of the Chilean sociologist Eugenio Tironi (2005) to the effect that, to decide what kind of education we need, we first have to decide what kind of society we want.

Higher education must engage in debates both on the future of society and on the future of education. Democratic education, particularly democratic higher education, is a prerequisite for a fair, inclusive and sustainable democratic society. The Covid-19 crisis will broaden our view of sustainability; it will make sustainability an even more urgent concern. We therefore think it essential that the ideal of the democratic civic university actively engaged with the life and problems of its community and society become the definitive model of higher education in the post-Covid-19 world. Certainly, positive steps have been taken over the past decades in this direction, but they have not been nearly sufficient and other models of higher education remain dominant.

EDUCATION FOR THE PUBLIC GOOD

The neoliberal "entrepreneurial university" is a model that has gained increasing currency and power throughout the world, contributing to increasingly savage inequalities and a diminished sense of public purpose. Education for profit, not virtue; students as consumers, not producers of knowledge; academics as individual superstars, not members of a community of scholars – all of these developments reflect the commercialisation of higher education, which contributes to an overemphasis on institutional competition for wealth and status and has a devastating impact on the values and ambitions of students (Bok 2003). When institutions prioritise commercialisation, their behaviour legitimises and reinforces the pursuit of economic self-interest by students and amplifies the widespread sense that they are in college or university exclusively to gain career-related skills and credentials for their personal benefit. Student idealism and civic engagement are strongly diminished when students see their universities abandon academic values and scholarly pursuits to function as if they were competitive, profit-making corporations. Commercialism and the development of the entrepreneurial university foster an environment in which higher education is seen as a private benefit, not a public good (Benson et al. 2017).

However, returning to a more traditional model, in which the university is detached from society, does not provide an effective counter to the neoliberal university. On the contrary, its internal, disciplinary focus and emphasis on elite education works against core democratic goals such as diversity, inclusion and equity. The quality and relevance of higher education also need to be measured by the extent to which it offers possibilities to all students in accordance with their talents and aspirations.

Our argument, simply put, is that to create a better post-Covid-19 world requires democratic civic universities dedicated to producing knowledge and educating ethical, empathetic students for just and sustainable democratic societies. It requires higher education to fulfil its four major purposes, as outlined above.

A democratic civic university would infuse democracy across all aspects of the institutions.

From a European perspective, seeing students as members of the academic community is established public policy as expressed by ministers responsible for higher education in 2001: "They [ministers] supported the idea that higher education should be considered a public good and is and will remain a public responsibility (regulations etc.), and that students are full members of the higher education community" (Bologna Process 2001).

Participatory democracy and a culture of democracy, not just democracy as defined by voting or a system of government, would be primary goals of a democratic civic university. The US educator and philosopher John Dewey defined democracy as "a way of life" (Dewey 1939/1993: 229) in which all citizens actively participate in all the communal, societal, educational and institutional decisions that significantly shape their lives (Benson, Harkavy and Puckett 2007). In line with that goal [democracy as a way of life], members of a democratic civic university would treat community members as ends in themselves rather than as means to an end.[11] The relationship itself and the welfare of the various partners would be the pre-eminent value, not simply developing a specified programme or completing a research project.

The democratic purpose of higher education has been increasingly recognised across the world. For example, at the previously mentioned Global Forum held in June 2019 in Strasbourg on Academic Freedom, Institutional Autonomy and the Future of Democracy, participants from 41 countries across Europe, North America, Latin America, Australia, Asia and the Middle East adopted a Declaration, which stated:

> Academic freedom and institutional autonomy are essential to furthering the quality of learning, teaching, and research, including artistic creative practice – quality understood as observing and developing the standards of academic disciplines and also quality as the contribution of higher education to democracy, human rights, and the rule of law. Higher education must demonstrate openness, transparency, responsiveness and accountability as well as the will and ability to work with and contribute to the communities in which colleges and universities reside. (Global Forum 2019: paragraph 2)

---

11. This approach resonates with Kant's second categorical imperative: "Act in such a way that you always treat humanity, whether in your own person or in the person of any other, never simply as a means, but always at the same time as an end" (Kant, 1785/1993: 30).

We strongly believe that working with and contributing to their local communities is essential if colleges and universities are to function as responsible democratic institutions that effectively teach their students citizenship and civic engagement through what they do in practice. We also believe, with the Global Declaration, that fulfilling their democratic purpose means that universities need to work with their local communities, demonstrating "openness, transparency, responsiveness and accountability" (ibid.).

GLOBAL CO-OPERATION

For over 20 years, a transatlantic and now global co-operation has been working to realise the democratic purpose and promise of higher education. Given the transnational impacts of Covid-19 on higher education, communities and societies, we must strengthen that co-operation as a means to develop and sustain democratic schooling, universities, communities and societies. The co-operation involves the Council of Europe, the International Consortium for Higher Education, Civic Responsibility and Democracy (IC), the Organization of American States (OAS) and the International Association of Universities (IAU).

The Council of Europe, established in 1949, defends human rights, democracy and the rule of law, develops continent-wide agreements to standardise member countries' social and legal practices, and promotes awareness of a European identity across cultures based on shared values. It comprises 47 member countries, and its Steering Committee for Educational Policy and Practice (CDPPE)[12] includes another three countries that are also signatories to the European Cultural Convention (Council of Europe 1954). This treaty provides the framework for the Council of Europe's work in education policy and practice.

The IC was created in 1999 to work with the Council of Europe. The purpose of the IC is to advance the contributions of institutions of higher education to democratic development on campus, in local communities and in the wider society. It is composed of the United States (represented by a Steering Committee from the American Association of State Colleges and Universities, American Council on Education, Anchors Institutions Task Force, Association of American Colleges and Universities, Campus Compact, Democracy Commitment and NASPA-Student Affairs Professionals in Higher Education); Australia (represented by Engagement Australia); the United Kingdom (represented by the National Co-ordinating Centre for Public Engagement); Ireland (represented by Campus Engage Ireland); South Africa (represented by Universities South Africa); and the Magna Charta Observatory based in Italy.

In spring 2018, the OAS joined the co-operation between the IC and the Council of Europe. The OAS, established in 1948, brings together all 35 independent states of the Americas to promote solidarity, collaboration and sovereignty, based on its main pillars of democracy, human rights, security and development.

In autumn 2019, the IAU joined the co-operation mentioned above. Created under the auspices of UNESCO in 1950, the IAU represents universities and other higher

---

12. See www.coe.int/en/web/education/cdppe, accessed 29 July 2020.

education institutions, organisations and affiliates across 130 countries. The IAU acts as the global voice of higher education and its organisations to UNESCO, advocating and advancing a dynamic leadership role for higher education in society. Articulating the fundamental values and principles that underpin education and the pursuit, dissemination and application of knowledge,[13] the Association advocates the development of higher education policies and practices that respect diverse perspectives. In addition, it promotes social responsibility and contributes to the development of a sustainable future.[14]

This global co-operation undertakes cross-national research projects, joint meetings and the sharing of best practices as part of its efforts to advance higher education's contribution to building democratic societies. The collaboration between IC and the Council of Europe first launched a cross-national research project on Universities as Sites of Citizenship and Responsibility. Beginning in 1999, a team of European and US researchers assessed the activities of institutions of higher education that supported democratic values and practices and that helped to disseminate those activities, and 14 European and 15 US universities completed the pilot study, whose US component was funded by the National Science Foundation (Harkavy, Hodges and Weeks forthcoming). The Council of Europe published the research findings in *The university as res publica: higher education governance, student participation and the university as a site of citizenship* (Bergan, 2004).

The co-operation has hosted six global forums, and the Council of Europe has published five monographs on the conference themes (see Huber and Harkavy 2008; Bergan and Damian 2010; Bergan, Harkavy and van't Land 2012; Bergan, Gallagher and Harkavy 2016; Bergan and Harkavy 2018; Bergan, Gallagher and Harkavy 2020). Additional partners were involved in planning the conferences, among them the European Wergeland Centre, the European Students' Union, the University of Oslo, Queen's University Belfast, the Australian Catholic University and LUMSA University (Harkavy, Hodges and Weeks forthcoming; Harkavy forthcoming).

FURTHERING THE DEMOCRATIC MISSION OF HIGHER EDUCATION IN THE AFTERMATH OF THE COVID-19 PANDEMIC

The next Global Forum, which will be held in 2021 or 2022 subject to the development of the Covid-19 pandemic, will focus on the democratic mission of higher education in the light of sustainable development. While not being a conference on the implications of Covid-19, of which there will presumably be many over the next few years, the Global Forum will of necessity incorporate the lessons of the Covid-19 pandemic as well as of the social justice movements – most notably Black Lives Matter, which originated in the United States but which also had repercussions in other countries.

---

13. See https://iau-aiu.net/Vision-Mission, accessed 29 July 2020.
14. See www.iau-aiu.net/, accessed 29 July 2020. The IAU maintains and develops the IAU-UNESCO World Higher Education Database, by which it reaches out to 20 000 higher education institutions around the world.

The Global Forum will seek to address questions such as:
- What values and commitments must underpin higher education and its appeal to public authorities for support?
- How does academia redesign its work in democratic collaboration with others, within and beyond its campus?
- What deeper or new relationships need to be built with the local communities of which higher education is a part, especially those most affected by the pandemic and its aftermath?
- What new institutional practices help sustain and engage the most at-risk students, while ensuring that all students are also educated to be ethical, empathetic, engaged democratic citizens?
- How can universities work together locally, nationally and globally to co-operatively respond to the complex multifaceted issues arising from the pandemic?

The 2021 Global Forum will aim to spark an intellectual and democratic movement to reimagine how democratic civic universities can co-create more just, equitable, inclusive, sustainable democratic societies with local and global partners. It will consider how higher education can best fulfil its mission to prepare students for democratic citizenship and develop a culture of democracy in them in the aftermath of the Covid-19 pandemic. The Global Forum will also look beyond campuses to reimagine how the higher education community and its members can work as actors of democracy in broader society. The commitment to democracy must be developed in individual members of the academic community but also in the community as a whole. Democracy cannot be developed through theoretical learning alone; it must also be practised as part of the day-to-day life of the institution. The principles of democracy remain but the way in which they are put into practice may need to be re-examined, both during and in the wake of the Covid-19 pandemic.

The higher education community has a responsibility to prevent the current Covid-19 crisis from developing into a deepening and pervasive crisis of democracy. This responsibility is also incumbent on public authorities as well as the broader civil society. While public health was for obvious reasons the immediate priority when the Covid-19 crisis emerged,[15] and will remain essential in its aftermath, education should be no less a societal priority in the years to come. Both public health and the public responsibility for education will be crucial to the health of our democratic societies. Uniquely, higher education needs to contribute to both.

It is therefore essential for our future that academics, students and their representatives, university administrators, government officials, public authorities and community partners work together locally, nationally and globally to create democratic civic universities dedicated to developing fair, decent, just, equitable, inclusive, sustainable democratic societies. We are committed to contributing to this development by strengthening our co-operation and sharpening our focus during the pandemic and beyond.

---
15. For a timeline and updated overview of the development of the pandemic, see www.who.int/emergencies/diseases/novel-coronavirus-2019/events-as-they-happen, accessed 29 July 2020.

REFERENCES

Benson L., Harkavy I. and Puckett J. (2007), *Dewey's dream: universities and democracies in an age of education reform*, Philadelphia, PA: Temple University Press.

Benson L. et al. (2017), *Knowledge for social change: Bacon, Dewey, and the revolutionary transformation of research universities in the twenty-first century*, Philadelphia, PA: Temple University Press.

Bergan S. (ed.) (2004), *The university as res publica: higher education governance, student participation and the university as a site of citizenship*, Strasbourg: Council of Europe.

Bergan S. (2005), "Higher education as a 'public good and a public responsibility': what does it mean?", in Weber L. and Bergan S. (eds), *The public responsibility for higher education and research*, Council of Europe Higher Education Series No. 2, Strasbourg: Council of Europe Publishing, pp. 13-28.

Bergan S. and Damian R. (eds) (2010), *Higher education for modern societies: competencies and values*, Council of Europe Higher Education Series No. 15, Strasbourg: Council of Europe Publishing.

Bergan S., Gallagher T. and Harkavy I. (eds) (2016), *Higher education for democratic innovation*, Council of Europe Higher Education Series No. 21, Strasbourg: Council of Europe Publishing.

Bergan S., Gallagher T. and Harkavy I. (eds) (2020), *Academic freedom, institutional autonomy, and the future of democracy*, Council of Europe Higher Education Series No. 24, Strasbourg: Council of Europe Publishing.

Bergan S. and Harkavy I. (eds) (2018), *Higher education for diversity, social inclusion and community: a democratic imperative*, Council of Europe Higher Education Series No. 22, Strasbourg: Council of Europe Publishing.

Bergan S., Harkavy I. and van't Land H. (eds) (2012), *Reimagining democratic societies: a new era of personal and social responsibility*, Council of Europe Higher Education Series No. 18, Strasbourg: Council of Europe Publishing.

Bok D. (1990), *Universities and the future of America*, Durham, NC: Duke University Press.

Bok D. (2003), *Universities in the marketplace: the commercialization of higher education*, Princeton, NJ: Princeton University Press.

Bologna Process (2001), "Towards the European Higher Education Area. Communiqué of the meeting of European Ministers in charge of Higher Education in Prague on May 19th 2001", available at www.ehea.info/page-ministerial-declarations-and-communiques, accessed 29 July 2020.

Council of Europe (1954), European Cultural Convention, available at www.coe.int/en/web/conventions/full-list/-/conventions/treaty/018, accessed 29 July 2020.

Council of Europe (2007), Recommendation CM/Rec(2007)6 of the Committee of Ministers to member states on the public responsibility for higher education and research, available at https://search.coe.int/cm/Pages/result_details.aspx?ObjectId=-09000016805d5dae, accessed 29 July 2020.

Council of Europe (2018), *Reference Framework of Competences for Democratic Culture*, Vol. 1: *Context, concepts and model*; Vol. 2: *Descriptors of competences*; Vol. 3: *Guidance for implementation*, Strasbourg: Council of Europe Publishing. Also available at www.coe.int/en/web/reference-framework-of-competences-for-democratic-culture/, accessed 29 July 2020.

Council of Europe (2020), European Qualifications Passport for Refugees, available at www.coe.int/en/web/education/recognition-of-refugees-qualifications, accessed 29 July 2020.

Dewey J. (1939), "Creative democracy: The task before us", in Morris D. and Shapiro I. (eds) (1993), *The political writings*, Hackett Publishing, Indianapolis, IN/Cambridge, MA.

Global Forum (2019), *Global Forum on Academic Freedom, Institutional Autonomy and the Future of Democracy Declaration* (21 June 2019), available at https://rm.coe.int/global-forum-declaration-global-forum-final-21-06-19-003-/16809523e5, accessed 29 July 2020.

Harkavy I. (2006), "The role of universities in advancing citizenship and social justice in the 21st century", *Education, Citizenship, and Social Justice*, 1(1), 5-37.

Harkavy I. (forthcoming), "The promise of higher education: 70 years of IAU (1950-2020) – Creating democratic civic universities in a post-Covid-19 world: the IAU and global collaboration", in Fredman P., van't Land H. and Pricopie R. (eds), *International higher education cooperation through the International Association of Universities*, New York/London: Palgrave McMillan/Springer Nature.

Harkavy I., Hodges R. A. and Weeks J. (forthcoming), "Towards creating the truly engaged, responsive university: Penn's partnership with West Philadelphia as an experiment in progress", in Brink C. (ed.), *The responsive university and the crisis in South Africa*, Boston/Leiden: Brill.

Harper W. R. (1905), "The university and democracy", in Harper W. R. (ed.), *The trend in higher education*, Chicago: University of Chicago Press, pp. 1-34.

Huber J. and Harkavy I. (eds) (2008), *Higher education and democratic culture: citizenship, human rights and civic responsibility*, Council of Europe Higher Education Series No. 8, Strasbourg: Council of Europe Publishing.

Kant, I. (1785/1993), *Grounding for the metaphysics of morals*, translated by J. W. Ellington (3rd ed.), Indianapolis/Cambridge: Hackett.

Lichfield J. (2020), "The next epidemic: resurgent populism", *Politico*, 4 June 2020, available at www.politico.eu/article/the-next-epidemic-resurgent-populism/, accessed 28 August 2020.

Tironi E. (2005), *El sueño chileno: comunidad, familia y nación en el Bicentenario* [The Chilean dream: community, family and nation at the bicentenary], Santiago de Chile: Taurus.

Chapter 2

Higher education, civic engagement, Covid-19 and the "new normal"

Ronaldo Munck

We hear repeatedly that we will have to live with Covid-19 and that there will be a "new normal". But what does that mean in the context of higher education? Many psychologists tell us there is a huge tendency after a crisis for people to want to "get back to normal" (see Taylor 2019). But is that even possible after Covid-19? Does it mean we should just strive to return to the status quo? Covid-19 is a health crisis but also a social, political and cultural one, and will, of course, have a major economic impact, not least on higher education (see preliminary survey in IAU 2020a).

What I will try to do here is lay out some of the broad parameters of the debates and decisions we face in higher education, while setting these issues within the broader context of democratic development and governance. I will also make an argument for the increased relevance of civic engagement and community-based research, seeking to initiate a conversation among this sector in our new post-Covid order. To be clear, all arguments are provisional and subject to change, more than is normally the case, in an era of supercharged complexity and risk. The debate on the post-pandemic university will also, necessarily, be an international collective endeavour to map a way forward and create a common strategy that will seek to ensure higher education contributes to the enhancement of democracy, in terms of society and international relations, but also of knowledge.

NORMAL AND PATHOLOGICAL

First, we might need to think through the relationship between the normal and the pathological, based on the seminal work on the subject by philosopher of science Georges Canguilhem, who argued that

> We shall say that the healthy man [*sic*] does not become sick insofar as he is healthy. No healthy man becomes sick, for he is sick only insofar as his health abandons him and in this he is not healthy. The so-called healthy man thus is not healthy. His health is an equilibrium which he redeems on inceptive ruptures. The menace of disease is one of the components of health. (Canguilhem 1991: 56)

How does this relate to the contemporary university? Was it healthy and then did it become pathological because of the coronavirus? For Canguilhem, being healthy and being "normal" are not altogether equivalent since the pathological is but one kind of normal. Being normal also implies being normative but then being healthy (as in a body) implies being able to transcend the norm. To be in good health means being able to fall sick and recover, according to Canguilhem. So, was the Western university really healthy before the coronavirus? Does the current pathology signal a simple accentuation of normal phenomena or does it lead to a "crisis" defined in medical terms as "the turning point of a disease when an important change takes place, indicating either recovery or death"?

The Covid-19 crisis has brought home the essential role that universities play in contemporary society, with their medical scientists playing a vital role in the search for a vaccine, for example, and in providing back-up for vital pandemic tasks. Universities are major research centres and significant employers in cities and even regions. If the present funding crisis were to result in their failure that would have a catastrophic impact on learning, research and employment. But, as publicly funded bodies, they need to reflect the common good and reconsider the path of marketisation they have been on in recent decades. We need to make sure that the university that emerges from the Covid-19 crisis is more sustainable and inclusive than the previous model.

We might also, at this point, take up a potentially positive reading of "crisis", which is implicit in its original definition as "the turning point for better or worse in an acute disease or fever" (Merriam-Webster 2020). There is good reason why democratic bodies and individuals generally reacted in horror at the curtailment of civil liberties that was, in some countries during the Covid-19 crisis, deemed the only way to deal effectively with the virus. In this paradigm, people, not the virus, are posed as the problem and behavioural economists advise governments on how to deal with them. An alternative scenario would be that these very same people learn from the crisis that they are living through and call for fundamental system change. Rebecca Solnit (2010) has argued that the Mexico City earthquake of 1985 and the 2005 Hurricane Katrina disaster in the US unleashed great reserves of human solidarity, energetic improvisation and purposeful intent that augured well for the future. In relation to the current Covid-19 crisis, Solnit argues that "ordinary life before the pandemic was already a catastrophe of desperation and exclusion for too many human beings, an environmental and climate catastrophe, an obscenity of inequality" (Solnit 2020) so that fundamental change is overdue and a return to "business as usual" is not an option. In other words, we may not wish to return to "normal", and the "pathological" period we are living through could help us create the conditions for a new, more humane social order.

SHOCKWAVES

It was within an already chaotic situation that the Covid-19 crisis emerged and sent real shockwaves through the global economy, now threatened imminently by a depression that would dwarf that of the 1930s (see IMF 2020). In March 2020 we witnessed a near-fatal crisis in the financial system, kept going only through spectacular interventions by the Federal Reserve in the US, the Bank of England and the European Central Bank. Production and employment plummeted with the enactment of Covid "lockdowns" and credit contracted dramatically. A historic drop in oil prices brought home the integrated and precarious nature of the global economy. The question now arises as to whether capitalism can once again rise from its sick-bed and recover its legendary animal spirits? For Adam Tooze, any notion of a unified global order has now dissipated: "we will somehow have to patch together China's one-party authoritarianism, Europe's national welfarism and whatever it is the United States will be in the wake of this disaster" (Tooze 2020). We are certainly a long way from the optimism of 1989-90 when the collapse of communism and the beginning of globalisation painted a rosy future for capitalism.

The social impact of the Covid crisis was very rapidly felt. According to the International Labour Organization (ILO 2020), by March 2020 almost half the global workforce – 1.6 billion people – were in immediate danger of having their livelihoods destroyed by the economic impact of Covid-19, and the International Monetary Fund forecast a 3% contraction (Guardian 2020). Of the total global working population of 3.3 billion, about 2 billion work in the "informal economy", often on short-term contracts or in self-employment, and suffered a 60% collapse in their wages in the first month of the crisis (ILO 2020). In this rapidly evolving crisis, the higher education system will not be immune.

Already we have seen signs that many universities are dismissing staff among the approximately 40% of their employees who are on precarious, temporary or part-time contracts. This will have a direct impact on the ability of universities to deliver high-quality education and will have a devastating impact on those employed at universities and their surrounding communities. In global terms, we are facing a crisis of livelihoods of unprecedented proportions where a future without income, food or security is on the horizon for many. It is not surprising that forward-thinking economists such as Mariana Mazzucato are calling for a re-think of the global economic order as and when it reboots (Mazzucato 2020). The universities cannot be separate from this debate if they are to rise to the challenge, not only as socially embedded organisations but also as "thought leaders".

EDUCATION DILEMMAS

At an online workshop to launch a new Economist Intelligence Unit report, Francisco Marmolejo (ex-tertiary-level specialist at the World Bank) stated that "unless we disrupt, and are willing to take risks, as soon as conditions return to some sort of normal, we may try to become the same as we were before. This crisis is telling us we no longer have the luxury of assuming things will be as they used to be" (EIU 2020). That is the overarching dilemma for higher education: seek a return to "normal" or accept the need for disruptive thinking. The Economist Intelligence Unit report (ibid.: 7) itself offered five supposedly "innovative" models:
- ▶ Online universities, which leverage the internet to offer higher education anytime, anywhere, to anyone. They tap into a growing desire for more flexible modes of learning and promise to dramatically increase access for long-marginalised groups. However, the past decade and, of course, the impact of Covid-19, has brought a much-needed reality check about the challenges of online learning.
- ▶ The cluster model, which eliminates the traditional siloed nature of university campuses by fusing multiple institutions. However, common priorities

do not always exist across or even within institutions, which can make collaboration difficult.
- ▶ Experiential institutions, which bring teaching out of the classroom, with learning driven by diverse experiences such as internships or hands-on projects. However, the experiential mode is also a new one and faces several challenges, including finding ways to align looser and longer-term projects with semester-time evaluation constraints.
- ▶ Liberal arts colleges, which are typically smaller institutions that aim to provide a highly personalised university experience with a lower teacher–student ratio. However, higher teaching and facility costs mean that funding remains a challenge.
- ▶ The partnership model, where institutions build relationships with external partners in order to secure long-term funding and improve job prospects for graduates. However, low entry-level requirements have led to criticism that some institutions are providing sub-par qualifications to students who would struggle to complete courses at more traditional institutions.

While this typology might represent the models familiar in the north Atlantic region, it does not strike me as sufficiently innovative, and I wonder if this scenario planning represents simply a tinkering with existing models. One other drawback of this modelling is that it explicitly assumes that higher education is an "industry" subject to simple cost–benefit analysis. There is a strong argument that we need to return to basics and ask (or re-ask) the question "what are universities for?" (Collini 2012).

There are also very specific challenges being faced by the higher education sector that will affect the way we do business, so to speak. What we have taken to be normal in higher education may not look so normal now. What we have called internationalisation has, in fact, in some countries been a narrow market-driven recruitment drive of fee-paying overseas students. We see now that the higher education system in the West had become dangerously dependent on this income. We also learn about the high environmental cost of this international travel: it is estimated that carbon emissions related to international student mobility doubled between 2000 and 2015. This vital aspect of "normal" functioning has been dubbed "the internationalisation revolution that isn't" (Altbach and de Wit 2020, see also White and Lee 2020).

As we now move into a post-mobility world, this flow of students across the globe will inevitably decrease. But that does not mean that internationalism is dead. On the contrary, the need for a sustainable internationalism will be even greater as the world recovers from the Covid-19 crisis. Already we see much sharing of medical and epidemiology information across countries, and higher education as a whole has become much more open to collaboration. The new internationalism will need to be constructed on a democratic basis, rather than a narrow cost–benefit analysis and the lure of a quick and easy financial injection. What does internationalism mean in higher education today? I would argue that we do need to go back to basics to answer that question, following up on the vital work of the IAU (see IAU 2020b).

Another area where we might reconsider the "normal" working of higher education is in relation to online learning. For some time, it has become clear that the famous MOOCs (massive online open courses) were not the panacea for a new model of online university in the era of globalisation. Where we are in terms of the Covid-19 crisis is a general enforced turn towards online teaching to deal with the physical closure of many universities. That has been necessary, but not necessarily successful and not necessarily a turn we would want to sustain in a post-Covid-19 situation where austerity and cutbacks lead to academic staff retrenchment. What has also now come to the fore is the depth of the digital divide, with many educators in the global South pointing out that the enforced turn towards online learning, in a context of poor connectivity and inadequate IT preparation, has only exacerbated existing inequalities (see Naidu 2020; Mbodila 2020; Mandal 2020). This situation has also been observed in the community teaching sector of the global North's higher education system, where hidden digital divides now come to the fore. What will be necessary "after" Covid-19 is a sustained effort to democratise access to digital technologies and not a market-driven turn to online teaching directed at the more affluent "connected" sectors of society, for example through a concerted effort around a suggested new 18th UN Sustainable Development Goal, which would include equitable internet access.

There is now a growing acknowledgement that "business as usual" is not an option for higher education post-Covid. University vice chancellors (presidents and rectors) tell us that higher education will change forever (see Mitchell 2020). But what does that mean in practice? If we recall the reaction after the last major crisis, the Great Financial Crisis of 2007-09, we saw then a doubling down on the very policies that caused the crisis in the first place. Banks and financial institutions were bailed out by the taxpayer, regulation was soon put to one side and the casino economy was going once again. After the Covid-19 crisis there will be calls for a return to strong states and free markets. Will the university just accompany that move or will it find a new moral purpose, as growing voices (Harkavy et al. 2020; Stückelberger 2020) are calling for? Are we actively exploring alternative scenarios for a post-Covid-era university and are we developing strategies to achieve our preferred option?

What we require is nothing short of a reinvention of the purposes of the university. That education is a public good should be part of this new common sense. That education, and not enterprise, is the driving force of the university mission should also be part of this. What we are seeing is a general recognition that universities need to reaffirm their role in terms of social responsibility. The myriad ways in which they have responded to the Covid-19 crisis have made that role very clear to those working at the university, but also to a wider public.

In particular, we see a growing recognition of the importance of community. The World Health Organization (WHO) has acknowledged that it is community resilience and coherence that has ensured to a large extent the success of the various "social distancing" measures taken by governments. Community engagement needs to come out of the Covid-19 crisis strengthened and empowered. If that happens, the crisis will have had one beneficial impact and we will all be stronger as a result of it. Community-based research will also be more important, as we realise that markets cannot do everything and we reject the notion that "there's no such thing as society", as Margaret Thatcher (in)famously put it in the 1980s (see Gamble 1994). Communities need to be involved more in setting the research agenda for the post-Covid-19 university. Social responsibility needs to be more than a slogan for mission statements and become a daily practice embedded across the university and its interactions with society and the political order.

It is worth noting in regard to the civic engagement mission that the Economist Intelligence Unit report referred to above declares that

> Today, civic engagement is needed more than ever, as societal trust continues to decline and common ties are fractured ... A boost to civic engagement could help to restore trust and connections between networks of individuals from diverse backgrounds. The benefits would be diverse and substantial. Beyond reducing political polarisation, academics have shown that social ties help to boost economic performance (business relies on trust) and reduce violence and mortality. More broadly, social capital helps to cushion society against the impact of major economic, environmental or societal challenges, crises or transformations–of which several are on the horizon. (EIU 2020: 15)

This seems a somewhat instrumental view of civic engagement, which is not simply about generating trust for the business world, but it does acknowledge clearly that there are more serious shocks on the way. Just as with the coronavirus, these threats are well known and the time to prepare is now. Engaging with society is clearly a vital part of this foresight exercise and will assist in building more resilience in to the current higher education order.

DEMOCRACY

Universities will also need to deal very openly and explicitly with the question of democracy, which is sometimes sidestepped as being "political". Democratic governance is, by and large, put on hold and many critics hold fire, given the health emergency we are all living through, albeit under very different conditions. A simplistic "authoritarianism" versus "democracy" narrative has taken root, reminiscent of the Huntingdon debate of the 1970s around the "dangers of democracy". There is a sense that democracy is not efficient when it is time to deal decisively with crisis; certainly Covid-19 plans are not being put up to public scrutiny. The Covid-19 crisis has effectively disciplined democracy and civil society worldwide, empowering authoritarian regimes and silencing their critics. But there has also been a flourishing of grassroots democracy through social solidarity and mutual support networks. Democracy cannot be "postponed" without damaging it. As Frances Brown and colleagues put it: "it is essential that supporters of democratic governance everywhere attend to this sweeping range of effects, both negative and positive, to identify entry points and interventions that can pre-empt long-term political damage and nurture potential gains" (Brown et al. 2020). The university needs to be part of that democratic movement and promote an alternative vision for a sustainable society.

Democracy cannot be built on the basis of deep and enduring social inequalities. We have already referred to the digital divide, a present and immediate form of social exclusion in the university of today. But the Covid crisis has also exposed a stark global divide between the insured and protected and the uninsured and vulnerable sectors of the population. The differential impact of the pandemic within the United Kingdom and the United States of America, for example, has been stark, with disadvantaged communities suffering twice the number of infections than the average, a difference that goes up to three times the average among black and ethnic minority populations (see, for example, the report by Public Health England 2020). The differences between the global North and South also lie in the open, with the latter seeing already depleted health systems and no ability to maintain basic income levels across the population. There has also been a deterioration of the democratic health of societies, with an emergence of a naked "survival of the fittest" mode of thinking and a return to a form of eugenics in regard to the elderly and vulnerable last seen in Germany in the 1940s (see Hearse 2020). Universities cannot pretend this is a normal situation; it is more akin to a post-war reconstruction moment when accepted nostrums need to be set aside and the emergency on our doorsteps addressed with all urgency.

One of the concepts coming to the fore in response to the present crisis is that of "resilience", with futurists such as Jeremy Rifkin arguing that with the Covid-19 crisis "we must enter a new era: the 'era of resilience'" (Rifkin 2020). Interestingly, this is a concept that has been at the fore in international development studies for some time (see Chandler 2014), signalling in general terms an ability to recover from or adjust more easily to misfortune or change. Individuals, communities and nations have varying capacities to recover from major catastrophes, be they famines, natural disasters, pandemics or financial crises. Resilience is often linked by development agencies to crises, disasters or risk management. At its simplest, it is about how communities respond to stress. But there is a more critical, less policy-oriented interpretation of resilience that posits it not so much as a policy goal but, rather, as a way of thinking and acting in a complex world. With traditional forms of political representation and even accepted versions of the right/left divide increasingly being seen as less relevant, the practice of resilience may act like a lens well placed to focus responses to an increasingly insecure form of life, where the real source of power lies in a diverse and plural community. It is precisely at this point that the strategy of civic engagement and community-based research needs to come to the fore to help articulate the debate on what the university after Covid-19 might look like.

REFERENCES

Altbach P. and de Wit H. (2020), "COVID-19: The internationalisation revolution that isn't", *University World News* (14 March 2020), available at www.universityworldnews.com/, accessed 1 July 2020.

Brown F. et al. (2020), "How will coronavirus reshape democracy and governance globally", Carnegie Foundation, available at https://carnegieendowment.org/2020/04/06/how-will-coronavirus-reshape-democracy-and-governance-globally-pub-81470, accessed 1 July 2020.

Canguilhem G. (1991), *The normal and the pathological*, New York: Zone Books.

Chandler D. (2014), *Resilience. The governance of complexity*, London: Routledge.

Collini S. (2012), *What are universities for?*, Harmondsworth: Penguin.

EIU (Economist Intelligence Unit) (2020), "New schools of thought. Innovative models for delivering higher education", available at https://pages.eiu.com/launch-folder_report-download-registration.html, accessed 1 July 2020.

Gamble A. (1994), *The free economy and the strong state: the politics of Thatcherism*, London: Macmillan.

Guardian (2020), "'Great Lockdown' to rival Great Depression", *The Guardian* (14 April 2020), available at www.theguardian.com/business/2020/apr/14/great-lockdown-coronavirus-to-rival-great-depression-with-3-hit-to-global-economy-says-imf, accessed 28 August 2020.

Harkavy I., Bergan S., Gallagher T. and van't Land H. (2020), "Universities must help shape the post-COVID-19 world", *University World News* (18 April 2020), available at www.universityworldnews.com, accessed 1 July 2020.

Hearse P. (2020), "Government 'herd immunity' strategy tipping Britain towards huge death toll", *Europe Solidaire Sans Frontières*, available at www.europe-solidaire.org/spip.php?article52431, accessed 21 September 2020.

IAU (International Association of Universities) (2020a), "Global survey: report on impact of Covid-19 in higher education", available at www.iau-aiu.net/IAU-releases-Global-Survey-Report-on-Impact-of-Covid-19-in-Higher-Education, accessed 21 September 2020.

IAU (2020b), "Internationalization", available at www.iau-aiu.net/Internationalization, accessed 21 September 2020.

ILO (International Labour Organization) (2020), "As job losses escalate, nearly half of global workforce at risk of losing livelihoods", available at www.ilo.org/global/about-the-ilo/newsroom/news/WCMS_743036/lang--en/index.htm, accessed 1 July 2020.

IMF (International Monetary Fund) (2020), "A crisis like no other, an uncertain recovery", available at www.imf.org/en/Publications/WEO/Issues/2020/06/24/WEOUpdateJune2020, accessed 21 September 2020.

Mandal S. (2020), "Emergency solutions are exacerbating the digital divide", *University World News* (18 April 2020), available at www.universityworldnews.com/, accessed 1 July 2020.

Mazzucato M. (2020), "The Covid-19 crisis is a chance to do capitalism differently", *The Guardian* (18 March 2020), available at www.theguardian.com/commentisfree/2020/mar/18/the-covid-19-crisis-is-a-chance-to-do-capitalism-differently, accessed 1 July 2020.

Mbodila M. (2020), "Online learning – the pandemic cannot change reality", *University World News* (23 April 2020), available at www.universityworldnews.com/, accessed 1 July 2020.

Merriam-Webster (2020), available at www.merriam-webster.com/dictionary/crisis#, accessed 1 July 2020.

Mitchell N. (2020), "COVID-19 crisis will change HE forever, IHEF hears", *University World News* (25 March 2020), available at www.universityworldnews.com/, accessed 1 July 2020.

Naidu E. (2020), "Concerned academics call for halt to online learning", *University World News* (23 April 2020), available at www.universityworldnews.com/, accessed 1 July 2020.

Public Health England (2020), *Disparities in the risk and outcomes of Covid-19*, available at https://assets.publishing.service.gov.uk/government/uploads/system/uploads/attachment_data/file/892085/disparities_review.pdf, accessed 22 September 2020.

Rifkin J. (2020), Interview, available at www.handelszeitung.ch/unternehmen/jeremy-rifkin-we-are-now-facing-real-time-how-fast-global-economy-can-collapse, accessed 1 July 2020.

Solnit R. (2010), *A paradise built in hell: the extraordinary communities that arise in disaster*, New York: Penguin.

Solnit R. (2020), "The impossible has already happened: what coronavirus can teach us about hope", *The Guardian*, available at www.theguardian.com/world/2020/apr/07/what-coronavirus-can-teach-us-about-hope-rebecca-solnit, accessed 1 July 2020.

Stückelberger C. (2020), "COVID-19 and the ethical responsibility of universities", *University World News* (11 April 2020), available at www.universityworldnews.com/, accessed 1 July 2020.

Taylor R. (2019), *The psychology of pandemics preparing for the next global outbreak of infectious disease*, Cambridge: Cambridge Scholars Publishing.

Tooze A. (2020), "Shockwave", *London Review of Books*, 42(8), available at www.lrb.co.uk/the-paper/v42/n08/adam-tooze/shockwave, accessed 1 July 2020.

White B. and Lee J. (2020), "The future of international HE in a post-mobility world", *University World News* (18 April 2020), available at www.universityworldnews.com/, accessed 1 July 2020.

Chapter 3

The pre-Covid-19 world: race and inequity in higher education

Henry Louis Taylor, Jr

INTRODUCTION

Higher education[16] must become an engaged, civic institution "dedicated to producing knowledge and educating ethical, empathetic students for just and sustainable democratic societies" to realise its promise of greatness (Harkavy et al. 2020). However, for this to happen, the university must become actively engaged with the life and problems of its community and society (ibid.). The purpose of this chapter is to explore race[17] and inequity in higher education before the pandemic. The "race" concept is viewed differently in various parts of the world, and there are unique ways that it is conceived in the United States, Latin America and Europe. However, regardless of one's theorising on race, the challenges of people of colour lie at the core of building just and sustainable societies (O'Flaherty 2018).

The building of an engaged, civic university is a process that unfolds over time, and the prototypical university is an aspiration and a reference point in assessing higher education. Davarian Baldwin reminds us that higher education is a duality, with a double consciousness. It is focused both on academic and on entrepreneurial activities to generate funds (Baldwin 2017). With the rise of the knowledge economy, universities, now more than ever, are expected to facilitate economic development. This non-traditional role has led universities both in the United States and Europe to increasingly build partnerships between government and the private sector and become involved in entrepreneurial activities (Dabić 2019). In the United States, these "business" activities are producing tensions between the academic and entrepreneurial dimensions within the academy (Knapp and Siegal 2009). The progressive, academic side of this contradiction must triumph if the university is to realise its

---

16. In this chapter, the terms "higher education" and "university" are used interchangeably, and both include an assortment of institutions, including community colleges, colleges and research universities.
17. Editors' note: the use of the term "race" reflects the diverging history of the United States and Europe. In the United States, race is a central concept in understanding the history of the country and reflects, in particular, the lingering results of the enslavement of Blacks. In Europe, the concept of "race" is largely avoided, in part because of its connotations of race theories of the 1930s and in part because societal divides are perceived more in terms of ethnicity and migration than as being linked to race.

promise. Within this conceptual frame, this chapter seeks to understand how higher education confronted the pre-Covid-19 race and equity challenge, by examining the recruitment of Blacks, Latinx[18] and Native Americans to US colleges and universities and by exploring higher education's relationship to communities of colour.

What is the meaning of this statement, which describes the higher education prototype? Definitions matter, and as the world moves toward a post-Covid-19 society, cogent, precise definitions of concepts and anchoring statements are more important than ever. Definitions enable us to describe accurately the world that we seek to change, as well as to identify those challenges that must be overcome to achieve our goals. The historian Ibram X. Kendi theorised that "definitions anchor us in principles" (Kendi 2019: 17). The problem of defining concepts is not a trivial issue, he said. Using vague, indeterminate, "wastebasket concepts" is popular because "imprecise" or cloudy meanings avoid debate and divisions, while creating superficial unity. Such imprecise terms also make it possible to sidestep transparency by pretending to implement one strategy while knowingly operationalising another (ibid.: 17). Therefore, the university, to realise its promise, must use a set of lucid definitions to guide its activities.

So, what is meant by the statement that the university must become a "civic institution that produces knowledge and creates educated, empathetic students for just and sustainable democratic societies and that it must be actively engaged in the life and problems of the 'community' and 'society'"? This statement refers to the university becoming an anti-racist institution that produces knowledge for radical social change that will inform and guide the construction of the neighbourly community (Benson et al. 2017). To realise in practice their aspiration of being democratic civic universities dedicated to producing knowledge and educating ethical, empathetic students for just and sustainable democratic societies, they must be "anti-racist" and produce knowledge for racial and social change. It is not enough to simply produce knowledge; they must produce knowledge for "social change" that can inform the creation and development of the "neighbourly community". An anti-racist university consciously seeks to dismantle the structures of racism and social class inequity while fighting to implement policies that promote the development of a racially equitable and just society (Tate and Bagguley 2017). In Dewey's dream (2007), the scholars Lee Benson, Ira Harkavy and John Puckett theorised that the secret to building a just society was the creation of "democratic, cosmopolitan neighbourly communities". Such communities, they posited, would function as the primary social unit in society.

I theorise that such "neighbourly communities" are multi-racial, cross-class places that are characterised by high-quality housing affordable to the lowest income groups and serviced by high-quality schools and social institutions that promote social, mental and physical well-being. They are anchored by community control, participatory democracy and collective ownership, along with the regulation and control of market dynamics. The community residents are bound together by a culture informed by the values of anti-racism, reciprocity, collectivism, solidarity and participatory democracy. The engaged university seeks to create students dedicated to the building of neighbourly communities and sustainable democracies (Luter and Taylor 2020).

---

18. "Latinx" is a gender-neutral term used to describe people of Latin American origin.

Building the neighbourly community brings us to the question of democracy. There exist multiple types of democracies, so the term must be carefully defined. In *Dewey's dream* (Benson, Harkavy and Puckett 2007), the authors define elitist, neoliberal democracies as democratic societies, such as the United States, where the mass of citizens have limited ability to influence the government, institutional decisions or the economy. In neoliberal democracies, the citizen's power to influence government is mainly through the vote, where they select between or among elites competing for office or authority. In these democratic societies, the citizenry has almost no power to influence the economy or large institutions, and racism, income inequality and wealth inequality are the norms (Mounk 2018).

Participatory democracy, posit Benson, Harkavy and Puckett (2007), is an alternative to neoliberal democracy. Participatory democracies reflect a way of life that actively involves its citizenry in all issues that affect their lives, from the family, school and economy to religion and government. The mass of citizens participates in the elaboration of systems that drive social development, along with the formulation of policies that guide their actions (Taylor H. L., Jr 2009). In advanced societies, citizens ought to integrate social democracy and participatory democracy, with participatory democracy driving neighbourhood-scale actions. Social democracies, then, are people-centred societies that seek to monitor and control market dynamics while promoting social entrepreneurship and human development with the intent of equitably distributing income and wealth while simultaneously raising the quality of life among all citizens. The intent of social democracies is thus to harness market forces and use them to produce socially and racially beneficial outcomes (Stuart 2016).

RACE AND INEQUITY IN HIGHER EDUCATION

Defining this prototype of the engaged, civic university is vital because it functions as the reference point in our discussion of race and inequity in higher education before the pandemic. Before 1968, the university was an exclusive, racist institution. The rise of the US university was thus rooted in the slave economies of the colonial world. The slavery industry was a huge economy that played a vital role in the building and functioning of many of the nation's most significant colleges and universities. Higher education not only extracted wealth from enslaved Black labour but also produced knowledge and an intellectual climate to support this economic system and way of life (Wilder 2013). In the years after the slave enterprise was outlawed, higher education continued to support Black exploitation and Jim Crow[19] racism, and to produce knowledge that justified it. In the age of Jim Crow, there were only a handful of Black students on white campuses. Most Blacks, if they wanted a college education, had to attend Black colleges, mostly located in the South.

In the era after the Second World War, the racist activities of higher education took the form of engaging in place-based neighbourhood development. The break-up of the colonial world led to a Cold War between the capitalist and socialist camps

---
19. The term "Jim Crow" refers to the age of legalised segregation in the United States. These laws were enacted following the Civil War in the United States and lasted until 1954, when the United States Supreme Court declared the doctrine of Separate but Equal to be unconstitutional.

and spawned the rise of a knowledge economy. The emergent knowledge economy ignited the explosive growth of higher education so that it could produce the new breed of knowledge workers: scientists, chemists, engineers, physicians, financiers, accountants, lawyers and stockbrokers, along with a cadre of cultural, clerical, sales and other white-collar workers. Between 1940 and 1980, college enrolment leaped from about 1.5 million to a little over 12 million (Snyder 1993).

The dramatic growth in enrolment led to a corresponding need for more faculty and staff members, as well as new facilities and new apartment buildings and houses to accommodate the enlarged campus community. The physical requirements to accommodate university growth created an intense struggle over land use between the university and its host community. Universities are landlocked anchor institutions that need to expand in place to accommodate growth. This need for physical expansion meant seizing land surrounding the university, then repurposing and converting it for higher education uses. The problem was that the growing Black and Brown populations surrounding universities needed that same land for community development.

The same forces that triggered the explosive growth of higher education also catalysed the Second Great Migration of Blacks to the city, along with significant increases in the Mexican and Puerto Rican populations and other immigrants of colour. This migration of oppressed populations to cities was part of the transformation of the industrial city into the knowledge city. Black migration led the way. Between 1945 and 1970, more than five million Blacks poured into northern, mid-western and western US cities, with New York and Chicago leading the way. Concurrently, even more whites rushed from cities to the new homeownership zones opening up in the suburbs.

Higher education believed that the urban crisis jeopardised its institutions. Administrators were fearful that the expanding Black and Latinx population, creeping blight and crime threatened their world-class reputation, assets and ability to recruit students, faculty and staff. Therefore, the university made transforming Black/Brown neighbourhoods into university communities their top priorities. This aspiration led to a marriage between gentrification and university growth and development. In the late 1940s and 1950s, the University of Chicago and Columbia University developed the university community prototype. The gentrified university community model was a chic, racially integrated and middle-class community imbued with a culture that reflected the lifestyle of white faculty, staff, students and knowledge workers.

In this gentrification model, the university intended to purge the university community of "undesirable" low-income Black and Brown workers, while retaining the Black middle class (Taylor K.-Y. 2019). University officials used an urban renewal strategy to halt blight and expand their campuses by usurping lands occupied by Black and Brown residents. By 1964, the federal Housing and Home Finance Agency reported that 154 urban renewal projects involving 120 colleges and universities and 75 hospitals had been implemented (Taylor, Luter and Miller 2018; Taylor, Luter and Uzochukwu 2018).

THE DISRUPTION

The 1968 assassination of Dr Martin Luther King, Jr disrupted the universities' racist expansion schemes and catalysed the process of dismantling systemic structural racism in higher education. In this turbulent setting, the intervention of Black students forced higher education to defer the university community dream. In retaliation for the King killing, Black rebellions occurred in more than 100 cities across the United States (Blakemore 2018). As cities burned, Blacks lost hope in the possibility of changing America. Blacks believed that America was beyond redemption after the killing of a preacher who spoke of love, peace and justice. Floyd McKissick, director of the Congress of Racial Equality, angrily stated that "nonviolence is a dead philosophy, and it was not the Black people that killed it. It was white people that killed nonviolence and white racists at that" (Johnson 1968: 26).

Higher education, in response to the growing anger and cynicism, sought to reignite hope among Blacks and atone for past racism by recruiting large numbers of African Americans and Latinx to higher education. The resultant influx sparked a revolution on campuses. Blacks, with aid from the radical white student movement, started to dismantle structural racism on campus and defer higher education's quest to build the university community. The movement started with Black students demanding the hiring of Black faculty members and administrators and calling for the establishment of Black Studies programmes. The students also demanded that the university create a welcoming campus environment for them.

To realise their demands, from 1968 to 1973, Black students staged protests on about 200 college campuses. These protests led to increases in Black enrolment, the recruitment of Black faculty and staff and the establishment of Black Studies programmes and departments at universities across the country. In 1968, San Francisco State University hired sociologist Nathan Hare to establish the nation's first Black Studies programme (Bondi 2012). Black militancy had a revolutionary multiplier effect on the broader freedom movement. It activated other groups, which led to the establishment of Women's Studies programmes and various ethnic studies programmes.

The revolutionary Black students also disrupted the university's quest to build the university community. The students demanded that higher education end its expansionist, colonial white settler relationship with the Black community. The land-use conversion struggle between Columbia University and Harlem over Morningside Park most dramatically illustrates Black student intervention in town–gown relations. Morningside Park separated Columbia and Harlem, and during the 1960s Columbia University tried to convert the parkland into recreational space for its students and a buffer zone between the university and the growing Black Harlem community. Columbia ignored the protests of community residents, including Black politicians, but the intervention of Black students in 1968 created an internal crisis on campus, which ended their effort to take over the park (Carriere 2011; Luter and Taylor, Jr. 2020). The revolutionary actions of Black and white students and their faculty allies forced the university to turn inwards and address its racism and sexism. These students catalysed a radical change in higher education and paved the way for the rise of the engaged university movement in the late 1980s.

COLOUR BLINDNESS AND THE RE-EMERGENCE OF RACISM

A convergence of three inter-related forces spawned the resurrection of racism in higher education. During the 1970s, the severe economic crisis became the midwife that delivered neoliberal capitalism and globalism. An economic recession followed this crisis in the 1980s and 1990s (Kalleberg 2018). The neoliberal "small government and limited taxes" mandate forced public universities to become more entrepreneurial in order to increase revenues and replace lost public dollars (Clark 1998). Neoliberalism thus caused higher education to re-evaluate its spending priorities while empowering its business and real estate and property management units to generate more funds (Etienne 2012).

Then, in 1978, the US Supreme Court made a landmark ruling that undermined the Black presence in higher education. In the *Regents of the University of California v. Bakke* case, the Supreme Court ruled that affirmative action was constitutional but invalidated the use of racial quotas to address historical oppression and exploitation. The Supreme Court insisted that race was only one of several criteria that universities could use in admission policies (Yosso et al. 2004). Significantly, the decision validated reverse discrimination, which refers to the discrimination against whites by institutions seeking to overcome the cumulative effects of Black and Brown oppression and exploitation. This decision opened the door for higher education to decelerate the recruitment of Black students and faculty (Spratlen 1979; Harris 2018).

Universities, to avoid exposure to legal risks, started to adopt a colour-blind diversity-equity-inclusion model to act as watchdog for the recruitment of students and faculty of colour (De Welde 2017). The results were disastrous. At the University at Buffalo, for example, the percentage of tenured Black faculty members fell from 4% (52) to 2.6% (31) between 2009 and 2019. By 2019, the combined number of Blacks, Latinx and Native American faculty was less than 6% of the tenure track[20] faculty members (Sinclair 2017; Office of the Provost 2020). The Buffalo experience became the norm for most institutions of higher education (Schneider and Saw 2016). The use of a diversity-equity-inclusion model to act as watchdog and support affirmative action on campus was an abject failure. The reason is that whiteness becomes the default group whenever race is not explicitly centred (Bonilla-Silva 2010). The typical definition of diversity helps to explain why: "while diversity is often used in reference to race, ethnicity, and gender, we embrace a broader definition of diversity that also includes age, national origin, religion, disability, sexual orientation, socio-economic status, language, and physical appearance" (National Council of Non-Profits 2020). In a society based on a racialised social system, colour-blind definitions, such as this one, render invisible the racial hierarchy, thereby hiding the position of whites at its top. The result is that whiteness is protected and prioritised.

Higher education, then, resurrected its university community dream in the 1990s and 2000s. The urban crisis persisted, and the university borrowed language from the community engagement movement to disguise its university community model (Ehlenz 2015; Etienne 2012). The engagement movement's naivety about land development economics made it possible for the university's real estate and property management offices to mask their gentrifying actions (Yamamura and Koth, 2018; Galster 2019). In city after city, masking its profit-making motives, higher education built the gentrified chic university community by masking it under the guise of neighbourhood improvement.

---

20. The "tenure track" is the professorial pathway to promotion and job security. An assistant professorship is the entry level to tenure-track positions. In the United States, lecturers and adjuncts are not on the tenure track.

WHERE DO WE GO FROM HERE? CAN HIGHER EDUCATION HELP SHAPE THE POST-COVID-19 WORLD?

The question undergirding this chapter is: "Can higher education play a leading role in shaping the post-Covid-19 world?" Higher education had serious issues before the pandemic, including the growing influence of the entrepreneurial spirit. The university must address these issues in this liminal period if it is to play a leading role in shaping the post-Covid-19 world. The American Awakening,[21] triggered by the Floyd Rebellions,[22] created the conditions to transform higher education. According to the New York Times, from 15 to 26 million people actively participated in the Floyd Rebellions, and millions more vigorously supported them (Buchanan, Bui and Patel 2020). When we add international participation to the count, it makes the Floyd Rebellions perhaps the greatest mass demonstration in history. This massive protest was against police violence and the failure of neoliberal society. The university must acknowledge the failure of neoliberalism to legitimise its capacity to lead.

Significantly, the Floyd Rebellions illustrate the importance of centring racial equity and anti-racism in the struggle for justice, and also provide evidence that the Black struggle always opens the door to the more massive struggle to change America (Taylor K.-Y. 2020). The rebellions are spawning conversations throughout society about radical social change, reimagining institutions and centring anti-racism in the battle for justice, democracy and revolutionary economic change. Across the globe, people are also talking about changing the calculus undergirding our institutions, culture and way of life (Women's Health Editors 2020).

The uncomfortable truth is that higher education must break with the elites and turn away from their vision of limited democracy and inequitable wealth distribution if it is to play a lead in shaping post-Covid-19 society. This uncomfortable truth poses the question: can the progressive campus forces dominate the business side of the university and defeat the nemesis of the engaged university – the entrepreneurial university? I believe they can. The Floyd Rebellions unleashed a cultural revolution on campus. If that revolution triumphs during this liminal age, then the university will lead the movement to reshape the post-Covid-19 world.

REFERENCES

Baldwin D. L. (2017), "When universities swallow cities", Chronicle of Higher Education (30 July 2017), available at www.chronicle.com/article/When-Universities-Swallow/240739?cid=at&utm_source=naicu, accessed 16 July 2020.

Benson L., Harkavy I. and Puckett J. (2007), Dewey's dream: universities and democracies in an age of education reform, Philadelphia: Temple University Press.

---

21. I use "American Awakening" to describe Americans' growing awareness of racial injustice and racial and social class inequality in the US.
22. The "Floyd Rebellions" refer to the street protests that took place in the United States and around the world in response to the police killing of the African American, George Floyd.

Benson L. et al. (2017), *Knowledge for social change: Beacon, Dewey, and the revolutionary transformation of research universities in the twenty-first century*, Philadelphia: Temple University Press.

Blakemore E. (2018), "Why people rioted after Martin Luther King, Jr.'s assassination", *History Shows* (2 April 2018), available at www.history.com/news/mlk-assassination-riots-occupation, accessed 16 July 2020.

Bondi M. (2012), *The Black revolution on campus*. Berkeley: University of California Press.

Bonilla-Silva E. (2010), *Racism without racists: color-blind racism and the persistence of racial inequality in the United States*, 3rd edn, New York: Rowman & Littlefield.

Buchanan L., Bui Q. and Patel J. K. (2020), "Black Lives Matter may be the largest movement in U.S. history", *New York Times* (3 July 2020).

Carriere M. (2011), "Fighting the war against blight: Columbia University, Morningside Heights, Inc., and counterinsurgent urban renewal", *Journal of Planning History*, 10: 5-29.

Clark B. R. (1998), *Creating entrepreneurial universities: organizational pathways of transformation*, New York: Pergamon Press.

Dabić M. (2019), "Entrepreneurial university in the European Union – EU in the EU", *Journal of Knowledge Economy* (4 January 2019), available at https://doi.org/10.1007/s13132-018-0579-0, accessed 23 September 2020.

De Welde K. (2017), "Moving the needle on equity and inclusion", *Humboldt Journal of Social Relations*, 39: 192-211.

Ehlenz M. M. (2015), "Neighborhood revitalization and the anchor institution; assessing the impact of the University of Pennsylvania's West Philadelphia initiatives on University City", *Urban Affairs Review*, 52: 714-50.

Etienne H. F. (2012), *Pushing back the gates: neighborhood perspectives on university-driven revitalization in West Philadelphia*, Philadelphia, PA: Temple University Press.

Galster G. (2019), *Making our neighborhoods, making our selves*, Chicago: University of Chicago Press.

Harkavy I., Bergan S., Gallagher T. and van't Land H. (2020), "Universities must help shape the post-COVID-19 world", *University World News*, available at www.universityworldnews.com/post.php?story=20200413152542750, accessed 16 July 2020.

Harris A. (2018), "The Supreme Court justice who forever changed affirmative action", *The Atlantic*, available at www.theatlantic.com/education/archive/2018/10/how-lewis-powell-changed-affirmative-action/572938/, accessed 16 July 2020.

Johnson T. A. (1968), "Scattered violence occurs in Harlem and Brooklyn", *New York Times* (5 April 1968).

Kalleberg A. L. (2018), *Precarious lives: job insecurity and well-being in rich democracies*, Cambridge UK: Polity Press.

Kendi I. X. (2019), *How to be an antiracist*, New York: One World.

Knapp J. C. and Siegal D. J. (2009), *The business of higher education: leadership and culture*, Santa Barbara, CA: ABC-Clio.

Luter G. and Taylor H. L., Jr (2020), "Building the neighborly community in the age of Trump: toward a university-community engagement movement 3.0", in Kronic R. F. (ed.), *Emerging perspectives on community schools and the engaged university*, Hershey, PA: IGI Global, pp. 98-116.

Mounk Y. (2018), "America is not a democracy", *The Atlantic* (March 2018), available at www.theatlantic.com/magazine/archive/2018/03/america-is-not-a-democracy/550931/, accessed 16 July 2020.

National Council of Non-Profits (2020), "Why diversity, equity, and inclusion matter for nonprofits", Washington DC: National Council of Non-Profits, available at www.councilofnonprofits.org/tools-resources/why-diversity-equity-and-inclusion-matter-nonprofits, accessed 16 July 2020.

O'Flaherty M. (2018), "Second European Union minorities and discrimination survey: being Black in the EU", Vienna, Austria: European Union Agency for Fundamental Rights, available at https://fra.europa.eu/en/publication/2018/being-black-eu, accessed 16 September 2020.

Office of the Provost (2020), "Faculty trends by race/ethnicity fall", Buffalo, NY: The University at Buffalo, available at www.buffalo.edu/provost/oia/facts-publications/factbook/faculty-and-staff/faculty-and-staff.html, accessed 16 July 2020.

Schneider B. and Saw G. (2016), "Racial and ethnic gaps in postsecondary aspirations and enrollment", *Journal of the Social Sciences*, 2(5): 58-82.

Sinclair T. (2017), *Report on the gender and ethnic composition of State University of New York Faculty, 1995-2015*, Albany, NY: State University of New York, University Faculty Senate, Operations Committee: pp. 1-122.

Snyder T. D. (1993), *120 years of American education: a statistical portrait*, Washington DC: Center for Educational Statistics, U.S. Department of Education, Office of Educational Research and Improvement.

Spratlen T. H. (1979), "The Bakke decision: implications for Black educational and professional opportunities", *Journal of Negro Fducation*, 48(4): 449-56.

Stuart S. (2016), "Are we moving from capitalism to socialism?", *HSC Wealth Advisors* (30 August 2016), available at www.hscwealthadvisors.com/capitalism-to-socialism/, accessed 16 July 2020.

Tate S. A. and Bagguley P. (2017), "Building the anti-racist university: next steps", *Race, Ethnicity and Education*, 20(3): 289-99.

Taylor H. L., Jr (2009), *Inside El Barrio: an inside view of Castro's Cuba*, Sterling, VA: Kumarian Press.

Taylor H. L., Jr, Luter G. and Miller C. (2018), "The university, neighborhood revitalization, and civic engagement: toward civic engagement 3.0", *Societies,* 8(106): 1-21.

Taylor H. L., Jr, Luter G. and Uzochukwu K. (2018), "The truthful mirror: reforming the civic engagement movement in higher education", in Kronick R. F. (ed.), *Community engagement: principles, strategies, & practices*, Hauppauge, NY: Nova Science, pp. 1-24.

Taylor K.-Y. (2019), *Race for profit: how banks and the real estate industry undermined Black homeownership*, Chapel Hill: University of North Carolina Press.

Taylor K.-Y. (2020), "How do we change America?", *New Yorker* (8 June 2020), available at www.newyorker.com/news/our-columnists/how-do-we-change-america, accessed 16 July 2020.

Wilder C. S. (2013), *Ebony and Ivy: race, slavery, and the troubled history of America's universities*, New York: Bloomsbury Press.

Women's Health Editors (2020), "These viral Instagram graphics explain the impact of Black Lives Matter protests so far", *Women's Health*, available at www.womenshealthmag.com/life/a32812120/black-lives-matter-protests-impact-instagram-graphics/, accessed 16 July 2020.

Yamamura E. K. and Koth K. (2018), *Place-based community engagement in higher education: a strategy to transform universities and communities*, Sterling, VA: Stylus Publishing.

Yosso T. J. et al. (2004), "From Jim Crow to affirmative action and back again: a critical race discussion of racialized rationales and access to higher education", *Review of Research in Education*, 28: 1-25.

Part II

CHALLENGES AND RESPONSES

Chapter 4

Some challenges facing higher education in Europe in view of the Covid-19 pandemic

Ellen Hazelkorn

PANDEMIC ACCELERATING TRENDS

The world's increasing interconnectedness means that countries, people and issues which were previously unfamiliar or distant have become immediate and challenging in ways we were previously able to ignore. The 2020 Covid-19 pandemic is a tragic case in point.

The effect of the pandemic has been unprecedented and dramatic, changing almost every aspect of our lives overnight. In fact, one of the most amazing features of the past months has been the way in which people around the world – with some worrisome exceptions – have responded so quickly to the new public health guidelines and adapted. Higher education has not been immune (Croucher and Locke 2020; Estermann et al. 2020; Marinoni, van't Land and Jensen 2020; *Higher Education in Southeast Asia and Beyond* 2020; *Inside Higher Education* 2020; *International Higher Education* 2020; UNESCO-IESALC 2020; World Bank 2020).

The emergency phase has generated truly heroic responses from higher education. But the next phases will be more uncertain. Much will depend upon economic and political circumstances – and on policy decisions. Rather than big bang changes, existing trends are likely to accelerate and underlying weaknesses and inequalities are likely to be exposed. We are already seeing evidence of these trends.

The role and responsibilities of higher education are likely to come under increasing scrutiny, especially its contribution to social and economic recovery. There will be requests for the type of nimbleness and responsiveness for which universities have received so much praise in responding to the pandemic to be mainstreamed. While individual institutions point to financial vulnerabilities, bigger questions will be asked about the sustainability of the overall system of tertiary/higher education. Universities are likely to get a better hearing from the public and the broader political system if they lead with innovative solutions and in genuine partnership with their regions. This will bring the strategic capacity of college and university leadership to the fore.

How should we begin to think about the future of higher education in Europe in the medium to longer term? What are the likely challenges and opportunities? The next sections focus on six broad themes and discuss some implications and opportunities. This chapter concludes with a short discussion about the role and responsibilities of higher education in the post-Covid-19 world.

HIGHER EDUCATION IN EUROPE IN A CHANGING WORLD – THE NEED FOR STRUCTURED INTERNATIONAL DIALOGUE AND CO-ORDINATION

The spirit of internationalisation and cultural and scientific exchange has been intrinsic to universities and the spread of, and discourse around, ideas since their origins. In recent times, beginning with the Sorbonne (Bologna Process 1998) and Bologna (Bologna Process 1999) declarations, the Bologna Process/European Higher Education Area has been pivotal in promoting mobility and the exchange of ideas and cultural understanding. Today, student, academic and professional mobility is a normal part of scholarly endeavour. While geographic, linguistic and historical ties remain strong, universities are simultaneously competitors and collaborators.

In the first instance, the centre of gravity of the global economy is shifting eastwards and southwards as new players and new mega-regions emerge and wield more power and influence. Global university rankings are highly criticised but they confirm this multi-polar trend. In 2004, a year after the Academic Ranking of World Universities first emerged, the Americas and Europe dominated, with 180 universities in the top 200; by 2019, they held 155 places (Hazelkorn 2021). Looking at the top-500 group, a pipeline of universities and scholars from a more diverse set of countries is coming through. The aftershocks of the pandemic may dent these projections, but they are unlikely to alter the overall geopolitical shifts (Allen et al. 2020). Indeed, there is the danger that balkanisation of the global economy into rival trading blocs, alongside protectionist measures, will have an impact on international student and research flows, creating volatility and difficulty for nations and institutions in managing risk.

At the same time, collaboration is strengthening. The Human Genome Project of 1990 involved 20 universities and research centres. The UN Sustainable Development Goals (SDGs) formally recognised that societal problems were territorially blind, and no country has the knowledge or research capacity/capability to solve them on their own. The search for a vaccine and therapies against Covid-19 reaffirms this. The Bologna Declaration embedded collaboration between the European Research Area (ERA) and the European Higher Education Area (EHEA), setting an example for other regions around the world.

In these and many other areas of activity we see the guidelines, protocols, frameworks and regulations which together form a "complex, evolving lattice" (Marginson 2018: 23) of multilateral co-operation sustained by formal, informal and non-formal arrangements.

If the pandemic teaches us anything, it is that we underestimate the value of ongoing structured international dialogue, co-ordination, processes and tools at our peril.

Crises highlight the necessity for practical solutions. The need for an international assembly bringing together governments, policy makers, non-state and societal actors, universities and other higher education institutions, academics and researchers to promote and sustain international dialogue and collaboration across international higher education and global science is more critical now than ever.

DANGER OF "SURVIVAL OF THE FITTEST" APPROACH DOMINATING POLICY

Current projections suggest the pandemic will cause a major shock to the global economy, with severe socio-economic consequences. EU forecasts suggest the total EU economy will contract by 8.3% in 2020 and 5.8% in 2021, with job losses projected to rise to almost 10% before beginning to decline – although these figures are almost certainly likely to fluctuate as the full impact of the pandemic is felt (European Commission 2020a; 2020c). The effect will also vary across regions, people and sectors, with impact being felt the most by younger workers and recent graduates, those in the informal economy and lower-skilled jobs (ILO 2020; JRC 2020). At a time of diminished tax revenues, governments face rising demands for state-led initiatives with respect to health and social services, labour-activation and other safety-net initiatives, economic supports and stimulus programmes.

These dramatic effects coincide with two other developments. Demographic changes account for Europe's shrinking population. By 2070, EU countries (these figures include the UK) are expected to represent less than 4% of the world's population, compared with about 6% today. As life expectancy increases, more than 13.2% of the population will be aged 80 years or older compared with only 5.8% today (European Commission 2020b). In addition, technological progress along with climate change will have a transformative effect on how people live, work and socialise (Centre for the New Economy and Society 2018). Precise information about which jobs are likely to be affected, automated, lost or displaced in the future is uncertain, but new opportunities will almost certainly require higher-order cognitive, communication and interpersonal skills, complex problem solving, creativity, fluency of ideas and active learning, requiring people to have broad-based skills alongside specialist knowledge.

Elite universities with strong(er) bank balances and robust reputations will be better able to weather the impacts of the pandemic. They are currently experiencing significant reductions in international students and associated income but are likely to return to buoyancy over the medium term (Altbach and de Wit 2020). But, too much attention is focused on one kind of university. In Europe in 2017, the universities ranked in the top 100 constituted only 4% of the total 19.8 million tertiary students (Eurostat 2018).

The bigger concern is the rest of the tertiary system, beyond the resource-intensive research universities. These are the colleges and universities – often in smaller cities and towns – that the overwhelming majority of our students attend. Public institutions are most dependent upon government resources, while private ones depend upon tuition fees, both of which are likely to be affected by current circumstances.

How do we ensure the sustainability of the whole tertiary system to ensure it provides diverse educational, research and student experiences for learners of all ages and abilities throughout their lives? One thing is clear, we cannot allow a "survival of the fittest" approach to dominate policy.

Traditional (semi-)rigid boundaries between, and biases about, academic, technical and vocational education and training (VET/TVET) are blocking innovative thinking. In many instances such boundaries have encouraged socio-economic stratification rather than mission differentiation, and unnecessary competition for resources and students. Instead, more emphasis should be placed on creating learning eco-systems, with closer links across the system through collaboration and networking, and deeper engagement with cities and regions. We should develop integrated and flexible pathways with genuine collaborative programmes and credit accumulation and transfer systems. Back-office facilities and infrastructure can be shared, overcoming gratuitous duplication.

Rather than piecemeal institutional actions or bilateral agreements, structured co-ordination, underpinned by innovative governance arrangements and funding, can encourage and support greater porosity, creating a system of more connected, horizontally diverse institutions (Hazelkorn 2016). The EU strategy for smart specialisation is a complementary policy approach. It promotes a place-based model characterised by leveraging strengths and potential, and embracing social, technological and economic innovation, with wide stakeholder involvement and supported by effective monitoring mechanisms (Edwards et al. 2017; Kempton et al. 2013). These initiatives could underpin a new social contract between higher education and society (Hazelkorn and Gibson 2019).

In the era of the Green Agenda, we should adopt the principles of biodiversity (Wilson 1988), recognising that each institution plays a critical role, all mutually supporting one another, without which the entire system may collapse.

RE-THINKING THE MODEL OF EDUCATIONAL PROVISION FOR HIGH-PARTICIPATION SOCIETIES

Even before the current crisis, questions were being asked about graduate outcomes, relevance and employability. While EU member states have made good progress towards the goal of increasing to at least 40% the share of the population aged 30-34 who have completed tertiary education by 2020, about one fifth of 15-year-olds show insufficient abilities in reading, mathematics and science – a backward step compared to 2012 (Eurostat 2018; European Commission 2019a). This is atop the unemployment situation we now find around us.

It is certain that higher education will now be asked to play a more direct role in social and economic recovery and to embrace a more diverse cohort of learners into the future. Can we re-think our current model of education provision, and teaching and learning? Is it still fit-for-purpose for "high participation societies" (Cantwell et al. 2018)? Should we not need to pay more attention to trying to balance supply (programmes offered) and demand (skills requirements) in recognition that they are interconnected and that both knowledge and skills are required in this rapidly changing world (Keep 2016).

We are only in the early stages of a learning revolution involving digitalisation and new teaching and learning pedagogies. The surge to digital platforms and online provision which we have just witnessed should be mainstreamed. This does not mean everything goes online, but the experience of borderless higher education (OBHE 2020) shows us we can deliver high quality in this format. But can we go further? The Erasmus programme and the European Credit Transfer and Accumulation System (ECTS) have not yet fulfilled their potential for credit accumulation and transfer, albeit that is a component of some of the European University initiatives. Work-based/work-informed learning, innovative modes of delivery, learner and career pathways, shorter and different types of courses/programmes and new forms of credentials should become the norm. Students should be empowered to tailor their entry, exit, assessment and qualifications to their personally determined needs with the introduction of competency-based education and micro-credentials rather than being required to fit a standardised model. Likewise, there should be growing involvement of enterprise and civil society in helping to shape learning outcomes, influence career guidance, provide internship programmes, advise on faculty appointments and promotion criteria, evaluate research projects and their impact, and undertake similar types of activity. These developments will facilitate a shift from traditional time-served education to just-in-time education, with implications for the organisation of the institutions and academic practices.

Should we also be looking at the curriculum development process itself? As a guesstimate, the timeline from ideation to (re)design, internal quality assurance, student entry and progression to graduation and into the labour force, and student feedback could take approximately 7-8 years. By this time the economy and job opportunities will have changed, in some cases very dramatically – as we are currently witnessing. Greater commitment to continuous flexibility and responsiveness is required.

REACHING PEOPLE AND COMMUNITIES MOST AFFECTED BY THE PANDEMIC AND ALIENATED FROM SOCIETY AND EDUCATION

The underlying assumption of social progress and massification (meaning, in higher education, a massive expansion in student numbers) was that each generation would be better off than the previous one. However, according to the OECD, income inequality is at its highest level for 50 years (OECD 2018). Every generation since the baby-boom era has seen the middle-income group shrink and its economic influence weaken (OECD 2019). Attention is also drawn to students who are gradually being left behind by current systems and those unable to access the system in any meaningful and sustained way. Disadvantaged students remain under-represented among those entering the system and, if they enrol, they are over-represented in less prestigious institutions and/or degree programmes (OECD 2017: 35-6). The issue is not simply access but "access to what?" (Bastedo and Gumport 2003). Too often governments have failed to address the broader equity agenda, providing insufficient support mechanisms to ensure active participation and successful completion (Salmi 2018). Universities have often acted as gatekeepers, as they pursue prestige at home and abroad, rather than as a gateway to opportunity (Cantwell et al. 2018; Carnevale, Schmidt and Strohl 2020; Piketty 2020).

Globalisation has brought benefits but it has also increased economic insecurity (felt by individuals, their families and communities), widening disparities of wealth, opportunities and political views according to educational attainment, institutional status and place. Despite the fact that demand is growing, more people feel left behind (Algan et al. 2017; Inglehart and Norris 2016).

The aim is to reach out to people and communities who have been affected by the pandemic, or who may be the first in their family to consider attending tertiary education or who feel deeply alienated from society. Reskilling and repurposing qualifications should coincide with concerted efforts to help overcome generational inequalities and disadvantage according to socio-economic, race, ethnicity, regional and digital-divide factors. And, as people live actively for longer, universities will need to adopt a lifelong learning approach and respond to ongoing requirements for education and training as the norm.

RISK OF EXCESSIVE FOCUS ON MEDICAL AND BIOLOGICAL SCIENCE AT THE EXPENSE OF A HOLISTIC APPROACH TO RESEARCH AND INNOVATION

Globalisation, mobility and the growing use of data sharing, open science platforms and other tools have contributed hugely to transnational partnerships, networks and cross-disciplinary collaboration. English as the *lingua franca* has been another, if controversial, enabler. The number of international research collaborations has tripled over the past 15 years (Crew 2019). Internationally co-authored papers, as a percentage of all scientific papers, have more than doubled over the past 20 years, accounting for all the output growth by scientifically advanced countries (Wagner, Park and Leydesdorff 2015; Salmi 2015; Adams and Loach 2015). International collaboration accounts for increased numbers of patents, with global teams featuring prominently, exceeding the performance of in-country patents and also being better cited within and outside the firm (Kerr and Kerr 2015). There is a strong correlation between science and economic policy with countries displaying high levels of openness, in other words being more internationalised, and having higher levels of impact (Popov and Sundaram 2017; Wagner et al. 2018). Unsurprisingly, international collaboration is now a key indicator of quality.

The global search for a vaccine and other therapies against Covid-19 highlights the benefits of global collaboration. Indeed, it is likely to accelerate initiatives around open science as envisaged by the EU's Plan S (Science Europe 2018). It is also likely to encourage further adoption of open research infrastructures based on FAIR (findable, accessible, interoperable, reusable) principles – albeit there are challenges in legal constraints, confidentiality issues, intellectual property rights, scientific recognition systems and quality assurance. However, there are worrying signs also of unnecessary competition and hoarding supplies (Sanger et al., 2020; Apuzzo, Gebrekidan and Kirkpatrick 2020; Boseley 2020; Cohen 2020).

Worrying also is that renewed interest in, and reliance on, science and experts has primarily focused on medical and biological science and epidemiology, with funding (re)oriented accordingly. Will the pandemic lead to wider appreciation of the value and contribution that all disciplines can make to our understanding of societal change?

Most countries have established a pandemic or public health advisory body – but how many of them are genuinely multidisciplinary, with experts from across the arts, humanities and social sciences alongside science, technology, engineering and mathematics (STEM) subjects? On the other hand, we should not get too comfortable. We have seen a return to the anti-expert lobby, especially in the USA and Brazil, posing a false dichotomy between public health and re-opening the economy.

INCREASED MONETISATION OF HIGHER EDUCATION AND RESEARCH DATA

The current environment has also re-focused attention on measuring the impact and benefit of publicly funded research. To paraphrase John F. Kennedy, it is not only what universities do for themselves that counts but the overall benefits they bring to their communities and citizens. Hopefully, renewed concerns about the distorting effect caused by exceptional attention given to high-impact journals and impact factors will kick-start a much-needed debate about the meaningfulness of indicators (DORA 2012; Hicks et al. 2015; Creus 2020; te Roller 2020; VSNU et al. 2019).

The debate around what constitutes "excellence" has encouraged rankings to jump on this bandwagon (Council of Europe 2012: para. 6). The *Times Higher Education* Impact Ranking measures university commitment to the UN SDGs but there are huge difficulties with the methodologies and use of paywalls, which should not surprise anyone (*Times Higher Education* 2019; Hazelkorn 2020). More interesting is the extent to which the global rankings will remain credible during and after the pandemic. Indeed, it could be argued that rankings incentivised universities to over-expand their share of international students, with the dire consequences we now see. As we ponder their fitness for purpose, we are likely to see continued corporate integration among rankings, publishing and big data, and hence the monetisation of higher education and research data (Fyfe et al. 2017; Posada and Chen 2018).

LEADING INNOVATIVE SOLUTIONS TO POST-COVID-19 CHALLENGES

Universities and colleges across Europe have had a strong relationship with their countries, cities and regions throughout the centuries. This mutually beneficial relationship ties together their futures. As the UNESCO *Global Education 2030 Agenda* recognises:

> Education is both a goal in itself and a means for attaining all the other SDGs. It is not only an integral part of sustainable development, but also a key enabler for it (UNESCO 2017: 1)

Because investing in higher education and research is an investment in our shared future, there is a special onus on higher education and research to be innovative and to lead change. This focuses our attention on the strategic capacity of college and university leadership. The quality of our system and its outcomes depends upon the quality of the people who lead, but do we spend sufficient time developing recruitment or succession strategies? In a 2019 survey of senior leaders in Irish higher education, only 20% believed institutional management had the capabilities appropriate to the standards required to meet current challenges and responsibilities facing higher education (Hazelkorn and Boland 2020). And, despite some impressive achievements, significant gaps persist between the rising number of women as students and those in leadership roles (European Commission 2019b). Organisational, academic culture and societal barriers to career opportunities continue to exist (O'Connor, Martin et al. 2019; O'Connor, O'Hagan et al. 2019).

The civic university agenda has received increasing attention over the years and is likely to take on greater urgency in the future, associated with quality assurance and funding (Farnell 2020; Goddard et al. 2016; UPP Foundation 2019). However, too often reference to civic engagement is rhetorical and episodic, with insufficient commitment at all levels of higher education and government. Too often pursuit of prestige through university rankings has fostered a false dichotomy between being globally competitive and being regionally rooted (Grau et al. 2017; Hazelkorn 2015). Too often "third mission" activity is envisaged as something disconnected from teaching and research. Instead, while approaching it in different ways, civic engagement must be embedded as a core component of all universities: helping people achieve their personal development goals, providing the skills needed to serve our economies and maintain and enhance our living standards, and providing the basis for a society rich in culture and social capital.

As we are currently witnessing, as the world becomes more interconnected, more complex societal challenges arise. Overcoming these challenges requires all citizens to have a better understanding of the issues in order to separate fact from fake news and hoaxes. Democracy depends upon active responsible citizenship (Hazelkorn et al. 2015). This is the role and responsibility that higher education and research must take on; it must seize the initiative and lead.

This is no time for sitting on the sidelines.

REFERENCES

Adams J. and Loach T. (2015), "Comment: a well-connected world", *Nature*, 527(7577), S58-S59, available at https://doi.org/10.1038/527S58a, accessed 23 July 2020.

Algan Y. et al. (2017), "The European trust crisis and the rise of populism", *Brookings Papers on Economy Activity* (Fall 2017), available at www.brookings.edu/wp-content/uploads/2018/02/algantextfa17bpea.pdf, accessed 23 July 2020.

Allen J. et al. (2020), "How the world will look after the coronavirus pandemic", *Foreign Policy* (March 2020): 1-12, available at https://foreignpolicy.com/2020/03/20/world-order-after-coroanvirus-pandemic/, accessed 23 July 2020.

Altbach P. G. and de Wit H. (2020), "Post pandemic outlook for HE is bleakest for the poorest", *University World News*, 4 April, available at www.universityworldnews.com/post.php?story=20200402152914362, accessed 23 July 2020.

Apuzzo M., Gebrekidan S. and Kirkpatrick D. D. (2020), "How the world missed COVID-19's silent spread", *New York Times* (27 June 2020), available at www.nytimes.com/2020/06/27/world/europe/coronavirus-spread-asymptomatic.html?nl=todaysheadlines&emc=edit_th_20200628, accessed 23 July 2020.

Bastedo M. N. M. and Gumport P. J. P. (2003), "Access to what? Mission differentiation and academic stratification in U.S. public higher education", *Higher Education*, 46(3): 341-59.

Bologna Process (1998), "Sorbonne Joint Declaration. Joint declaration on harmonisation of the architecture of the European higher education system", available at www.ehea.info/page-ministerial-declarations-and-communiques, accessed 19 July 2020.

Bologna Process (1999), "The Bologna Declaration of 19 June 1999", available at www.ehea.info/page-ministerial-declarations-and-communiques, accessed 19 July 2020.

Boseley S. (2020), "US secures world stock of key Covid-19 drug remdesivir", *The Guardian* (30 June 2020), available at www.theguardian.com/us-news/2020/jun/30/us-buys-up-world-stock-of-key-covid-19-drug, accessed 23 July 2020.

Cantwell B., Marginson S. and Smolentseva A. (eds) (2018), *High participation systems of higher education*, Oxford: Oxford University Press.

Carnevale A., Schmidt P. and Strohl J. (2020), *The merit myth. How our colleges favor the rich and divide America*, Washington DC: The New Press.

Centre for the New Economy and Society (2018), *The future of jobs report 2018*, Geneva: World Economic Forum, available at www3.weforum.org/docs/WEF_Future_of_Jobs_2018.pdf, accessed 23 July 2020.

Cohen J. (2020), "Unveiling Warp Speed, the White House's America-first push for a coronavirus vaccine", *Science* (12 May 2020), available at https://doi.org/10.1126/science.abc7056, accessed 23 July 2020.

Council of Europe (2012), Recommendation CM/Rec(2012)7 of the Committee of Ministers to member states on the responsibility of public authorities for academic freedom and institutional autonomy, available at www.refworld.org/pdfid/50697ed62.pdf, accessed 25 September 2020.

Creus G. J. (2020), "Will others follow China's switch on academic publishing ?", *University World News* (21 March 2020), available at www.universityworldnews.com/post.php?story=2020031810362222, accessed 23 July 2020.

Crew B. (2019), "The top 10 countries in research collaboration", *Nature Index* (12 July 2019), available at www.natureindex.com/news-blog/data-visualization-top-ten-countries-research-collaboration, accessed 23 July 2020.

Croucher G. and Locke W. (2020), *A post-coronavirus pandemic world: some possible trends and their implications for Australian higher education*, retrieved from https://melbourne-cshe.unimelb.edu.au/__data/assets/pdf_file/0010/3371941/a-post-coronavirus-world-for-higher-education_final.pdf, accessed 14 October 2020.

DORA (2012), *San Francisco Declaration on Research Assessment*, available at https://sfdora.org, accessed 23 July 2020.

Edwards J. et al. (2017), *Higher education for smart specialisation: Towards strategic partnerships for innovation* (No. 23/2017), Luxembourg: Publications Office of the EU, available at https://doi.org/10.2760/376572, accessed 16 September 2020.

Estermann T. et al. (2020), *The impact of the Covid-19 crisis on university funding in Europe: Lessons learnt from the 2008 global financial crisis*, Brussels: European University Association, available at https://eua.eu/downloads/publications/eua%20 briefing_the%20impact%20of%20the%20covid-19%20crisis%20on%20university%20 funding%20in%20europe.pdf, accessed 23 July 2020.

European Commission (2019a), *Pisa 2018 and the EU: Striving for social fairness through education*, retrieved from https://ec.europa.eu/education/sites/education/files/document-library-docs/pisa-2018-eu_1.pdf, accessed 23 July 2020.

European Commission (2019b), *She figures 2018*, Luxembourg: Publications Office of the EU, available at https://op.europa.eu/en/publication-detail/-/publication/9540ffa1-4478-11e9-a8ed-01aa75ed71a1, accessed 23 July 2020.

European Commission (2020a), *EU Spring 2020 economic forecast: a deep and uneven recession, an uncertain recovery*, available at https://ec.europa.eu/info/sites/info/files/economy-finance/ecfin_forecast_spring_2020_overview_en_0.pdf, accessed 23 July 2020.

European Commission (2020b), *Report from the Commission on the impact of demographic change* (No. COM(2020) 241 final), available at https://doi.org/10.1017/CBO9781107415324.004, accessed 23 July 2020.

European Commission (2020c), *EU Summer 2020 economic forecast: an even deeper recession with wider divergences*, available at https://ec.europa.eu/commission/presscorner/detail/en/ip_20_1269, accessed 23 July 2020.

Eurostat (2018), Tertiary education statistics, available at https://ec.europa.eu/eurostat/statistics-explained/index.php?title=Tertiary_education_statistics, accessed 14 July 2020.

Farnell T. (2020), *Community engagement in higher education: trends, practices and policies. NESET report*, Luxembourg: Publications Office of the EU, available at https://nesetweb.eu/wp-content/uploads/2020/07/NESET_AR1-2020_analytical-report.pdf, accessed 23 July 2020.

Fyfe A. et al. (2017), *Untangling academic publishing: A history of the relationship between commercial interests, academic prestige and the circulation of research*, available at https://doi.org/10.5281/zenodo.546100, accessed 23 July 2020.

Goddard J. et al. (2016), *The civic university: the policy and leadership challenges*, Cheltenham, UK: Edward Elgar Publishing.

Grau F. X. et al. (eds) (2017), *Towards a socially responsible university: balancing the global with the local*, Higher Education in the World No. 6, Girona, Spain: Global University Network for Innovation (GUNi).

Hazelkorn E. (2015), *Rankings and the reshaping of higher education: the battle for world-class excellence*, 2nd edn, Basingstoke, UK: Palgrave Macmillan.

Hazelkorn E. (2016), *Towards 2030: a framework for building a world-class post-compulsory education system for Wales*, Cardiff: Welsh Government, available at http://gov.wales/topics/educationandskills/publications/reports/

review-of-the-oversight-and-regulation-of-post-compulsory-education-and-training-in-wales/?lang=en, accessed 23 July 2020.

Hazelkorn E. (2020), "Should universities be ranked for their SDG performance?", *University World News* (21 March 2020), available at www.universityworldnews.com/post.php?story=20200317145134326, accessed 23 July 2020.

Hazelkorn E. (2021), "What do global university rankings tell us about US geopolitics in higher education?", in J. J. Lee (ed.), *U.S. power in international higher education*, New Brunswick, NJ and London: Rutgers University Press.

Hazelkorn E. and Boland T. (2020), "How does Irish higher education see itself?", *International Higher Education*, 103(Summer): 29-30.

Hazelkorn E. and Gibson A. (2019), "Public goods and public policy: what is public good, and who and what decides?", *Higher Education*, 78(2): 257-71.

Hazelkorn E. et al. (2015), *Science education for responsible citizenship*, Luxembourg: Publications Office of the EU.

Hicks D. et al. (2015), "Bibliometrics: the Leiden Manifesto for research metrics", *Nature*, 520(7548): 429-31, available at https://doi.org/10.1038/520429a, accessed 16 September 2020.

Higher Education in Southeast Asia and Beyond (2020), "How is COVID-19 impacting higher education?", Special Issue (June), available at https://headfoundation.org/wp-content/uploads/2020/06/HESB-8-COVID19_2020.pdf, accessed 23 July 2020.

ILO (2020), "A policy framework for tackling the economic and social impact of the COVID-19 crisis", *Policy Brief*, Geneva: International Labour Organization, available at www.ilo.org/wcmsp5/groups/public/@dgreports/@dcomm/documents/briefingnote/wcms_745337.pdf, accessed 23 July 2020.

Inglehart R. F. and Norris P. (2016), *Trump, Brexit, and the rise of populism: economic have-nots and cultural backlash*, Harvard Kennedy School (HKS) Working Paper No. RWP16-026, Cambridge, MA: Harvard University, available at https://papers.ssrn.com/sol3/papers.cfm?abstract_id=2818659, accessed 23 July 2020.

Inside Higher Education (2020), *Responding to the COVID-19 crisis, Part III: a survey of college and university presidents*, Washington, DC: Inside Higher Education and Hanover Research, available at www.insidehighered.com/booklet/responding-covid-19-crisis-part-iii-new-survey-college-and-university-presidents, accessed 23 July 2020.

International Higher Education (2020), Special Issue on Covid-19, Issue 102, available at www.internationalhighereducation.net/en/handbuch/gliederung/#/Gliederungsebene/811/No.-102-Special-Issue-2020, accessed 23 July 2020.

JRC (2020), "The impact of COVID confinement measures on EU labour market", *Science for Policy Briefs* (May 2020): 5, available at https://ec.europa.eu/jrc/sites/jrcsh/files/jrc.120585_policy.brief_impact.of_.covid-19.on_.eu-labour.market.pdf, accessed 23 July 2020.

Keep E. (2016), *Improving skills utilisation in the UK – some reflections on what, who and how?* (No. 123), Oxford: Centre on Skills, Knowledge and Organisational Performance (SKOPE), University of Oxford.

Kempton L. et al. (2013), *Universities and smart specialisation* (No. S3 Policy Brief Series No. 03/2013), Luxembourg: Publications Office of the EU, available at https://op.europa.eu/en/publication-detail/-/publication/cc0c282a-3f69-4c78-bf8e-7a61c1587556/language-en, accessed 23 July 2020.

Kerr S. P. and Kerr W. R. (2015), "Global collaborative patents", in *Harvard Business School Working Paper* (No. 16-059), Cambridge, MA: Harvard Business School, available in *The Economic Journal*, 128(612): F235-F272 at https://doi.org/10.1111/ecoj.12369, accessed 16 September 2020.

Marginson S. (2018), *The new geopolitics of higher education*, Centre for Global Higher Education Working Paper Series No. 34, Oxford and London: CGHE, available at www.researchcghe.org/perch/resources/publications/wp34final.pdf, accessed 23 July 2020.

Marinoni G., van't Land H. and Jensen T. (2020), *The impact of Covid-19 on higher education around the world*, IAU Global Survey Report, Paris: International Association of Universities, available at www.iau-aiu.net/IMG/pdf/iau_covid19_and_he_survey_report_final_may_2020.pdf, accessed 23 July 2020.

O'Connor P., Martin P. Y. et al. (2019), "Leadership practices by senior position holders in higher educational research institutes: stealth power in action?", *Leadership*, 15(6): 1-22, available at https://doi.org/10.1177/1742715019853200, accessed 16 September 2020.

O'Connor P. O'Hagan C. et al. (2019), "Mentoring and sponsorship in higher education institutions: men's invisible advantage in STEM?", *Higher Education Research and Development*, 39(4): 764-77, available at https://doi.org/10.1080/07294360.2019.1686468, accessed 16 September 2020.

OBHE (The Observatory on Borderless Higher Education) (2020), "OBHE is closing at the end of 2020", available at www.obhe.ac.uk/who_we_are/about_the_observatory, accessed 14 July 2020.

OECD (2017), *Report on benchmarking higher education system performance: conceptual framework and data*, Paris: OECD, available at www.oecd.org/education/skills-beyond-school/Benchmarking%20Report.pdf, accessed 23 July 2020.

OECD (2018), *Inequality*, Paris: OECD, available at www.oecd.org/social/inequality.htm, accessed 14 July 2020.

OECD (2019), *Under pressure: the squeezed middle class*, Paris: OECD, available at www.oecd-ilibrary.org/social-issues-migration-health/under-pressure-the-squeezed-middle-class_689afed1-en, accessed 23 July 2020.

Piketty T. (2020), *Capital and ideology*, Cambridge, MA: Belknap Press of Harvard University Press.

Popov V. and Sundaram J. K. (2017), "Convergence? More developing countries are catching up", in V. Popov and P. Dutkiewica (eds), *Mapping a new world order: the rest beyond the West*, pp. 7–22, Cheltenham, UK: Edward Elgar Publishing.

Posada A. and Chen G. (2018), *Inequality in knowledge production: the integration of academic infrastructure by big publishers*, 0–21, available at https://hal.archives-ouvertes.fr/hal-01816707/document, accessed 23 July 2020.

Roller E. te (2020). "Dutch funders move away from journal impact factor" (27 March 2020), available at www.researchprofessionalnews.com/rr-news-europe-netherlands-2020-3-dutch-funders-move-away-from-journal-impact-factor/, accessed 23 July 2020.

Salmi J. (2015), *Study on open science: impact, implications and policy options*, Luxembourg: Publications Office of the EU, available at https://ec.europa.eu/research/innovation-union/pdf/expert-groups/rise/study_on_open_science-impact_implications_and_policy_options-salmi_072015.pdf, accessed 23 July 2020.

Salmi J. (2018), *All around the world – higher education equity policies across the globe*, Indianapolis, IN: Lumina Foundation, available at https://worldaccesshe.com/wp-content/uploads/2018/11/All-around-the-world-Higher-education-equity-policies-across-the-globe-.pdf, accessed 23 July 2020.

Sanger D. E. et al. (2020), "Search for coronavirus vaccine becomes a global competition", *New York Times* (19 March 2020), available at www.nytimes.com/2020/03/19/us/politics/coronavirus-vaccine-competition.html, accessed 23 July 2020.

Science Europe (2018), "Plan S: accelerating the transition to full and immediate open access to scientific publications", available at www.coalition-s.org/wp-content/uploads/Plan_S.pdf, accessed 23 July 2020.

Times Higher Education (2019), "Impact ranking", available at www.timeshighereducation.com/rankings/impact/2019/overall#!/page/0/length/2, accessed 14 July 2020.

UNESCO (2017), "Education for sustainable development goals: learning objectives", in *The Global Education 2030 Agenda, Objectives Learning*, available at https://unesdoc.unesco.org/ark:/48223/pf0000247444, accessed 23 July 2020.

UNESCO-IESALC (2020), *COVID-19 and higher education: today and tomorrow. Impact analysis, policy responses and recommendations*, available at https://bit.ly/34TOSvu, accessed 23 July 2020.

UPP Foundation (2019), *Truly civic: strengthening the connection between universities and their places. The final report of the UPP Foundation Civic University Commission*, available at https://upp-foundation.org/wp-content/uploads/2019/02/Civic-University-Commission-Final-Report.pdf, accessed 23 July 2020.

VSNU et al. (2019), *Room for everyone's talent*, available at www.vsnu.nl/files/documenten/Domeinen/Onderzoek/Position%20paper%20Room%20for%20everyone's%20talent.pdf, accessed 23 July 2020.

Wagner C. S., Park H. W. and Leydesdorff L. (2015), "The continuing growth of global cooperation networks in research: a conundrum for national governments", *PLoS ONE*, 10(7): 1–15, available at https://doi.org/10.1371/journal.pone.0131816, accessed 23 July 2020.

Wagner C. S. et al. (2018), "Openness and impact of leading scientific countries", *Frontiers in Research Metrics and Analytics*, 3(March): 1-10, available at https://doi.org/10.3389/frma.2018.00010, accessed 23 July 2020.

Wilson E. O. (ed.) (1988), *Biodiversity*, available at https://doi.org/10.17226/989, accessed 23 July 2020.

World Bank (2020), *The COVID-19 crisis response: supporting tertiary education for continuity, adaptation, and innovation*, (April 2020): 9, available at http://pubdocs.worldbank.org/en/621991586463915490/WB-Tertiary-Ed-and-Covid-19-Crisis-for-public-use-April-9.pdf, accessed 23 July 2020.

Chapter 5

Challenges to US higher education in performing local missions during and after the Covid-19 pandemic

David Maurrasse

INTRODUCTION

The Covid-19 pandemic has dramatically altered institutions of higher education and their surrounding localities in the United States. The relationship between institutions of higher education and their communities has been strained at times, but colleges and universities and the neighbourhoods, cities and regions in which they are situated are interdependent. They exist within a similar ecosystem in which institutions of higher education, to varying degrees, rely on their surroundings in order to function.

In recent years, we have begun to see an increase in active attempts by institutions of higher education to collaborate with local community-based organisations, governments and other partners to strengthen local communities, and to address issues such as education, health and economic development. A movement to enhance the role of institutions of higher education and other anchor institutions[23] in democratic community partnerships has continued to grow. This development has helped institutions of higher education draw upon their human, intellectual, social, physical and economic capital to reduce inequities in their communities.

The advent of Covid-19 has challenged institutions of higher education to advance their local missions even further. Communities across the US and the globe have been experiencing an extraordinary public health and economic crisis. Various inequities that already existed have been exacerbated. This has become particularly pronounced racially, as Black, Latinx[24] and Native American populations have been

---

23. For the concept of "anchor institutions" and the Anchor Institutions Task Force, see AITF 2020.
24. "Latinx" is used as a gender-neutral term for Latin Americans. The US Office of Management and Budget (OMB) defines "Hispanic or Latino" as a person of Cuban, Mexican, Puerto Rican, South or Central American, or other Spanish culture or origin, regardless of race. See www.census.gov/topics/population/hispanic-origin/about.html, accessed 22 July 2020.

contracting and dying from the virus at higher rates. Many are confronting greater economic instability on top of already vulnerable circumstances.

Institutions of higher education bring a vast array of resources to their local community. In addition to knowledge capital, they bring economic, physical and other forms of capital. During the pandemic, local needs for these resources have become particularly apparent, as colleges and universities provided, for example, physical locations for testing and treatment. The pandemic also revealed the economic interdependency between local communities and institutions of higher education. Many towns and neighbourhoods depend on the purchasing power of university students and staff. While more local residents are expecting resources from colleges and universities, especially for the most under-served populations, institutions of higher education themselves have faced declining tuition, layoffs, a transition to online learning, uncertainty about how to re-open and numerous other disruptions to the fundamental dimensions of how they function (DePietro 2020; German Academic Exchange Service 2020). Just as the pandemic has further illuminated inequities in society, it has highlighted disparities among institutions of higher education (Sorenson Impact Center Staff 2020). Well-endowed institutions are certainly disrupted along with everyone else, but for a significant number of institutions of higher education, particularly those that depend on tuition, the pandemic has caused more serious financial stress. Furthermore, many of the community colleges, historically black colleges and universities,[25] Hispanic Serving Institutions,[26] Tribal Colleges and Universities[27] and various public (and also some private) universities that are economically vulnerable serve many of the more disadvantaged populations. Additionally, higher education and other sectors are facing a racial reckoning, as a racial justice movement has been significantly expanding during the pandemic due to the murder of George Floyd and other African Americans.[28]

---

25. According to the U.S. Department of Education, "Historically black colleges and universities (HBCUs) were established to serve the educational needs of black Americans. Prior to the time of their establishment, and for many years afterwards, blacks were generally denied admission to traditionally white institutions. As a result, HBCUs became the principle means for providing postsecondary education to black Americans"; see www2.ed.gov/about/offices/list/ocr/docs/hq9511.html, accessed 22 July 2020.
26. The U.S. Department of Education says that "A Hispanic-Serving Institution (HSI) is defined as an institution of higher education that is an eligible institution; and has an enrollment of undergraduate full-time equivalent students that is at least 25% Hispanic students at the end of the award year immediately preceding the date of application"; see https://sites.ed.gov/hispanic-initiative/hispanic-serving-institutions-hsis/, accessed 22 July 2020.
27. Tribal Colleges and Universities are unique institutions that offer opportunities for Native Americans to pursue higher education within their own cultural and regional contexts. According to the U.S. Department of Education, "there are 32 fully accredited Tribal Colleges and Universities (TCUs) in the United States, with one formal candidate for accreditation. Three are in Associate Status"; see https://sites.ed.gov/whiaiane/tribes-tcus/tribal-colleges-and-universities/, accessed 22 July 2020.
28. George Perry Floyd Jr (14 October 1973–25 May 2020) was a Black American man killed by a white police officer during an arrest after allegedly using a counterfeit $20 bill in Minneapolis. Floyd's death triggered global protests against racially motivated violence and police brutality. The shooting death of African-American teen Trayvon Martin in February 2012 and the acquittal of policeman George Zimmerman in 2013 triggered the #BlackLivesMatter movement, which returned to national headlines and gained further international attention after Floyd's death. A couple of other prominent examples of African Americans who were murdered in acts of racist violence in 2020 include Breonna Taylor and Ahmaud Arbery.

Amidst the many challenges facing institutions of higher education, society cannot navigate the duration and aftermath of the pandemic without colleges and universities. Many institutions of higher education have been contributing to finding a cure for the virus, serving as sites for testing, advancing testing, graduating medical students early to allow them to help care for patients in local hospitals, developing and distributing personal protective equipment (PPE), housing patients and the homeless, treating patients through medical campuses, raising awareness about pandemics, providing mental health services, publishing pandemic situation information and instructions, and more. They have also been collaborating with local governments on plans for their regions, providing access to technology for children and young people forced to learn remotely, creating new training programmes in fields likely to grow due to the pandemic, and providing technical services to small local businesses and beyond. In public health and many other realms, institutions of higher education have been significantly contributing to their communities. The Anchor Institutions Task Force has been gathering examples of how colleges, universities and other anchor institutions have been advancing their local missions amidst Covid-19, some of which are shared herein (AITF 2020).

IMMEDIATE CHALLENGES TO US HIGHER EDUCATION INSTITUTIONS

As institutions of higher education and their communities are interdependent, they have both faced simultaneous challenges from the pandemic (Gavazzi 2020). While colleges and universities have faced tremendous disruptions and economic insecurities, nearby communities have been experiencing repercussions of these changes in addition to other difficulties due to the crisis. Institutions of higher education, which drove local economies in some instances, suddenly were no longer providing economic activity, as dormitories closed and students, faculty and staff were no longer actively purchasing locally (Nicholson and Semmler 2020; Anonymous 2020). As many businesses have been forced into permanent closure, not having been able to withstand months without revenue, the nature of communities around colleges and universities has been gradually altered for the short term.

At the time of writing, as the autumn semester 2020 approaches, colleges and universities are confronted with determining how to resume activities. Since the virus continues to spread in the US, many institutions will have to continue operating virtually to a substantial extent, which will further adversely impact local economies. The US is clearly experiencing greater difficulty than some other countries in managing the pandemic. The US never had a national strategy to shut down or to adhere to particular guidelines (e.g. wearing masks). Each state has developed its own policies for shutting down as well as re-opening, which has led to some confusion. This considerable variation in policy and practice has also led to recent outbreaks, which have influenced decisions by colleges and universities for the autumn semester 2020. For example, institutions typically join athletic "conferences" such as the Ivy League or Big Ten for regular competitions, under governing bodies like the National Collegiate Athletic Association, National Association of Intercollegiate Athletics or United States

Collegiate Athletic Association, and some athletic conferences have decided to forego intercollegiate sports, influenced by the country's inability to control the spread of the virus (Nietzel 2020).

A public health crisis on a campus can also affect the community. If students and staff contract the virus, their contagion can transcend campuses to spread in the community as well, and vice versa. Therefore, the combined public health and economic effects of the pandemic can directly affect the local community (World Bank 2020). One area in which we have seen recent growth in higher education–community partnerships has been in institutions' deliberate efforts to hire and buy locally. The pandemic has significantly harmed institutions' finances, straining their ability to employ local workers and purchase from local businesses.

It is important to reiterate that the financial constraints faced by colleges and universities are not equal. Those without large endowments (Rosenberg 2020) are more vulnerable. Declining public budgets during the pandemic have led to cuts in public higher education (Kilgore 2020). These public institutions typically play significant roles in serving their local communities, as many of them serve largely low-income areas and communities of colour, and they tend to have limited resources. For public urban universities, such as Rutgers University–Newark (Cantor et al. 2019), strengthening local, lower-income communities is central to their mission. Community colleges also enrol a higher proportion of local residents. Overall, these public colleges and community colleges are more severely affected by the pandemic because of their vulnerable financial conditions and their limited access to resources, yet these are the institutions upon which under-served communities tend to rely. Additionally, some private colleges and universities are facing a looming financial crisis due to sharp declines in investment income and tuition revenue (Anderson et al. 2020).

LONG-TERM IMPACT OF COVID-19 ON US ANCHOR INSTITUTIONS AND THEIR LOCAL PARTNERS

The pandemic's impact on higher education and surrounding communities is significant, and likely to be long-lasting and far-reaching. In many communities, populations that were already vulnerable are now even more precariously situated. Increased unemployment will not lead to the re-employment of all who lost jobs during the pandemic. Some industries (retail, hospitality, travel) are forever altered by this crisis, which will lead to further layoffs (McKinsey and Company 2020). Lower-income children and youth, who were thrust into virtual learning, will be further behind in their schooling.

Some have not paid rent or mortgage for months, thanks to a moratorium on these payments. But this reprieve, along with extended unemployment benefits, has an approaching expiration date. Thus we could see noticeable increases in homelessness (Kendall 2020). As some communities, especially communities of colour, have been disproportionately affected by the virus, evidence is surfacing about the long-term health consequences of those who contracted Covid-19 and recovered. The US suffered from propaganda at the highest levels, suggesting the pandemic was over in May 2020. But the reality is that the pandemic rages on at the time of writing (mid-July 2020). It is still spreading, and it remains challenging for those who are unable to socially distance. This is often the case in lower-income communities.

Higher education, a sector that is not known for rapid change, will have to adapt quickly. In order to fulfil their missions, higher education institutions will have to be creative about how to engage students, conduct research and serve communities. As industries and demand for goods and services continue to evolve, institutions of higher education will have to take note and reshape curricula where necessary.

As the breadth and depth of systemic racism has been so apparent in recent months, colleges and universities will have to be better equipped to leverage their resources to reduce racial inequities as well as transform themselves into anti-racist institutions. Institutions of higher education will have to be equipped to meet the needs of all of their students and develop more focused efforts to meet the needs of students of colour and recognise economic disparities in their midst. They will have to be able to, for example, address the digital divide on their campuses as well as in their communities if they hope to be equitable entities.

The pandemic has led to federal policies and policy ideas that have influenced some aspect of diversity and inclusion on campuses. The recently introduced, and somewhat quickly rescinded, immigration policy that requires international students to leave the US if their campuses are conducting mostly remote learning is one more example of how institutions of higher education have been targeted by federal policy (Perper 2020). There has been some discussion at the federal level about withdrawing funding for institutions of higher education that do not re-open in person in autumn 2020. The language of "re-opening in person" has been used by the Trump administration on various occasions, referring to a desire for schools at all levels to have students and teachers physically on campus and in classrooms for face-to-face teaching and learning. The science suggests that restoring total in-person education to the extent prior to the pandemic would make classrooms spreaders of the virus. But external policy (or the threat thereof) is pushing for something else. US higher education has been periodically ensnared in tense exchanges with certain policy makers over a range of issues. The relationship between higher education and state and federal governments will be a major long-term priority because colleges and universities will be challenged to do more with less. It seems it is more expensive to add more frequent and widespread disinfection, spacing in classrooms, plexiglass, PPE and so on. Yet, the policy conversation is about cutting higher education. It appears that the long term will include strained budgets for institutions of higher education, coupled with increased expectations.

External communities, having been confronted with their own economic devastation, will need colleges and universities and other anchor institutions more than ever. Local schools will need external partners, such as institutions of higher education, to help strengthen educational outcomes and overall social mobility, especially for the most under-served children and youth (The Netter Center for Community Partnerships at the University of Pennsylvania 2020). Local economies will need institutions of higher education to bring an infusion of resources after months of shutting down.

But this is increasingly looking like more of a long-term reality, because much of higher education will be conducted online until the end of the year.

How colleges and universities engage in community partnerships has already been significantly revised. In many ways, such partnerships have been forced to operate virtually. Overall, in the face of various challenges, institutions of higher education in the US have been responding to the pandemic on numerous levels. Here are a few examples drawn from the ongoing research of the Anchor Institutions Task Force.

HOW SOME US HIGHER EDUCATION INSTITUTIONS HAVE RESPONDED TO COVID-19 IN THEIR COMMUNITIES

Some universities have deployed clinical faculty to local hospitals to help confront the pandemic

At Yale University, 1400 clinical faculty in the School of Medicine have been serving as front-line health care providers, treating the patients at Yale New Haven Hospital.[29]

Some universities have been manufacturing/collecting medical equipment and supplies to meet local needs

The Robotics programme faculty of Lake Area Technical College, a community college, has been assisting health care providers and first responders by using its 3D printers to produce protective face shields and facemasks. The college also called for physical and financial resources to support its community efforts.[30]

Some higher education institutions have provided testing services for local communities

Howard University Faculty Practice Plan began offering free coronavirus testing at its Benning Road Clinic on 5 May 2020. The testing site was funded by a grant from the Bank of America and provides a critical resource in an area that needs testing the most. The Bank of America has awarded a US$1 million grant to the Faculty Practice Plan (HUFPP) to improve access to Covid-19 testing in the diverse Washington, DC communities located east of the river.

Some university libraries continue to serve local community

Since the pandemic outbreak, the University of New Mexico Libraries have continued to provide services to the University and the wider Albuquerque community. From curb-side checkout services to computer rentals and online research consultations, the university libraries have been pivoting to the needs of their users (Velasquez and Whitt 2020).

---

29. See https://news.yale.edu/2020/04/14/yale-stands-new-haven-responding-covid-19, accessed 22 July 2020.
30. See www.lakeareatech.edu/covid-19/, accessed 22 July 2020.

In the re-opening stage of the pandemic, universities planned to adapt to various safety measures, such as distancing measures and virus testing

In May 2020 Rice University announced its plans to re-open the campus for the autumn 2020 semester, which would begin in mid-August with the full population on campus, but with safety protocols in place. Such measures include contact tracing, precautionary isolation of individuals with possible exposure to the virus and testing protocols. Appropriate social distancing measures will be required. Classes are to be delivered in dual-mode, available in person and remotely. Similar to other university models, Rice's autumn semester will end before Thanksgiving break (end of November), with no autumn break.

Some universities have helped local community organisations to recruit volunteers

The University of Pennsylvania School of Nursing had posted a message on its website[31] asking for those interested in helping to contribute directly to two of its community partners (Families Forward Shelter and Puentes de Salud).

Coronavirus funds have been established to support community-based organisations and address other matters

University of California San Francisco has created the UCSF Covid-19 Response Fund to support its efforts of co-ordinating with colleagues across the Bay Area and northern California to care for patients while also protecting the health of their faculty, staff, students, patients and visitors.

Harvard University announced the formation of a grant programme to provide emergency funding to non-profit organisations and community groups serving the Allston-Brighton neighbourhood of Boston. The Harvard University Allston-Brighton Emergency Response Grant will allow recipient organisations to quickly mobilise and respond to the needs of the community during this unprecedented global health crisis.

Some universities have addressed the urgent need for demographic data and impact surveys during the pandemic

In response to the Covid-19 pandemic, faculty members of the School of the Public Affairs and Administration (SPAA), Rutgers University – Newark, have been working with the Urban League of Essex County to assess the impact of Covid-19 by surveying Newark residents.

---

31. See www.nursing.upenn.edu/news-events/coronavirus-covid-19-information-and-resources/, accessed 14 July 2020.

The Association of American Medical Colleges is calling for a national standardised data-collection system to accurately capture information about race, ethnicity, social conditions and environmental conditions affecting the spread of illness.

Universities have organised events to help students explore issues of community compassion during pandemic

At the University of Texas at San Antonio, the Civic Leadership Integrative Seminar class, an undergraduate course in UTSA's College for Health, Community & Policy,[32] partnered with SA2020[33] and Compassionate San Antonio[34] to host the event "Compassion in the Time of Covid-19: San Antonio Community Conversations" from 2 to 18 April 2020 (Bustamante 2020).

Some universities have provided remote technical assistance for local businesses and organisations

At the University of San Diego, the current inventory of faculty implementing online community engagement continued. To help community-based organisations and local residents, faculty continued to have students provide critical support functions such as marketing and communication support, data analysis and programme impact, compiling court briefs for asylum seekers, court case transcription services and online fitness and wellness courses for seniors.

Some university leaders have shared experience in discussions on Covid-19 and the future of higher education

Mary Schmidt Campbell, President of Spelman College, an HBCU, has shared Spelman's experience in community engagement with educational leaders at a conference. In the last year, Spelman students have made a marked improvement in the literacy levels of Atlanta middle school students by volunteering as tutors in SpelReads,[35] the college's literacy programme with local schools. Dr Campbell recommended that higher education institutions share resources and collaborate to share costs and improve efficiencies for the Atlanta University Center Consortium.

THE PANDEMIC AND THE FUTURE

The pandemic has had an impact on the non-profit sector as a whole. Many of the community partners to colleges and universities are also making do with limited finances. Institutions of higher education have been thrust into accelerating their digitalisation processes, relying not only on teaching and learning online, but engaging the community virtually as well. In the future, we will likely see practices such as

---

32. See https://hcap.utsa.edu/, accessed 14 July 2020.
33. See www.sa2020.org/, accessed 14 July 2020.
34. See https://sacompassion.net/, accessed 14 July 2020.
35. See www.spelman.edu/about-us/news-and-events/news-releases/2020/01/21/spelreads-helps-atlanta-public-school-students-improve-reading-skills, accessed 22 July 2020.

collaboration on K-12 education,[36] technical assistance to local businesses, and other common forms of higher education – community partnerships, as online endeavours.

Certainly, the need to close the digital divide in local communities and on campuses will become a central component of higher education–community partnerships. At many levels, the pandemic has exacerbated systemic racism and other inequities. These realities have always loomed over higher education–community partnerships. But they are now more important than ever (Bradley 2020).

As the economy continues to change, placing greater pressure on lower-income communities, institutions of higher education must be prepared to provide education and training, particularly in growing industries, to assist access to employment and overall social mobility in their communities. Providing higher education opportunities for under-served communities will be fundamental to the longer-term sustainability of many of the neighbourhoods and cities that host colleges and universities.

Overall, institutions of higher education will have to demonstrate their role as anchor institutions in their communities more than ever in order to help communities rebuild in the wake of the pandemic. The various ways in which colleges and universities have been engaging in their communities in recent months is only the beginning. In all aspects of life – education, health, economic development and others – disparities have deepened. The value that institutions of higher education can bring to society in the years to come centres on their ability to strengthen the most disadvantaged populations, through democratic community partnerships. This pursuit must not only draw upon higher education, it must be a function of collaboration across sectors to harness resources that can transform lives and livelihoods. Recent months have also demonstrated the depths of the systemic dimensions of societal inequalities and disparities. Higher education must not only engage locally, but directly confront the pervasive systems, internally and externally, that drive inequality. It is clear that societies with such tremendous disparities cannot withstand a pandemic, nor function well after one.

REFERENCES

AITF (Anchor Institutions Task Force) (2020), *AITF Strategic Plan 2020-2023*, available at www.margainc.com/aitf, accessed 25 September 2020.

Anderson N., Gabriel D. and Svrluga S. (2020), "Rising expenses, falling revenues, budget cuts: Universities face looming financial crisis", *Washington Post* (23 April 2020), available at www.washingtonpost.com/education/2020/04/23/rising-expenses-falling-revenues-budget-cuts-universities-face-looming-financial-crisis/, accessed 14 July 2020.

Anonymous (2020), "US college towns lose vital revenue as graduation ceremonies are shelved", *The National* (25 May 2020), available at www.thenational.ae/business/us-college-towns-lose-vital-revenue-as-graduation-ceremonies-are-shelved-1.1024274, accessed 14 July 2020.

---

36. K-12 stands for schooling from kindergarten through to twelfth grade. The term is used in the United States and Canada, and possibly other countries.

Bradley E. (2020), "Higher ed's role in tackling two pandemics, Covid-19 and racism", *Forbes* (1 July 2020), available at www.forbes.com/sites/elizabethbradley/2020/07/01/higher-eds-role-in-tackling-two-pandemics-covid-19-and-racism/#382070854da7, accessed 14 July 2020.

Bustamante V. (2020), "Students explore issue of community compassion during pandemic", *UTSA Today* (2 April 2020), available at www.utsa.edu/today/2020/04/story/covid-compassion-conversations.html, accessed 14 July 2020.

Cantor N. et al. (2019), "Tackling 'the two Americas' with city-wide collaboration in Newark", *Journal on Anchor Institutions and Communities*, 2(1): 27-38, available at www.margainc.com/wp-content/uploads/2019/05/AITF-Journal-2019.pdf, accessed 20 July 2020.

DePietro A. (2020), "Here's a look at the impact of coronavirus (COVID-19) on colleges and universities in the U.S.", *Forbes* (30 April 2020), available at www.forbes.com/sites/andrewdepietro/2020/04/30/impact-coronavirus-covid-19-colleges-universities/#3fa71e161a68, accessed 14 July 2020.

Gavazzi S. (2020), "In sickness and in health: university-community partnerships and the COVID-19 pandemic", *Forbes* (12 May 2020), available at www.forbes.com/sites/stephengavazzi/2020/05/12/in-sickness-and-in-health-university-community-partnerships-and-the-covid-19-pandemic/#3f8e40892630, accessed 14 July 2020.

German Academic Exchange Service (2020), *COVID-19 impact on international higher education: studies & forecasts*, available at www.daad.de/en/information-services-for-higher-education-institutions/centre-of-competence/covid-19-impact-on-international-higher-education-studies-and-forecasts/, accessed 14 July 2020.

Kendall M. (2020), "Report: coronavirus crisis could leave tens of thousands of Californians homeless", *Mercury News* (15 May 2020), available at www.mercurynews.com/coronavirus-could-make-tens-of-thousands-of-californians-homeless-according-to-report, accessed 14 July 2020.

Kilgore E. (2020), "The coming COVID-19 higher-ed disaster", *New York Magazine* (6 May 2020), available at https://nymag.com/intelligencer/2020/05/the-coming-covid-19-higher-ed-disaster.html, accessed 14 July 2020.

McKinsey and Company (2020), *COVID-19: Implications for business*, available at www.mckinsey.com/business-functions/risk/our-insights/covid-19-implications-for-business, accessed 14 July 2020.

Nicholson Z. and Semmler E (2020), "No students. No graduation. 'Total devastation' in college towns during coronavirus pandemic", *USA Today* (22 May 2020), available at www.usatoday.com/story/news/education/2020/05/15/coronavirus-unemployment-2020-college-graduation-economy/5205202002/, accessed 14 July 2020.

Nietzel M. (2020), "Will Covid-19 cause the collapse of intercollegiate athletics?", *Forbes* (12 July 2020), available at www.forbes.com/sites/michaeltnietzel/2020/07/12/will-covid-19-cause-the-collapse-of-intercollegiate-athletics/#6822563b2e51, accessed 14 July 2020.

Perper R. (2020), "ICE says international students taking online courses have to transfer or leave the US, as dozens of schools shift to remote learning in response to COVID-19", *Business Insider* (7 July 2020), available at www.businessinsider.com/international-students-visas-cant-take-only-online-classes-ice-2020-7, accessed 14 July 2020.

Rosenberg B. (2020), "Will the coronavirus kill liberal arts colleges?", *Times Higher Education* (10 April 2020), available at www.timeshighereducation.com/opinion/will-coronavirus-kill-liberal-arts-colleges, accessed 14 July 2020.

Sorenson Impact Center Staff (2020), "COVID-19's disparate impact", *Inside Higher Ed* (11 June 2020), available at www.insidehighered.com/views/2020/06/11/pandemic-will-affect-different-institutions-and-students-unequally-opinion, accessed 14 July 2020.

The Netter Center for Community Partnerships at the University of Pennsylvania (2020), *University-assisted community schools network*, available at www.nettercenter.upenn.edu/what-we-do/national-and-global-outreach/university-assisted-community-schools-network, accessed 14 July 2020.

Velasquez S. and Whitt R. (2020), "University Libraries pivots to continue serving local community", *UNM Newsroom*, 26 May 2020, available at news.unm.edu/news/university-libraries-pivots-to-continue-serving-local-community, accessed 14 July 2020.

World Bank (2020), *The COVID-19 crisis response: supporting tertiary education for continuity, adaptation, and innovation*, Washington, DC: World Bank, available at http://pubdocs.worldbank.org/en/621991586463915490/WB-Tertiary-Ed-and-Covid-19-Crisis-for-public-use-April-9.pdf, accessed 4 July 2020.

Chapter 6

Public responsibility for higher education in the time of Covid-19

Sjur Bergan

INTRODUCTION

In the early days of the Bologna Process, European ministers responsible for higher education stated twice that higher education is a public good and a public responsibility (Bologna Process 2001, 2003). This statement raises at least two important questions.

The first is why ministers found it necessary to make the same statement at two successive ministerial conferences. It is unlikely ministers made a determined effort to state the obvious. As a participant in the two ministerial conferences as well as in the preparation of them, it is this author's clear perception that ministers were concerned that what had been seen as a defining feature of higher education in Europe could no longer be taken for granted. Rather than stating a fact, ministers were therefore expressing a concern and an aspiration.

The second question is seemingly simple but requires a more elaborate response: what did ministers mean more precisely? Phrased differently: how could their aspiration be transformed into reality?

THE NOTION OF PUBLIC RESPONSIBILITY

It may be interesting to debate where, on the continuum between a purely public and a purely private good, higher education would or should be located. The more important question, at least in terms of policy, is, however, what we mean by public responsibility. This is a question that the Council of Europe has explored in some detail (Bergan 2005; Council of Europe 2007).

Public responsibility is in this context understood as the responsibility of public authorities for higher education. The responsibility of higher education institutions and the academic community at large towards society is an important topic that is explored by, among others: the Council of Europe; the International Consortium for

Higher Education, Civic Responsibility, and Democracy;[37] the International Association of Universities;[38] and other partners in a long-standing project on the democratic mission of higher education.[39] It is, however, not comprised in the notion of "public responsibility" as explored in this contribution, which focuses on the responsibility of public authorities.

Public authorities are responsible for a specific education system, which comprises all institutions and programmes recognised as part of that system. The Danish Ministry of Education is responsible for the Danish education system, including the part of the system covering higher education. In some countries the situation is more complex, either because responsibility for the education system may be divided between a Ministry of Education and a separate ministry responsible for higher education and – often – research, or because responsibility for the system is divided among different levels of governance, for example between national and regional authorities. For example, in Spain competence for education is shared between the central authorities and those of the autonomous communities, whereas in Belgium it lies with the three Communities (Flemish, French and German). In Bosnia and Herzegovina, this competence falls mainly to cantons within the Federation and in the Republika Srpska, with quite limited competence at national level vested in the Ministry of Civil Affairs. In the United States, where the role of public authorities in higher education is less important than in Europe, competence lies with states more than with the Department of Education.

One of the responsibilities of public authorities is to ensure that education does not turn into a single-purpose undertaking but rather that the system caters to all major purposes of higher education. As defined by the Council of Europe (2007: paragraph 5), these are:

- preparation for sustainable employment;
- preparation for life as active citizens in democratic societies;
- personal development;
- the development and maintenance, through teaching, learning and research, of a broad, advanced knowledge base (see also Bergan 2005).

Responsibility and provision

To be effective, the public responsibility for higher education needs to be nuanced, and the different elements need to be considered specifically. Thus, public authorities should have:

- exclusive responsibility for the framework within which higher education and research is conducted;
- leading responsibility for ensuring effective equal opportunities to higher education for all citizens, as well as ensuring that basic research remains a public good;

---

37. See www.internationalconsortium.org/, accessed 8 July 2020.
38. See www.iau-aiu.net/, accessed 8 July 2020.
39. See www.coe.int/en/web/higher-education-and-research/democratic-mission-of-higher-education, accessed 8 July 2020.

> substantial responsibility for financing higher education and research, the provision of higher education and research, as well as for stimulating and facilitating financing and provision by other sources within the framework developed by public authorities (Council of Europe 2007: paragraph 7).

As will be seen, a distinction must be made between responsibility and provision. Institutions may be public or private, and the latter may be non-profit or for-profit. Provided that the institutions and programmes belong to a national education system, however, they operate within the framework established by the public authorities responsible for that particular system, regardless of the profile and ownership of the institution. They need to follow the national legislation in question, both specific education legislation and general legislation such as labour legislation, safety regulations for laboratories and laws regulating accounting. They also need to undergo quality assurance in accordance with national requirements; the qualifications they provide must comply with the national qualifications framework; and the public authority responsible must recognise the institution and/or programme in question as part of its education system, as stipulated in the Lisbon Recognition Convention, Section VIII (Council of Europe and UNESCO 1997).

PUBLIC RESPONSIBILITY IN THE COVID-19 PANDEMIC

As shown through the chapters of this book, the Covid-19 pandemic demonstrated the fragility but also the resilience of higher education systems and institutions, as well as of individual members of the academic community, in the face of a sudden health crisis.

The first observation is that the impact of the pandemic has not called into question the basic proposition that there is a public responsibility for higher education or its major components as outlined above. If anything, and this is also true in areas beyond education, the crisis has strengthened the notion of public responsibility. This is true for the health sector, where no public authority – at least in Europe – could assume only partial responsibility for health care during the crisis. As is the case for education, health care could be provided by non-public actors, but within the framework established by public authorities, who were responsible for ensuring that all residents in the country had adequate access to health care. In the same way that some of the difficulties in ensuring adequate education provision during the Covid-19 crisis originated in weaknesses in education systems prior to the crisis, the pre-crisis state of public health systems to some degree determined their ability to respond to the crisis.

This was an important part of the reasoning behind the confinement measures taken in many countries to prevent further spread of the disease as much as possible. Such measures were of course taken to protect the health of individuals, but also to seek to ensure that the number of patients with serious Covid-19 infection did not surpass the capacity of health systems to cater for them. In some countries where the numbers of serious Covid-19 cases were unevenly distributed across the territory, patients were transferred from more to less affected areas. This was, for example, the case in France, where patients were transferred from Alsace – a region with a very high number of cases from the earliest phases of the pandemic – to less affected regions as well as to Germany, Luxembourg and Switzerland. The latter cases were a very welcome practical show of European solidarity at a time when responses to the crisis were national more often than European.

An increased role for public authorities was observed in several other sectors also, including some that have been subject to sharp ideological debates. There has, for example, been considerable disagreement over the extent of public involvement in the economy, and this disagreement is still one of the political dividing lines in most countries. There was, however, little disagreement about whether public funds should be used to bolster private companies struggling under the impact of the Covid-19 crisis, for the dual purpose of ensuring the survival and longer-term viability of those companies but also of the jobs they offer. There was debate about the efficacy of specific measures as well as about the longer-term viability of specific companies or sectors, even with extensive public financial support, but there was little or no debate about whether it was proper or legitimate for public authorities to intervene to bolster sectors of the economy considered important for strategic reasons or to preserve employment. This author is also unaware of any businesses declining public financial support for ideological reasons. The aviation sector and, more broadly, tourism are evident examples of sectors that were particularly badly affected and that most national authorities saw a need to support with massive public funding while also finding it proper, for example, to differentiate the support provided for different airlines.

The second observation is that a strengthened role for public authorities did not amount to a takeover. Public authorities provided support as well as the overall framework within which activities were conducted, but for the most part they did not take over the running of hospitals that had so far been privately run or of private businesses.

Public authorities did modify rules and regulations where this was considered necessary and in compliance with the need to ensure public safety. The health sector is again an obvious example, and one that also affects higher education. In some areas of Europe, the necessary health care for Covid-19 patients could not be ensured by the health professionals already working in the region. The need could then be met through the temporary transfer of licensed health professionals from other regions, by encouraging retired and other staff who had left active service but kept their licences up to date to resume service and by enabling qualified but not (yet) licensed persons to work under the supervision of duly licensed health professionals. In this context, it is important to keep in mind that practitioners of most but not all health professions require a professional licence in addition to the stipulated academic qualifications. Medical doctors and nurses are obvious examples, but the list of regulated health professions is long and varies somewhat from country to country.

To expand the pool of available health professionals beyond those holding a valid licence, three measures may be envisaged, and all were explored in Europe in spring 2020.[40] One is to make sure that the licensing of medical staff proceeds without delay, even if the crisis conditions make it difficult or impossible to organise examinations in

---

40. See "Thousands of medical students being fast-tracked", *CNN News* (20 March 2020), available at https://edition.cnn.com/2020/03/19/europe/medical-students-coronavirus-intl/index.html, accessed 8 July 2020.

the classic format. Final examinations in health-related academic disciplines could be replaced by alternative assessment methods. A second measure is to call on advanced students in health-related disciplines. Countries such as Ireland, Italy and France appealed to medical and nursing students to help out, and the appeals were answered.

The third option is to identify those who have the required qualifications but do not have a professional licence in their country of residence. The refugee community is an obvious place to look, and early in the Covid-19 crisis the Secretary General of the Council of Europe and the United Nations High Commissioner for Refugees (UNHCR) called on health authorities to make it possible for refugees with health-related qualifications to contribute.[41] Through the European Qualifications Passport for Refugees (EQPR),[42] the Council of Europe, in co-operation with the UNHCR and the recognition centres of 10 member states, also provides a practical instrument for assessing the qualifications held by refugees, even when these cannot be adequately documented (Bergan and Skjerven 2020). Of the 454 refugees who had received the EQPR by the end of 2019, 46 had health-related qualifications, and some worked in fields related to their qualifications (McDonald-Gibson 2020). In spring 2020, further assessment sessions were organised in France and Italy, focusing specifically on health-related qualifications.

As stated, the purpose of encouraging public authorities to enable qualified but unlicensed health professionals to help meet the challenges of the Covid-19 crisis is not to seek to bypass the professional licensing process but rather to make it possible for such persons to work under the supervision of licensed professionals. Advanced students in health-related fields will gain experience that will be of great value in their further – and licensed – career, and the EQPR could hopefully help guide qualified refugees into the professional licensing procedure.

THE CASE OF HIGHER EDUCATION

Both the Covid-19 crisis itself and its aftermath illustrate important aspects of the public responsibility for higher education. In particular, the crisis illustrates issues related to academic freedom, institutional autonomy and the relationship between public authorities and higher education institutions (Bergan, Egron-Polak and Noorda 2020).

The point that higher education is provided within the general framework established by public authorities, which goes beyond the framework established specifically for higher education, such as higher education legislation or the national qualifications framework, is driven home by the enhanced safety regulations for public areas. Regulations on physical distancing, requiring masks to be worn in public spaces or limiting the number of persons who can assemble in a closed physical space apply

---

41. See Council of Europe Education Department News, press release on bringing refugee health workers into the fight against Covid-19, available at www.coe.int/en/web/education/-/council-of-europe-and-unhcr-support-member-states-in-bringing-refugee-health-workers-into-the-fight-against-covid-19, accessed 16 September 2020.
42. For details, see www.coe.int/en/web/education/recognition-of-refugees-qualifications, accessed 8 July 2020.

as much to higher education institutions, despite their autonomous status, as they do to any other public space. General regulations on travel to and from the country in which an institution is located apply also to students and staff.

Together, these two elements – rules on public spaces alongside rules on travel to and from other countries – and the decisions that institutions make to adapt to those rules mean that higher education students are less likely to return to lectures as soon as primary and secondary school students return to classrooms. Higher education institutions are generally larger than schools; learning and teaching are partly conducted in areas assembling large groups of people, such as auditoriums and libraries; student residences often provide relatively limited space for each resident; and the proportion of students and staff from other countries is relatively high. Many institutions will continue online learning into the new academic year 2020-21, many will explore blended learning, and international student and staff exchanges are unlikely to resume to any considerable extent until spring or even autumn 2021. This holds true even in the absence of a second wave of the Covid-19 pandemic, which would prolong the exceptional Covid-19 measures for a period that cannot be foreseen at the time of writing (July 2020).

While it would be improper for public authorities to seek to regulate the details of teaching, learning and research within institutions, they would generally be considered to act within their competence if they sought to ensure higher education provision in under-served parts of the country or to stimulate teaching and research in academic areas considered of particular importance (Bergan, Egron-Polak and Noorda 2020). Public authorities are likely to act in this sense in the aftermath of the Covid-19 crisis. If a higher education institution catering mostly to a peripheral area of the country were to require additional financial and other support to avoid closure, public authorities would act within their remit if they decided to provide such support. This kind of support, which would in principle not be different from helping to bolster a struggling airline, could be important in ensuring continued societal, economic and cultural development in areas of a country that might otherwise be further exposed to marginalisation and depopulation. In the same vein, public authorities might provide support and incentives for some or all institutions in its higher education system to explore new methods of teaching and learning, for example blended or online, in the expectation that such measures would help ensure the viability of the education system in the aftermath of the Covid-19 pandemic.

Among other things, the pandemic has altered perceptions of priorities in public policies. In part, this has translated into changed voting patterns in the few elections that have so far been held during or after the pandemic. In the second round of the local elections held in France on 28 June 2020, election lists associated with environmental protection, notably the Green Party, scored very well in larger and medium-sized cities. A second, and worrying, tendency of these elections was an exceptionally low participation rate.[43] In part, the voters' changed priorities reflect the relative importance to different sectors of society of health, where (unsurprisingly) health concerns have become more prominent, and the environment.

---

43. For analysis, see https://c.dna.fr/politique/2020/06/28/defections-et-grosses-surprises, accessed 8 July 2020.

It would therefore not be surprising if one outcome of the Covid-19 crisis were to be increased public investment, not only in health care and the environment but also in related study programmes and research. Investment in research would be most likely to favour epidemiology in particular, including research to develop new vaccines. Such action would be entirely within the remit of public authorities, as long as it was not overly directive.

EDUCATION FOR DEMOCRACY IN THE TIME OF COVID-19

A broader concern is that higher education should continue to fulfil its four major purposes, as outlined above. While it may be tempting to focus public support for higher education on measures and programmes likely to give immediate results in terms of economic output and improved health services, a unilateral focus on these objectives would disregard the public responsibility for ensuring a broad and advanced knowledge base as well as for preparing students to play an active role as citizens of democratic societies.

During the Covid-19 crisis, we have seen tendencies in several countries for authorities to take advantage of the crisis to challenge aspects of democracy, human rights and the rule of law. In Europe, the Hungarian emergency legislation giving the government considerably enhanced powers, not limited in time, was of particular concern,[44] but there were developments of concern also in several other countries. In some countries, when considering the relevant legislation, parliaments reduced the time for which emergency powers would apply, demonstrating the importance of parliamentary control.

There are two overall lessons of the Covid-19 pandemic. The first lesson is that, while education is obviously of immediate importance to society, it is equally important in the medium to longer term. This point has been made by both educationalists and public figures in positions of political responsibility, former UK Prime Minister Gordon Brown among them (speaking in an online meeting of UNESCO's SDG-Education 2030 Steering Committee Meeting on 4 June 2020). The second key lesson is that we must not allow the current health crisis to become a crisis of democracy.

The commitment of higher education is vital to ensure that our societies draw the appropriate lessons from the Covid-19 crisis and to help us develop the kind of society in which we would like to live. This will require sound public policies, with public authorities playing a proper role. It will also require that higher education institutions and the academic community of scholars and students engage in public space, and put their advanced knowledge and understanding of specific issues at the service of broader society and into the broader context of societal development. Higher education must play a major role in helping to shape the post-Covid-19 world and it must do so by reshaping higher education itself (Harkavy et al. 2020).

---

44. Concern at the Hungarian emergency legislation was expressed by, among others, the Secretary General of the Council of Europe; see www.coe.int/en/web/portal/-/secretary-general-writes-to-victor-orban-regarding-covid-19-state-of-emergency-in-hungary, accessed 8 July 2020.

This would ideally be done in co-operation between higher education, public authorities and other stakeholders. Any absence of such co-operation would, however, not free the higher education community from its responsibility to work for democratic, sustainable and healthy societies.

REFERENCES

Bergan S. (2005), "Higher education as a 'public good and a public responsibility' – What does it mean?", in Weber L. and Bergan S. (eds), *The public responsibility for higher education and research*, Higher Education Series No. 2, Strasbourg: Council of Europe, pp. 13-28.

Bergan S., Egron-Polak E. and Noorda S. (2020), "Academic freedom and institutional autonomy – What role in and for the EHEA?", in Bergan S., Gallagher T. and Harkavy I. (eds), *Academic freedom, institutional autonomy and the future of democracy*, Higher Education Series No. 24, Strasbourg: Council of Europe, pp. 41-55.

Bergan S. and Skjerven S. A. (2020), "A way to enable refugees to help in the COVID-19 crisis", *University World News* (2 May 2020), available at www.universityworldnews.com/post.php?story=20200501142822238, accessed 8 July 2020.

Bologna Process (2001), "Towards the European Higher Education Area", available at www.ehea.info/Upload/document/ministerial_declarations/2001_Prague_Communique_English_553442.pdf, accessed 8 July 2020.

Bologna Process (2003), "Realising the European Higher Education Area", Communiqué of the Conference of Ministers responsible for Higher Education (Berlin, 19 September 2003), available at www.ehea.info/Upload/document/ministerial_declarations/2003_Berlin_Communique_English_577284.pdf, accessed 8 July 2020.

Council of Europe (2007), Recommendation CM/Rec(2007)6 of the Committee of Ministers to member states on the public responsibility for higher education and research, available at https://search.coe.int/cm/Pages/result_details.aspx?ObjectId=09000016805d5dae, accessed 8 July 2020.

Council of Europe and UNESCO (1997), *Convention on the Recognition of Qualifications concerning Higher Education in the European Region* (Lisbon Recognition Convention), available at www.coe.int/en/web/conventions/full-list/-/conventions/rms/090000168007f2c7, accessed 8 July 2020.

Harkavy I., Bergan S., Gallagher T. and van't Land H. (2020), "Universities must help shape the post-COVID-19 world", *University World News* (18 April 2020), available at www.universityworldnews.com/post.php?story=20200413152542750, accessed 8 July 2020.

McDonald-Gibson C. (2020), "Healthcare workers from refugee backgrounds want to help fight COVID-19: one man's journey shows how that might be possible", *TIME*, online edition (28 April 2020), available at https://time.com/5826166/refugees-coronavirus-healthcare/, accessed 8 July 2020.

Chapter 7

Past, present, future: re-thinking the social responsibility of US higher education in light of Covid-19 and Black Lives Matter

Ira Harkavy and Rita A. Hodges

INTRODUCTION

The founding purposes of colleges and universities in the United States, including colonial colleges, historically black colleges and universities, community colleges and research universities, focused on service and social responsibility.[45] The Covid-19 pandemic, the murder of George Floyd (and many others) and the Black Lives Matter movement[46] have graphically exposed the extreme poverty, persistent deprivation and pernicious structural racism embedded in 400 years of history afflicting communities across the United States. These developments have also raised troubling moral questions, including what is higher education's actual contribution to the public good?

In this chapter, we provide brief overviews of US higher education's responsibility to society from both a legal and an historical perspective. We conclude by proposing a strategy that would, in our judgment, better fulfil the university's social responsibility, significantly improve academic work and increase higher education's contributions to democracy.

---

45. For an overview of US higher education and its different types of institution, see Helms et al. 2019.
46. The murder of George Floyd at the hands of police officers (one in a long tally of Black Americans) in Minneapolis on 25 May 2020 ignited a wave of national and international protest. Black Lives Matter, a global movement to help "eradicate white supremacy" and counter acts of "violence inflicted on Black communities", has been at the forefront of protests against racial injustice (see Black Lives Matter 2020).

TAX-EXEMPT STATUS OF HIGHER EDUCATION, SOCIAL RESPONSIBILITY AND DEMOCRACY

US higher education institutions, by and large, are tax-exempt, a status significant for their operation and survival. Higher education's tax exemption is based on its social responsibility and contributions to democracy. The educational purposes of colleges and universities, including research, teaching and service, are "recognized in federal law as critical to the well-being of our democratic society" (AAU 2019: 2). The federal law applies to the vast majority of public and private universities, providing important tax exemptions on corporate income tax, financial investments, gifts, property and more, while in turn requiring certain federal and state regulations and oversight (AAU 2019; Courant et al. 2006).

The modern federal role in US higher education finance took shape following the Second World War, beginning with the GI Bill of 1944 and the National Defense Education Act of 1958 (Zumeta et al. 2012). Both policies provided increased education opportunities across the income spectrum. By the mid-1970s, "Pell grants" (direct financial assistance to students) fully covered the costs of education at public universities and about one third of the cost at the average private four-year institution (Mettler 2014). The primary funding of public institutions through federal and state subsidies up until 1980 would indicate that society was seen as the primary beneficiary (Hossler 2006).

By the 1980s, however, things had begun to shift. Rising tuition levels, expansion of financial aid for middle- and upper-income families and the shift from grants to loans pointed to a new belief that individuals were the primary beneficiaries of higher education and should thus shoulder most of the costs. Moreover, continual decline in state appropriations since the early 1980s have led to increasing similarities in finance and function of public and private non-profit colleges and universities (Courant et al. 2006). Student debt has only escalated since that time (Mettler 2014). Financial aid advocates are again calling for a dramatic increase in federal Pell grants, given the economic crisis related to the Covid-19 pandemic (Murakami 2020a).

Covid-19 has also renewed debates in the US about the tax-exempt status of higher education institutions. It has increasingly been argued that elite private universities, in particular, should make Payments in Lieu of Taxes (PILOT), in the form of voluntary payments to local governments, to reflect their use of local services without paying property taxes (Hanna 2020). The Trump Administration has also threatened to take away tax exemption (Murakami 2020b).

THE UNREALISED DEMOCRATIC PUBLIC PURPOSE OF HIGHER EDUCATION

The critical past and current roles of historically black colleges and universities, other minority-serving institutions, community colleges and state comprehensive institutions, in educating a majority of US undergraduate students (particularly minority populations) and serving their communities, cannot be overemphasised. Our primary focus, however, is on US research universities. This is not only because we work at one but also because research universities are extraordinarily influential, significantly shaping how the rest of the higher education system functions (Benson et al. 2007).

The founding purpose of every colonial college – except for the University of Pennsylvania – was largely to educate ministers and religiously orthodox men capable of creating good communities built on religious denominational principles,[47] whereas Benjamin Franklin founded the University of Pennsylvania (Penn) as a secular institution to educate students in a variety of fields. In 1749, envisioning the institution that would become the University of Pennsylvania, he wrote of developing in students "an *Inclination* join'd with an *Ability* to serve Mankind, one's Country, Friends and Family; which *Ability*. ... should indeed be the great *Aim* and *End* of all Learning" (Franklin 1749: 150-1).

Franklin's call to service is echoed in the founding documents of hundreds of private colleges established after the American Revolution, as well as in the speeches of many college presidents (Rudolph 1962). A similar blend of pragmatism and idealism found expression in the subsequent century in the Morrill Act of 1862, which established land-grant colleges and universities whose purpose was to advance the mechanical and agricultural sciences, expand access to higher education and cultivate citizenship. Using language typically found in documents from these institutions, the trustees of the Ohio Agricultural and Mechanical College (now The Ohio State University) in 1873 stated that they intended not just to educate students as "farmers or mechanics, but as men, fitted by education and attainments for the greater usefulness and higher duties of citizenship" (Boyte and Kari 2000: 47). Later, the University of Wisconsin's "Wisconsin Idea" broadened the concept of civic engagement from preparing graduates for service to their communities to developing institutions intended to solve significant, practical problems that affected citizens across the state (McCarthy 1912; Maxwell 1956: 147-8; Stark 1995-6).

The Second Morrill Act of 1890 required southern states to establish and fund what are known today as historically black colleges and universities, or HBCUs, as well as provide funding for research experiment stations (Dubb and Howard 2007; Thelin 2004). The land-grant institutions eventually came to adopt a three-part mission that included research, teaching, and extension for the public good (Dubb and Howard 2007; Fribourg 2005).

Political scientist Charles Anderson highlights the democratic purpose behind the creation of the research university in the late 19th and early 20th centuries:

> With deliberate defiance, those who created the American university (particularly the public university, though the commitment soon spread throughout the system) simply stood this [essentially aristocratic] idea of reason on its head. Now it was assumed that the widespread exercise of self-conscious, critical reason was essential to *democracy*. The truly remarkable belief arose that this system of government would flourish best if citizens would generally adopt the habits of thought hitherto supposed appropriate mainly for scholars and scientists.

---

47. Harvard (Congregationalist), William and Mary (Anglican), Yale (Congregationalist), Princeton (Presbyterian), Columbia (Anglican), Brown (Baptist), Rutgers (Dutch Reformed) and Dartmouth (Congregationalist) were all created with religiously based service as a central purpose.

> We vastly expanded access to higher education. We presumed it a general good, like transport, or power, part of the infrastructure of the civilization. (Anderson 1993: 7-8)

Simply put, strengthening democracy at the expense of old social hierarchies served as the central mission for the development of the US research university, including both land-grant institutions and urban universities. In 1876 Daniel Coit Gilman, in his inaugural address as the first President of Johns Hopkins, the first modern research university in the United States, expressed the hope that universities would "make for less misery among the poor, less ignorance in the schools, less bigotry in the temple, less suffering in the hospital, less fraud in business, less folly in politics" (Long 1982: 184). Belief in the democratic purposes of the research university echoed throughout higher education at the turn of the 20th century. In 1908 Harvard's President Charles Eliot wrote:

> At bottom most of the American institutions of higher education are filled with the democratic spirit of serviceableness. Teachers and students alike are profoundly moved by the desire to serve the democratic community. …This is a thoroughly democratic conception of their function. (Veysey 1965/70: 119)

University presidents of the late 19th and early 20th centuries worked to develop major national institutions capable of meeting the needs of a rapidly changing and increasingly complex society. Imbued with boundless optimism and a belief that knowledge could change the world for the better, these "captains of erudition" (Veblen 1918) envisioned universities as leading the way towards a more effective, humane and democratic society for all, particularly for residents of the city. Academics at this time also viewed the city as their arena for study and action. They seized the opportunity to advance knowledge, teaching and learning by working to improve the quality of life in cities that were experiencing the traumatic effects of industrialisation, immigration and large-scale urbanisation. This animating mission to advance knowledge for the continuous improvement of the human condition is readily identified in the histories of leading urban universities at the turn of the 20th century, including Columbia University, the University of Chicago and the University of Pennsylvania.[48]

Few Progressive Era (1890-1920) university presidents and academics, however, viewed local communities as reciprocal partners from whom they and their students could learn in the complex process of identifying and solving strategic community problems. University–community engagement was essentially a one-way enterprise motivated by elitism and *noblesse oblige*. University "experts" armed with scientific knowledge would identify community problems and authoritatively prescribe solutions, not work collaboratively with community members in a mutual relationship from which both groups might benefit and to which both groups would contribute knowledge, ideas and insights. The expert's role was to study and assist, not to learn from and with, the community (Benson et al. 2017).

---

48. For detailed histories of these and other leading urban universities at the turn of the 20th century, see Benson et al. 2017 and Puckett and Lloyd 2015.

In 1899, W. E. B. Du Bois, in his classic study *The Philadelphia negro*, written while an instructor at the University of Pennsylvania's Wharton School, succinctly captured the purpose of Progressive Era research "as the scientific basis of further study, and of practical reform" (Du Bois 1899/1996: 4). Yet, scholarship focused on producing direct and positive change had largely vanished from universities after 1918. The First World War was the catalyst for a full-scale retreat (Harkavy and Puckett 1994). The brutality and horror of that conflict ended the buoyant optimism and faith in human progress and societal improvement that had marked much of the so-called Progressive Era of the late 19th and early 20th centuries (Ross 1991).

As our close colleague Lee Benson observed in 1997:

> In the decades after World Wars I and II, American higher education ... increasingly concentrated on essentially scholastic, inside-the-Academy problems and conflicts rather than on the very hard, very complex problems involved in helping American society realize the democratic promise of American life for all Americans.[49]
> As a result, they increasingly abandoned the public mission and societal engagement that had powerfully, productively inspired and energized them during their pre-World War I formative period of great intellectual growth and development. (Benson 1997: 2)

Since the end of the Cold War, there has fortunately been a substantive and public re-emergence of what might be termed "engaged scholarship" designed to contribute to democracy. The academic benefits of community engagement have been illustrated in practice – and the intellectual case for engagement effectively made (Bok 1990; Boyer 1990; Cantor 2018; Gutmann 1999; Padrón 2013). That case, simply stated, is that higher education institutions would better fulfil their core academic functions, including advancing knowledge, teaching and learning, if they focused on improving conditions in their societies, including their local communities.

More broadly, a burgeoning democratic, civic and community engagement movement has developed across higher education in the United States to better educate students for democratic citizenship and to improve schooling and the quality of life. Service learning, engaged scholarship, community-based participatory research, volunteer projects and community economic development initiatives are some of the means that have been used to create mutually beneficial partnerships designed to make a positive difference in the community and on the campus (Benson et al. 2017). In addition, the impacts of increased black presence on campus and student unrest, beginning in 1968 in the wake of the assassination of Martin Luther King Jr, also helped pave the way for the civic and community engagement movement in higher education (Taylor and McGlynn 2008).

Granting that progress, university engagement has been, in our judgment, woefully insufficient.

---

49. The phrase "promise of American life" is taken from Herbert Croly's 1909 progressive manifesto, *The promise of American life* (New York: Macmillan, 1909).

WHERE DO WE GO FROM HERE?

In the early 1990s, one of us (Harkavy) wrote that "[Universities] can no longer try to remain an oasis of affluence in a desert of urban despair" (Benson and Harkavy 1991: 14). The impacts of Covid-19 and the powerful lessons of Black Lives Matter, among other things, make this statement seem even more true today.

Conditions in Philadelphia – the city where the University of Pennsylvania (Penn), our home institution, is located – are an example of a more general phenomenon of severe distress. At 25.7%, the poverty rate is the highest among the country's 10 largest cities. About 400 000 residents – including roughly 37% of the city's children under the age of 18 – live below the federal poverty line, which is an annual income of US$19 337 for an adult living with two children. In addition, nearly half of all poor residents are in deep poverty, which is defined as having an income of 50% below the federal poverty line. African Americans in Philadelphia account for 40% of the total population but over half of the coronavirus-related deaths (City of Philadelphia 2020). At the same time, Philadelphia (like many other cities) is home to a key resource that can help to change these conditions. It has one of the highest concentrations of anchor institutions, with higher education institutions and academic medical centres or hospitals representing 12 of the 15 largest private employers, and the Philadelphia metropolitan area contains more than 100 colleges and universities (Select Greater Philadelphia Council 2016; Pew Charitable Trusts 2017).[50]

As indicated by the above data, there is simply no "return to normal" in the post-Covid-19 world, because "normal" was abnormally cruel and degrading. Among the institutions that must change, do better and do things differently are universities, including our own. To begin with, changes in "doing" will require recognition by higher education institutions that, as they now function, they – particularly research universities – have not made the kind of contribution they could and should to improving human life for the better. In fact they, albeit often unintentionally, contribute to racial and socio-economic inequalities and systemic racism. Among other indicators of the work left to be done, a 2017 *New York Times* study revealed that at least 38 elite universities in the US, including Penn and four other Ivy League institutions, enrolled more students from the top 1% of the income scale than from the entire bottom 60% (Aisch et al. 2017). Analysis by the *New York Times* also revealed that, at the top 100 US colleges and universities, Black and Hispanic students are even more under-represented than they were in 1980 (Ashkenas, Park and Pearce 2017).

Stated directly, social responsibility needs to be, as Chis Brink has argued, "the soul of the university", not rhetorically, but in practice (Brink 2018). We are applying John Dewey's seminal proposition that major advances in knowledge tend to

---

50. The significant role of anchor institutions, particularly colleges and universities, in working in and with their local communities has been increasingly recognised. For the Anchor Institutions Task Force (AITF), see AITF 2020. The Council of Europe, in collaboration with AITF, has held conferences in Rome (2017), Dublin (2018) and Strasbourg (2019) to discuss creating a European entity inspired by AITF.

occur when human beings consciously work to solve the central, highly complex problems confronting their society (Benson et al. 2007). The main priority of higher education, in our judgment, should be eradicating injustice and racism on campus and in the community through democratic, mutually transformative partnerships with their neighbours. If US colleges and universities were to adopt and act on that priority, they would realise their historic purpose, better advance research, teaching and learning, fulfil their social responsibility and make a powerful contribution to creating a genuinely inclusive, equitable, democratic society where Black Lives finally Matter.

REFERENCES

AAU (Association of American Universities) (2019), *Tax-exempt status of universities and colleges: Internal revenue code section 501(c)(3) and section 115* (February 2019), available at www.aau.edu/sites/default/files/AAU-Files/Key-Issues/Taxation-Finance/Tax-Exempt-Status-Universities-post-TCJA.pdf, accessed 27 July 2020.

Aisch G. et al. (2017), "Some colleges have more students from the top 1 percent than the bottom 60. Find yours", *New York Times* (18 January 2017), available at www.nytimes.com/interactive/2017/01/18/upshot/some-colleges-have-more-students-from-the-top-1-percent-than-the-bottom-60.html, accessed 26 July 2020.

AITF (Anchor Institutions Task Force) (2020), *AITF Strategic Plan 2020-2023*, available at www.margainc.com/aitf, accessed 25 September 2020.

Anderson C. W. (1993), *Prescribing the life of the mind*, Madison, WI: University of Wisconsin Press.

Ashkenas J., Park H. and Pearce A. (2017), "Even with affirmative action, Blacks and Hispanics are more underrepresented at top colleges than 35 years ago", *New York Times* (24 August 2017), available at www.nytimes.com/interactive/2017/08/24/us/affirmative-action.html, accessed 27 July 2020.

Benson L. (1997), "Comments on William Sullivan's keynote address, Philadelphia Higher Education Network for Neighborhood Development Conference", Swarthmore College, Swarthmore, PA (23 October 1997), in Harkavy I. (1998), *School-community-university partnerships: effectively integrating community building and education reform*, paper presented to conference on Connecting Community Building and Education Reform: Effective School, Community, University Partnerships, a Joint Forum of the U.S. Department of Education and U.S. Department of Housing and Urban Development, Washington, DC, available at https://community-wealth.org/sites/clone.community-wealth.org/files/downloads/paper-harkavy.pdf, accessed 16 September 2020.

Benson L and Harkavy I. (1991),"Progressing beyond the welfare state: a neo-Deweyan strategy", *Universities and Community Schools* (Spring-Summer 1991), 2(1-2).

Benson L., Harkavy I. and Puckett J. (2007), *Dewey's dream: universities and democracies in an age of education reform*, Philadelphia, PA: Temple University Press.

Benson L. et al. (2017), *Knowledge for social change: Bacon, Dewey, and the revolutionary transformation of research universities in the twenty-first century*, Philadelphia, PA: Temple University Press.

Black Lives Matter (2020), available at https://blacklivesmatter.com/about/, accessed 29 July 2020.

Bok D. C. (1990), *Universities and the future of America*. Durham, NC: Duke University Press.

Boyer E. L. (1990), *Scholarship reconsidered: priorities of the professoriate*, Princeton, NJ: Carnegie Foundation for the Advancement of Teaching.

Boyte H. C. and Kari N. N. (2000), "Renewing the democratic spirit in American colleges and universities: higher education as a public work", in Ehrlich T. (ed.), *Civic responsibility and higher education*, Westport, CT: American Council on Education/Oryx Press, pp. 37-60.

Brink C. (2018), *The soul of a university: why excellence is not enough*, Bristol, UK: Bristol University Press.

Cantor N. (2018), "Of mutual benefit: democratic engagement between universities and communities", *Liberal Education* 104(2), available at https://aacu.org/liberaleducation/2018/spring/cantor, accessed 28 July 2020.

City of Philadelphia (2020), COVID-19 data, available at www.phila.gov/programs/coronavirus-disease-2019-covid-19/testing-and-data/#demographic-data-of-cases, accessed 15 July 2020.

Courant P. N., Mcpherson M. and Resch A. M. (2006), "The public role in higher education", *National Tax Journal*, LVIV(2): 291-318.

Du Bois W. E. B. (1899/1996), *The Philadelphia negro: a social study*, Philadelphia: University of Pennsylvania Press.

Dubb S. and Howard T. (2007), *Linking colleges to communities: engaging the university for community development*, College Park, MD: The Democracy Collaborative.

Franklin B. (1749): "Proposals relating to the education of youth in Pennsilvania" [sic], in Best J. H. (ed.) (1962), *Benjamin Franklin on education*, New York: Teachers College Press.

Fribourg H. (2005), "Where are land-grant colleges headed?", *Journal of Natural Resources and Life Science Education*, 34: 40-43.

Gutmann A. (1999), *Democratic education*, Princeton, NJ: Princeton University Press.

Hanna M. (2020), "Penn professors call for universities to support Philly schools", *Philadelphia Inquirer* (8 July 2020), available at www.inquirer.com/education/university-of-pennsylvania-pilot-taxes-schools-petition-20200708.html, accessed 27 July 2020.

Harkavy I. and Puckett J. L. (1994), "Lessons from Hull House for the contemporary urban university", *Social Service Review*, 68: 299-321.

Helms R. M. et al. (2019), *U.S. higher education: a brief guide,* Washington, DC: American Council on Education.

Hossler D. (2006), "Students and families as revenue: the impact on institutional behaviors", in Priest D. M. and John E. P. S. (eds), *Privatization and public universities*, Bloomington: Indiana University Press, pp. 109-28.

Long E. L. Jr. (1982), *Higher education as a moral enterprise*, Washington, DC: Georgetown University Press.

Maxwell R. S. (1956), *La Follette and the rise of the Wisconsin progressives*, Madison, WI: State Historical Society of Wisconsin.

McCarthy C. (1912), *The Wisconsin idea*, New York: Macmillan.

Mettler S. (2014), *Degrees of inequality: how the politics of higher education sabotaged the American dream*, New York: Basic Books.

Murakami K. (2020a), "A new call to increase Pell", *Inside Higher Ed*. (21 July 2020), available at www.insidehighered.com/news/2020/07/21/amid-concerns-about-college-affordability-call-increase-pell, accessed 27 June 2020.

Murakami K. (2020b), "Will push to reopen threaten aid?" *Inside Higher Ed*. (16 July 2020), available at www.insidehighered.com/news/2020/07/16/uncertainty-over-aid-higher-education-possible-next-coronavirus-relief-bill, accessed 25 July 2020.

Padrón E. (2013), "Reimagining democratic societies: a new era of personal and social responsibility", in Bergan S., Harkavy I. and van't Land H. (eds), *Reimagining democratic societies: a new era of personal and social responsibility*, Strasbourg: Council of Europe, pp. 55-61.

Pew Charitable Trusts (2017), *Philadelphia 2017: the state of the city*, available at www.pewtrusts.org/~/media/assets/2017/04/pri_philadelphia_2017_state_of_the_city.pdf, accessed 26 September 2020.

Puckett J. L. and Lloyd M. F. (2015), *Becoming Penn: The pragmatic American university, 1950–2000*, Philadelphia: University of Pennsylvania Press.

Ross D. (1991), *The origins of American social science*, New York: Cambridge University Press.

Rudolph F. (1962), *The American college and university: a history*, Knopf Publications in Education, New York: Alfred A. Knopf.

Select Greater Philadelphia Council (2016), *At the heart of good business: Greater Philadelphia, the place to establish and grow your business*, available at www.selectgreaterphiladelphia.com/wp-content/uploads/2016/06/SGP-Report-2016-lowres.pdf, accessed 27 July 2020.

Stark J. (1995-6), *The Wisconsin idea: the university's service to the state*, reprinted from the 1995-1996 Wisconsin Blue Book, available at www.scifun.org/WisIdea/WI-Idea_Legislative-Ref-Bureau.pdf, accessed on 6 August 2019.

Taylor H. L. and McGlynn L. (2008), "Solving the Dewey problem: what is to be done?", *Good Society* 17(2): 56-62.

Thelin J. R. (2004), *A history of American higher education*, 2nd edn, Baltimore, MD: Johns Hopkins University Press.

Veblen T. (1918), *The higher learning in America: a memorandum on the conduct of universities by business men*, New York: B.W. Huebsch.

Veysey L. R. (1965/70), *The emergence of the American university*, Chicago: University of Chicago Press.

Zumeta W. et al. (2012), *Financing American higher education in the era of globalization*, Cambridge, MA: Harvard Education Press.

Chapter 8

Beyond a "new normal": Covid-19, Black Lives Matter and the remaking of higher education

Peter Englot and Nancy Cantor

"What do we want? Justice! When do we want it? Now!" "Black Lives Matter!" "Enough is enough!" "No justice, no peace!" "Shut it down!"

Thunderous chants like these, born of pain, exasperation, incredulity, anger and resolve have been reverberating through the streets of communities of every size across the United States and around the world. Communities everywhere have been jolted into renewed awareness of systemic racism by the doubly deadly convergence of the Covid-19 global pandemic, whose impacts disparately affect people of colour, and a new concatenation of killings of Black and Brown people by police, examples of which are all too easy to find seemingly in every country (Inclusion Project 2020).

After the pandemic first exploded in the United States in March 2020 (it is growing again at a record pace as we write, in mid-July 2020), the global higher education community's angst was focused on how and when universities would "recover" from the financial crisis wrought by the pandemic and establish a "new normal" in operations. We have argued elsewhere that such concerns, while no doubt important, fail to address the enduring challenges we face that have been thrown into sharp relief by the pandemic, whose disparate impacts lay bare the structural inequities embedded in the US educational system, reflecting broader and deeper structural inequities that remain pervasive (Cantor and Englot 2020).

US colleges and universities now are demonstrating awareness of this imperative (Anderson 2020). Only time will tell if today's well-intentioned statements of support signal genuine commitment to join with others to do the hard work of dismantling the architecture of segregation that permeates our culture. But at a moment of clarity like this, when the truth is so raw and undeniable, the higher education community must take swift action to build the momentum needed to effect lasting change reflecting renewed awareness that a "new normal" is far too modest a conception of what is needed (Carnevale et al. 2020a).

A RECKONING WITH SOCIETAL TRANSFORMATION

"Institutional transformation" is a more apt description of what is needed, transcending boundaries within the academy and between the academy and the world, with an eye towards collective work to advance equity and impact, to cement the identity of our institutions – each in its own way – and to build their role as indispensable partners in improving the human condition. We suggest that there are four inextricably intertwined aspects to the necessary transformation, all aimed at the public good (Cantor 2020). First, we need to diversify the student body and faculty, building a critical mass of representation so that our demographics better reflect those of our communities. Second, we need to recognise and reward publicly engaged scholarship, giving scholarship "a richer, more vital meaning", in the words of the late great Ernest L. Boyer (Boyer 1990). Third, we need to cultivate genuinely reciprocal, sustained relationships between our universities and our communities (as the stable, committed anchors of equitable growth and opportunity). Fourth, we need to learn to overcome our competitive instincts and collaborate across an ecosystem of institutions, organisations and sectors (all committed to a movement of change).

Yet resisting the urge to merely return to normal is no small matter, especially when the consistent message from US political leaders flies in the face of every truth there is about what we need to do to continue saving lives during a still-active pandemic that has already killed on the order of 130 000 people in the US and more than a half-million worldwide, while also denying the very existence of systemic racism (Baker and Haberman 2020; Scherer and Dawsey 2020). As Nicholas Kristof wrote in a column titled, "Crumbs for the hungry, windfalls for the rich", even US Government efforts purportedly aimed at helping those most gravely affected by the economic collapse caused by the pandemic are being twisted to reinforce prevailing power structures (Kristof 2020). This is occurring side by side with more than the usual recognition of the disparate impact of the pandemic on precisely the communities most disadvantaged by that very status quo – black and brown urban centres; Indigenous tribal communities; Asian American communities facing the bigotry of stigmatisation; immigrant farmworkers; rural towns with meat-packing plants; and "essential workers" in grocery stores and nursing homes (Artiga et al. 2020) – reflecting decades of systemic failure to embrace the safety nets needed in the United States, not to mention failure to level the path to prosperity (Porter 2020).

Proactive and innovative investments are needed to create genuine opportunity beyond a safety net – investments that, prior to the pandemic, were being proposed to change the future educational, social and economic outlooks (Tienda 2016) for the fastest growing parts of the US population (Frey 2015). Even before the toll of the pandemic, many in the US recognised that to pay for the next generation's social and economic security in retirement would require constructing a more equitable educational and economic roadmap for social mobility among that next generation (Carnevale and Smith 2016). As Mary Kay Henry, President of Service Employees International Union, asked David Gelles in an interview for the *New York Times*, "Are we going to return to a status quo that was not good for the majority of US families? Or are we going to use this shock to our system to create the real structural change that we need?" (Gelles 2020).

We wish, here, to ask those same questions about the road to recovery vis-à-vis the educational status quo and the new majority being educated in our primary and secondary schools that needs and deserves a genuinely viable path to post-secondary attainment and the social mobility that it affords (Carnevale et al. 2020b). What does that kind of transformation look like?

On the ground in Newark, New Jersey, we can see that it must start with the fundamental realities of everyday life. Newark is a city that characterises the gross inequities of the US: 85% of residents are Black or Brown, the poverty rate is 28% and nearly one in five people do not have health insurance – all in a city situated in the New York City metropolitan area, one of the most prosperous areas in a country where nationally the rates of poverty and lack of access to health care are less than half what they are in Newark, while the State of New Jersey's rates are even lower (U.S. Census Bureau 2020a). These disparities in life circumstances reflect gross disparities in opportunity that are intensely racialised. They play out every day in the form of constraints that people of colour face in access to housing, education, technology, legal representation, and health care – every domain of life – but very tangibly in cumulative disparities in wealth. In New Jersey, for example, white families have a median net worth of US$352 000, which stands in staggering contrast to the US$7 300 median for Latinx[51] families and US$6 100 median for Black families (New Jersey Institute for Social Justice 2020: 1).

The Covid-19 pandemic and resurgent Black Lives Matter movement are demonstrating unequivocally that these are not just challenges for Black and Brown people; they are challenges for us all. For US higher education, this acceptance of responsibility must go back at least to the Morrill Acts of the late 1800s, which enabled higher education to benefit directly from the theft and re-appropriation of land from Indigenous nations to found the nation's system of land-grant universities (Lee and Ahtone 2020), as well as to the slave labour that built many universities (Georgetown University 2015; Rutgers University 2015). Transparency about the past must motivate commitments in the present to leverage our physical, financial, human and intellectual capital in partnership with others to combat racism and advance social mobility in the communities where we are located.

Doing this entails engaging deeply with public, private and non-profit sector partners in collective, place-based work that focuses on the roots of racism and social stagnation. In a city like Newark, working on housing opportunity is an obvious choice because housing is the source of much of US citizens' wealth, accumulating over a lifetime and across generations through the acquisition of real estate. Yet despite civil rights legislation that has been in effect for upwards of a half-century, progress in assuring equal opportunity in housing remains a distant dream. Today's segregation of neighbourhoods in cities across the US is the result of a combination of *de facto* choices of individuals with regard to where they want to live, abetted by generations of *de jure* federal, state and local laws designed to segregate white families from families of colour (Rothstein 2017). For example, while 77% of New Jersey's white households own a home, only 41% of Black households do. Building

---

51. "Latinx" is a term increasingly used in the US to refer to people of Latin American background, employing a gender-neutral "x" rather than the gendered "o" or "a" ending.

on the legacy of slavery, structural factors that have suppressed real estate wealth accumulation by Black and Brown people while creating patterns of deeply segregated neighbourhoods include racially restrictive land covenants, exclusion from certain veterans' benefits, exclusionary real estate sales and financing practices – known collectively as "redlining" – and predatory lending practices (New Jersey Institute for Social Justice 2020: 2).

While many US cities have grappled for decades with the degree to which such policies and practices continue to mire progress towards eliminating housing inequities, Newark's Mayor Ras J. Baraka has made achieving equitable growth one of the city's highest priorities. He has formed an Equitable Growth Commission to advise him and the city's elected Municipal Council on developing policies to mitigate gentrification in Newark, as housing costs rise with population growth in the New York City metropolitan area and more people are being priced out of living in the area's core. The highly inclusive commission includes Rutgers-Newark law professor David Troutt, whose Center for Law, Inequality, and Metropolitan Equity received strategic support from the university to conduct the policy research that ultimately led to the commission's founding. The commission also includes appointees from global corporations such as Prudential, which is headquartered in Newark; real estate developers; community-based non-profit organisations that provide essential services to lower-income residents; state and regional housing advocate groups; and Rutgers-Newark business professor Kevin Lyons (City of Newark 2018).

Housing opportunity goes hand in hand with educational opportunity in the US because primary and secondary schools are funded primarily by taxes paid by residents on their real estate. This creates inequalities that can last generations. New Jersey's primary and secondary schools are among the most segregated in the US, more so than any of the former Confederacy of southern states that fought in the US Civil War to preserve slavery. Today, nearly half of New Jersey's 585 000 Black and Latinx public school students attend schools that are more than 90% Black and Latinx (Boddie 2019). Ultimately, then, schools in New Jersey tend to be doubly segregated – by race and class – with poorly funded schools being found disproportionately in communities where residents are predominantly Black and Brown.

Cognisant of this, and with strategic financial support from Rutgers-Newark, law professor Elise Boddie created the Inclusion Project, which explores legal avenues to create more inclusive communities. Among them is research into the extent and deleterious effects of segregated schools on students of all backgrounds, as well as how to desegregate them. That work has become foundational for the legal strategy adopted by the New Jersey Coalition for Diverse and Inclusive Schools, a non-profit organisation that has filed a lawsuit against the State of New Jersey to desegregate the schools. Their two-pronged argument is that inclusive schools with diverse student bodies are demonstrably better for all students than segregated schools, and that a New Jersey state law requiring students to attend school in the local school district in which they live is a root cause of the segregation. So, the coalition is suing the state to change that law, a case which is currently being adjudicated (Stein 2020).

An even broader coalition, the Newark City of Learning Collaborative (NCLC), is working to increase college-going among students in Newark's schools, where, as of 2018, only 21% of Newark residents had earned an associate's (two-year) degree or higher, compared with 46% of all New Jersey residents and 40% of US citizens (U.S. Census Bureau 2020b). With backbone administrative leadership and support provided by Rutgers-Newark, NCLC's cross-sector partnership of community-based organisations, K–12 schools, local government, foundations, corporations and higher education, shares the goal of increasing the proportion of Newark residents with a degree, or credential beyond high school, and ultimately sustaining an ecosystem of support for post-secondary degree attainment. Initiatives driven by NCLC to build that ecosystem include:

- pre-college mentoring and co-curricular engagement to assist high school students in the transition to college;
- a partnership with the Rutgers University–Newark School of Public Affairs and Administration (SPAA) to create a city-wide data project assessing post-secondary trends in Newark that produced *Post-secondary outcomes of Newark high school graduates*, the first comprehensive analysis of college-going patterns for high school graduates from district, charter, county and parochial school sectors (Backstrand and Donaldson 2018);
- a partnership with the Newark Public Library that helps residents build their knowledge base of what it takes to prepare for college throughout the primary and secondary school years;
- a city-wide challenge in co-ordination with the Newark Board of Education and the United Way of Essex County to support high school seniors and their families applying for federal financial aid programmes;
- a city-wide dual enrolment initiative, allowing Newark high school students to earn college credit while still pursuing their high school diplomas, all at no cost to their families.

NCLC's 10 higher education partner institutions in the region work to make the transition to college seamless and affordable for Newark students. For Rutgers-Newark, that includes a funding programme guaranteeing that full tuition and fees will be covered by financial aid for any Newark resident or New Jersey County College transfer student with an adjusted family income of US$60 000 or less. Known as Rutgers University–Newark Talent & Opportunity Pathways (RU-N to the TOP), it has helped more than double the representation of students from Newark at the university since 2013 to the present level of 14.5% of all undergraduates.

Complementing these hyper local initiatives are collaborative efforts to increase educational opportunity for other groups statewide who face systemic racism. One such group is undocumented students – individuals who were brought to the US as children without standard immigration documentation, but who effectively know no other home country. Living with the recurring threat of deportation owing to torturous vicissitudes of US immigration policy, undocumented students number nearly half a million in the US and 20 000 in New Jersey alone (Presidents' Alliance 2020). Rutgers-Newark advocates for them nationally, along with several hundred other college and university leaders, through the Presidents' Alliance on Higher Education and Immigration for policy changes that will remove the threat of deportation and create a pathway to US citizenship for undocumented students. Like some other institutions, Rutgers-Newark also deploys significant resources to provide financial support for them, as current US policy makes them ineligible for federal financial aid for college.

Likewise, there are clusters of institutions collaborating to increase educational opportunity for incarcerated and formerly incarcerated individuals through a small handful of programmes across the US (RAND Corporation 2020). Rutgers-Newark is the hub of one of the largest such networks, the New Jersey Scholarship and Transformative Education in Prisons (NJ-STEP) Program, which is co-ordinating "stackable" two-year and four-year higher education institutions to grant college degrees (Kendall 2020). In addition to teaching in seven New Jersey prison facilities, NJ-STEP is working with non-profit groups like the New Jersey Institute for Social Justice and the Vera Institute, as our publicly engaged faculty and staff advocate for voting rights, train re-entry entrepreneurs and push the state and our nation to provide equitable growth pathways, especially for those from Black and Brown communities that have disproportionately high incarceration rates.

Indeed, mass incarceration warrants collective action in and of itself, having eviscerated communities across the US, where one in three Black men nationally is projected to serve time in prison at some point in their lives, reflecting a rate of imprisonment two-and-a-half times that of Latino men and six times that of whites (La Vigne et al. 2015). There is no shortage of partners in our community eager to engage with our faculty, staff and students in taking collective action on policing and criminal justice reform, as well as increasing educational opportunities for incarcerated and formerly incarcerated individuals to build the skills and rightfully gain employment, so that their communities can reap the benefits of their talents (Davis et al. 2013). Such partnerships include the Newark Public Safety Collaborative, in which faculty and staff members from the Rutgers-Newark School of Criminal Justice have joined with local law enforcement and neighbourhood groups to collect and analyse hyper-local data on the characteristics of crime hotspots, then collectively focus on changing those characteristics as a way to strengthen neighbourhoods while reducing crime, supported by community-based "street teams" – community members who help the aggrieved find ways forward because they empathise with the struggle to survive in a world where the odds always seem to be stacked against you (Newark Public Safety Collaborative 2020).

Indeed, the hyper-local knowledge and credibility of the street teams work on a much larger scale, too. When Newark's own recent protest in support of the Black Lives Matter movement drew 12 000 people onto the streets of downtown, the marchers' combination of rage and peaceful resolve – and the protest's virtual absence of violence – were noted by observers whose familiarity with such events in Newark was limited to the 1967 Rebellion that resulted in 26 deaths and millions of dollars in damage (Tully and Armstrong 2020). That was due in no small part to street teams dispersed in groups throughout the crowd, righteously enraged as everyone else, as protest organiser Larry Hamm attested, but also righteously resolved to help their fellow marchers maintain their focus on the real reason they were there: to make the case for justice and for peace.

If universities are to play a meaningful role on the other side of the inflection point in history the world is experiencing right now, when up until now we have been part and parcel of the social systems that have perpetuated racism and inequity, we should aspire to that level of empathy for and with our communities, and to that level of commitment to working in true partnership with them to achieve justice, equity and peace (Maurrasse 2020).

REFERENCES

Anderson G. (2020), "Growing recognition of Juneteenth", *Inside Higher Ed* (19 June 2020), available at www.insidehighered.com/news/2020/06/19/colleges-acknowledge-juneteenth-holiday, accessed on 21 July 2020.

Artiga S. et al. (2020), "Growing COVID-19 hotspots in the U.S. south and west will likely widen disparities for people of color", Kaiser Family Foundation, available at www.kff.org/coronavirus-policy-watch/growing-covid-19-hotspots-in-south-and-west-likely-widen-disparities-people-of-color/, accessed 21 July 2020.

Backstrand J. and Donaldson K. (2018), *Post-secondary outcomes of Newark high school graduates (2011-2016)*, Newark, NJ: Rutgers University–Newark SPAA.

Baker P. and Haberman M. (2020), "Trump praises 'great' police, rebuffing protests over systemic racism", *New York Times* (8 June 2020), A15, available at www.nytimes.com/2020/06/08/us/politics/defund-police-trump.html?searchResultPosition=3, accessed 21 July 2020.

Boddie E. (2019), Testimony to New Jersey State Legislature Joint Committee on Public Schools (19 March 2019), Trenton, NJ.

Boyer E. L. (1990), *Scholarship reconsidered: priorities of the professoriate*, Princeton, NJ: Princeton University Press.

Cantor N. (2020), "Transforming the academy: the urgency of recommitting higher education to the public good", *Liberal Education*, Winter/Spring 2020, 106(1/2): 48-55.

Cantor N. and Englot P. (2020), "What are we going to do about structural inequities highlighted by pandemic?", *NJSpotlight* (15 April 2020), available at www.njspotlight.com/2020/04/op-ed-what-are-we-going-to-do-about-structural-inequities-highlighted-by-pandemic/, accessed 21 July 2020.

Carnevale A. and Smith N. (2016), "The economic value of diversity", in E. Lewis and N. Cantor (eds), *Our compelling interests: the value of diversity for democracy and a prosperous society*, Princeton, NJ: Princeton University Press, pp. 106-60.

Carnevale A., Schmidt P. and Strohl J. (2020a), "How higher ed can stop affirmative action for rich white people", *Chronicle of Higher Education* (8 July 2020), available at www.chronicle.com/article/How-Higher-Ed-Can-Stop/249140, accessed 21 July 2020.

Carnevale A., Schmidt P. and Strohl J. (2020b), *The merit myth: how our colleges favor the rich and divide America*, New York: The New Press.

City of Newark (2018), "Newark announces creation of commission to prevent gentrification and assure equitable growth", City of Newark (6 December 2018), available at www.newarknj.gov/news/newark-announces-creation-of-commission-to-prevent-gentrification-and-assure-equitable-growth, accessed 21 July 2020.

Davis L. M. et al. (2013), *Evaluating the effectiveness of correctional education*, Santa Monica, CA: RAND Corporation.

Frey W. H. (2015), *Diversity explosion: how new racial demographics are remaking America*, Washington, DC: Brookings Institution.

Gelles D. (2020), "'Working people want real change': a union chief sounds off on the crisis", *New York Times* (24 May 2020), available at www.nytimes.com/2020/05/22/business/mary-kay-henry-seiu-corner-office.html, accessed 5 December 2020.

Georgetown University (2015), *Georgetown University: slavery, memory, and reconciliation*, Georgetown University, available at http://slavery.georgetown.edu/, accessed 21 July 2020.

Inclusion Project (2020), *Snapshots of COVID-19: structural inequity and access to justice*, Newark, NJ: Rutgers University Law School, available at http://theinclusionproject.rutgers.edu/wp-content/uploads/2020/07/snapshots-of-covid-19-structural-inequity-and-access-to-justice-2020.pdf, accessed 21 July 2020.

Kendall T. (2020), "He started his college education behind bars. Now he wants to help kids avoid prison", *CBSNews* (17 January 2020), available at www.cbsnews.com/news/he-started-college-education-in-prison-now-he-wants-to-help-kids-avoid-prison-2020-01-17/, accessed 21 July 2020.

Kristof N. (2020), "Crumbs for the hungry, windfalls for the rich", *New York Times* (24 May 2020), available at www.nytimes.com/2020/05/23/opinion/sunday/coronavirus-economic-response.html?searchResultPosition=1, accessed 21 July 2020.

La Vigne N. G., King R. and Fontaine J. (2015), "Want to reduce mass incarceration? Do no harm and invest in people and communities", Urban Institute, available at www.urban.org/urban-wire/want-reduce-mass-incarceration-do-no-harm-and-invest-people-and-communities, accessed 21 July 2020.

Lee R. and Ahtone T. (2020), "Land grab universities: expropriated Indigenous land is the foundation of the land-grant university system", *High Country News* (30 March 2020), available at www.hcn.org/issues/52.4/indigenous-affairs-education-land-grab-universities, accessed 21 July 2020.

Maurrasse D. (2020), "Anchor institutions task force strategic plan", New York: Marga Inc., available at www.margainc.com/covid-19/, accessed 21 July 2020.

New Jersey Institute for Social Justice (2020), *Erasing New Jersey's red lines: reducing the racial wealth gap through homeownership and investment in communities of color*, Newark, NJ: New Jersey Institute for Social Justice.

Newark Public Safety Collaborative (2020), *Newark Public Safety Collaborative*, Newark, NJ: Rutgers University–Newark School of Criminal Justice, available at https://newarkcollaborative.org/, accessed 21 July 2020.

Porter E. (2020), *American poison: how racial hostility destroyed our promise*, New York: Alfred A. Knopf.

Presidents' Alliance (2020), "Undocumented students in higher education", Presidents' Alliance on Higher Education and Immigration (1 April 2020), available at https://2wslav2505mz1d7rci3uuem8-wpengine.netdna-ssl.com/wp-content/uploads/2020/04/2020-04-16-NAE-PA-Report-Undocumented-Students-in-Higher-Education.pdf, accessed 21 July 2020.

RAND Corporation (2020), *Correctional education*, RAND Corporation, available at www.rand.org/well-being/justice-policy/portfolios/correctional-education.html, accessed 21 July 2020.

Rothstein R. (2017), *The color of law: a forgotten history of how our government segregated America*, New York: Liveright Publishing.

Rutgers University (2015), *Scarlet and Black Project*, Newark, NJ: Rutgers University (10 November 2015), available at https://scarletandblack.rutgers.edu/, accessed 21 July 2020.

Scherer M. and Dawsey J. (2020), "Trump says GOP will look to move convention out of North Carolina", *Washington Post* (2 June 2020), available at www.washingtonpost.com/politics/gop-looks-beyond-north-carolina-for-convention-as-relations-deteriorate-with-state-leaders/2020/06/02/e9cf9106-a4fa-11ea-b619-3f9133bbb482_story.html, accessed 21 July 2020.

Stein G. (2020), "Racial healing begins by admitting our schools are segregated", *NJ.com* (23 June 2020), available at www.nj.com/opinion/2020/06/racial-healing-begins-by-admitting-our-schools-are-segregated-opinion.html, accessed 21 July 2020.

Tienda M. (2016), "Diversity as a strategic advantage: a socio-demographic perspective", in Lewis E. and Cantor N. (eds), *Our compelling interests: the value of diversity for democracy and a prosperous society*, Princeton, NJ: Princeton University Press, pp. 192-205.

Tully T. and Armstrong K. (2020), "How a city once consumed by civil unrest has kept protests peaceful", *New York Times* (2 June 2020), available at www.nytimes.com/2020/06/01/nyregion/newark-peaceful-protests-george-floyd.html?searchResultPosition=1, accessed 21 July 2020.

U.S. Census Bureau (2020a), *American community survey 2019*, U.S. Census Bureau, available at www.census.gov/search-results.html?q=city+of+newark+nj&page=1&stateGeo=none&searchtype=web&cssp=SERP&_charset_=UTF-8, accessed 21 July 2020.

U.S. Census Bureau (2020b), *Educational attainment in the United States: 2019*, U.S. Census Bureau, available at www.census.gov/content/census/en/data/tables/2019/demo/educational-attainment/cps-detailed-tables.html, accessed 21 July 2020.

Chapter 9

University challenge – The role of research-intensive universities in crisis management

Åse Gornitzka and Svein Stølen[52]

INTRODUCTION

Only a semester ago, it would have been hard to believe that research-based knowledge at the forefront of science would soon become an everyday topic of conversation. Media are saturated with data and statistics on the nature and state of a virus. Reproduction rates and theories of viral origin and spread are discussed at kitchen tables around the globe – and perhaps most urgently around the cabinet tables of national decision makers. Politicians and government officials are on a steep, at times brutal, learning curve, as they make extremely urgent and consequential choices about how to deal with the Covid-19 crisis by weighing a plethora of doubtful premises while balancing conflicting priorities. In dealing with a crisis of such a magnitude and as fateful as this, the stream of problems to address is overwhelming, and the effectiveness of the available solutions is not easy to predict. Decision makers are caught up in a whirlwind. Striking features of the crisis are how diverse the national responses to the crisis turned out to be and how scientific knowledge has been at the heart of the process of crisis management at different stages. In this respect, the 2020 spring semester will for a long time stand out as the semester when the world practically turned into an ominous laboratory for studying human and institutional action under conditions of extreme time pressure and uncertainty amid high expectations that science should provide the solutions. Consequently, universities were also challenged to engage in the collective response.

In this chapter, we direct attention to how research-intensive universities were coupled and decoupled from governmental crisis management. By crisis management we mean "the sum of activities aimed at minimizing the impact of a crisis" (Boin, Kuipers and Overdijk 2013: 81). We examine the implications for the current and future role of research-intensive comprehensive universities in a democratic political order.

---

52. This chapter is based on an article published in *Times Higher Education* and available at www.timeshighereducation.com/blog/coronavirus-can-improve-societal-understanding-universities-role, accessed 22 July 2020.

In this respect, our arguments are of a general nature. We draw nonetheless on the experiences of one single country – Norway – a case characterised by conditions that are hard to replicate in other national political orders with smaller resources and weaker institutions. Yet, the case is of broader interest because the country's response has so far been among the high-performing systems when it comes to this episode of public crisis management (Christensen and Lægreid 2020).

WHAT KIND OF RESPONSE TO WHAT KIND OF CHALLENGE?

The Covid-19 crisis shook the roots of institutions that govern societies across the globe – irrespective of their democratic value. Covid-19 is a massive challenge to societal institutions, to collective action, a problem cutting deeply into the fabric of social, economic and academic life. Under strong time and media pressure, decision makers faced questions of life and death, literally and undeniably. Pressure for collective action was felt in the urgency attached to the Covid-19 crisis. Government doing nothing was also a fateful kind of response. Coping with the crisis relied on early recognition of the problem, that is, identifying the situation as a threat requiring attention. In this respect, in Norway the role of expertise was considerable: having two expert agencies, the Norwegian Directorate of Health and the Norwegian Institute of Public Health, under the aegis of the Ministry of Health and Care Services, was key at this early stage. These agencies had close connections to international and multilateral institutions that were crucial in coping with executive tasks of crisis management (Boin, Kuipers and Overdijk 2013).

On 12 March 2020, the Norwegian Government announced its response to the threatening virus. The first cases of infection within national borders had been identified already in February. The action plan was introduced to the public at a government press conference – an event dramatically staged and held in a tone of voice full of fundamental alarm. After a period of fence-sitting in response to the first reports of infected cases, the Norwegian Government now introduced draconian measures (Christensen and Lægreid 2020). The prime minister was flanked by the Minister of Health and Care Services and the directors of both health agencies.

This set-up signalled that the task of making sense of the threat would rest with the core political and executive leadership with the support of the expert bodies. These also became the core set of decision-making actors in the weeks to come. The measures introduced on 12 March contained standard measures to avoid the spread of infectious disease, developed from the perspective of the health sector. Yet, the complete list of regulatory measures, especially with respect to social distancing, cut deep into the social and economic order: the lockdown of day care centres, schools and universities and university colleges was unprecedented – and so was the closure of businesses involving close contact with clients, such as hairdressers, gyms and hotels. The collective understanding of the nature of the threat the government communicated to the general public was as a threat to our way of life – a mega threat only surpassed in modern times by the Second World War. The gravity of the situation was such that maintaining the national way of life had to yield to concern about virus spread and the capacity for treating Covid-19 patients, exemplified most iconically by the ban on spending weekends and holidays in a cottage.

Moreover, it became blatantly clear that the threat was transboundary – in terms of its global spread, but even more importantly how it transcended boundaries between sectors of society, although not all sectors were hit equally hard.

The public saw the measures to stop the virus as not only a health issue, but also as a policy problem affecting all other sectors of society. The responsibility for co-ordinating crisis management was transferred from the Ministry of Health and Care Services to the Ministry of Justice and Public Security (Christensen and Lægreid 2020: 2), which could symbolise the understanding of the transboundary nature of the crisis. The initial suppression strategy of the government was followed up by this broader understanding, introducing financial support for businesses and laid-off employees. The number of infected citizens peaked in late March and early April.[53] Gradually, parts of social and economic life were unlocked, and the intrusive emergency regulations terminated. Approaching the end of the troublesome semester, the government announced that the situation was "under control".

KNOWLEDGE-BASED GOVERNANCE IN TIMES OF MEGA CRISIS MANAGEMENT – CAPACITY AND LEGITIMACY

Two main factors affect societies' ability to tackle and respond to such a crisis with good governance: government capacity and government legitimacy (cf. Christensen and Lægreid (2020), who make this argument based on an analysis of the Norwegian case). Government capacity includes how prepared governments are, and the resources they have at their disposal, for analysing the problem and devising relevant solutions. Government legitimacy, that is, maintaining citizens' trust in government as well as the sense of what are normatively appropriate actions to take, is equally important for crisis management to be successful.

We argue here that the research-intensive university contributes to both of these key elements in crisis management. Research-intensive universities can be seen as institutionalised knowledge reservoirs or an emergency repository that can be activated as part of the government's capacity for crisis management. It is especially important that public health agencies and their leadership adhere to high professional and scientific standards with a high level of scientific literacy. This played a key role in the crisis-management response and demonstrates (once again) that the biggest impact that research-intensive universities make in terms of utilisation of specialised expertise for the benefit of society is providing public institutions with competent professionals. This includes the ability to convey and discuss the considerable uncertainty attached to the core problem – in this case the problem of stopping the virus and dealing with the side effects of available solutions. Even though government had to devise measures whose effectiveness and consequences they could not easily predict and with the added pressure of urgency, the call for the "one-armed adviser" was less of an issue than one might expect. Decision makers were fairly open about how choices were at times drenched in uncertainty. Professional concerns were not always a requirement (e.g. closing of schools or banning the use of holiday houses)

---

53. See www.vg.no/spesial/2020/corona/, accessed 22 July 2020.

but the cabinet as the key decision maker collaborating closely with the health agencies built on the "precautionary principle" (Christensen and Lægreid 2020).

The case also demonstrates how research-intensive universities engaged in crisis management despite not being part of the core set of actors making the decisions on the specific measures to be taken, because the responsibility for and attention to those decisions were anchored in the political executive leadership.

The University of Oslo, as the main research-intensive comprehensive university, contributed with relevant scientific knowledge to ensure informed discussion and the identification of effective solutions. This applied to the early stages of crisis management, when actors were trying to develop an understanding of the nature and extent of the threat. Moreover, academics joined the national conversation in the public sphere as to the effectiveness and legitimacy of the measures taken by government after the main decisions were made. The breadth of academic research fields has become highly relevant. Research-based evidence and controversy have not been sidelined in Norway as they have in some other countries, but nor have professionals taken over, or been delegated, the power to make decisions, as has happened for instance in the Swedish case. We can also see the contours of how basic research in comprehensive universities is becoming increasingly important in the reflection stage of crisis management. Critical analytical capacity will be key for learning, for the legitimacy of the actions taken, and for evaluation and accountability of decision makers.

The University of Oslo's response to the national research council's call for Covid-19 research is illustrative in this respect. It showed the relevance of core health science and research to medical and biological aspects such as virological, clinical and immunological characterisation, risk and protective factors, including assessing contact/proximity risk and mental health. The role of the humanities and social sciences was demonstrated in research on human aspects including pandemic rhetoric, public response, trust and the role of social media. The same goes for research on the experiences of patients and primary health care professionals and the ethical dimensions of public measures.

Technological contributions include new information systems utilising big data and statistical analyses. A prominent example is the District Health Information System (DHIS2),[54] an open-source, web-based software platform for data collection, management and analysis. The platform developed under the leadership of Professor Kristin Braa is in use by ministries of health in 72 low- and middle-income countries and released a digital data package to accelerate case detection, situation reporting, active surveillance and response for Covid-19.

The role of critical analytical capacity, building on interdisciplinary research and expertise, is illustrated in the role played by Professor Steinar Holden. Holden, an economist and chair of the Department of Economics, was appointed by the government to chair the expert committee that analysed the economic effects of different specific measures against the Covid-19 pandemic. This kind of expertise

---

54. For the District Health Information System, see www.dhis2.org/about, accessed 22 July 2020.

was used in political decision making as an input for assessing the balance between protecting the economy and protecting the public from the virus, a core dilemma in this case of crisis management.

Professor Hans Petter Graver's criticism of rule of law aspects of a crisis law proposed by the government on 18 March resulted in major amendments during the parliamentary deliberations, and Norway ended up with a crisis law giving far less authority to the government than initially proposed. In this case, the critical function of independent academics affected the public's and the political community's perspective and view on the normative and legal justification for an emergency law.

Professor Anne Spurkland is one of many researchers engaged in public outreach activities, blogging as an experienced immunologist on the basic mechanisms of the virus and why she herself was afraid of getting the disease. Her work is a clear example of how academic expertise interacts with the public sphere and can contribute not only to the effectiveness but also to the legitimacy of expert-based crisis management. As Christensen and Lægreid observe in their study of the Norwegian case, crisis communication was "characterized by clear, timely and repeating messages and advices for action informed by expert knowledge and delivered by credible political and administrative executives and experts" (Christensen and Lægreid 2020: 4).

LESSONS FOR THE UNIVERSITY IN AN AGE OF UNCERTAINTY

Academics have responded massively to the challenge, and disciplinary knowledge is demonstrating the great value of its scientific depth. Yet, faced with the truly dreadful problems thrown up by the pandemic, the importance of multidisciplinary and interdisciplinary collaboration becomes obvious, too.

The Covid-19 crisis highlights the importance of scientific multilingualism. This is a clear challenge to the research-intensive comprehensive university. The crisis goes far beyond medical issues to factors such as the spread of infections, how it can be limited and how vaccines can be developed. We are also acutely dependent on gaining insight into how factors such as culture, demographics, the organisation of national health services, public administration and industry work together to influence the effectiveness of government efforts to combat the spread of the virus.

The same applies to the societal, economic and political consequences of partial lockdowns. The world has become an uncomfortable laboratory for the study of such complex inter-relationships. Urgency presents us with a major challenge, however. Speed is necessary but cannot override the need for reliable studies that adhere to principles of research ethics and scientific methodology. Yet the huge amount of personal, institutional and national prestige potentially on offer for making the decisive scientific contribution, such as a Covid-19 vaccine, may challenge the adherence to academic standards. Under such conditions, there is a real fear that researchers could take shortcuts and in so doing also affect the trust in scientific expertise and the authority of experts.

We already see tendencies for research results to be presented more quickly in the daily newspapers than through peer-reviewed channels, and we see institutions controlling what their researchers publish. High-speed quality assurance, via peer review, is necessary when political action cannot be put on hold, but it remains a challenge.

Yet researchers cannot replace politicians as decision makers. This is not merely because it would breach democratic norms but also because – as we know from studies of the relationship between public administration, politics and research in general – it is rare that complex phenomena can be reduced to one scientifically unambiguous piece of advice. Uncertainty regarding the effects of infection prevention and control measures gives rise to different political narratives around the world about what is the most durable strategy for combating the virus. Scientific advice enters a crowded place when it comes to decision making. Among the other factors that need to be quickly weighed are legality, legitimacy and the economic and redistributive consequences of alternative strategies.

However, this does not make scientific advice less important. In a "knowledge democracy", there are high expectations that political decisions should be science-informed and justifiable with reference to professional standards. Only very rarely have we in modern times seen such a clear demonstration of the crucial importance of having a scientific "knowledge reservoir" that decision makers can draw from in acute and high-risk situations.

Therefore, it matters how we, on a long-term basis, organise research and connect it to politics and public administration in a sustainable way at the local, national and – no less importantly – global level.

CRISIS MANAGEMENT AND POST-PEAK REFLECTIONS: OPEN ADVICE, OPEN DEMOCRACIES

We must reflect on post-Covid-19 policies and measures at many levels, including in academia. The academic community and its leaders have taken part in the speedy transformation of its educational delivery through "overnight" digitalisation of teaching. One key dimension is the continued need to work towards open science. Attention so far has mostly focused on journals (at least in Norway), yet the Covid-19 crisis shows that other dimensions of open research are just as important. Data, results and insights must be made available for utilisation and assessment. This applies not just to the final data; approaches, methods and interpretations must also be released. It is evident that researchers need to share their data with the political decision makers and the general public under specific terms and rules of engagement. And they must be open about scientific controversies, risks and uncertainty. There is nothing to fear from this: surveys show that the population largely trust science and, amid all of its devastating consequences, the pandemic may even increase that trust further (Norges Forskningsråd 2020).

It already seems a long while ago that "we've had enough of experts" was the dominant refrain; anti-vaccine arguments, for instance, are being given very short shrift. A preliminary analysis of the Covid-19 crisis indicates that there are high expectations that political decisions must be open and professionally justified. The latter is a major challenge to research-intensive universities and academic communities. Trust in science cannot be taken for granted and the role of research-intensive universities needs to be nurtured and renewed. The same goes for the terms under which academic expertise takes part in the policy-making process. This needs to be part of the reflections on the effects of chosen courses of action in post-crisis learning.

The UK Government has claimed that it is "following the science",[55] but few people knew what "the science" was, who sat on its scientific council or what kind of advice they gave. The case of Norway tells a different story – a case of research-based advice being open, for the most part. Attempts at strategic presentation of data and studies, or postponing sharing of information, have increasingly met with public discussion over transparency.

The public knows which agencies, committees and research groups have provided the basis for crisis management, and we gradually gain access to their knowledge summaries and their research-based advice. We can, of course, understand the government's need to co-ordinate communication in a time of crisis. But when the crisis is so extensive, affecting all sectors and affecting people's fundamental rights and quality of life, it is crucial that the knowledge base is open, that it is debated – and before decisions are made.

Quick and open publication of facts and analyses is a democratic right, but also essential when expert communities give advice in an emergency situation – and transparency is vital to both the effectiveness and legitimacy of crisis management. Better mutual understanding of the roles, needs and interests of all parties involved in decision making, from politics and public agencies to civil society and industry, may also result in a clearer societal understanding of the role and responsibilities of universities. This would be an important element in better preparing ourselves for future crises.

One clear lesson from the hits and misses of public policy and regulation at the different stages of the Covid-19 crisis is how a scientific knowledge base needs institutional autonomy and academic freedom to prevent short-sighted instrumentality and to ensure the integrity and legitimacy of science in crisis management. The critical function of academic institutions in particular is key to the role that academic expertise can play. Liberal democracies need independent watchdogs that direct attention towards governments' crisis management when they make biased factual claims, take democratic shortcuts, take and keep power beyond what is reasonable and justifiable or allow strong economic interests to unduly trump the rights and interests of vulnerable groups. For that we need autonomous universities with a strong understanding of their societal role.

The response to the Covid-19 pandemic should stimulate some reconsideration of the current understanding of institutional autonomy. The European University Association ranks universities according to four dimensions: organisational, staffing, academic and financial autonomy. Norway as a country is ranked as number 8, 15, 9 and 27 in the four categories, with an unweighted financial autonomy of 27%.

---

55. See www.theguardian.com/world/2020/apr/23/scientists-criticise-uk-government-over-following-the-science, and www.theguardian.com/world/2020/may/04/rival-sage-group-covid-19-policy-clarified-david-king, accessed 22 July 2020.

One major reason is that there are no tuition fees. An analysis of the University of Oslo by an international strategic advisory board chaired by former Finnish prime minister Esko Aho found that Norwegian universities are profoundly dependent on public funding, which is increasingly earmarked for specific purposes. Private funding is rare. The group chaired by Mr Aho saw this as an impediment to university autonomy, suggesting that the university is severely constrained in the allocation and use of financial resources. The impact of the Covid-19 pandemic on universities suggests quite the opposite: this funding mechanism gives stability to the institutions and institutionalises the country's need for academic expertise. This type of credible commitment of governments seems to be a more resilient model for university funding and for universities to fulfil their mission and "bend without breaking" in the midst of a severe crisis.

REFERENCES

Boin A., Kuipers S. and Overdijk W. (2013), "Leadership in times of crisis: a framework for assessment", *International Review of Public Administration*, 18(1): 79-91, available at https://doi.org/10.1080/12294659.2013.10805241, accessed 17 September 2020.

Christensen, T. and Lægreid, P. (2020), "Balancing Governance Capacity and Legitimacy: How the Norwegian Government Handled the COVID-19 Crisis as a High Performer", *Public Admin Rev, 80 (5)*: 774-779; available at doi:10.1111/puar.13241, accessed 17 September 2020.

Norges Forskningsråd (2020), *Befolkningens tillit til og syn på forskning* ("Citizens' trust in and view of research"), Norges Forskningsråd (The Research Council of Norway) and KANTAR, April 2020, available at www.forskningsradet.no/contentassets/96ad9ee96f7a460cada4501ad0b3502d/pm-rapport-befolkningens-tillit-til-forskning---april-2020.pdf, accessed 22 July 2020.

Chapter 10

Maireann na daoine ar scath a chéile: Dublin City University, Covid-19 and the creation of the "next normal"

Daire Keogh

INTRODUCTION

In the aftermath to a previous crisis, Ireland's Great Famine (1845-50), John Henry Newman visited Dublin and delivered an address in which he developed the "Idea of a university" (published 1852), which would nourish in its students the critical skills necessary for life as he saw it. In the aftermath of Covid-19 it is incumbent on universities to engage in that dialogue once more, and to redefine our purpose in a post-pandemic world. At Dublin City University (DCU) we are determined to harness our energies and connections to meet the great challenges of our age, captured so clearly in the sustainable development goals.

In the ancient Irish language (*Gaeilge*), we have a reservoir of proverbs called *Seanfhocail*, two of which are most favoured by educators. The equivalent of John Donne's "no man is an island", *Maireann na daoine ar scath a chéile*, translates literally as "people live in one another's shadow", while the second, *Ní neart go chur le cheíle*, suggests that there is no strength without unity. Both are employed to the point of cliché, but the island's response to the coronavirus pandemic has vindicated the insight of the ancients. In contrast to other regions, Covid-19 elicited a united response in Ireland as the nation rallied to the cause of solidarity beneath the banner of "Save Lives – Stay at Home". Science, health and safety considerations set the tone, creating an environment in which experts became popular heroes and universities embraced their civic mission. The crisis inspired conversations about the prospect of a new "better normal", while the 1920s Civil War rival political parties joined with the Greens to form an historic coalition government. Certainly, Covid-19 exposed the stark inequalities within Irish society, and the consequences of a decade of austerity were manifest within education. Yet the new government broke ground, inaugurating a Ministry of Higher Education with ambitions to "drive inclusion and equality". Higher education, having proved vital in Ireland's emergency, had been identified as critical in its recovery.

COVID-19 IN IRELAND

Ireland's national holiday, 17 March, is a global celebration when the world goes green for "St Paddy's Day". Ministerial delegations ply the planet promoting culture and trade, while the highlight of the annual mission is the celebrated Shamrock exchange between the Taoiseach (Prime Minister) and the President at the White House. Irish universities exploit the festival, too, and each year visit alumni, donors and partners in the United States. March 2020 was like no other, however, since the pall of the rising crisis cast a sombre and tentative mood over the visit. In hindsight, it was surprising it happened at all, with the emergency escalating and leaders responding "in real time".

On 11 March, the World Health Organization formally designated Covid-19 as a pandemic; that night, President Trump abruptly announced a European travel ban and almost simultaneously Irish health officials recorded the island's first Covid-19 death. Within hours, Ireland followed Italy into an unexpected lockdown. The context of the Taoiseach's announcement to the nation, while still in Washington DC, was a powerful symbol of the global nature of this scourge, but more significantly, the subdued tenor of his address set a tone, which characterised the nation's subsequent response:

> I know that this is coming as a real shock and it is going to involve big changes in the way we live our lives.
> I know that I am asking people to make enormous sacrifices.
> We're doing it for each other.
> Together, we can slow the virus in its tracks and push it back. (Varadkar 2020)

Even though the coronavirus threat was known by epidemiologists, it acted effectively as a "black swan" event in terms of its impact and consequences, compounded by its duration with no end in sight.[56] Ireland's geopolitical context minimises risks of disruption or natural disasters, although an increasing number of extreme weather events in recent years has provided test runs for our crisis-management teams.

At DCU, we employed valuable learnings from these events to great effect. Critically, the university leadership was in transition from President Brian MacCraith to myself, but from the outset our co-ordination of the response was led by the Chief Operations Officer, Dr Declan Raftery, who had begun to implement Covid-19 prevention measures already in January. The President's "cabinet", the Senior Management Team, morphed into a Covid Crisis Management Team (CMT), which created a textbook response; the group projected a shared university voice, leaders across the system were empowered, decision making was expedited, responsibility rolled out and the crisis was effectively managed across the university. We were also fortunate in having emergency planning specialists in the DCU Business School – many of whom were supporting key decision makers in the health, defence and emergency response sectors as the crisis evolved – who informed the university approach.

---

56. A "black swan" is a major development or event which had not been predicted and which disrupts conventional wisdom and assumptions. The European assumption that all swans were white was overturned by explorers' first encounter with the Australian black swan.

DCU, "Ireland's University of Enterprise", prides itself on a culture and dispositions to which the Civic University movement aspires. We are a values-based university, determined to foster an environment that is open, collegial, collaborative, student-focused and ambitious. Our mission is to "Transform lives and society", and our strategic plan *Talent, discovery, and transformation* (2017-22) commits us "to address the major challenges facing the world ... today and to develop the talent and knowledge that society needs" (DCU 2017). A feature of our strategy process was the adoption of a rolling planning model, echoing Churchill's dictum that "plans are of little importance, but that planning is essential". At no point did DCU anticipate a catastrophe of the magnitude of Covid-19, but the culture of planning facilitated an ability to flex in ways which demonstrated the "DCU-DNA", our values and strategic objectives.

From the outset, our CMT moved through a sequence of operational states, from active crisis management on a daily basis through scenario planning and associated decision making to the current steady-state situation. The current emphasis (mid-July 2020) of our CMT is on the adjustment to the "next normal", the implications of hybrid delivery for the coming year and the monitoring of our readiness barometer. We are doing so, however, in the context of an unprecedented institutional budget deficit and alarming financial projections. Fortunately, significant investment had been made in the digital infrastructure of the university in advance of the crisis. That additional capacity, combined with the expertise of our National Digital Learning Institute, facilitated the rapid translation of almost 1 400 modules to our online platform in the lockdown. Next year, our hybrid delivery will move beyond emergency remote learning, and our intention is to offer quality blended learning in what will in effect be an acceleration of our strategic intentions to move towards greater online delivery.

DUBLIN CITY UNIVERSITY'S RESPONSE

DCU's immediate response to the Covid-19 pandemic mirrored emergency measures adopted by universities elsewhere. The priority was the safety of our people, students and staff. Working from a philosophy articulated by Dr Michael Ryan (Irish-born Executive Director of the World Health Organization's Health Emergencies Programme) at a WHO press conference on 13 March 2020 that "perfection is the enemy of the good when it comes to emergency management" and "in a crisis, good now is better than perfect too late", DCU adopted a practical approach, focused on the needs of the community (Ryan 2020). In both our internal and external communications, our emphasis has been on providing clarity and certainty (for staff, students and prospective students) as early as possible and on reflecting an institutional culture that is both agile and empathetic in its response to unprecedented, complex circumstances. In particular, the core messages, that have also been the decision drivers, have focused on providing a safe environment, and on optimising both the formal learning and the broader student experience. Evaluations have recorded broad student satisfaction with this compassionate response. Disadvantaged students, however, have been impacted disproportionately by Covid-19, not merely financially, but also by digital inequity, personal circumstances and increasing pressures from mental health issues. In response, DCU has launched an appeal to meet the increasing incidence of student hardship.

Human Resource colleagues have also observed disproportionate consequences of Covid-19 for the carers among our staff, and particularly women, who – in the words of Sheryl Sandberg, Facebook Chief Operations Officer – have been subjected to a "double-double-shift" in the pandemic (Sandberg 2020). During the crisis the HR Department developed Working from Home protocols and an elaborate Return to Work Policy. Health and well-being have been a priority and, conscious of the additional burden and stress which the pandemic has imposed, the university has created a four-week window to facilitate staff taking time off for physical and mental rest.

The responsibility of universities clearly extends beyond their walls, and for DCU, which defines itself as the engaged antithesis of the Ivory Tower, the crisis proved an opportunity to test the veracity of that statement. From the outset, in the first-phase response, the university provided vital logistical supports to the national response to Covid-19 and front-line workers. These included the creation of a contact-tracing call centre on campus, staffed by volunteers from DCU, hosting a Covid-19 Clinical Assessment Hub and the provision of personal protective equipment (PPE) to a number of partner hospitals and community care centres. In advance of the massive airlift of resources from China, this included the urgent provision of hand sanitiser, manufactured in our Nano Research Facility, and the 3D printing of face visors and other resources by colleagues in I-Form, our Research Centre for Advanced Manufacturing, funded by Science Foundation Ireland (SFI).

In the second-phase response, DCU brought the additional application of research expertise to address the new challenges associated with the pandemic. DCU researchers, for example, together with colleagues from the Royal College of Surgeons, applied their knowledge to improve the current mathematical modelling for the disease. As varied research activities emerged across campus, and principal investigators proactively lobbied national funding agencies, the university established a dedicated Covid-19 Research and Innovation Hub to leverage DCU's research expertise across multiple disciplines, in collaboration with national and international stakeholders, with a view to developing immediate solutions. A call for proposals received 74 applications. Of these, 15 have been funded by DCU's philanthropic arm, the DCU Educational Trust, addressing five key areas: technologies for rapid diagnostics for Covid-19; the challenges faced by front-line health-care workers in hospitals and nursing home areas; developing novel solutions to enhance the national testing strategy; mitigating the impact on organisations, workers and the economy; and tackling societal issues in a Covid-19 world, including education, business and the citizen.

Consistent with DCU's commitment to equality and inclusion, too, several research programmes prioritised the experience of citizens with additional needs. Health Research Board Covid-19 Rapid Response funding was secured for a project examining interventions to support young people with Autism Spectrum Disorder during the pandemic. Another project will investigate observations by parents of children with special needs that their children have regressed during the period of Covid-19 lockdown. A Corona Citizens' Science Study unites research teams at DCU, National University of Ireland Galway and the Insight SFI Centre for Data Analytics (NUI Galway) to examine the impact of the pandemic and the associated restrictive measures (lockdown, social distancing) on daily life in Ireland. In parallel, DCU launched the Irish Covid-19 Oral History Project, in collaboration with Indiana University-Purdue University Indianapolis, focused on orally archiving the Irish lived experience of the Covid-19 pandemic and detailing the Irish experience of the Covid-19 pandemic in communities both at home and abroad to inform historians, researchers and policy makers responding to future epidemics.

Education is the profession of hope and, uniquely among the Irish universities, DCU possesses a full faculty of education, the Institute of Education. Their expertise, in the realm of teacher education and research, was applied to support the displaced millions of learners across the globe as classrooms and early years settings migrated to virtual spaces for learning. This displacement has given rise to a new appreciation for education and schooling as a social connection; parents who were initially worried about their children missing learning quickly realised that the real loss was interaction and engagement. The Institute of Education responded with a series of Facebook Live events on supporting children and young people learning at home. The From a Distance series addressed themes such as children online, the challenges of the under sixes, supporting children with special needs and thinking about the future of education.

In all of these virtual events the theme of the social and emotional well-being of children and young people was to the fore, and this will certainly be the new focus for debates about the future direction of education in a post-Covid-19 world. Our work – in student well-being, on the experience of homeless children, on children who experience educational disadvantage, on student voice and agency, on the quality of early childhood education, on empowering children as writers, mathematicians and scientists – has set the tone for the debates to come. Worthy of note, too, was the agency of our student teachers. When post-primary schools closed, some of our students who were on school placement as part of their teacher education programme, found themselves at the online learning front line, working with their classes on whatever emergency platform the school had mobilised. They had received no preparation for this from their Institute lecturers and mentors; they had to jump right in. But they did, and their experience will inform programme redesign to future-proof our student teachers, whose own careers and influence as teachers have been honed by the human insights and empathy acquired in 2020.

CONCLUSION

Higher education is at its very best when it is most connected. Indeed, the most successful universities are those that are globally interconnected but locally rooted. If nothing else, Covid-19 has convinced us of our common humanity and the vulnerability of our shared planet. The crisis provided an opportunity for an affirmation of the essential civic mission of the university in the "next normal", and in June 2020 we captured that in *DCU Volunteer*, a new strategy developed to support student self-awareness "as civic anchors in society – nurturing a sustainable future of active engagement and contribution to the public good" (DCU 2020). In essence, *DCU Volunteer* is intended to act as a bridgehead linking the university community, students, staff, facilities and resources with our connected communities locally, nationally and internationally.

As a place-based university that developed Ireland's first civic engagement strategy, DCU is focused on its social responsibility. It is committed to a curricular reform to provide the very best learning environment to develop smart graduates, self-aware individuals, who are emotionally intelligent, loving and lovable. We will extend our collaboration with industry, within the government of Ireland's new Human Capital Initiative framework, to provide programmes which support lifelong learning and flexible delivery. We are committed, too, with our international partners, such as Arizona State University and the European Consortium of Innovative Universities, to deliver curiosity-driven research focused on the great societal challenges. Finally, we are determined to provide even greater engagement to drive our society, education and the arts, not as a "third mission", but intrinsic to our very purpose.

At the height of the Northern Ireland Troubles, in 1972, the Ulster poet Seamus Heaney, himself an educator, remarked that "if we winter this one out, we can summer anywhere" (Heaney 1972). The same might be said of Covid-19. As we waken from that nightmare we can do so with a greater confidence in the influence (and responsibility) of the university, and confidence in education more broadly, as a focus of creativity and citizenship, and as an instrument for equity and social cohesion. Our universities, their staff and students have made an invaluable contribution to conquer Covid-19. More than that, they have modelled a vision of a better, sustainable and just world, and of how, with universities and communities as co-creators, that world could be delivered.

REFERENCES

DCU (Dublin City University) (2017), *Talent, discovery, and transformation* [strategic plan 2017-22], available at www.dcu.ie/sites/default/files/iss/pdfs/web_version_combined.pd, accessed 23 July 2020.

DCU (Dublin City University) (2020), *Dublin volunteer strategy* (June 2020), available at https://www.dcu.ie/sites/default/files/community/pdfs/dcu_volunteer_strategy.pdf, accessed 13 October 2020.

Heaney S. (1972) [interviewed], "New book of poems launched", *Cork Examiner* (22 November 1972).

Ryan M. (2020), contribution at WHO Coronavirus press conference (13 March 2020), available at www.who.int/docs/default-source/coronaviruse/transcripts/who-transcript-emergencies-coronavirus-press-conference-full-13mar2020848c48d2065143bd8d07a1647c863d6b.pdf?sfvrsn=23dd0b04_2, accessed 23 July 2020.

Sandberg S. (2020), comment on a May 2020 survey published by LeanIn.org, her advocacy organisation, available at https://edition.cnn.com/2020/05/07/success/sheryl-sanderg-coronavirus-women-burnout/index.html, accessed 23 July 2020.

Varadkar L. (2020), [reported in] "Coronavirus: Full text of Leo Varadkar's speech: Taoiseach announces closure of schools, colleges and other public facilities", *Irish Times* (12 March 2020), available at www.irishtimes.com/news/health/coronavirus-full-text-of-leo-varadkar-s-speech-1.4201041, accessed 15 July 2020.

Chapter 11

Public work and reclaiming the democratic impulse of higher education in these pandemic times

Paul C. Pribbenow

THE INTERSECTION OF THREE PANDEMICS

Here we find ourselves in 2020 living at the intersection of three pandemics. The novel coronavirus Covid-19 pandemic has disrupted all aspects of how we live and work and has pointedly illustrated the tension between public health and economic well-being. Following in the wake of the Covid-19 pandemic, an economic pandemic threatens our social fabric with massive unemployment and business closures worldwide. And, most recently, the racial inequities exacerbated by the senseless murder of George Floyd by Minneapolis police officers have created a third pandemic that threatens to tear the United States apart. Surely this uncharted terrain presents unique challenges for all of us as citizens, trying to imagine how we will navigate to some as yet unknown future.

I experience the intersection of these three pandemics with anger and resolve as President of Augsburg University, one of the most diverse institutions in the United States and located in one of the most diverse neighbourhoods in the country. The impact of these pandemics on our students, faculty and staff – and on the immigrant neighbours we cherish – is stark. Their health, their economic well-being and their safety are all threatened. And I feel an urgent responsibility to act in response to those threats.

There is much we can – and will – do as a university to accompany our community as we deploy our many resources to work on health, economic and safety challenges. In fact, Augsburg University possesses, in its 150-year history, threads of democratic and public work commitments that will shape our efforts in the days and years ahead (Adamo 2019). This, then, is an important moment for our university and all of higher education to lean into the impact of these pandemics with a powerful response grounded in our democratic commitments.

THE DEMOCRATIC IMPULSE OF US HIGHER EDUCATION

There are a variety of pathways in the US system of higher education, each of which illustrates what I would call a "democratic impulse" in mission and purpose. It is an impulse that embraces a commitment to the integration of dignified work and citizenship for the well-being of our commonwealth. It is an impulse present in the founding charters and in many forms throughout the history of these diverse institutions (see Association of Governing Boards 2019), and yet there is also evidence of how that democratic impulse has been eroded over the years – eroded by both institutional neglect and external forces.

For example, private liberal arts institutions were originally founded as "democracy colleges", meant to educate citizens to lead and pursue their work with a sense of purpose and dignity. Private research universities were organised as knowledge creators, contributing to the scientific and professional communities. And yet, in both cases, these institutions today are often seen as elite and disconnected from the communities in which they are located.

Another example is the US land-grant institutions, which were chartered by the federal government in the late 19th and early 20th centuries to pursue applied learning and community outreach, and yet now compete for rankings often based on metrics unrelated to the needs of the communities they serve. Consider also our community and technical colleges, established after the Second World War to provide universal access for students to pursue vocational opportunities; these colleges were often buffeted by public disagreements about goals, funding and mixed outcomes for students. In both land-grant institutions and community colleges, the founding commitments to the dignity and centrality of work contributing to community capacity have been eroded, often replaced with an instrumental economic focus.

My point is twofold: the democratic work-centred impulse for higher education is present in the founding and history of institutions, but it has also been eroded and challenged to the point where that impulse may not be evident in the life of institutions today.

So, what to do? As a long-time university leader committed to the democratic impulse in the history of my institution, I believe that I must identify resources – especially intellectual resources – that can help renew that democratic impulse. The urgency of that renewal has been made more pressing by the intersecting pandemics of our time, each of which in its own way threatens the mission and work we pursue.

THREE LESSONS FROM THE SETTLEMENT HOUSE TRADITION

I believe that one compelling source of those intellectual resources is found in the settlement house tradition.

The settlement house tradition, born in the east end of London in the late 19th century by Oxford-educated young people, sought to model how taking up residence in the midst of immigrant neighbourhoods, engaging neighbours in exploring how best to respond to the realities of their lives and then working co-operatively alongside each other to make the neighbourhood safer, cleaner and more just, could help solve urban problems and ultimately shape public policy to be more respectful of the value and dignity of work (Toynbee Hall 2018).

In other words, settling in a neighbourhood, becoming a neighbour, was seen as the most effective way to ensure healthier and more vibrant urban communities. This was in juxtaposition to the idea of experts coming into a neighbourhood to offer and/or impose their solutions. The well-educated settlement residents certainly had expertise to offer, but it was offered in the context of neighbourhood-wide engagement and participation. The lessons learned from these neighbourhood efforts then became the impetus for social policies that would shape urban life for decades to come.

In the United States, the settlement house tradition took root initially in New York and then Chicago, where Jane Addams and her colleagues founded Hull House in 1889 on the near west side of the city and sought to transform a troubled immigrant neighbourhood. Their work at Hull House – including educational programmes, community centres, libraries, music schools, theatres, sanitation, work on child labour practices and honouring cultural heritages – illustrated the wide range of efforts pursued in response to the needs of neighbours, the richness of immigrant cultures and the value and importance of immigrant work traditions (Addams 1910).

Though the settlement houses themselves were gradually abandoned, the tenets of the settlement house tradition took root in other forms in the late 20th and early 21st century. As Ira Harkavy and John Puckett argued in 1994, the idea of applied sociology which the early settlement leaders wrote about and practised offers a moral and pragmatic framework for colleges and universities to "function as perennial, deeply rooted settlements, providing illuminated space for their communities as they conduct their mission of producing and transmitting knowledge to advance human welfare and to develop theories that have broad utility and application" (Harkavy and Puckett 1994: 312).

Especially for urban, place-based institutions like Augsburg University, the settlement house tradition (and specifically the work of Jane Addams and her colleagues at Hull House in Chicago) offers three key ideas that inform our response to the pandemic and help us renew the democratic impulse of our institutions.

Democracy as a social ethic

Democracy, for Jane Addams, was not simply a creed or a sentiment or a political system, but an ethic that challenges us to balance individual needs and interests with the common good. In her *Democracy and social ethics* (Addams 1902 2002), Addams describes the idea of democracy as a social ethic with a simple image: we are all travellers on a thronged road, she said, and our minimum responsibility to each other is to understand the burdens we bear (ibid.: 7) – in other words, to know each other's stories and circumstances. That is the basis for a democratic social ethic. The genius of democracy is that the self does not go away but enters into a relationship with others in mutual need and aspiration.

This is not a utopia, but a way of negotiating our lives together in a messy world. As we all recognise, things will not always go well, but with a democratic way of life they will go forward towards a horizon of shared purpose and dignified work that inspires and energises our community.

Similarly, in his recent essay entitled *With the people: an introduction to an idea*, David Mathews argues that "Democracy is us – The People. And we can restore our sense of sovereignty … by what we produce every day using the abilities and resources of our fellow citizens. And when the things that happen frustrate, disappoint and anger us – as they will – the question we have to ask ourselves is not what is wrong with democracy, but what are we going to do about it? That question can only be answered *with* one another" (Mathews 2020: 34).

As universities committed to this idea of democracy as a social ethic, this "with" way of living together, we embrace the work we do – teaching, scholarship and service – with a clear regard and a sense of humility about how we might do that work alongside our neighbours – neighbours who may not share our ideological, religious or political commitments – not apart from them.

This concept of democracy as a social ethic has informed our work as part of two anchor partnerships in our metropolitan area. Anchor institutions are universities, hospitals and other enduring organisations that play a vital role in their local communities and economies. They tend to remain in their geographical settings, even as conditions change around them (AITF 2020). In both the Cedar-Riverside Partnership and the Central Corridor Anchor Partnership, Augsburg University comes to the table with our neighbourhood partners, stating our self-interest as an institution while we explore the potential for shared value for our neighbourhood. Over the past decade, our anchor work has addressed neighbourhood safety, workforce, youth programmes, transportation, infrastructure and place-making. The results are examples of how higher education institutions can lean into pressing community challenges as authentic partners, with our neighbours (Walljasper 2020).

Our public work in the 21st century is informed by the Norwegian-American Haugean Lutherans who founded Augsburg University in 1869. Inspired by the spirit of community practised by the early Christians, Hans Nielsen Hauge[57] was a lay preacher and skilled entrepreneur who believed that the established Lutheran church in Norway did not create healthy and just communities. He sought to put the ideal of a common and shared economy into practice in Norway, preaching the gospel on Sundays and living out the gospel through the week by creating new businesses in which work was valued. As followers of his ideas, our founders believed deeply in the ways in which work and citizenship were inextricably linked by building sustainable communities (Adamo 2019).

An expansive understanding of knowing and knowledge

One of the most striking characteristics of the settlement house tradition was the embrace of various forms of knowing and knowledge. In this way, the settlement houses helped immigrant neighbours assimilate to new surroundings,

---

57. For more information about Hauge, see www.britannica.com/biography/Hans-Nielsen-Hauge, accessed 1 July 2020.

while at the same time helping them hold onto cultural practices and wisdom that might disappear in a new setting.

For example, at Hull House, Jane Addams recognised that certain ethnic and cultural craft practices were difficult to maintain without the materials and equipment to pursue them. In order to create opportunities to continue these craft practices, she created the Labour Museum (Addams 1910: 171-8), where neighbours practised these cultural arts and also passed them along to the next generation and to neighbours unfamiliar with the practices. This was a means of sustaining cultural knowledge and thereby enriching neighbourhood life.

For colleges and universities, the concepts of what constitutes knowledge and ways of knowing are often limited to particular traditions such as the scientific method with its evidence-based claims or Western concepts of what constitutes truth and beauty. The settlement house tradition reminds us that there is knowledge and wisdom from many sources, and our openness to diverse forms of knowledge and ways of knowing has the potential to enrich our lives.

An example of this openness to different forms of knowledge for Augsburg is linked to our now regular practice of "land acknowledgements" at public events. This is one example:

> Augsburg's spirit is propelled by a heartbeat that started long before us. That heartbeat was present even before our founding 150 years ago – it was present when the land where Augsburg today stands was stewarded by the Dakota people. The Dakota are the original inhabitants of this area, and they are still here today. We honour their wisdom about this place, their recognition that we are all part of the same creation. We share their sense of obligation to the larger community, including to future generations. (Augsburg University 2020)

We acknowledge that the land we occupy was originally settled by the Lakota and Ojibwe peoples, and we go further to lift up the ways in which Indigenous peoples teach us important lessons – lessons we have forgotten – about how to be good stewards of the land. Knowledge and wisdom from native peoples expand and enhance our stewardship, understanding and practices.

An openness to new social arrangements

Throughout the history of settlement houses, a crucial strategy was to listen to the needs of neighbours and neighbourhoods before organising ways of responding to those needs. In other words, there was an openness to what I would call diverse "social arrangements" and there were no predetermined ways to organise.

At Hull House in early 20th-century Chicago, this sometimes meant a patchwork of organisational models, as the needs of neighbours overrode any static, bureaucratic responses. A museum for labour and crafts here, a youth centre there; a kindergarten here, a library there; a neighbourhood sanitation team here, a safe labour practices group there. And perhaps most compelling about this openness to various social arrangements was the willingness of Addams and the neighbours to admit when a particular arrangement did not work and search for a better option (Addams 1910: 109).

For American colleges and universities, the idea of fluid social arrangements flies in the face of a fairly conservative, hierarchical bureaucracy, marked by many silos and layers, making it difficult to adjust to shifting needs. Yet, it is incumbent upon us to explore different organisational forms that create fluid boundaries within campuses and between campuses and the wider community, undoing the often privileged and static forms of organisational life that become obstacles for access and opportunity (Association of Governing Boards 2019).

At Augsburg, this openness to fluid social arrangements has taken various forms. For example, we have reviewed all institutional policies and practices through an equity lens, identifying where long-standing policies create obstacles to student progress and success. We also have partnered with various organisations, such as the Urban Debate League (MNUDL 2020), to bring them as permanent residents to our campus. Based on shared commitments to education, civic engagement and diversity, these partner organisations benefit from our material infrastructure, freeing them to use their resources more directly in areas of common interest, while the Augsburg community benefits from staff and programming that enrich our work in the community. Fluid organisational boundaries make it possible to obtain mutual benefit in pursuit of common values and commitments.

RENEWING THE DEMOCRATIC IMPULSE OF HIGHER EDUCATION IN THESE PANDEMIC TIMES

So, we return to these pandemic times, looking for evidence of this public work in our community – evidence that these ideas from the settlement house tradition can make a difference. And here I find Professor Katie Clark from Augsburg's Nursing faculty, leading our Health Commons in the midst of the Covid-19 outbreak, meeting the needs of those in our community experiencing homelessness. And there I see our students, responding to a pandemic of systemic racism, putting their black and brown and white bodies at risk protesting for racial equity and law enforcement reform. And there I find our faculty and staff, seeing the distressing impact of unemployment and economic unrest in our immediate neighbourhood, stepping outside of their daily routines to provide food and housing and security to our immigrant neighbours so at risk.

Surely there are a multitude of intellectual resources that might help inform how colleges and universities embrace their democratic work. My examples have made a significant impact on our work at Augsburg and continue to shape my leadership, especially in these pandemic times. My challenge to my colleagues in higher education is to (as I tell our incoming students each autumn) show up, pay attention and do the work, because our presence, our attention and our public work are more urgently important for our democracy than ever before.

REFERENCES

Adamo P. (2019), *Hold fast to what is good*, Minneapolis: Augsburg University.

Addams J. (1910), *Twenty years at Hull-House*, New York: Macmillan.

Addams J. (1902 2002), *Democracy and social ethics*, Urbana IL/Chicago: University of Illinois Press.

AITF (Anchor Institutions Task Force) (2020), *AITF Strategic Plan 2020-2023*, available at www.margainc.com/aitf/, accessed 1 July 2020.

Association of Governing Boards (2019), "Renewing the democratic purposes of higher education," *AGB Reports*, available at https://agb.org/reports-2/democratic-purposes/, accessed 22 June 2020.

Augsburg University/Luther Seminary (2020), Editorial Style Guide, 2020, pp. 20-21, https://inside.augsburg.edu/marketing/style_guidelines/, accessed 5 January 2021.

Harkavy I. and Puckett J. (1994), "Lessons from Hull House for the contemporary urban university," *Social Service Review*, 68/3: 299-321.

Mathews D. (2020), *With the people: an introduction to an idea*, Dayton, OH: Kettering Foundation Press.

MNUDL (Minnesota Urban Debate League) (2020), available at www.augsburg.edu/urbandebateleague/, accessed 22 June 2020.

Toynbee Hall (2018), "History of Toynbee Hall", available at www.toynbeehall.org.uk/our-history, accessed 22 June 2020.

Walljasper J. (2020), "Augsburg deeply involved in innovative effort to keep Twin Cities vital", available at www.augsburg.edu/president/blog/, accessed 22 June 2020.

Chapter 12

Higher education should embrace this liminal moment because there will be no "new normal"

James T. Harris and Nicholas R. Santilli

Colleges and universities face a liminal moment. Two significant forces, one new and one old, have emerged to challenge the status quo, namely, Covid-19 and the struggle for social justice. In the early days of the pandemic a new term to describe a desired future started to emerge, a term that has now become part of the lexicon in American culture: "the new normal". The use of the word "new" itself acknowledges that it is unlikely we will return to the same state of affairs we had at the beginning of the 2019/20 academic year. When we consider the science behind the virus, and the possibility of at least another two years before we will fully relax restrictions, as well as the growing civil unrest in light of renewed violence against Black Americans, it is highly unlikely that we will return to "normal" any time soon (CNBC 2020).

On 11 June 2020, Scott Carlson of *The Chronicle of Higher Education* and Michael J. Sorrell, President of Paul Quinn College, hosted a virtual event focused on "the maladies of race and class in the United States". *The Chronicle* published an article from the event on 15 June. We were struck by an opening comment by Sorrell:

> We have to start by just acknowledging a very basic point, which is that we are where we are as a country because this is what higher education has produced. All of our leaders are products of our institutions. They sat in our classrooms, they walked our campuses, they absorbed what we taught them. (Carlson and Sorrell 2020: 2)

If this is an accurate portrayal of the role of higher education over the past years, then a "new normal" will simply not do. The normal that existed for decades prior to the pandemic did not serve everyone equitably. As the pandemic progressed, Covid-19 data demonstrated a disproportionate number of infections and deaths among the poor and Black, Indigenous, Persons of Colour (BIPOC), shining a bright light on unequal access to quality health care. According to a report from the Centers for Disease Control and Prevention (2020), Non-Hispanic American Indian, Alaska Native and Non-Hispanic Black Americans were five times more likely to be hospitalised for the virus than their fellow White Americans.

These clear disparities within the health-care system, coupled with the continuing dehumanisation and unjust killings of Black Americans at the hands of police, have shed a light on the need for the United States of America to actually atone for institutionalised racism, to address the truth of its long-term impact on our democracy and meaningfully reconcile those damages. It is abundantly clear the United States must find a new path forward for a more democratic and just society, and that higher education must lead the way.

A SHIFTED LANDSCAPE

Today, higher education is faced with a radically different societal environment that requires a radically different response. Unless we view this as a liminal moment in history and an opportunity to change, substantially, we will miss an opportunity to evolve and to be better prepared to meet the needs of society. Before the pandemic, the environment for higher education was volatile, uncertain, complex and ambiguous. With decreasing government investment in higher education, soaring discount rates, and the public perception of higher education at an all-time low, any attempt by higher education leaders to return to old ways of thinking would both be irresponsible and ensure that their institution will no longer be relevant to the needs of society.

We all understand that there are few organisations in society as multifaceted as colleges and universities. As complex organisations we must evolve with society. We propose that the pandemic has presented universities with an existential choice: adapt or become irrelevant to the promotion of democratic ideals in the 21st century. Enlightened leaders will recognise that what we are facing is a liminal moment and that a modest reorganisation of existing practices is not enough. The present environment demands a more radical reformation if our institutions and our democracy are to survive. We must remember that higher education not only educates individuals for citizenship in a democracy but is also the engine for innovation and creativity that helps the US, and the globe, thrive. What, then, should higher education do?

A new way of proceeding is emerging in higher education. This new form is not a "new normal" but instead a movement towards an educational experience not bounded by limits such as seat time, a rigid calendar, bricks and mortar and stereotypic notions of learning. What is emerging is an educational experience that works to advance social equity, protects the rights of the poor and under-served and acts as a catalyst for meaningful societal change through democratic ideals.

While universities rose to the challenge of moving from classroom instruction to online teaching and learning when the pandemic hit, it is clear that engagement with community partners became difficult during the health crisis. As universities focused on delivering academic content, supporting local community partners became less of a priority. At the University of San Diego, where we had developed deep community partnerships over many years, we were able to pivot and find ways to serve the most urgent needs of the local community when the pandemic struck. For example, as it became clear that the low-income neighbourhoods near our campus did not have access to county Covid-19 testing sites due to a lack of adequate transportation, the university worked closely with San Diego County health officials to bring a Covid-19 testing site to our campus. With the ability to serve over 150 local neighbours a day with direct access to Covid-19 tests, this site has been instrumental in helping health officials to quickly identify active cases and has kept the local community from developing into a Covid-19 hotspot.

A WAY FORWARD: RELEVANCE, COST, INNOVATION

How should institutions of higher learning respond? By doing what the sector does best: embrace the opportunity that has emerged and find a new level of adaptation. Not just a "new normal" but a novel adaptation that sets up the sector for not just surviving but flourishing. The type of flourishing that is necessary to promote the enduring goals of a democratic society dedicated to social mobility, freedom and civil society.

The pandemic has revealed dark truths about American society. We are a country with a large percentage of citizens who are both scientifically illiterate and incapable of discerning fact from fiction, or unwilling to do so. We have leaders and a majority of Americans who cannot comprehend the science behind the spread of disease or who lack a basic knowledge of history to navigate current events. When large segments of our society lack access to the resources that reveal the noble truths that have comforted civilised society in times of uncertainty for over a millennium, we know this is a society that cannot endure. Higher education has an opportunity at this moment to evolve – as it has in the aftermath of previous "black swan" events: those rare, unexpected and unpredictable events that change the direction of history – and to help recapture its leadership role in society.

We propose that the advancement of democratic ideals and practices through higher education should occur in three ways: a greater focus on the relevance of the liberal arts and sciences in the US primary, secondary and post-secondary educational experience, a transformation of the financial model for higher education that reins in the cost of education and provides greater access, and the creation of innovative solutions to advance teaching, learning and scholarship that are tied to an institution's role as a stable fixture or anchor institution in its own community. To do this it is not enough for an institution to prepare students for their roles as responsible citizens but the university itself must practise these ideals by building democratic and reciprocal partnerships with organisations outside the academy to enhance the long-term viability of the communities where they reside.

The evolution of our relevance

We have a responsibility as a sector to evolve in the way we educate future leaders. Higher education must reclaim its core purpose: namely, to provide a public good that advances the well-being of all members of society. To accomplish this, we must accept that US institutions of higher education have played a role in the devaluation and dismantling of the liberal arts and sciences, which has left the United States behind the knowledge curve globally. This is not a recommendation to return to some past era, but rather a clarion call that we must clearly demonstrate the relevance of the liberal arts and sciences for the 21st century for primary, secondary and post-secondary education in the US. For example, since higher education in the US produces the teachers for primary and secondary education, we must accept that it has to more firmly direct the way it prepares teachers and lead the charge for an educational renaissance in the United States.

To accomplish a renaissance in US education, a new level of adaptation is required, to ensure the delivery of higher education that reclaims this core purpose. We acknowledge that a number of institutions of higher education have formed strong partnerships with local school systems. However, these partnerships must become broader and deeper, and they must include a wider commitment to the expertise of a diverse set of scholars, especially in the areas of human learning and development, the STEM (science, technology, engineering and mathematics) fields, the humanities and civics. This commitment must be a standard way of proceeding, a compact between higher education and primary and secondary education; it must be a compact grounded in the pursuit of diversity, equity and inclusion for students, faculty, staff and the curriculum delivered in our colleges and universities. At its core, this is a call for a renewal of higher education's commitment to the liberal arts and sciences.

The Association of American Colleges and Universities has offered a vision for how liberal education might lead the way. In a recent publication (AAC&U 2020: 22-7) titled *What liberal education looks like*, AAC&U outlines five "frontline challenges" facing universities in delivering on the promise of liberal education:

- First, it will require advocacy, and a determined effort to rally the higher education community around the vision and carry it with confidence, integrity and persuasive force into the public square.
- Second, it will require renewed and reinvigorated commitment to the civic and democratic purposes of higher education.
- Third, it will be necessary to make equity a pervading focus of educational reform and innovation, moving beyond the goals of access and compositional diversity to design and deliver educational experiences that support the success of all students.
- Fourth, it will be necessary to take proactive steps to ensure that college and university campuses are places of welcome where all students are, and feel themselves to be, safe and places of belonging where no students are, or feel themselves to be, marginalised.
- Fifth, if the emerging vision of liberal education described here is to be fully realised, it will be necessary to address issues of affordability.

There must be no compromising by college and university leaders in the pursuit of these five challenges. If the leadership of our great American institutions of higher education back away from these actions they risk losing the moral authority to lead the social changes that will serve students now and society into the future. Ultimately, US education must produce graduates who are civically engaged, scientifically literate critical thinkers who know how to act with compassion, lead with integrity and live for justice.

The evolution of our cost structure

Prior to the pandemic, the public and elected officials were laser-focused on the growing amount of debt that recent college graduates have accumulated and what needs to be done to address it. While myriad plans have been proposed to lower debt among future college graduates, there is no viable solution likely from the US Government in the aftermath of the pandemic. At the local level in San Diego, this belief that higher education is not accessible to students from low-income communities led to very few students from those neighbourhoods applying to the university for admission.

One solution, in the spirit of the fifth challenge above, is for US higher education to completely reset its financial model so students understand what it actually costs to attend and how long it will take to graduate. For the case of public higher education in the US, tuition and fees at public institutions are often differentiated by in-state and out-of-state pricing: namely, in-state residents pay a lower rate than individuals residing outside the state. This preferential pricing takes into account the fact that in-state residents help subsidise public education within the state. Although this pricing model exists, students from low-income families continue to struggle to afford the tuition and fees to cover in-state higher education (Education Trust 2020). We need to evolve a new model of access for low-income students that crosses sectors within higher education. Higher education needs to reconsider its fundamental mission and determine whether it is truly meeting its objectives of advancing knowledge and educating citizens, particularly those from low-income families. What does it say about the values of a state institution when a low-income student who is a resident of the state cannot be admitted or even afford the local state institution because its admissions standards and costs are too high, all in the name of chasing higher rankings?

Private, selective institutions, like the University of San Diego, have their own set of challenges. First, these institutions need to completely reset their pricing. With average discount rates at private institutions across the country well over 50%, and much of that money going to students from families who can afford to attend in the form of "merit" scholarships, private colleges and universities must reconsider their entire financial model and commitment to students from lower-income families, especially in neighbourhoods near their campuses. Private institutions need to take a hard look at the academic and administrative programmes they offer and establish priorities in alignment with their mission and vision for the future. Too many institutions have implemented programmes that add little value to the student experience and have led them to abandon their commitment to their local communities.

Mission creep has pushed institutions to stray from their core purpose of educating students for their roles as responsible citizens because too often the institution itself is no longer acting as a good citizen in its local community. Institutions should instead focus on delivering mission-critical programmes and services with quality and intention. As outlined by AAC&U, institutions need to implement rigorous academic and administrative programme review processes to cut costs and align strategy with resources to ensure the prosperity of the institution and the communities it serves.

At the University of San Diego, we created an integrated strategic planning process that included not only key university constituents but also local community partners as we determined our vision for the future. At one point we asked key community leaders, faculty and university board members to meet to discuss how the university could better fulfil its mission as an anchor institution. The conversation was difficult at times, as community leaders expressed their deep concerns that the university was not doing enough to support community partners. This led directly to specific university strategic goals to increase diversity at the university from local under-served populations.

One concrete step towards achieving that goal was to create the Torero Promise, a scholarship designed to meet the full financial need of students from low-income families locally. The university also developed a new scholarship programme through philanthropic support for local high school students covered by the Deferred Action for Childhood Arrivals (DACA) policy[58] who are ineligible for federal financial aid.

Three years later, in 2020, the number of students from under-represented communities in San Diego had grown 20% and the retention rates for first-year African American students at the university grew from 84% to 91%. The number of DACA students enrolled had tripled. When the pandemic hit, the university knew that direct outreach to students from local neighbourhoods would be difficult. So, the university worked directly with community partners to find different ways to identify qualified students for these scholarship programmes since the students enrolled in these high schools would no longer have access to school counsellors. In autumn 2020, the university anticipates an increase in both the number of DACA students enrolling and the number of students of colour from local neighbourhoods. Thankfully the university had developed strong democratic partnerships with community leaders prior to the pandemic or the university would have likely lost access to those student populations.

Innovation: is accreditation reform the key to the evolution of anchor institutions?

The University of San Diego offers some guidance as to how an institution of higher learning may work collaboratively with its local community to be a force for good. An important question to ask relative to broadening the influence of an anchor institution among residents in its vicinity may be, "What is holding them back?" We suggest that few entities are holding institutions accountable for providing evidence of how they create more equitable educational outcomes for the under-served. One avenue left to encourage institutions to not just promote equity but actually provide evidence of equity outcomes may be through the vehicle of institutional accreditation. For this to work, however, the accreditation process needs some reformation to align equity outcomes with institutional review (Coleman 2020).

---

58. DACA students were brought to the US as children but have no right of residence. See these resources on the University of San Diego website: www.sandiego.edu/president/writings-addresses/immigration-and-DACA-follow-up.php and www.sandiego.edu/immigration-dialogue/undocumented/, accessed 22 July 2020.

It is well reported that the relationship between institutions of higher education, accrediting bodies and the U.S. Department of Education is tense (Anguiano and Flores 2020; Kelchen 2017; U.S. Department of Education 2018). A rather calculated dance has been underway between higher education institutions, accreditors and the Department of Education regarding the accreditation process. There have been calls for reform, including the elimination of the present system, revising this system to allow more innovation on campuses and changing the system to incentivise institutions to quickly adjust to market forces. The recent decision to allow institutions to seek accreditation by any of the regional accrediting bodies only makes the process more complex and potentially threatens to accelerate a race to the bottom regarding institutional quality.

Why is the evolution of accreditation important? We certainly agree that some form of oversight is necessary to ensure quality and equity and to protect constituents. But is the present system really directed towards quality improvement and consumer protections, or is it simply promoting old ideas about quality and ultimately raising costs? The process of maintaining accreditation has added layers of administrative processes that occupy the attention of campus leaders and demand the commitment of institutional resources that should be directed towards the work of scholarship, teaching and learning. Reformation of the criteria for accreditation to amplify the work of equity, serving as an anchor to the local community, and civic engagement tied to the curriculum, may provide the needed incentive for institutions to prioritise accomplishing the outcomes that promote life and work in a democratic society.

We are reminded of a simple refrain that emerged during the 2008 recession: "Don't waste a good crisis". Our response should not simply rearrange the deck chairs on the ship known as higher education. We must view this as a liminal moment, not as a return to some glory days or a "new normal". Rather, we must view this as a time of evolutionary change and use this as an opportunity to fulfil the full democratic promise of higher education in the 21st century.

REFERENCES

AAC&U (Association of American Colleges and Universities) (2020), *What liberal education looks like: what it is, who it's for, and where it happens*, available at www.aacu.org/advocacy-liberal-education-0, accessed 7 July 2020.

Anguiano V. and Flores A. (2020), *The Accreditation Reform Act of 2020: a path toward a more equitable and high-quality higher education system*, Center for American Progress, available at www.americanprogress.org/issues/education-postsecondary/news/2020/02/11/480338/accreditation-reform-act-2020/, accessed 20 July 2020.

Carlson S. and Sorrell M. J. (2020), "Higher ed's reckoning with race: a conversation about bigotry, diversity, and opportunity", *Chronicle of Higher Education* (15 June 2020), available at www.chronicle.com/article/Higher-Ed-s-Reckoning-With/248988, accessed 15 June 2020.

Centers for Disease Control and Prevention (2020), *COVIDView: a weekly surveillance summary of U.S. COVID-19 activity*, available at www.cdc.gov/coronavirus/2019-ncov/covid-data/covidview/past-reports/07032020.html, accessed 13 July 2020.

CNBC (2020), *Coronavirus outbreak likely to go on for two years, scientists predict*, available at www.cnbc.com/2020/05/01/coronavirus-pandemic-likely-to-last-for-two-years-scientists-predict.html, accessed 21 July 2020.

Coleman A. (2020), *Data, accreditation and equity*, presentation at the CHEA Annual Conference, 28 January 2020, available at www.chea.org/data-accreditation-and-equity, accessed 11 July 2020.

The Education Trust (2020), *"Segregation forever?" The continued underrepresentation of Black and Latino undergraduates at the nation's 101 most selective public colleges and universities*, available at https://edtrust.org/resource/segregation-forever/, accessed 22 July 2020.

Kelchen R. (2017), *Higher education accreditation and the federal government*, Urban Institute, available at www.urban.org/sites/default/files/publication/93306/higher-education-accreditation-and-the-federal-government.pdf, accessed 20 July 2020.

U.S. Department of Education (2018), *Rethinking higher education: accreditation reform*, available at www.insidehighered.com/sites/default/server_files/media/White%20Paper%20on%20Accreditation%20Reform%2012.19.18.pdf, accessed 20 July 2020.

Chapter 13

Covid-19 and "the crises in higher education"

Liviu Matei

A REFERENCE FRAMEWORK FOR UNDERSTANDING THE COVID-19 CRISIS IN HIGHER EDUCATION

This chapter attempts to shed light on the crisis in higher education induced by the Covid-19 pandemic. It searches for insight regarding possible ways to address the crisis by placing this far-reaching, yet individual, catastrophe in the context of the history of crisis, or crises, in higher education in the massification era and the discourse about these crises.

At the time of writing (mid-July 2020), the Covid-19 pandemic has been unfolding for only a few months. The immediate effects are severe, in and beyond public health. It is not yet clear how long this crisis will last. It is too early to gauge its full impact on the fabric and functioning of societies, locally and globally. In higher education too, the effect is shattering. Universities, more than public authorities or other stakeholders in higher education, are struggling to cope with the crisis. They feel as it they have been ambushed, with no clear end in sight. Scenario planning for the short term has become a semi-permanent condition, another name for the need to deal with, and plan under, an oppressing uncertainty and unprecedented constraints and risks. For now, higher education institutions are forced to focus on surviving today and tomorrow – to make sure they teach effectively and have students (and staff) this last term of the academic year just ending, next term or the entire next academic year. They are worried and feel isolated.

This has been declared, once again, a time of crisis in higher education and it is impossible to deny the reality of the crisis.

We can ask, however, what kind of crisis is it. Is it transient or long-lasting? Is it existential? The end of the university has been prophesied already a few times before. Is this a "real crisis"? This is a term used frequently in the literature (Sovern 1989; Ogden 2002; Geiger 2006; Qadeer 2006; Meyerhoff et al 2011; Brown 2014; Against the Grain 2019/20) and it exposes the inflationary nature of the discourse on the crisis in higher education and its particular dimensions and areas. Is this a comprehensive crisis in higher education or does it touch only one or a few discrete dimensions, such as enrolment, funding and mode of delivery? Is this a time of danger for the entire higher education paradigm as we have come to know it in the age of internationalisation and globalisation? Or is it rather an opportunity for a necessary and decisive transformation, for example with regard to the use of educational technology to "harness fully" its promise for online educational activities (EY 2020), and for which a clearly articulated vision and strategy are needed (Stokes and Johnson 2020)?

Some of these questions are being asked already. Most others are not. Can such an exercise help: put the present crisis in the context of the history of crises in higher education and the discourse about them? Most probably, it can indeed contribute, be it only to a limited extent, to understanding the crisis, its nature, manifestations, current and possible future effects. At the same time, it might help avoid certain mistakes, both at the analytical and actional level, in tackling the crisis.

The discourse on the crisis in higher education is convoluted, confusing, potentially misleading. The "crisis in higher education" is often prophesied, anticipated, and then it does not happen. On the other side, as certain studies claim, there is so much talk about a crisis, even when there is none, really, that in the end the rhetoric itself triggers one, as in Aesop's fable of the shepherd boy and the wolf (Openo 2020). The crisis in, or of, higher education is frequently over-analysed, in part owing to the exceedingly self-reflective, even narcissistic, nature of this discourse. Some scholars (Brown 2014) have argued that what is called a crisis is in fact one or a set of stress factors (where "stress" is meant to imply less than "crisis"), or even only the reflection of the anxiety generated inside higher education communities by these stress factors (Tight 1994).

A careful review of the literature reveals, therefore, that the notion of "crisis in higher education" has only a limited conceptual and analytical purchase. Even the definition of "crisis" is fluctuating and ambiguous. And yet, crisis scholarship can provide both useful information and analytical references for understanding specific developments and states of affairs in higher education because, as in the current situation, real crises do occasionally occur and their study can be informative. On the other hand, mere scrutiny of the discourse on the crisis can be valuable too. Discerning its shortcomings can be helpful in the present situation of pandemic, one that has given a fresh impetus to new prophecies and soul-searching in higher education, along with the pragmatic efforts to address the crisis.

The most serious shortcoming of the discourse on the crisis in higher education, it can be stated, is that it often tends to blow out of proportion certain challenges, stress factors or trends, and overlook or devalue other factors and trends. This may be analysed as a version of the existential fallacy (Scalambrino 2018): if certain characteristics of an assumed object or reality exist, it does not necessarily follow that that particular object is real or that reality exists as such, and that they are correctly described.

THE DISCOURSE ON THE CRISIS IN HIGHER EDUCATION: SYNOPSIS AND A BRIEF TYPOLOGY OF CRISES

The literature on the crisis in higher education, is vast: thousands of articles and books have been written on this subject. There is so much written on this subject and so persistently that one might think that higher education had been in a permanent crisis at least since the beginning of massification after the Second World War, as has been noted already (Tight 1994).

Why higher education is so prone to an apparent state of permanent crisis (if that is really the case) is an interesting question, as is why there is so much talk about a crisis. Several explanations have been proposed. One of them stipulated that the university is an institution of modernity, ill equipped for the post-modern age and for this reason permanently in a state of crisis, even in danger of disappearing altogether (see, for example, Scott 1988). Others (Carr 2012) see universities as a type of institution that is too complex, in terms of the functions they are expected to fulfil and their internal organisation, to be capable of smooth operation and that is therefore prone to a continuous state of crisis. In a version of this explanation, Tight (1994) hypothesised that multiple changing pressures and demands on the members of the higher education communities, combined with reduced resources and an intrinsically slow reaction time in higher education, result in anxiety, in the perception (but not reality) of a permanent crisis in higher education institutions.

This discourse is not about a crisis, in the singular, but about many different crises, in the plural, whether simultaneous or consecutive. A historical analysis of this discourse shows that at least some key topics, forms of manifestations and causes of the crises are shifting in time. In the 1960s, the crisis was understood in Europe and the US to be mostly about student movements and protests. The World Bank's policies in Africa, beginning in the immediate post-colonial period and lasting for a few decades, generated a crisis in higher education in several countries of this continent, which even led to, allegedly, a "starvation cure" of the university (Samoff and Carrol 2003). Changes in political regimes have led to further assertions about a crisis in higher education, for example with the rise and fall of the communist regimes of Central and Eastern Europe. Other changes of political winds, like the stalled European integration of the current decade, are perceived as another situation of crisis in higher education, not only in certain countries, such as post-Brexit United Kingdom, but on the entire European continent. Unfolding demographic downturns are testing universities hard in many countries, to the point of raising the spectre of another crisis. The Syrian civil war that started in 2011 has generated a refugee crisis in higher education (Kamyab 2011). In fact, this is part of a much broader and, if we look closely, ongoing refugee crisis in higher education in Europe (Streitwieser et al. 2016), if not globally. The terrorist attacks of 11 September 2001 generated a crisis in higher education in the US and beyond, centred originally around issues of security. Technological advances from the late 20th century are also sometimes assumed to have led to a crisis, which involves "existential" questions, such as how much teaching should move online or could MOOCs (massive open online courses) take over everything? We know the answer to the latter question by now, and it is negative.

Crises appear to come and go; they last for a short while or a little longer. There are fewer crises that seem more "enduring". The most salient of these is the crisis of funding: since the beginning of massification, the tension between the expansion of enrolment and the lack of a corresponding increase in funding, or simply insufficient funding to support the expansion, has been consistently portrayed as a kind of built-in characteristic of the contemporary university and a form of crisis.

The nature, scope and gravity of the various crises (real or alleged) are assessed differently by different scholars. Certain strands of the crisis discourse gain significant strength in the public imaginary and, at times, play a significant role in the everyday lives of many people and in the broader public policy or political debates. Such are, for example, the student debt crisis in the United States (Lazerson 2010) or the crisis having to do with the alleged "death of expertise" and dwindling of meritocracy in the context of populism (Nichols 2017; Krastev 2017). Other crises in higher education are subjects of concern only in smaller public policy contexts or higher education circles. Such is, for example, the crisis pertaining to liberal arts education.

The discourse on the crises in higher education is vast and multifarious. It is also somewhat disconcerting. But it is not completely uninteresting or unhelpful. We can try a brief systematisation in the form of a succinct taxonomy of crises. This, in turn, may help to analyse and understand the current crisis and, at least partially, to orient the response and avoid certain mistakes along the way.

ORIGIN/SOURCES OF THE CRISES

A simple criterion can distinguish between internal and external sources of a crisis. The crises in higher education triggered by the 9/11 terror attacks or by the vast demographic changes in Central and Eastern Europe currently can be seen as having external causes. The same can be said about the crisis induced by the great economic recession of 2007-09. The crisis in the university understood as an institutional crisis, on the other hand, might be considered as having internal, or primarily internal, causes. In the second half of the 20th century, the university as it used to be known in the 19th and early 20th centuries expanded vastly: in terms of demography (enrolment exploded through massification) and geography (higher education extended significantly beyond the global North and also beyond the larger urban centres and traditional university cities in many countries); disciplinarily (new disciplines have emerged); and organisationally and functionally (new forms of higher education institutions emerged and their missions diversified). It has been stated that, or asked whether, the university model itself, as an institution of the modernity, has become imprecise and ineffective, "epistemologically confused" (Scott 1988), leading to, or just expressing, a crisis.

It can be difficult to distinguish precisely between external and internal sources. If we are trying to explain the crisis of funding in higher education, we can ask whether the source of this crisis is external (ideologies, policies, economic developments) or internal (obsolete organisation of the university). The same can be said about the impact of technology. Is that an external stress factor? Or are the sources of any crisis in this area (expressed, for example, in the hesitations and controversies about the mode of delivery) to be found at the intersection of both external and internal developments and constraints?

What may also be useful in this context is an analysis using the concept of locus of control, borrowed from social psychology and education sciences (Lefcourt 2014). That would help investigate how actors in higher education represent the factors that control success or failure in a situation of crisis, and what they consider as being internal factors (that they can control themselves) or external (that they cannot control).

GEOGRAPHICAL SCOPE OF THE CRISES

Some crises are limited to a specific country or region. Others may be international, even global. There is plenty of literature about the crises in higher education in particular countries on all continents, from Brazil (Schwartzman 1988) to Taiwan and China (Hwang 2016), and from Finland and West Germany (Gardin 2015) to Japan (Pool 2003). Regional crises are more rarely analysed but they are not absent from the literature, whether they refer to entire continents or just sub-regions. For example, Banya and Elu (1997) have written about the crisis of higher education in sub-Saharan Africa at the end of the 20th century. In another example, a case has been made recently (just before the pandemic) about the crisis of academic freedom in the entire European Higher Education Area (EHEA)[59] region, arguing that this crisis has distinct European characteristics and requires a European solution, despite academic freedom being at the same time a global challenge and a matter in which national legislation and policies play crucial roles as well (Matei 2020).

Are there global crises in higher education? The crisis induced by the pandemic seems to be global; it affects already almost all countries and higher education institutions directly and will almost certainly affect the rest at least indirectly. While some challenges of this global crisis are common, however, others are not; they are different in different countries and for different categories of institutions.

AREAS OF OPERATION AND ORGANISATION OF HIGHER EDUCATION IMPACTED

The literature about the crises in higher education may appear as too unfocused in part because it touches unsystematically on diverse aspects that are impacted by a crisis. These aspects, or factors, can be systematised. They refer to the organisation or areas of operation of the university: funding, enrolment, access, completion, curriculum and pedagogy, disciplinary areas, completion and graduation rates, employability and careers, mode of delivery, governance models and practices, and relationships with society and the immediate environment. Sometimes, the main foci of a crisis are substituted for explanations of that crisis. Brown (2014), for example, argues that the crisis of higher education consists in and is explained by the fact that higher education institutions, their leaders and the professoriate are concerned exclusively with pursuing status and positions for themselves, their subjects and their institutions, at the expense of their core activities of educating students and conducting research.

WHO RESPONDS TO THE CRISIS?

It is also interesting to systematise the responses in the literature as to who does or should answer when a crisis strikes. These responses appear to align with the main traditions of governance and leadership in higher education. In the US,

---

59. See www.ehea.info/, accessed 20 July 2020.

higher education institutions themselves and their leaders are expected to play a larger role. In Europe, the state and national public policy makers are allocated more responsibility than in the US. Given the *sui generis* nature of the EHEA as a regional (continental-wide) space for dialogue and action in higher education, and its corresponding governance arrangements, transnational policy makers and international organisations can and should also play a key role in addressing a crisis, including the current one.

It also matters who is asking the question about who should be working to address the crisis – scholars, policy makers or university administrators, for example. In the case of the current crisis, international consulting firms have provided influential analyses of the crisis, offering particular projections about who should be in charge of answering it (EY 2020).

THE COVID-19 CRISIS IN HIGHER EDUCATION

A question frequently asked in the literature about crises in higher education is whether they are real or just rhetorical. The Covid-19 crisis appears to be real by any measure. The evidence collected in this volume attests to the fact that it is certainly a crisis, but a more pertinent question is whether this will be a temporary disruption, or a more sustained challenge to some of the taken-for-granted ways in which higher education institutions have traditionally operated. In other words, we can ask what kind of crisis is it, in view of the short taxonomy outlined above, and how is it being addressed?

In terms of geographical scope, the pandemic affects higher education virtually everywhere in the world. It affects institutions, higher education systems and the interactions between and among stakeholders. This is evident, for example, if we look at how health restrictions, social distancing and lockdowns, travel and visa restrictions have affected teaching and learning, assessment, the international flows of students, educational co-operation and joint research endeavours and exchanges. This is a major shock locally and globally, still unfolding, and it is not clear when and how universities will recover from it.

Are the causes of this crisis internal or external? How are people in higher education and the policy makers representing the factors that control current evolutions and the locus of control for the efforts to address the crisis and their chances of success? Given that the crisis emerged as a result of a major epidemiological situation, it can be easily stated that the cause is external. Accordingly, the way out should be through public health measures, not at all or only partially controllable by universities themselves. In reality, of course, the picture is more complicated. It is uncertain to what extent and by when the public health situation could be contained or resolved by public authorities, and universities themselves need to act anyway. They all need to address not only the source of the crisis but also its manifestations and consequences in higher education.

The picture is more complicated also because this externally induced crisis interacts with pre-existing "conditions" and challenges (other crises?) in the university.

The main factors or areas affected currently, and some of the main questions and challenges related to them, appear to be as follows:

- ▶ Pedagogy and mode of delivery. There is much anxiety, pondering and controversy around the issue of online teaching, in spite of the fact that the crisis has shown that online methods are not only useful but in fact inevitable now. These questions touch on the immediate but also on the long term, looking beyond the crisis. How much online teaching is possible, effective and educationally healthy? For universities that are new to teaching online a large portion of the curriculum (which is most of them), is it possible to train the instructors over the summer, and design and put in place the infrastructure for "proper" online teaching by autumn 2020?
- ▶ Enrolment and access. At the time of writing, universities are concerned whether students will enrol at all in autumn 2020, whether those who need visas can get them, whether their parents will allow them to travel away from home, whether students will agree to online teaching or rather prefer to defer until the pandemic clears up. If teaching is to take place mainly online, will there be new issues of access as well?
- ▶ Funding. Will universities relying on tuition fees for a large part of their income even survive? Will public budgets be cut, thus affecting universities that are publicly funded, as in the economic recession of 2007-09? Will universities relying to a significant extent on income from international students be disproportionately affected?

In terms of who is expected to answer this crisis in higher education, universities are not only on the front line, but they seem to be largely isolated from each other and insufficiently supported by the public authorities and other stakeholders. Even some private foundations have cut funding already committed for higher education projects in order to redirect resources to addressing the public health emergency directly. Potentially influential international organisations and institutions, such as the EU Commission, have done very little to stimulate and support a co-ordinated answer to the crisis in higher education. Even new and daring constructions, based on the idea of taking solidarity and co-operation in higher education to a new level, such as the European Universities Initiative,[60] have proposed very little so far by way of helping universities to act together rather than in isolation.

As in any other situation of crisis, there is a natural tendency to concentrate on the immediate and the most visibly dangerous and ignore the rest. While this is understandable, it can also be costly. When some universities in Europe are fighting for their survival, should they care about the continental crisis of academic freedom? Is that a luxury now? At a time when Myanmar's economy is at a standstill and the country is in lockdown, should the public authorities proceed with an autonomy pilot project designed before the crisis or just focus on keeping universities in Myanmar afloat, as they are, still almost fully deprived of autonomy?[61] Is the discussion about

---

60. Sometimes called the European University Alliances or the European University Networks initiative; see https://ec.europa.eu/education/education-in-the-eu/european-education-area/european-universities-initiative_en, accessed 10 July 2020.
61. The author has been involved in designing this project in Myanmar and advocates for its prompt implementation in spite of the Covid-19 crisis.

reforming the student loan system still on the agenda in the US, now that universities and colleges are concentrating on whether and how they can open their real or virtual gates in autumn 2020? Is it still technically possible and morally requisite to think about, and act on, the refugee crisis, or is the pandemic a so much bigger calamity that it will obscure the smaller one (which nevertheless severely affects millions of people as well) in the minds and activities of everybody working in, or having responsibility for, higher education?

CONCLUSIONS

The present analysis shows that placing the crisis induced in higher education by Covid-19 in the context of the broader discourse on the crises in higher education helps understand the nature of this crisis and its manifestations. This analysis, based on a taxonomy of crises, also helps us recognise who is responding to the crisis and how; it uncovers limitations, even mistakes in the efforts to tackle the current crisis; and it allows us to identify or confirm recommendations for action.

Although the primary source of the crisis is external, it touches on important internal aspects of university operations. Higher education institutions alone cannot control or resolve the public health situation or address fully its broader effects on society. They can, however, make a contribution through research (in a variety of areas and fields), some of their degree and non-degree programmes, and public advocacy, and by adapting their internal operating modes. It is important for higher education institutions to clarify what they can control, and must act on, internally, in their particular contexts.

Although the crisis appears to impact more severely a few selected areas of operation and organisation of the universities, it also brings about challenges in most if not all other areas, sometimes in connection with or adding to pre-existing conditions. We can ask whether this is becoming a comprehensive crisis in higher education.

Universities appear to be largely left alone, addressing the crisis in isolation, institution by institution, at least for now. It is imperative for the public authorities, who tend to concentrate exclusively on matters of health, security and economic outlook (if at all), and other stakeholders to work with and support universities in tackling the crisis. Where governance traditions and arrangements allow it, national and transnational actors (such as the EU Commission, the Council of Europe, ASEAN and the ASEAN University Network, regional university associations in all parts of the world, etc.) should assume a function of co-ordination of both reflection on and action to address the crisis. This is almost completely missing at present, in the first months of the crisis, and affects the capacity to respond. It is also important for universities not to abandon but to cultivate their existing higher education alliances and networks, or even form new ones, and rely on them systematically and programmatically, be it only partially, for addressing the crisis. This is not happening at present either – at least not yet.

The efforts to address the crisis, and its analysis to date, tend to overlook important ongoing challenges and pre-existing conditions in higher education, which may come at a significant cost in the mid and long term. It is important, therefore, for universities and policy makers not to abandon but rather strive to continue – while acknowledging the new conditions – previous efforts and projects, such as those aiming at addressing the ongoing "crises" of governance (academic freedom and university autonomy), access (including refugee education) or equity (whether considering social background or gender aspects).

The nature of the Covid-19 crisis makes the pressure of the immediate both real and momentous. It is also important, however, to try to calibrate the action to address it while considering long-term challenges and aspirations as well.

REFERENCES

Against the Grain (2019/20), "Back talk – the real crisis in higher education", *Against the Grain* (28 February 2020), 31(6): 86.

Banya K. and Elu J. (1997), "The crisis of higher education in sub-Saharan Africa: the continuing search for relevance", *Journal of Higher Education Policy and Management*, 19(2): 151-66.

Brown R. (2014), "The real crisis in higher education", *Higher Education Review*, 46(3): 4-25.

Carr N. (2012), "The crisis in higher education", *MIT Technology Review* (27 September 2012), available at www.technologyreview.com/2012/09/27/182834/the-crisis-in-higher-education/, accessed 10 July 2020.

EY (2020), "Beyond Covid-19 lies a new normal–and new opportunities", *MIT Technology Review* (30 June 2020), available at www.technologyreview.com/2020/06/30/1004575/beyond-covid-19-lies-a-new-normal-and-new-opportunities/, accessed 10 July 2020.

Gardin M. (2015), "Higher education in crisis: post-war lessons from Finland and West Germany", *Journal of Contemporary European Research*, 11(2): 196-211.

Geiger R. L. (2006), "Real crisis or unpleasant realities?", *Society*, 43(4): 35-40.

Hwang K. K. (2016), "Academic self-colonization and the crisis of higher education in Taiwan and Mainland China", in Chou C. and Spangler J. (eds), *Chinese education models in a global age. Education in the Asia-Pacific region: issues, concerns and prospects*, vol. 31, Singapore: Springer.

Kamyab Sh. (2017), "Syrian refugees higher education crisis", *Journal of Comparative & International Higher Education*, 9: 10-14.

Krastev I. (2017), "The rise and fall of European meritocracy", *New York Times* (17 January 2017), available at www.nytimes.com/2017/01/17/opinion/the-rise-and-fall-of-european-meritocracy.html, accessed 10 July 2020.

Lazerson M. (2010), *Higher education and the American dream: success and its discontents*, Budapest/New York: Central European University Press.

Lefcourt H. M. (ed.) (2014), *Locus of control: current trends in theory and research*, New York: Psychology Press.

Matei L. (2020), "Academic freedom, university autonomy and democracy's future in Europe", in Bergan S., Gallagher T. and Harkavy. I. (eds), *Academic freedom, institutional autonomy and the future of democracy*, Higher Education series no. 24, Strasbourg: Council of Europe, pp. 29-40.

Meyerhoff E., Johnson E. and Braun B. (2011), "Time and the university", *ACME: an international e-journal for critical geographies*, 10(3): 483-507.

Nichols T. (2017), *The death of expertise and the campaign against established knowledge and why it matters*, New York: Oxford University Press.

Ogden W. R. (2002), "The real crisis in the classroom: where have all the teachers gone?" *Education* (Winter 2002), 123(2): 365-9, 374.

Openo J. (2020), "The discourse of crisis in higher education: fake news or real emergency?" (7 May 2020), available at www.jasonopeno.com/blog/2020/5/7/discourse-of-crisis-in-higher-education-fake-news-or-real-emergency, accessed 10 July 2020.

Pool G. S. (2003), "Higher education reform in Japan: Amano Ikuo on 'the university in crisis'", *International Education Journal*, 4(3): 149-76.

Qadeer I. (2006), "The real crisis in medical education", *Indian Journal of Medical Ethics*, III(3): 95-6.

Samoff J. and Carrol B. (2003), *From manpower planning to the knowledge era: World Bank policies on higher education in Africa*, UNESCO Forum Occasional Paper No. 2.

Scalambrino F. (2018), "Existential fallacy", in Arp R., Barbone S. and Bruce M. (eds), *Bad arguments: 100 of the most important fallacies in Western philosophy*, Hoboken, NJ/ Chichester, West Sussex: John Wiley & Sons, pp. 332-4.

Schwartzman S. (1988), "Brazil: opportunity and crisis in higher education", *Higher Education*, 17: 99-119.

Scott P. (1988), "The end of the European university?", *European Review*, 6(4): 441-57.

Sovern M. I. (1989), "Higher education: the real crisis", *New York Times Magazine* (22 January 1989), 138(4760): 24-6.

Stokes P. and Johnson M. (2020), "Lead from the future", *Inside Higher Ed.* (1 April 2020), available at www.insidehighered.com/views/2020/04/01/how-higher-education-can-overcome-crisis-induced-backlash-against-online-education, accessed 10 July 2020.

Streitwieser B., Miller-Idriss C. and de Wit H. (2016), *Higher education's response to the European refugee crisis: challenges, strategies, and opportunities*, Working Paper, Graduate School of Education & Human Development, Washington, DC: George Washington University, available at https://gsehd.gwu.edu/sites/default/files/documents/bernhard_streitwieser_working_paper_10.2016_final.pdf, accessed 10 July 2020.

Tight M. (1994). "Crisis, what crisis? Rhetoric and reality in higher education", *British Journal of Educational Studies*, 42(4): 363-74.

Chapter 14

Resilience and resistance: the community college in a pandemic

Brian Murphy

INTRODUCTION

All universities and colleges in the United States were deeply and immediately affected by the sudden appearance of Covid-19. What began as incredulity at the severity and rapidity of the virus' spread was quickly followed by incredulity at the failure of the federal government to act responsibly. States and municipalities were on their own, and universities and colleges were largely left adrift to seek their own ways of acting quickly to protect their students, campuses and communities.

The result was a patchwork of closures and re-openings. Initially, in March 2020, there was an almost universal move to distance learning in lieu of on-campus teaching and research, with the closure of campus services and operations and a hurried gathering of advice and guidance on how best to honour the requirements of "stay at home" and "keep students enrolled".

The two-year public community colleges suffered the same fate as their university neighbours: the immediate needs were to close up operations, shift instruction to online and distance modalities and keep students engaged and focused when all around them collapsed. But the community colleges suffered under constraints not shared by many of their university neighbours: limited discretionary dollars, little or no funding from endowments to fall back on and students whose limited economic resources and constrained family circumstances made any transitions much more difficult and stress-inducing.

But it would be an error to look at the experience of US community colleges or their students during the pandemic only through the lens of their constraints or their limited resources. This is instead a story of resilience and engagement, and the remarkable ability of poor and first-generation students to adapt and then resist despair and isolation. More critically, it is a story of what happens when equity drives college practice, and commitments to participation and democratic governance matter.

NATIONAL CONTEXT

The 1 050 US community colleges enrol over 11 800 000 students, 44% of all undergraduate students in the United States (AACC 2020). These are "open access" institutions, accepting students whose credentials would not allow entrance to university, students without admissions requirements beyond some English-language competence. This means that community colleges enrol the vast majority of low-income, first-generation or immigrant students in the United States and offer a pathway to either vocational employment or transfer to four-year universities. Indeed, over 50% of all bachelor level (first degree) graduates of public comprehensive universities in the United States[62] are transfer students from the community colleges. And at the most selective of the public research universities in the United States – the nine campuses of the University of California – over a third of all graduates are transfer students from the state's community colleges.

Community college students are diverse in all ways. Among all students enrolled in credit courses in US community colleges, 26% are Latino, 13% are Black, 45% are white, 6% are Asian/Pacific Islanders, 4% are two or more races and 1% are Native American (ibid.). This is a diversity which reflects the changing demographics of the United States, where non-white persons are projected to be the numerical majority by 2042.

More critically, the community colleges are the entry point for communities long marginalised in the United States: 57% of all Native Americans attending college are in the public community colleges, 52% of all Latinos, 42% of all African American students and 39% of all Asian/Pacific Islander students are enrolled in these colleges (ibid.). And among all the students who complete a four-year degree at US universities, 49% have enrolled in a community college at some point in their academic career (Community College Research Center 2020).

Community college students are older than the 18- to 22-year-old cohort typically found in private colleges and universities, they often have families and jobs and they most often have fewer resources with which to pursue their education. Two thirds of them attend part-time, the vast majority do not attend residential colleges with available student housing and over 60% of them receive financial aid. And, the vast majority of them work while being students: 62% of all full-time students are employed, 72% of all part-time students are employed (AACC 2020). But, because they are more likely to be poor and first-generation, their employment is most often low-wage and insecure.

These demographics matter in the daily life of the colleges, where there is no presumption that education is an expected privilege, or that students and their families can easily manage the financial obligations, commitments of time or focus that more elite institutions often presume about their students. Yet, the daily reality is that these students do the work, complete the credits and the programmes, transfer into

---

62. State-funded "comprehensive universities", serving regional and state constituencies, offer baccalaureate and master's degrees and some doctorates; Research 1 universities have research as one of their primary functions.

university or get employment. At the University of California, community college transfer students perform the same as or better than so-called "native" or first-year admits.

RESPONDING TO THE PANDEMIC

The diversity and resilience of community college students provide a framework for understanding the experience of the colleges during the pandemic, and the degree to which the students' own agency and engagement have mattered in confronting the indignities and dangers of the pandemic. At the same time, the colleges' commitments to equity and to democratic participation were critical to the nature and scope of their institutional response.

I will refer almost exclusively to the experiences of California's community colleges and I focus particularly on De Anza College. California's 116 public community colleges enrol over 2 200 000 students, more than 20% of all community college students in the United States. De Anza College, located in Cupertino, California, is one of the state's larger colleges, with 21 000 students. De Anza has a long tradition of superb teaching, a commitment to equity and civic engagement, and activist students. It is located at the epicentre of California's first major outbreak of Covid-19, in Santa Clara County.

When De Anza shut down its on-campus instruction and operations on 16 March 2020, virtually overnight, the overriding concern was to establish continuity of instruction via distance learning. But the college faced some immediate challenges. They needed to train their faculty and staff in online modalities if they had not yet done so, and their students also needed immediate training in these modalities, while many students did not have sufficient internet access or the necessary equipment to access the internet. In state-wide surveys, almost 20% of California community college students reported a lack of equipment and internet access (Student Senate 2020).

At almost all community colleges, there was an immediate mobilisation on two fronts: communication and access. At De Anza College, the college used all available communication tools to reach its students, alerting them to the emergency measures required by new regulations. Two surveys were conducted to determine the depth and range of needs among students, and this information, in turn, prompted a new emergency fund for students. The college then distributed over US$1.8m in CARES Act funding (i.e. federal relief funds made available to colleges and universities)[63] to students for emergency financial aid, laptops and tablets and leveraged free internet access through partnerships with local internet providers.

---

63. The Coronavirus Aid, Relief, and Economic Security (CARES) Act provided over US$16 billion in funding for emergency relief to American universities and colleges and their students. The U.S. Department of Education established the criteria and protocols by which the colleges applied for assistance; a common complaint was that the Department kept changing and revising its processes and delayed the money ultimately available to students. As a result, many colleges, including De Anza, used their own emergency funds, and those donated to the college, to offer emergency funds until the federal dollars finally arrived.

At De Anza, one of the few California community colleges on a quarter-term programme (i.e. three main sessions per year, plus a summer term, rather than a semester programme of two main terms), the college declared a one-week delay in opening the spring term and devoted that entire week to training faculty and staff in distance learning and off-site service delivery. The extra week gave time for students to regroup and figure out their options for continuing their education.

The results of the college's survey work were often startling and highlighted the particular difficulties faced by poor students. At De Anza, 44% of students reported losing their employment in the first month of the pandemic; 48% reported anxiety and depression. Of the students with food insecurity, 63% had either lost their employment or had their hours reduced (De Anza 2020). In a survey of California community college students conducted by the state-wide Student Senate, 67% of students reported serious anxiety or depression (SERU 2020; Student Senate 2020).

In the face of these findings, the college sought to provide counselling and other services, but those remained limited in scope and capacity. What has been less remarked upon is the resilience of those same students, however burdened by both unemployment and legitimate anxiety, and the critical role they played in pushing the colleges to respond to the pandemic in ways that acknowledged the particular burdens carried by low-income and first-generation students. At De Anza, it was, in fact, the elected student leadership that first asked for the campus closure to protect the community's health, two weeks before the campus closed, despite the obvious burden this would place on students. It was the students who first raised policy changes in grading and course withdrawals that later became state-wide policy.

These acts of agency and initiative are often overlooked in the narratives of "service" that mark how colleges responded – in good faith and with good effect – to the pandemic. And it is of course hard to tease apart what initiatives made which difference, but the proof of the students' resilience was in their persistence in the face of the dislocations of the virus. At De Anza College, the persistence rate (i.e. students continuing from term to term) fell only two percentage points between the winter and spring terms, which means that the vast majority of students persisted, remained enrolled and continued their education. And when the summer term opened, Mallory Newell, supervisor of college research at De Anza, confirmed that enrolment was up 26% (Newell 2020).

Our students did this, one must add, in the face of the pandemic's cruel demographics: low-income and poor communities, especially Black and Latino communities, were and are disproportionately represented in the awful numbers of Covid-19 illnesses and death. In neighbourhood after neighbourhood, poverty and race determined the odds of illness, and this was true of our students and their families. Almost all students from the poorest communities served by the college had family members laid off from work or had other family members employed in front-line jobs in hospitals, grocery stores or public services. Among those who were compelled to leave school, there was a disproportionate number of Black and Latino students. But many among them persisted.

How can we better understand the resilience of our students? At De Anza, there is a long tradition of student mobilisation and political leadership. There is a strong student government with its own independent funding; there is a superb elected student trustee with organising skills representing the students on the locally elected Board;[64] there is a certificate programme in "Social change leadership" which educates students seeking careers in organising and community leadership; there are over 70 student organisations and clubs where students group together; there are talented faculty and staff committed to the political and social activism of students; there are offices and projects that enlist students as mentors and leaders (VIDA 2020). In short, the college has a deep commitment to the active political and community engagement of its students and their engagement in the life of the college. And when the pandemic hit, these students did not fade into the woodwork; they did their own organising, they did their own outreach, they joined with faculty and staff in keeping the college focused on their needs.

At the same time, the administrative leadership at De Anza made a serious effort to broadly engage the faculty and staff unions and senates, to seek their guidance and agreement regarding the transition to online learning and the timing of any return to campus. This engagement came out of traditions and protocols developed over years, in which the advice and leadership of faculty and staff are valued not only for process reasons but for substantive reasons: they know the students and the college's capacities, and their views count. As a practical matter, this means endless meetings and protracted conversations. This means sacrificing speed in the name of broad participation. And, it is never good enough for some. Indeed, some faculty and staff at De Anza felt there had not been enough consultation and participation, and that too many decisions in the heat of the emergency had been made without adequate consultation. Similarly, student leaders complained at what they thought was inadequate communication, in a context where this expectation came up against the need to act immediately.

It was, in short, messy and contradictory. But no one can understand the efficacy with which a college serving 21 000 students reacted to a completely unexpected set of circumstances, or the astonishing resilience of those students, without understanding the depth of commitment to democratic action and equity at the college.

THE REBELLION IN THE STREETS

Three months into the pandemic, George Floyd was murdered by policemen in Minneapolis, and the streets of US cities exploded in grief and rage. Across the country, in the largest set of public demonstrations in its history, college and university students joined with younger students and their elders in a mass repudiation of police violence and the deeper structures of racism in the country. Risking their own health in an ever-widening health crisis, hundreds of thousands demanded both justice and a confrontation with racism.

These demonstrations were notable for the diversity of their participants and for the deep expression of solidarity that reverberated through them. At the same time, the

---

64. In California, all public community colleges are governed by locally elected boards of trustees, in geographically defined districts, subject to the legal and policy frameworks from the state Board of Governors. In the district governing De Anza College, each college has an elected student trustee.

demonstrations confronted the national embarrassment of a reactionary president whose pathological failure to lead the country during the Covid-19 pandemic was now compounded by his embrace of white supremacy and his demonising of the demonstrators.

While all accounts of the demonstration talk of tens of thousands of "young people", or tens of thousands of students, we need to point to the obvious: the health risks for young people of colour, especially Black and Latino, are significantly higher than for most people. And yet they took those risks, while at the same time focusing their energy and attention on what they could change close to home – and that included their colleges and universities. The most immediate focus of their energy was the police forces of colleges and universities and the demand that these forces either disband or transform into agents of community service.

At the same time, students were concerned to demand that colleges provide better and more responsive resources to students of colour, particularly African American. Student organisers, in short, did not see their lives as students divorced from their lives as actors in the streets. At De Anza College, this meant making demands on the administration, in concert with multiple faculty groups, to fund positions in support of Black students and (successfully) demanding that the local elected Board of Trustees pause in hiring two police positions. In the midst of an ever-worsening pandemic, under stay-at-home orders and required to organise through Zoom and Google Meet, our students were effective and powerful.

Community colleges conventionally judge themselves, and are judged, by the metrics of course completion, degree attainment and transfer to university, set against metrics of cost and ease of access. Almost never is a college judged for the political efficacy of its graduates or their capacity to forge enduring relationships across differences of race and ethnicity and class. Yet, a growing number of colleges across the United States judge themselves by the degree to which their students demonstrate the sort of resilience and action I have described among De Anza students. At Allegany College of Maryland, Tarrant County Community College and Lone Star College in Texas, at Monroe and Broome colleges in New York state, at LaGuardia College in New York City and Miami-Dade in Miami, regardless of local politics or partisan factionalism, students are showing that even a devastating pandemic cannot stop their development as community actors and activists.

A COMMITMENT TO EQUITY AND DEMOCRACY

I have described two arcs of action as colleges responded to the pandemic and the ensuing movement for racial justice: the institutional response of colleges seeking to support students – particularly low-income and first-generation students – and the response of students themselves when confronted with the deepest interruption of their lives and communities in living memory. In each instance, the commitment to equity – namely that poor and marginalised students be supported and engaged to the fullest extent possible – defines the actual work on the ground.

This commitment is maintained despite the absence of funding and resources. As Larry Galizio, President and CEO, Community College League of California, has pointed out, of all the federal resources provided for US higher education through the CARES Act, only 27% went to community colleges, even though they enrol 44% of undergraduates (Galizio 2020). And in state after state, the economic collapse during the pandemic means fewer and fewer state dollars for colleges and universities, even as the need for their services expands. This countercyclical budget problem – more students seeking education when resources shrink – means that community colleges simply cannot serve all who seek enrolment. So, as deep as the commitment to equity for marginalised students might be, it cannot compensate for a lack of resources. It is estimated that California's community colleges left 600 000 potential students unable to enrol during the 2008-09 recession (ibid.), who were disproportionately low-income, working-class, non-white.

If the crisis prompted by the pandemic deepens and the state of California cannot adjust its revenue streams (i.e. generate greater tax revenues), the programmatic and staffing commitments that a college must make if it is to support student civic engagement become harder to balance against the demands of maintaining the broader curriculum.

Maintaining a balancing act between institutional survival and broader commitments to student engagement and democratic life may depend, ironically, on the political capacity of students and their families to vote, participate in local, state and national political debate, support the taxation proposals required to keep colleges healthy and refuse a history that marginalises them. The colleges may depend on the students and their families as much as the students depend on the colleges.

This mutual dependence will become more critical as the national elections in November 2020 approach. As Eloy Ortiz Oakley, the Chancellor of the California State Community Colleges, puts it, our students are "under constant attack by a hostile administration" in Washington, referring not only to education policy but changes in immigration, environmental and health policy (Oakley 2020). If the elections are determined by voter turnout, surely the votes of younger citizens will matter greatly, and community colleges that have devoted themselves to the civic engagement of their students will have played a role beyond the immediate and local.

Finally, a note on the "narratives" through which we understand our work. Any review of the national organisations representing higher education in the United States will see little reference to the political capacity of our students. Almost without exception, there is lavish attention to student success, equity for all, occasionally a reference to social responsibility. In those organisations representing the community colleges there is much attention to equity of access and student success and no reference to the democratic purposes of college beyond a vague notion that a "vibrant democracy" requires greater economic access.

That a vibrant democracy might require attention to the political and community engagement of our students is often unacknowledged, partly due to a fear of partisanship and reprisal by reactionary forces. Yet, despite that avoidance, the pandemic and the demands for racial justice have thrown into sharp relief that young people across the country, including our students, are providing political and community leadership anyway. And our experience at De Anza demonstrates that a more intentional commitment to these dimensions of our mission serves us all.

REFERENCES

AACC (American Association of Community Colleges) (2020), "Fast Facts 2020", available at www.aacc.nche.edu, accessed 16 July 2020.

Community College Research Center (2020), "Community College Facts," New York: Teachers College, Columbia University, available at https:ccrc.tc.columbia.edu/Community-College-FAQs.html, accessed 16 July 2020.

De Anza (2020), College Office of Institutional Research, "Survey of basic needs – spring 2020", available at http://deanza.edu/ir/deanza-research-projects/surveys/BasicNeeds2020.pdf, accessed 10 July 2020.

Galizio L. (2020), President and CEO, Community College League of California, commentary, "Challenges and opportunities; California community colleges responding to COVID-19", Symposium sponsored by the Center for Studies in Higher Education, University of California, Berkeley (17 July 2020), available at https://cshe.berkeley.edu, accessed 20 July 2020.

Newell M. (2020), interviewed, Office of Institutional Research, De Anza College, July 2020.

Oakley E. O. (2020), Chancellor, California Community Colleges, commentary, "Challenges and opportunities; California community colleges responding to COVID-19", Symposium sponsored by the Center for Studies in Higher Education, University of California, Berkeley (17 July 2020), available at http://cshe.berkeley.edu, accessed 20 July 2020.

SERU (Student Experience at the Research University) consortium (2020), "Being a student during the pandemic", Public presentation of results of undergraduate and graduate surveys by Igor Chirikov, Director, sponsored by the Center for Studies in Higher Education, University of California, Berkeley (18 June 2020).

Student Senate (Student Senate for California Community Colleges) (2020), "COVID-19: California Community College student challenges", Student Senate for California Community Colleges Survey Report, May 2020.

VIDA (Vasconcellos Institute for Democracy in Action) (2020), available at www.deanza.edu/vida/, accessed 28 July 2020.

Chapter 15

The University of Bologna during the Covid-19 pandemic: protect, provide and innovate – Responses from a resilient community

Elena Luppi, Elena Consolini, Alessandra Scagliarini, Mirko Degli Esposti and Francesco Ubertini

The health emergency caused by the spread of Covid-19 had a profound effect on higher education institutions, forcing them to promptly move all academic activity online. The University of Bologna (Unibo) promptly switched to distance mode to ensure continuation of its services, projects and activities. This situation required, and still requires strong academic commitment and co-ordination among the different actors involved and an increasing investment in innovation of teaching and learning processes, mobilising the university system at several levels and increasing the importance of research-based activities.

COPING WITH THE EMERGENCY

At the end of February 2020, following the spread of the Covid-19 pandemic in Italy – in agreement with the Italian Ministry of University and Research, the Region of Emilia-Romagna and other public authorities – the University of Bologna ordered the suspension of teaching activities to reduce the danger of contagion. In the following weeks, the university put into place a list of policies and actions aimed at protecting the university community, providing prompt answers to its needs and innovating processes, practices and tools to cope with the emergency. This process, still in progress, has highlighted the strong resilience of the academic community and its members, as well as its capacity to consider this ground-breaking situation as an opportunity for self-assessment, reflection and innovative design, for the future of our institution.

A steady flow of communication was quickly provided to keep the whole academic community up to date on a daily basis during the lockdown. This included:
- daily emails from the rector with updates on the situation and the actions undertaken;
- the activation of an email address for giving prompt answers to any question or need related to the emergency (coronavirus@unibo.it);
- periodic emails for international students;
- support to students abroad attending mobility programmes and students from the Buenos Aires campus to cope with the emergency (such as travel, health issues, administrative duties);
- the activation of a multilingual medical support service for international students;
- the activation of online groups for mobility students, divided by geographic area, to provide support and information, as well as help for returning home;
- the online transfer of the Psychological Support Service and the Cross-cultural Counselling Service for international students (Unibo Support 2020; Unibo Counselling 2020).

LEARNING AND TEACHING

During the months since the pandemic began, the University of Bologna has worked to ensure all learning and teaching activities while complying with safety regulations and protocols. The transformation involved the transition to online platforms and the reorganisation of learning and teaching for the first, second and third cycle degree programmes, including lessons, oral and written examinations, admission tests, seminars and internships.

After the suspension of all teaching activities on 24 February 2020, 70% of the lectures were provided online one week later and 100% after two weeks, in synchronous mode, using the Microsoft Teams platform. In general, all teaching and learning activity has been transferred online, from the beginning of March 2020 to date, with the following figures:
- 3 667 lectures within our 221 degree programmes;
- 215 880 examinations;
- 10 069 graduations.

Thanks to very prompt and effective co-ordination among the governing, technical and administrative authorities of the university, and an extremely reactive and flexible response from the teaching staff, this transition was able to start and be completed in a very short time, considerably earlier than at the vast majority of other universities in Italy and across Europe.

Internships have been carried out remotely, through agreements with the hosting organisations and the provision of alternative activities monitored by the academic supervisors. Administrative services have also been ensured at a distance: student secretariats and all the administrative offices have provided their services online, by email or by telephone.

The Fair of the University of Bologna for future students also took place virtually: students enrolled in the first cycle degrees, and future students living in Italy or in any other country around the world, could discover the 221 Alma Mater[65] degree programmes. Moreover, the online orientation tests, which are required for application to many degree programmes, were redesigned in order to make it possible for applicants to take the tests from home.

For the first six months of the academic year 2020/21, the University of Bologna will offer blended synchronous teaching held in classrooms but also accessible remotely, with the aim of guaranteeing to any student, wherever they live, the possibility to start or continue their own study path without risks to health, delay, postponement or suspension, regardless of the evolution of the pandemic.

The blended synchronous method allows students to follow the total course of lessons or part of them, face to face or remotely. Each department tailors this model in a collegial way, taking into account the context, resources and characteristics of the study programme. Teaching and learning programmes should include blended solutions: combining blended synchronous teaching with a smaller amount of full distance e-learning, in case this choice can improve innovation and the quality of the teaching and learning proposal.

The development of this model requires specific organisational measures that are consistent with the principles of security, inclusion and quality, and that guarantee flexibility to adapt to different learning environments. This model should also ensure higher resilience for teaching and learning in view of the uncertainty linked to the evolution of the pandemic.

A specific security protocol has been designed in order to guarantee the safety of the whole academic community: students, teaching staff, technical-administrative staff and external collaborators.

To plan activities in compliance with health regulations, students will be asked to specify, using a dedicated app, the learning activities they intend to follow and the chosen method for attendance. This will enable the university to manage room capacity safely and efficiently and, if necessary, plan turnover. All students will have their lecture timetable and the method of attendance constantly updated.

For the second semester of the academic year 2020/21, meetings with students, exams and graduation sessions will be provided face to face again, but these activities will also be available remotely. This choice will allow the attendance of all students, even those encountering difficulties in coming back to university (for health or economic reasons) and, at the same time, will ensure the continuation of teaching activities even in the event of further lockdowns.

---

65. The University of Bologna, which can claim to be the oldest in the world, is often referred to as the Alma Mater Studiorum.

Quality and innovation in learning and teaching

In order to support the quality and innovation of teaching in an emergency, the University of Bologna has developed a plan consisting of monitoring, research and training (Unibo Innovation 2020). All these actions are inspired by a working method based on research and, in particular, by the model of Formative Educational Evaluation, an evaluation process focused on moments of data analysis, reflection and re-planning, with a view to improvement. This approach promotes the diagnostic, decision-making and design skills of the professors involved and enables them to increase their teaching skills.

The process can be summarised in the following phases: needs analysis, macro- and micro-planning, the planning and delivery of training activities, mid-term and final evaluation.

Steps that regulate the design and delivery of training proposed in the field of quality and educational innovation (Unibo Innovation: research 2020).

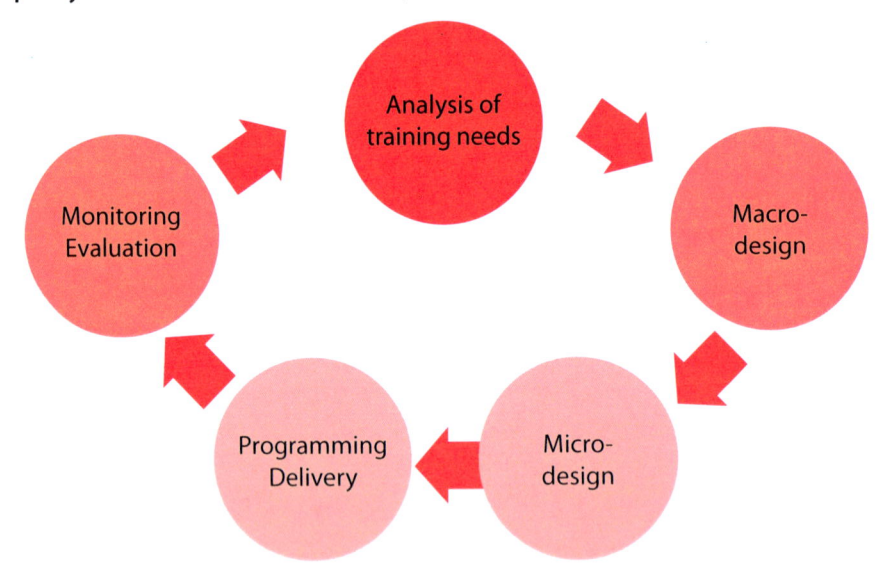

The cycle consists of: Analysis of training needs → Macro-design → Micro-design → Programming Delivery → Monitoring Evaluation → (back to Analysis of training needs).

Consistent with this working method, specific monitoring and training activities were launched with the aim of supporting teachers in developing innovation in their practice. In the period February to June 2020, research and evaluation were carried out and 21 training initiatives with 81 hours of training were delivered, involving a total of 590 teachers. Further training offers are being planned, based on the analysis of online teaching experiences, taking into account the results of the research that has been conducted (Unibo Innovation: in the Pandemic 2020).

Surveys of students

Two weeks after the start of online teaching, the University developed a survey addressed to students, through a short questionnaire on online teaching. Almost 10 000 students from all study programmes and subject areas answered. The results were presented in a formative video distributed to the entire University community, with the aim of guiding teachers in developing innovation in their practice in response to the emergency (ibid.). The survey was repeated at the end of the semester, and the results and needs for improvement will be incorporated into the design of the training action plans to be offered to the teaching staff in the second semester.

A survey on living conditions of the University's students was also conducted, promoted and carried out by the Student Council and the student associations and supervised by a team of professors in social sciences and humanities. The study aimed to assess the impact of the Covid-19 pandemic on students' experience, in particular the psychological, financial and housing dimensions, students' projects or expectations for the future, and their learning experiences.

Surveys of teaching practices

In order to analyse learning and teaching practices and encourage a collegial debate on them, a survey on teaching experiences was carried out. Professors and lecturers were asked to describe their experiences, using a specific template for project design. Almost 600 respondents described their practices, and the results were analysed and clustered by scientific and thematic areas. The initiative aimed to establish a network for sharing experiences and encouraging reflection, in order to test and disseminate online teaching strategies and methodologies.

A questionnaire on the teaching staff's opinions, attitudes and practices during the pandemic emergency is under development. The results will inspire further training programmes for professors and lecturers.

Training activities for the innovation of learning and teaching practices

On the basis of the analysis of learning and teaching practices, five training workshops were designed and delivered, each addressed to professors or lecturers from the scientific, technological, humanities, social science and medical faculties. These workshops took place in May and June 2020 and were conducted remotely by an expert in disciplinary didactics and a facilitator. The initiative was aimed at preparing teachers for the new blended synchronous phase. Indirectly, the project was intended to encourage the sharing and dissemination of online teaching experiences, to increase teachers' networks for innovation. Some specific learning needs emerged and, aiming to give an answer to and enhance innovation, specific videos for training were produced on the following topics: student's point of view, communication, teaching and learning strategies, and assessment and evaluation of online teaching. The theoretical and methodological inputs presented in the videos represented the method that has guided and will guide the design of teaching innovation in online and blended synchronous mode. The outcomes of the workshops provided inspiration for further training actions to be delivered from September 2020.

RESEARCH ACTIVITIES ON COVID-19

The University of Bologna is engaged in many kinds of research addressing the Covid-19 emergency. Not only its medical departments but also those of technology, and even social sciences, are involved in many areas of research aimed at responding to the emergency. Here are just a few examples:

- prototyping of a machine for filtering viruses and bacteria;
- mapping of Covid-19-activated proteins to understand how the virus attacks human cells and how the latter respond to these attacks;
- setting up a new laboratory to test masks and protection devices;
- development of an electrochemiluminescence-based technique in which the light-emitting chemiluminescent reaction is preceded by an electrochemical reaction for quicker, more cost-effective and ultra-sensitive serological tests (Unibo Chemistry 2020);
- meta-analysis of the sequenced genomes of the virus;
- development of a device doubling up on lung ventilators, allowing one ventilator to provide oxygen for two patients;
- clinical study of ultraviolet light for Covid-19 treatment;
- clinical study on the effectiveness of hydroxychloroquine in treating Covid-19;
- a regional study to improve the identifiability of Covid-19 in asymptomatic populations;
- development of a model to keep hospital admissions under control;
- health and educational research in schools during and after the emergency;
- comparative analysis of government measures to safeguard employment.

Many other studies are being conducted with the involvement of interdisciplinary teams from the University, all committed to providing prompt research-based responses to the emergency.

CULTURAL EVENTS AND COMMUNICATION

During the lockdown, the University put into place an intense programme of events and activities for communication, cultural entertainment, sports activity and community networking. The University's social profiles were constantly animated by text messages and videos addressed to the university community and open to any other interested persons.

From Monday to Friday, each day at 9 p.m., #UniboSera offered the opportunity to follow short reflective lectures on the "waiting time"[66] of lockdown, to invite the academic community, as well as citizens, to think about their changing habits, fears, new forms of socialising, the perception of time and our common future.

Every day until 26 April, at noon anyone could listen to "Words for us": great artists of cinema and theatre interpreting the words of Homer, Virgil, Aeschylus, Plato, Sophocles, Aristotle, Seneca, Augustine, Lucretius and Marcus Aurelius; words that have resisted time and can now help nourish a new hope.

---

66. This project described the time of lockdown as "waiting time": a time of suspension, reflection and expectancy.

The University choir, Collegium Musicum of the Alma Mater, suddenly switched to a virtual choir, offering concerts on their dedicated YouTube channel and showing how choral activity does not stop during quarantine.

The Bologna Business School organised a daily event called "QuaranTalks", with live broadcasts involving many Italian and international guests.

Every morning at 8.30 a.m. from Monday to Friday, the University provided online video training lessons on total body workouts, pilates, yoga and much more, to promote excercise before working from home.

The University Museum System posted videos and texts on its Facebook page, with reflections on history and on the present time. Space online was also dedicated to the Botanical Garden, to discover through photos and videos the blooms of March, and some videos offered educational activities easily replicable at home with children.

CREATIVITY IN THE EMERGENCY

During the lockdown, the University launched a programme of initiatives focused on creativity and innovation.

#SocialMakersforCovid19 is the name of a hackathon (SocialMakersforCovid19 2020), open to all Alma Mater members, to design projects to help girls and boys with mild intellectual disabilities and their families during the period when all day-care centres for disabled persons were closed down. Four teams of students were involved in designing projects with high social impact to support families with children with Down syndrome or other forms of intellectual disability. The students were supervised by a tutor supporting them in the adoption of a "Learning by Helping" approach. The solutions designed are also opened to prototyping through AlmaLabor and Almacube maker spaces (Almacube 2020; AlmaLabor 2020).

The initiative OPER.TEN – Transform Emergency Now! 10 Days for Change (OPER.TEN 2020) consisted of a design path, planned within the Open Innovation activities promoted by the University, in collaboration with Almacube and AlmaLabor, in response to the health emergency. OPER.TEN was conceived to develop possible solutions, of immediate application, to some of the most urgent problems that citizens were facing. Four teams of students from Emilia-Romagna universities were asked to conceive and design, in 10 days, solutions that could be further implemented thanks to the involvement of some strategic stakeholders, both in the corporate world and in public bodies, adopting the design-thinking approach and supervised by a coach.

Furthermore, the University launched the international hackathon UNA.TEN Transform Emergency Now! 10 Days for Change, an open innovation programme promoted by the UNA Europa alliance. UNA Europa is a network set up to create "the European university of the future" (UNA Europa 2020), where students can travel around Europe and attend integrated courses in different countries and languages, and researchers, professors and university staff can move freely among multiple locations, according to their professional needs. UNA Europa includes, together with the Alma Mater, eight prominent European universities: KU Leuven (Belgium), Helsingin Yliopisto (Finland), Université Paris 1 Panthéon-Sorbonne (France), Freie Universität Berlin (Germany), Uniwersytet Jagielloński (Poland), University of Edinburgh (UK) and Universidad Complutense de Madrid (Spain).

The UNA.TEN hackathon involved more than 100 students, who worked together in 19 teams from the UNA Europa Network. The student teams decided to deal with the following challenges related to the Covid-19 emergency: re-thinking cultural and entertainment activities, ensuring online privacy, information about the correct use of digital tools, ensuring the possibility of safe travel and avoiding food waste due to difficulties in the food chain.

The Univerty's Advanced Design Unit launched the project Creativity in Emergency, international research aimed at identifying and analysing design-driven solutions and initiatives developed by private companies to cope with the Covid-19 emergency (ADU 2020). Any start-up, organisation or company interested in participating could offer its contribution to the research by answering an online questionnaire. The research started from the premise that

> we're facing a 'new normal' era we were not prepared [for] as citizens, researchers, professionals and entrepreneurs. As we believe in culture and creativity as necessities for companies and the whole society, the research has the ambition to bring out how creativity and design processes have enabled organizations to progressively adapt to the emergency. (ibid.)

EXTRAORDINARY MEASURES IN RESPONSE TO THE COVID-19 EMERGENCY

A few measures were established to cope with the emergency and to provide support to students experiencing financial difficulties in the current situation. Due to the online transfer of any teaching and learning activity, the University provided SIM cards for students who did not have the means to attend online classes.

An agreement on short-term accommodation rentals has been made between the University and the Municipality of Bologna, and funds have been set up to offer rental contracts at affordable prices, in support of students and property owners.

Starting from the 2020/21 academic year, the project Almabike is to provide 600 bicycles to students under a free loan agreement (as well as bicycles for university staff), and student subscriptions to public transport will be particularly subsidised.

A crowdfunding campaign (Protect and Cure 2020) has also been launched to support health projects on Covid-19. Protect and Cure supports the following projects: the creation of a laboratory for the assessment of sanitary protective equipment for health; remote follow-up of Covid-19 patients; diagnosis, prevention and containment of the spread of Covid-19; production of respiratory systems for the treatment of respiratory syndromes; development of nanostructured materials for virus protection masks and machines for their production.

CONCLUSION

This contribution summarises the main actions that the University of Bologna carried out to cope with the Covid-19 emergency. Starting from February 2020, following the provisions to address the health emergency induced by the spread of Covid-19, which suspended the teaching activities of education institutions and universities at all levels, the University put in place a radical transformation of its organisation to ensure the continuation of teaching activities for the second semester of the academic year 2019/20. This was to ensure that all students had the opportunity to attend classes regularly and take final exams. Research activities did not stop but were instead often converted into studies aiming to provide responses to the pandemic. Activities related to the Univeristy's third mission were also redesigned as projects aimed at coping with the emergency. Cultural and communication projects were developed to sustain not only the University community but also all members of the local community.

The changes and innovations which have been put into place, in learning and teaching, research and the third mission, are the result of different processes characterising the University of Bologna: bottom-up empowerment, peer learning, research-based models, project design and actions based on assessment, monitoring and redesign.

Such innovation processes are still in progress and the results demonstrate the strong resilience of the Alma Mater community. Students, teaching staff, administrative staff and all members of the University community showed the capacity to transform this situation into an opportunity for ground-breaking self-assessment, reflection and innovation, for designing the future of our institution.

REFERENCES

ADU (Advanced Design Unit) (2020), University of Bologna, "Creativity in the emergency", available at https://site.unibo.it/cricc/it/ricerca/creativity, accessed 12 August 2020.

Almacube (2020), University of Bologna [maker space], available at https://en.almacube.com, accessed 12 August 2020.

AlmaLabor (2020), University of Bologna [maker space], available at www.unibo.it/en/services-and-opportunities/entrepreneurship/AlmaLaBOr, accessed 12 August 2020.

OPER.TEN (2020), "Transform Emergency Now! 10 days for change", crowdfunding campaign, available at www.una-europa.eu/stories/una-ten, accessed 12 August 2020.

Protect and Cure (2020), University of Bologna, crowdfunding campaign, available at https://sostienilaricercaunibo.ideaginger.it, accessed 12 August 2020.

SocialMakersforCovid19 (2020), available at https://site.unibo.it/almaengage/en/news/socialmakersforcovid19-a-hackaton-to-help-coping-with-mild-intellectual-disabilities, accessed 12 August 2020.

UNA Europa (2020), available at www.una-europa.eu, accessed 12 August 2020.

Unibo Chemistry (2020), University of Bologna, available at www.unibo.it/en/notice-board/increasingly-efficient-serological-tests-thanks-to-a-study-led-by-researchers-at-the-university-of-bologna, accessed 21 September 2020.

Unibo Counselling (2020), University of Bologna Cross-cultural Counselling Service, available at www.unibo.it/en/services-and-opportunities/guidance-and-tutoring/cross-cultural-counselling-service-for-international-students, accessed 12 August 2020.

Unibo Innovation (2020), University of Bologna, available at www.unibo.it/en/teaching/innovation-in-teaching-and-learning/innovation-in-teaching-and-learning, accessed 12 August 2020.

Unibo Innovation: research (2020), University of Bologna, available at https://centri.unibo.it/centroinnovazionedidattica/it/visione/ricerca, accessed 12 August 2020.

Unibo Innovation: in the Pandemic (2020), University of Bologna, available at https://centri.unibo.it/centroinnovazionedidattica/it/docenti/innovazione-didattica-nell-emergenza, accessed 12 August 2020.

Unibo Support (2020), University of Bologna Psychological Support Service, available at www.unibo.it/en/services-and-opportunities/health-and-assistance/the-psychological-support-service-sap, accessed 12 August 2020.

Chapter 16

Re-thinking African higher education in the post-Covid-19 era

Barnabas Nawangwe

No other global pandemic in modern history has shaken the world like Covid-19. What started as a small outbreak in central China, with the deceptive perception that it would be contained there, spread like wildfire across the globe, spreading panic in communities in practically every country. The devastation was huge, damaging all citadels of confidence even in the most advanced economies and societies. The pandemic did more damage to the psychological balance of nations than to the health of their people. As I write this article in summer 2020, it is still too early to say what the final death toll and other impacts will be, but it is clear that the confidence of entire nations in their invincibility is terribly shaken. Few sectors have been hit more than the education sector, particularly higher education. Africa, used to bracing itself against the devastation of many epidemics, including Ebola, HIV/AIDS, cholera and others, was extremely fragile in the face of this monstrous pandemic caused by Covid-19.

AFRICA CLOSED AGAIN

For over 15 centuries, most of Africa remained closed to the rest of the world due to a variety of factors, including thick impenetrable forests, harsh deserts, tropical diseases like malaria, and the sheer vastness of the continent. Africa slowly opened up to the rest of the world, albeit with some savage intrusions like slavery, which left severe bruises on the continent. The wounds of Africa are taking very long to heal, and the damage to her human resources will take many more years to be repaired. But Africa has started moving on, and many scholars and leaders have seen in Africa the next growth region of the world (World Bank 2020; Brookings Institute 2019; and others). Despite the damage done to African higher education by the disastrous World Bank policies of structural adjustment in the 1980s and 1990s, African universities registered steady growth in enrolment and in contribution to research (Mamdani 2007). Many African countries began seeing hope for a brighter future in their universities and began investing in them.

But the spread of the coronavirus on African soil led to the closure of borders, once again closing off Africa from the rest of the world. The closure of borders, even if only for three months after the arrival of the coronavirus, has already had devastating effects on the economies of most African countries, seriously dampening the hopes for the African renaissance declared by former South African President Thabo Mbeki (Ajulu 2001).

CONTRADICTIONS IN AFRICAN HIGHER EDUCATION

Many scholars have written about African higher education and its role in Africa's development. In their report to the OECD on higher education in Africa, Jowi et al. (2013: 8) assert: "Under this frame of analysis, the expansion of higher education served both political and economic aspirations of the newly independent governments. Hence, the governments were willing to allocate resources and invest in higher education". In the same report the authors quote Coleman and Court: "Further, public universities in these countries also 'symbolized national pride and self-respect' (Coleman and Court, 1993) and self-reliance" (Jowi et al. 2013: 8).

The enthusiasm with which governments of newly independent African countries established universities in the 1960s and 1970s was slowly eroded by a lack of appreciation of the universities as agents of change, and many governments started seeing them as citadels of opposition. The structural adjustment programmes of the World Bank simply helped further divert resources from the already resource-constrained universities. Resources were diverted from higher education to basic education, leading to the collapse of the critical tertiary institutions that provided the technical cadre so badly needed for a country's technological development. At the same time, as has been severally reported in the mass media, African governments were shouting loudly that African universities were producing "half-baked" graduates who were unfit for the job market (Babalobi 2019).

The World Bank policy shift on higher education in the early 2000s breathed some fresh air into higher education in Africa. African governments resumed prioritising higher education, and universities were given a new lease of life. After two decades of neglect, African universities struggled to regain stature and walk straight. During the period of deprivation, ironically many private institutions sprang up on the continent. Africa now had quantity, but did she have quality as well?

A NEW LEASE OF LIFE FOR AFRICAN UNIVERSITIES

In their OECD report, Jowi et al. (2013) quote Varghese: "The countries which have an expanded system of higher education with higher levels of investment in research and development (R&D) activities have higher potential to grow faster in a globalized knowledge economy." (Varghese, 2013, p. 12) When discussing the role of universities in socio-economic development, many Western scholars try to compare what universities in the West do and what their peers in Africa do. But it is not reasonable to try to compare the role of universities in completely different environments, with very different levels of socio-economic development. While arguably universities in both settings must have the development and dissemination of knowledge for socio-economic advancement as their main goal, the contexts are different and the roles of the universities in the two environments must hence be identified with some qualification. While a small farmer in the West wakes up to plough his field using a tractor, a peasant in rural Africa wakes up to yet another day of hard labour using the most rudimentary tools for tilling the soil. The farmer in the West retires to a rich lunch with a balanced diet, while the African peasant will most likely retire to a poor meal, if at all, devoid of a balanced diet.

A scholar in the two contexts cannot treat the problems faced by the two people in the same manner. The problem statements and methodology cannot be the same, if good results are to be obtained. While an African university must look for ways of pulling the African peasant from abject poverty, the university in the West is most likely concerned with how the wealth of the farmer in the West can be protected and improved. Should therefore the focus of the universities in the two socio-economic environments be similar? The answer is probably "no".

While universities in Africa may and must use all available technology to help leapfrog Africa's economy, the methods will certainly differ from those applied by a university in the West. The United Nations Sustainable Development Goals (UN 2020) may read exactly the same in Norway as they read in Uganda, but the realities are completely different. African universities have come to terms with this reality and have invested massively in mindset change.

For a long time, African universities were referred to as colonial institutions in an African setting. This perception was driven by the nature of the curricula at African universities, which were seen as inappropriate to solving Africa's problems. Many African leaders complained about what they termed "useless courses" taught at African universities. These leaders wanted to see only those courses that would produce tangible goods and not courses that were viewed as mere theory and philosophy. But African universities have fought hard to maintain the basic sciences and basic arts on their curricula. Failure to do this would relegate these universities to some sort of advanced technical schools, for the sciences and arts contribute tremendously to the development of critical thinking at a university.

The resuscitation of African universities by governments and, to some extent, with the help of external donors, has seen many of the universities reclaim their positions in the global fraternity of knowledge creators. Research is booming at many of the universities on the continent. Innovations in teaching and learning have been implemented. The future of these universities has started looking bright.

RESPONSES BY AFRICAN UNIVERSITIES TO THE COVID-19 PANDEMIC

Covid-19 has probably had a less devastating effect on Africa than on other continents as far as people's health is concerned. But Covid-19 could have the worst effect on the continent as far as its economy is concerned. Already suffering a worse burden of disease than any other region on earth, Africa's economy has had to struggle with diseases like malaria, which still remains the leading cause of death in Africa, Ebola, tuberculosis and, more recently, non-communicable diseases including cancer, diabetes, obesity and others. Increasingly, African countries have to make the painful decision whether to take money away from very demanding economic activities to deal with diseases that cripple their economic activities. The arrival of Covid-19 was therefore the last thing any government would have wished to deal with. And yet African governments had no choice but to divert resources from other activities to try to stop the spread of the coronavirus. The cost of laxity with the virus would be much higher, since most African countries do not have the facilities to deal with a major outbreak of a pandemic like Covid-19.

The first victims of the pandemic were the education institutions. Schools, colleges and universities across the continent were closed and they remain closed at the time of writing, three months after the first cases of Covid-19 were identified in Africa. The reaction by African universities to the Covid-19 pandemic is unprecedented. In their article in *University World News*, Abbey et al. (2020) point out that African universities under the African Research Universities Alliance quickly responded to the Covid-19 outbreak. The response by the African universities took several forms, including provision of clinical services in hospitals, testing for the coronavirus, conducting studies on the epidemiology of the virus and innovations to help with management of the disease. The universities also provided advisory services to national task forces on the response to Covid-19. Already several journal articles on Covid-19 in Africa have been published (Emmanuel et al. 2020; Kigotho et al. 2020). It is worth noting here that Africa still lags behind the rest of the world in the volume of scientific publications, still standing between 2% and 3% (Jowi et al. 2013: 18). Has Covid-19 finally triggered the unlocking of African universities' potential for research?

COVID-19 AND ITS IMPLICATIONS FOR HIGHER EDUCATION IN AFRICA

Covid-19 has very important lessons for Africa and for its higher education institutions. The global outbreak of the pandemic left Africa exposed. Whereas, in the recent past, epidemics were largely confined within Africa and the international community offered help to deal with them, Covid-19 spread very fast around the globe. The concern of every country was to protect its own people and apparently no country had the capacity to deal with its own problem and still help others. Africa was left on her own. The reaction by African governments is commendable. They gave a high proportion of their scarce resources to the fight against the spread of the coronavirus. What are the implications for higher education in Africa?

Since independence, African higher education has gone through difficult moments and to a large extent survived those moments. There is general anxiety in the world that Covid-19 will lead to the collapse of many education institutions, and that they will not survive the economic hardship brought about by the pandemic. A situational analysis of African universities, their locations and their funding mechanisms shows that many may indeed be forced to close, unless their governments intervene. One month into the lockdown as a result of the Covid-19 pandemic, several private universities in Uganda announced that they would not be able to pay the salaries of their staff since they were unable to collect fees from students. The situation was not different in many other African countries.

At the time of writing this article (summer 2020), universities are still closed, and it is not clear when they will re-open. The financial constraints facing private universities in Africa are now likely to continue for some time even after the universities re-open. While public universities get most of their funding from governments, private universities depend entirely on the fees paid by students. Private and public universities in Africa depend a lot on fees paid by students and, if fees are not paid, the universities may face serious constraints in providing services to their students.

The number of universities in Africa has risen exponentially in the last two decades. According to the uniRank database, in 2020 there are currently 1 225 officially recognised higher education institutions in Africa.[67] The majority of these institutions are privately owned and they most likely are facing the challenges highlighted above. Even public universities will most probably face serious constraints as many governments have cut their budgets as a result of the Covid-19 pandemic. The question we must therefore ask is: will higher education in Africa survive Covid-19?

Universities in Africa have shown a high level of innovation following the outbreak of the Covid-19 pandemic. They have demonstrated the capacity to adjust to adverse situations in a short time. Several things are likely to happen if African higher education institutions are to survive. It is likely that fees payable by students may have to decrease in the short run. To face this challenge, universities will have to devise ways of offering the same education at a lower price, hence the need to move to online education. Many universities are already moving to online education and are taking full advantage of opportunities provided through the various consortia promoting online education on the continent, including the Partnership for Enhanced and Blended Learning (PEBL 2020), an initiative of the Association of Commonwealth Universities, and training of lecturers on management of online courses offered by the International Institute of Online Education (IIOE 2020), an initiative of the UNESCO International Centre for Higher Education Innovation based at the Southern University of Science and Technology in Shenzhen, China.

Many African universities have realised the urgent need to move to online education and are putting resources there. There are discussions around the possibility of sharing online courses among the universities in order to cut costs, as well as other initiatives aimed at enhancing online education in Africa. Covid-19 will go away some time, but by that time higher education in African countries will have suffered some devastation as a result.

But Covid-19 has also brought new energy to African universities. The new energy is driven by the realisation that African universities cannot continue relying on solutions from elsewhere. They must innovate to survive. The challenge now is how best to harness this new energy and the new opportunities to pull higher education in Africa from the current pit caused by Covid-19 and raise it to new international levels. There is no doubt that African higher education institutions are equal to the task, as has already been demonstrated by the rapid response to Covid-19.

Fortunately, African universities can take advantage of opportunities provided by international associations, including the International Association of Universities, the African Research Universities Alliance, the Association of Commonwealth Universities and others. These associations provide a platform for sharing resources by the member

---

67. See www.4icu.org, uniRank, accessed 16 June 2020.

universities, as well as links to research grant agencies. With careful use of these opportunities, African universities will surely emerge from obscurity and prosper.

REFERENCES

Abbey E., Abu-Danso E. and Aryeetey E. (2020), "Research universities' multiple responses to COVID-19", *University World News*, available at www.universityworldnews.com/post.php?story=20200420091917110, accessed 16 June 2020.

Ajulu R. (2001), "Thabo Mbeki's African renaissance in a globalising world economy: the struggle for the soul of the continent", *Review of African Political Economy*, Civil society, kleptocracy and donor agendas: what future for Africa?, (March 2001) 28(87): 27-42.

Babalobi B. (2019), "Nigeria: why graduates are unemployed and unemployable", Vanguard column, *AllAfrica* (17 December 2019), available at https://allafrica.com/stories/201912240618.html, accessed 17 June 2020.

Brookings Institute (2019), *Africa's untapped business potential*, Foresight Africa series, 11 January 2019, available at www.brookings.edu/research/spotlighting-opportunities-for-business-in-africa-and-strategies-to-succeed-in-the-worlds-next-big-growth-market, accessed 26 June 2020.

Coleman J. and Court D. (1993), *University development in the Third World: the Rockefeller Foundation experience*, Oxford: Pergamon.

Emmanuel E. J. et al. (2020), "Fair allocation of scarce medical resources in the time of Covid-19", *New England Journal of Medicine* 382:2049-55, first published online 23 March 2020, available at www.nejm.org/doi/pdf/10.1056/NEJMsb200511410.1056/NEJMsb2005114, accessed 3 October 2020.

IIOE (International Institute of Online Education) (2020), available at http://en.ichei.org/2020/04/03/international-institute-of-online-education-co-launched-online-to-support-remote-learning-in-developing-countries/, accessed 26 June 2020.

Jowi J. O., Obamba M. O. and Sehoole C. (2013), "Internationalisation, research, innovations and management in Africa's higher education: an overview", in J. O. Jowi et al. (eds), *Governance of higher education, research and innovation in Ghana, Kenya and Uganda. Programme on Innovation, Higher Education and Research for Development (IHERD)*, Paris: OECD.

Kigotho W., Waruru M. and Sawahel W. (2020), "Universities pull their academic weight in fight against COVID-19", *University World News* (23 April 2020), available at www.universityworldnews.com/post.php?story=20200423073646854, accessed 16 June 2020.

Mamdani M. (2007), *Scholars in the marketplace – the dilemmas of neo-liberal reform at Makerere University, 1989-2005*, Dakar: Codesria.

PEBL (Partnership for Enhanced and Blended Learning) (2020), available at www.acu.ac.uk/get-involved/pebl/#:~:text=The%20Partnership%20for%20Enhanced%20and,courses%20delivered%20through%20blended%20learning, accessed 26 June 2020.

UN (United Nations) (2020), Sustainable Development Goals, available at https://sustainabledevelopment.un.org/?menu=1300, accessed 26 June 2020.

Varghese N. V. (2013), "Governance reforms in higher education in Africa", paper presented at policy forum in Nairobi, 16 May 2013, revised and published as *Governance reforms in higher education: a study of selected countries in Africa*, Paris: International Institute for Educational Planning.

World Bank (2020), "Overview", *The World Bank in Africa*, 23 April 2020, available at www.worldbank.org/en/region/afr/overview, accessed 26 June 2020.

Chapter 17

Leveraging the Covid-19 crisis to advance global sustainable universities: re-creation of valuable higher education

Kiyoshi Yamada and Koji Nakamura

INTRODUCTION

At present, the world is facing the effects of the coronavirus (Covid-19), and most countries are taking every step possible to prevent the spread of infection, including suspending economic activities and certain industries. Similarly, at Japanese universities, education and research activities on campus are suspended, and most classes are being conducted online. Since the beginning of the pandemic, we have been making trial-and-error efforts and prioritising "learning security" in an attempt to maintain the quality of education for students. Economic support and other actions have been implemented for students in financial difficulty due to the spread of Covid-19. These efforts in higher education in Japan are still underway to minimise the negative impact on students.

In the future, we will have to tackle the various issues that have become apparent due to the Covid-19 pandemic, such as adapting to a "new normal" and the digital transformation (DX) at the university. We believe that there is no going back to the situation before the Covid-19 pandemic began. It is essential not to take a break after overcoming this crisis but to push forward in the aftermath with the spirit of Build a Better Future, further strengthening realisation of the sustainable university.

In this chapter, we would like to give an overview of the efforts of Japanese universities and consider what universities around the world should do to develop new learning methods that are necessary to survive a post-coronavirus world.

HOW JAPANESE UNIVERSITIES HAVE BEEN RESPONDING TO THE COVID-19 CRISIS

The coronavirus crisis has transformed the way education is accessed for students around the world. According to UNESCO, more than one billion students in preschool, primary, lower and higher education are still affected by school and campus closures (UNESCO 2020). In Japan, the government declared a state of emergency on 7 April 2020 because of the spread of Covid-19. Each municipality responded to the issue by requesting that specific facilities – entertainment facilities (such as bars), schools, sports facilities, theatres, convention and exhibition facilities, hotels, department stores and shopping malls – close or stop operations. This state of emergency continued until the end of May, and then socio-economic activities resumed gradually.

However, the number of confirmed Covid-19 cases in Japan began rising again in early July, mainly in Tokyo and its metropolitan area. In response to the declaration of a state of emergency, most universities in Japan had postponed the starting date of the new academic year from early April to May. Then, many universities adopted measures for restricting access to the campus, with faculty members and administrative staff working in a reduced capacity because the Japanese Government had promoted an 80% reduction in direct social contact as well as shifting all classes, lectures, seminars and on-campus meetings to online platforms. Also, all extracurricular activities for students were suspended due to the campus closure. For everyone, it has been a first-time experience in preparing and creating teaching materials for online classes and academic orientation. Immediately after the start of the online classes, several universities, including Tokai University, experienced an outage with the learning management system (LMS) when students accessed the webserver all at once. However, now they can access the LMS without trouble.

In general, most university classes are held face to face, so online classes are much less prevalent. Therefore, recognition of the importance of online teaching and learning would most likely have been delayed further if the Covid-19 crisis had not happened. We can assume that one of the factors helping universities and colleges to overcome the Covid-19 crisis and transition smoothly to an adequate and qualitative online class environment was the experience of the government and universities in responding flexibly to the Great East Japan Earthquake of March 2011 by changing the start date of the new semester and providing support for study among the devastated students.

As of 1 June 2020, most universities in Japan are providing classes that are either all online or are a blend of online and in-person instruction. According to the Ministry of Education, Culture, Sports, Science, and Technology (MEXT), 95% of national and public universities and 88.3% of private universities offer online classes. Among all universities, 60% conduct classes entirely online and 30% offer blended learning opportunities. Only 10% of universities provide classes entirely in person (MEXT 2020). Tokai University, a private institution, is offering all of its classes online this semester. This was many faculty members' first experience with online classes. They learned about the advantages of online classes – for example, the students can learn in their own room or any other environment where they can concentrate on their study, and both faculty and students no longer have to commute on a packed train. Conversely, faculty members learned about the disadvantages, such as the difficulty of conducting classes that include practical skills, experiments and active learning.

Let us consider the reasons why universities are not able to resume classes on campus by examining the circumstances of the coronavirus crisis at Tokai University.

First, we would like to note the positive aspects of the shift to online teaching and learning. The Standards for the Establishment of Universities in Japan (in Articles 25 and 29) stipulate that the number of credits acquired in online classes shall not exceed 60 out of 124 credits as graduation requirements. As a special exception, to both prevent spreading Covid-19 and ensure learning opportunities for students, MEXT has removed the cap on the maximum number of credits that can be earned through online teaching and learning, subject to strict class attendance verification and submission of assignments. This special exception by MEXT will be effective until the end of the 2021 academic year. Also, many faculty and students felt that they were more active online than in classes in person, with more questions coming up through online chatting.

Next, we would like to comment on the difficulties with resuming in-person classes. The biggest dilemma is class size. First, there are many large classes, usually with hundreds of students, in which it would be complicated to control and prevent infection. Second, many students are staying away from the university and remaining at home, while many international students are still in their home countries, unable to enter Japan because of strict immigration control measures. Tokai University has about 30 000 students on seven campuses across the country, and the Shonan Campus in Hiratsuka, Kanagawa, the university's flagship campus, has 22 000 students. Around 300 of the 1 100 international students have not been able to enter the country.

However, the most pressing reason why universities in Tokyo and its metropolitan area might hesitate to re-open their campuses is that most of the newly confirmed cases of Covid-19 are among young people. In fact, the number of cases in Tokyo was about 1 000 in the week before 11 July 2020, and nearly half of the total cases were people in their twenties (Tokyo Metropolitan Government 2020). As mentioned above, the Shonan Campus has 22 000 students, of whom approximately 15 000 (70%) commuted from Tokyo and its metropolitan area every day (mainly using public transport) before the coronavirus crisis. From the perspective of ensuring the safety of faculty and staff in this challenging situation, resuming in-person classes becomes problematic. Furthermore, we at the university live together with the surrounding community. The university is responsible for considering the impact on the surrounding area and neighbouring residents before making a decision on re-opening the campus.

THE CHALLENGE TO UNIVERSITY REFORMATION: LEVERAGING THE COVID-19 CRISIS

Covid-19 has shed new light on many higher education operations and practices. The crisis has taught us that close person-to-person communication is severely limited in this kind of emergency. Among the benefits of globalisation, dynamic student–faculty–staff mobility across borders and international education and research exchanges with global partners are not possible at this point. We have also seen that international logistics are dysfunctional in emergencies. Previously, we never doubted that in-person meetings, commuting to the office, and business travel and business operation were necessary, but the rapid digital transformation of higher education has caused a paradigm shift.

From the perspective of institutional complementarity, it is difficult to rebuild something when there is no need for change. Major institutional reforms in Japan have occurred only a few times in Japanese history, such as the arrival of the US "Black Ships" in 1853 and the Meiji Restoration in 1868, the 1940s wartime system and the post-war reforms from 1945 (Encyclopaedia Britannica 2020). To move from a conspiracy equilibrium – i.e. Nash equilibrium[68] – to a new one, a "big push" is necessary. This coronavirus disaster could be the big push that opens up an opportunity for reform. If so, we have no choice but to leverage the disruption to create significant change. We believe that is the only way to ensure the coronavirus tragedies will not be in vain. In response, Tokai University has launched the Crisis Leveraged Actions for Revitalization (CLEAR) project, which aims to leverage this crisis to reform previously unchangeable issues in the university. Some changes achieved by the project are described below.

Establishing a smoke-free campus has been a long-standing concern for the university, which has a medical school and affiliated hospitals. By leveraging the strong recommendation by the World Health Organization (WHO 2020), stating that no smoking is an important countermeasure to Covid-19, all seven campuses became smoke-free as of 1 April 2020. As part of the services available for students, faculty and staff members who are unable to enter campus, the university started online counselling, led by the health promotion division, and installed additional electronic books and online databases to support learning and research from off-campus locations. Given that online classes will continue for the foreseeable future, the new LMS server was installed and will not go down even if it is accessed by many people from off campus. Also, the university has been providing approximately US$100 for each student (costing a total of US$3 million) as a request-based grant to improve the learning environment of online classes.

The above examples of changes may be far behind global standards in the view of innovative and cutting-edge universities around the world. However, we believe that a series of small changes will contribute to disruptive creation and transformation, and that faculty and staff will feel a sense of success, which will break through the collusive situation and atmosphere. It will require the entire university to come together to Build a Better Future, along with a pledge not to return to a pre-coronavirus society.

AVOIDING DEVALUATION OF HIGHER EDUCATION: BEYOND THE PROSPERITY OF ICT

In 1996, Paul Krugman pretended that he was living 100 years in the future and looking back at the past century (Krugman 1996). He outlined the "five great economic trends that observers in 1996 should have expected but missed", and one of the trends he stressed was "the devaluation of higher education". Krugman noted that. in the 1990s, everyone believed that education was the key to economic success for both

---

68. The Nash equilibrium is one of the solutions to non-cooperation in game theory. It refers to a situation where each player is maintaining the optimal reaction to each other. In other words, no one is willing to do anything because they have no incentive to change their strategy any further (Chakravorti 2004).

individuals and nations as a whole. A college degree, and maybe even a postgraduate degree, was essential for anyone who wanted an excellent job. However, Krugman predicted that the development of computers would displace many occupations that required a high level of education because more people around the world were able to access computers. Despite this, Krugman noted that in 1996 skilled machinists and other blue-collar workers were in high demand, while college-educated white-collar workers were being fired and their wages began to fall. Krugman commented that fears of a drastic decline in compensation for higher education would lead to a decline in the number of college-educated students, and he anticipated a future in which many institutions of higher education would not survive.

Let us translate Krugman's predictions into the present. If universities are simply places to provide knowledge and information, will people still come to traditional universities with high tuition fees and long enrolment periods to compete with the affordable online universities that are spreading globally? During the coronavirus crisis, the University of Cambridge announced that it would continue to offer online classes until the summer of 2021. Both Harvard and the Massachusetts Institute of Technology stated that they would continue to teach online for some time. The US and British university systems have found high value in communal living among people who do not know each other and have integrated it into their education. Having students living together in the dormitory poses a risk of generating Covid-19 clusters, and it is complicated to know how to deal with this while the coronavirus crisis continues.

There is no doubt that fully online classes or blended classes at university will continue for some time during the coronavirus crisis. With online classes becoming more mainstream among universities all over the world, classes may become more efficient, but we are concerned about the uniformity of class content in the future. Thus, we should caution that using information and communications technology (ICT) will turn into an educational objective in itself, rather than into an educational tool. In other words, increasing uniformity will raise the question of offering general education courses on a university-by-university basis. Alternatively, it could be argued that general education classes could be replaced by massive open online courses (MOOCs) or by classes offered by distance learning institutions such as the Open University.

Martin Trow was also worried about the university's ability to sustain itself in a future where the internet would come to dominate (Trow 1999). Again, quoting Krugman (1996), he stated that many institutions of higher education would not survive in this challenging environment in 2096. Krugman guessed that many famous universities would survive, but the role of universities such as Harvard would be transformed into "more of a social institution than a scholarly one" in 2096.

In recent years, Minerva Schools at Keck Graduate Institute, which does not have a campus, has gained the world's attention. Minerva is known as one of the most competitive universities in terms of acceptance. Minerva's students are required to study entirely online and to travel around the world, learning and living together. It is uncertain whether the value of higher education will have declined by the year 2096, as Krugman predicts. On the other hand, it can be presumed that the world's top universities believe that face-to-face stimulus is essential for students' growth. If that is the case, then we should at least avoid the devaluation of higher education for the future, but what should institutions of higher education do to survive?

It is important for faculty and students to cultivate closeness in their learning environment, whether online or in person in class. In terms of realising the depth of learning, it is essential that faculty and students share a unified space, even if it is in an online class. For the sake of becoming a sustainable university, we need to provide an environment in which faculty members and students can explore a sense of intimacy and can easily reach out to living knowledge. It is no longer a world where large universities can continue as before and survive safely. As Salim Ismail, Founding Executive Director of Singularity University pointed out, size does not always work to their advantage, and they could become extinct like the dinosaurs:

> [When] the asteroid of digitized information has hit, the global economy has changed forever. The era of traditional, hierarchical market domination by dinosaur companies is coming to an end. The world now belongs to smarter, smaller and faster-moving enterprises. This is certainly true now for information-based industries, and it will soon be true for more traditional industries as well. (Ismail et al. 2014: 135)

Therefore, it might be certainly a matter of operating the university in the smallest possible segment that can respond flexibly and quickly to cope with changes in any kind of environment.

New knowledge, information and technology are dramatically increasing in importance as the basis for all areas of society. At the same time, the consequences of globalisation, such as widening income disparities, national particularism and Brexit, are becoming apparent. It has also been suggested that the Covid-19 crisis has made each country feel the need to become self-reliant and not dependent on other countries and that this will lead to a further increase in inward tendencies (Word 2020). In the post-coronavirus era, the question will be how universities should address these challenges. To this question, Toshiya Yoshimi of the University of Tokyo pointed out that universities should be "universities for the benefit of global society" (Academist Journal 2018). Assuming that Yoshimi's statement comes true, what kind of knowledge and education should the universities provide? It would be desirable to provide knowledge and education that would make global society sustainable.

Individually, the universities would be better for students and for society if they combined the knowledge they have acquired, the sustainable development goals, because new global efforts to reduce poverty and hunger, improve health, enable equality and protect the earth are needed. We also should consider the role of the university to provide knowledge for the global community and to provide the students with the kind of education and research skills required to address global issues such as measures against unknown infectious diseases (e.g. coronaviruses) and cybersecurity. Also, it will be difficult to prevent the devaluation of higher education institutions themselves unless they improve the appropriate environment of their classes and change both the knowledge acquisition models and the way they educate students, who can create the knowledge required for the betterment of our future. These might be possible answers to Krugman and Trow's concerns and questions.

CONCLUSION: TOWARDS GLOBAL SUSTAINABLE UNIVERSITIES

As mentioned, the Covid-19 crisis has had a profound impact not only on the workings of global society and on the customs and culture around us but also on the very existence of higher education institutions. Even during this coronavirus crisis, the big push of digital transformation has provided an excellent opportunity to change what had to be changed while maintaining the Build a Better Future spirit. Moreover, higher education has benefited from advances in ICT, and has been able to continue to offer online classes and learning opportunities for students. However, if the coronavirus crisis continues for some time, there are some concerns that online classes could lead to uniformity among higher education institutions. Eventually, this uniformity might bring a devaluation of higher education, and many institutions might be unable to survive. To avoid this situation, universities should provide a more personalised learning environment for each student, no matter whether classes are online or offline. Also, universities should offer "living knowledge" while relating to and contributing to global society. These are the keys to the sustainable growth of higher education institutions.

REFERENCES

Academist Journal (2018), "Is the University dead? An interview with Toshiya Yoshimi, Professor of the University of Tokyo", *Academist Journal* (18 October 2018), available [in Japanese] at https://academist-cf.com/journal/?p=8751, accessed 1 August 2020.

Chakravorti B. (2004), "The new rules for bringing innovations to market", *Harvard Business Review*, 82(3): 58-67.

Encyclopaedia Britannica (2020), "Meiji Restoration", *Encyclopædia Britannica*, available at www.britannica.com/event/Meiji-Restoration, accessed 1 August 2020.

Ismail S. et al. (2014), *Exponential organizations: why new organizations are ten times better, faster, and cheaper than yours (and what to do about it)*, New York: Diversion Books.

Krugman P. (1996), "White collars turn blue", *New York Times Magazine* (29 September 1996), Section 6, p. 106.

MEXT (Ministry of Education, Culture, Sports, Science, and Technology) (2020), *Survey on implementation of classes at universities and HEIs in Japan under the COVID-19 pandemic (as of June 2020)*, available at www.mext.go.jp/content/20200605-mxt_kouhou01-000004520_6.pdf, accessed 15 July 2020.

Tokyo Metropolitan Government (2020), *Updates on COVID-19 in Tokyo*, available at https://stopcovid19.metro.tokyo.lg.jp/en, accessed 14 July 2020.

Trow M. (1999), "From mass higher education to universal access: the American advantage", *Minerva*, 37(4): 303-28.

UNESCO (2020), *COVID-19 impact on education*, available at https://en.unesco.org/covid19/educationresponse, accessed 11 July 2020.

WHO (World Health Organization) (2020), *Smoking and COVID-19*, available at www.who.int/news-room/commentaries/detail/smoking-and-covid-19, accessed 15 July 2020.

Word J. (2020), "Pandemic is last nail in globalization's coffin, says Carmen Reinhart", *Bloomberg* (21 May 2020), available at www.bloomberg.com/news/articles/2020-08-02/dollar-steady-asian-stocks-set-to-open-mixed-markets-wrap, accessed 30 July 2020.

Chapter 18

Leadership and opportunities for sustainable higher education vis-à-vis the pandemic

Santiago Acosta

INTRODUCTION

The turbulence created by the Covid-19 pandemic has shaken the foundations of our societies. The saying "the only thing that is permanent is change" has become a harsh reality in this globe-spanning disaster. Universities themselves, as an institution, have been in crisis for a long time. Subjected to previously unknown external pressures, they have been relegated to an increasingly marginal position and have been losing prestige in society. As educational institutions, universities are swamped by this disorientation: very seldom do they address education as enabling students to flourish as people, holding a worthy vision of the world, because this requires a solid foundation of what we mean by "human being" that involves definitions that, in the post-truth age, are seen as suspect. Our universities barely educate citizens insofar as local and global citizenship also call for explicit values and attitudes; they merely train professionals. Burdened by multiple tasks and increasingly heavy management chores, universities have been losing more and more autonomy to political powers.

The following is a personal reflection from the Private Technical University of Loja, in southern Ecuador, regarding the impact of the worst crisis humankind has faced for over a century in peacetime. I will attempt to provide insights envisioning a sustainable future for higher education after the pandemic.

OVERALL EDUCATIONAL LOSSES AND OPPORTUNITIES

In a context of crisis, there will inevitably be unfavourable situations and opportunities that unexpectedly unfold. Among the adverse consequences that the emergency has brought for higher education, I feel that two are outstanding:
- ▶ Educational chaos
  Closing higher education institutions has sent millions of on-campus-mode students home, and they were not ready for distance study: 23.4 million

university students in Latin America, meaning 98% of the region's post-secondary students (UNESCO-IESALC 2020: 12). Private homes have abruptly been turned into parents' workplaces and children's classrooms, with all the hurdles posed by households which are not usually well prepared to handle such activities. Nor do families have enough electronic devices for all members' remote work and study, and many homes also lack the connectivity that such a heavy workload requires. These deficiencies are worse for low-income families, so the pandemic has thus intensified existing inequalities (Kanwar and Daniel 2020: 6). The tensions of this situation are aggravated by homework overloads, resulting from the sudden virtualisation of in-classroom teaching. This generates anxiety and exhaustion, deepened when family members lose their jobs: in summary, educational and emotional chaos have invaded millions of students' lives (World Bank 2020: 16).

▶ Open and distance education has acquired a poor image
The educational material that classroom-based institutions have turned into digital form has often used a methodology reproducing regular in-class teaching on online learning platforms. The emergency allowed no time to incorporate virtual teaching methodologies, so synchronous online classes presented by teachers have been predominant. The shortcomings are acute: poor educational design; few virtual learning resources; no adequate tutorial support has been organised, or assistance with solving technology issues; and evaluation strategies are not designed for the new environment (García-Peñalvo et al. 2020: 9). This all results in an educational situation that cannot be called "online education" but only "emergency remote education" (Bozkurt et al. 2020: 2). If users of this kind of educational activity confuse it with actual digital learning, this mistake is terribly negative for the public image of distance education.

Nevertheless, some opportunities have been created for higher education in this new situation, as set out below.

▶ Re-thinking higher education
The educational emergency opens up the possibility to re-think higher education, not only its teaching and learning, but also its higher purpose and its relationship with society: how can we place human beings at the centre of the curriculum? The crisis involves not only public health or economics, but also the social and human domains. Without basic values, shared by all, it is impossible to overcome global challenges. There are also challenges on a personal scale: how to help people live a full life with dignity, so graduates can understand their professional career as a way of nourishing others' lives.

▶ Vindicating the university in society's eyes
I would argue that the university as an institution has begun to recover its reputation in the eyes of public opinion, after losing prestige by forfeiting its dominant position in vocational training and knowledge generation. Universities are rising, in the crisis, to meet their educational responsibility and social mission. Students have not missed out on an academic period. Further, universities have joined in serving the needs of public health; they are, for example, involved in social assistance activities. In Ecuador, universities have provided health personnel, including experts in epidemiology, have given tests to detect the

virus in the hospitals and laboratories, and have provided telemedicine services. They have even organised brigades to distribute food aid.

▶ Revaluing research

It has become evident that only science, seriously pursued, and knowledge generated by research, can overcome the pandemic, so governments and societies at large have regained their belief in research, leading to the expectation that public funding for priority lines of research will resume. This aspect is even more important when contrasted with the wave of fake news on social networks and publications making claims without any scientific rigour. Society's appreciation for serious information, backed by universities' scientific authority, has been revived.

▶ Online education has taken the lead

Distance education, with various names (online, digital, open, virtual), has moved into a dominant position after having been marginal to the educational system for so long, with its validity often questioned. No one could have foreseen this and, though one might argue that this situation is temporary, we know it will not vanish quickly. It is time to prepare for a considerable period of time during which online education and blended education will predominate. Educational institutions will have to make this modality of study normal, by training their teachers, designing their educational activities, improving their technology and incorporating educational resources. Then, when they have achieved all of that, they will have to think about whether they are willing to lose what they have achieved. From now on, it will be hard to argue that technology-mediated learning is second-rate, though this will demand putting in place robust quality-assurance arrangements. Distance-education critics have been silenced by the overwhelming evidence that this modality was able to suddenly take in millions of students and help keep them from missing a year of studies.

▶ Blended education will become mainstream

While online education has peaked in an exceptional manner due to the sudden need to move face-to-face classes online, it is likely to decline as the pandemic recedes. Instead, blended education will predominate over face-to-face teaching if universities are to retain the lessons learned during the crisis. But the challenges posed by this educational approach are especially demanding for institutions with no previous scaled-up experience, ranging from reskilling teachers and supporting students to learning in a more self-regulated way, through to implementing major curricular changes (Lim and Wang 2017).

▶ Strengthening co-operation and association

The pandemic has fostered linkages between schools, to join forces and create relationships of collaboration between universities and the public sector, and to build action fronts to cope with the pandemic. These good practices will surely persist when the emergency is behind us.

A CHALLENGE FOR UNIVERSITY LEADERS

The dual health and education crises have set the stage for university leaders to seize the reins of their organisations and set a clear course going forward. The first reflection must therefore address leadership: university leaders must be clear what needs to be done in terms of inescapable key missions, and they cannot delay institutional transformation. Universities must change, not only because of external pressures, but because reality changes, and these mutations call for responses unlike the traditional strategies. Just as learning cannot be the same as 30 years ago, universities cannot operate in the same way forever.

Although, as suggested above, universities have rehabilitated their image, undermined in society's eyes by factors on which we have scarcely touched, and do not have space to elaborate here, it is also true that universities must take a critical look at themselves for not having been able to act together, with greater weight in society. They have settled for competition with each other to attract more students or a greater market share, and they have not clearly explained to public opinion what they do. We must emerge from the maelstrom of the current situation and make our presence better known to society.

Although leaders must react to the pandemic, they must also adopt a proactive attitude and ask how the social and educational crisis that has led us to the pandemic may become an opportunity to set a new course. This approach will not be easy, because of the complexity of the situation and the hazards looming ahead for universities, especially with funding cutbacks and the confusion engendered by the emergency, which has hindered the search for motivating ideas to move ahead or even adequately identify the problems we face. A leader must combine all these actions: reflecting, discussing, defining problems, finding solutions, making decisions, all without haste, but also without losing the sense of urgency.

What proposals must university leaders make to cope with the health, social, and educational crisis? The following seem to be the most important.

- ▶ Rehumanising education and reorganising ethically
  The crisis has exposed sordid truths about humankind, such as governments' lack of transparency in managing the pandemic; many government officials who are out of touch with the reality of citizens; lack of compassion for the ailing and infirm to the point of stigmatising them; the greed of those who have sought to profit from the epidemic; and so many more. Education must resume its mission of training whole human beings as persons, as local and global citizens, in addition to graduating ethically, technically and scientifically competent professionals. We must teach about living and about living together, returning to the ethical values and attitudes that will make human progress viable.
- ▶ Taking a stance regarding digital transformation
  Leaders must take advantage of this huge experiment that humankind and its own institutions are undergoing by immersing in digital learning. In the eyes of other professional domains (health, journalism, commerce and finance among others), digitalisation of education must earn the respect of academics and policy makers who may still distrust technology-mediated learning. The future of education, even in the classroom, cannot remain unchanged. Hybridisation of learning modes is the future of schooling. Educational innovation must no longer be an individual adventure by committed educators and move on to properly managed institutional projects, allocating resources and measuring institutional impact, keeping students always at the centre.

▶ **Choosing educational quality**
The abrupt transition to emergency remote learning has unveiled a major quality deficit in educational services. We must assess how our offerings have evolved and propose improvements. Quality assurance agencies must develop and implement standards for improvement that do not emphasise punishment for errors, but focus on motivation for ongoing improvement and respect for institutions' autonomy to apply their own teaching models.

▶ **Impact on our local territory**
Universities' responses to the state of exception have reflected the needs and characteristics of each social and geographical context. Not all cities are the same, nor are their interactions with rural communities. Medium-sized cities have more fluid contacts with the countryside. Universities must learn from the crisis that their social commitment lies in helping transform their own local territories, so projects framed within "intelligent cities" and surrounding areas are an ideal channel to project their efforts. Further, it is indispensable for each university to align with productive and social capacities in their own context. If, for example, a specific territory has a culture-related potential, with activities already oriented towards creative industries, what repercussion does this reality have on the university's academic life and societal engagement? Leaders must watch out for such potentially enriching dynamics.

▶ **Influencing public policies**
Governments have been forced to make laws and regulations more flexible to enable a quick reaction to the crisis, both in education and in other realms of life. Ecuador has lived through a decade of hyper-regulation. Now that governments understand that regulatory excess stifles citizens' initiatives and breeds bureaucracy, it is indispensable for university leaders to rise to the occasion and urge policy makers to enact less invasive laws and more streamlined normative frameworks.

▶ **Consolidating inter-university alliances**
During the pandemic, universities have often responded by partnering to join forces, networking with the assistance of their constituency in the field, to expand the effect of aid activities. This good practice must continue so that universities can identify their shared points of interest. Some goals have already been mentioned: achieving legal reforms, working on research projects, helping each other in economic reactivation initiatives. Partnerships will be among universities, but also with other public and private societal stakeholders. This will help weave the social fabric, integrating networks to co-operate through shared values, building trust and commitment towards common social-impact goals.

▶ **Reaching ever-larger audiences**
University actions have repercussions in many of society's most remote places. University leaders are always present in multiple debates about the pandemic's effects and the future vision of a "new normal". This has been because universities have been among the institutions that have most clearly spoken out about the impacts of the crisis. There is renewed interest in hearing scholars' voices. Universities must seize this moment to maintain their presence in the public eye: with families, business, politicians, the media. Our proposals for these outside

players must be grounded in universities' main thrust: building capacities, forging opinion, fostering social innovation, designing pathways for lifelong learning, helping retrain out-of-date professionals, offering proposals for research and training that are innovative for the world of business.
- ▶ Encouraging shared leadership
University leaders have seen that many initiatives to assist society during the pandemic have emerged not from personal decisions, but from different areas in university schools and departments. New leaders have arisen in universities who have demonstrated lofty social consciousness, perseverance in addressing difficulties and commitment to social well-being. These leaders must not be lost in the phase of recovering post-pandemic normality. Such heavy tasks can be dealt with only by "distributed leadership" (Villa 2019: 308): administrators must give new leaders a hearing, give them a chance and dare to let them lead.
- ▶ Pushing for entrepreneurship and innovation
A university that embraces institutional, educational, social and productive innovation will be prepared for a future in which only those who are willing to venture forward and take risks will make any difference. Universities must be enterprising, tapping their innovative capacity and teaching entrepreneurial skills to professional sectors that are lagging behind. Ecuador as a country has a high rate of entrepreneurship, but also a high rate of failed enterprises. If universities do not equip these young entrepreneurs with the entrepreneurial, financial and commercial capacities they need, much of that energy for progress will be wasted and lost, with negative consequences for generating employment and wealth.

CONCLUSIONS

To summarise then, these are my conclusions about the future of higher education after the pandemic:
- ▶ Leadership is the key factor. We are facing the opportunity to re-think universities' mission and our responsibility to each human being and to society.
- ▶ Leaders must help the university community to navigate uncertainty, identify opportunities and turn these into mobilising challenges.
- ▶ We must return to the human being as the focus of education. Without people who have made sense of their own lives and their role in other people's lives, there can be no effective responses to crises.
- ▶ Digital transformation must revolutionise learning in all institutions, and a new hybrid modality must become the norm.
- ▶ Quality control systems must accompany educational change to ensure the system's reliability and equality (Ferreyra et al. 2017: 2).
- ▶ Public policies must underpin all these changes, allowing autonomous universities and social stakeholders to take the lead.
- ▶ Universities must work together and with all societal sectors: partnering, building the social fabric and consolidating local territories.
- ▶ It is necessary to innovate, and promote enterprise with a social foundation.

Universities will themselves choose whether to be left by the wayside or to help shape our future; there is potential that was emerging prior to the crisis, but the crisis has driven this potential to the fore. Without determined leadership, all may be lost for higher education institutions.

REFERENCES

Bozkurt A. et al. (2020), "A global outlook to the interruption of education due to COVID-19 pandemic: navigating in a time of uncertainty and crisis", *Asian Journal of Distance Education*, 15(1): 1-126.

Ferreyra M. et al. (2017), *Momento decisivo: La educación superior en América Latina y el Caribe* [At a crossroads: higher education in Latin America and the Caribbean], Washington, DC: Banco Mundial/World Bank, available at https://openknowledge.worldbank.org/bitstream/handle/10986/26489/211014ovSP.pdf?sequence=5&isAllowed=y, accessed 16 June 2020.

García-Peñalvo F.J. et al. (2020), "La evaluación online en la educación superior en tiempos de la COVID-19" [Online assessment in higher education in the time of COVID-19], *Education in the Knowledge Society* 21: 1-26.

Kanwar A. and Daniel J. (2020), *Report to Commonwealth Education Ministers: from response to resilience*, Commonwealth of Learning, available at https://static1.squarespace.com/static/5b99664675f9eea7a3ecee82/t/5ed626ce9204901023d0a5be/1591092958247/Report+to+Commonwealth+Education+Ministers.pdf, accessed 24 June 2020.

Lim C. P. and Wang T. (2017), "A framework and self-assessment tool for building the capacity of higher education institutions for blended education", in Lim C. P. and Wang L. (eds), *Blended learning for quality higher education: selected case studies on implementation from Asia Pacific*, Paris: UNESCO, pp. 1-38, available at https://unesdoc.unesco.org/ark:/48223/pf0000246851, accessed 28 July 2020.

UNESCO-IESALC (2020), *Informe COVID-19 y educación superior: De los efectos inmediatos al día después. Análisis de impactos, respuestas políticas y recomendaciones* [COVID-19 and higher education report: from immediate effects to the day after. Impact analysis, policy responses and recommendations], available at www.iesalc.unesco.org/wp-content/uploads/2020/05/COVID-19-ES-130520.pdf, accessed 20 June 2020.

Villa A. (2019), "Liderazgo: una clave para la innovación y el cambio educativo" [Leadership: a key to innovation and educational change], *Revista de Investigación Educativa*, 37(2): 301-26.

World Bank (2020), *COVID-19: Impacto en la educación y respuestas de política pública* [COVID-19: shocks to education and public policy responses], New York: World Bank Group, available at http://pubdocs.worldbank.org/en/143771590756983343/Covid-19-Education-Summary-esp.pdf, accessed 20 June 2020.

Chapter 19

American higher education: rescuing democracy's purpose and policies

Martha J. Kanter and Carol Geary Schneider

INTRODUCTION

On 29 April 2009, ministers from the then 46 countries of the Bologna Process affirmed that colleges and universities should

> have the resources to continue to fulfil their full range of purposes such as preparing students for life as active citizens in a democratic society; preparing students for their future careers and enabling their personal development; creating and maintaining a broad, advanced knowledge base and stimulating research and innovation. (Bologna Process 2009, para. 4)

Today, as a pandemic sweeps across the globe, democracy itself is under siege. Citizens in all countries must rally to ensure its survival, vitality, justice and capacity to solve society's urgent and often tragic problems. As cultural anthropologist Morgan Liu wrote:

> Democracy simply does not make sense to many people in the world today. For those living outside of north Atlantic countries, there appears to be a limit to what a democratic political system can accomplish in addressing their societies' deepest problems, founded on systemic inequality and injustice. (Liu 2017)

Higher education cannot alone rebuild citizens' broken faith in the promise of democracy. But – in partnership with the wider community – it has a critical role to play.

We know from decades of deep experience that solutions to big challenges always are enacted in particular societal contexts. Accordingly, while we embrace the larger goal of renewing democracy addressed in this book, we explore the meaning of that goal in the arena we know best: US democracy and American higher education.

In the United States, no problem is more urgent than closing the historic race, class and income divides that have engendered suspicion, fear, violence and even a presidency marked by deliberate fomenting of racial, ethnic and cross-border hostility. US disparities were deepened by the pandemic but long pre-dated it.

Further, US students and their families are burdened with more than $1.5 trillion in college debt (Looney et al. 2020), and with millions reeling from a battered economy, most Americans are struggling to find everyday solutions to the many challenges they face. We see a growing danger: can the US uphold a sacred element central to its historic vision and values as a democratic society where everyone with ability and drive can prosper, not only those with privilege?

Collectively, these issues have become what we call "fierce urgencies" for US democracy. This chapter explores the role US higher education should play in building new capacity to solve these fierce urgencies and create a more just, inclusive and globally responsible democracy.

In this US context, we see two overarching higher education pathways for rescuing and re-engaging with democracy's fundamental purpose – creating a society in which all are respected, all have access to political and social power and citizens themselves provide guidance on key issues to their legally elected governments.

▶ Pathway 1: The College Promise movement
Making college[69] universal, freely available and affordable for all who seek it, not just those who can afford it.

▶ Pathway 2: The Democracy Learning movement
Providing all learners with a robust, civic-enabling and problem-engaged post-secondary education.

Each of these pathways has gained widespread reach and momentum. The College Promise movement has been embraced in many communities and states and has made its way into pending federal legislation (U.S. House of Representatives 2019). The Democracy Learning movement is our simplified title for a broad array of civic-enabling educational reforms that also are moving forward.

▶ Connecting the Pathways
Educators and policy leaders should work to align and interconnect College Promise and Democracy Learning.

In what follows, we describe defining themes in each movement. After examining the available resources for a rededication to democracy learning, we propose near-term and longer-term initiatives to bring the two movements together as dynamic and mutually reinforcing catalysts for democratic rescue and renewal.

PATHWAY 1: THE COLLEGE PROMISE MOVEMENT – MAKING COLLEGE UNIVERSAL, FREELY AVAILABLE AND AFFORDABLE FOR ALL

Building cohesive, inclusive communities that ensure a quality education for all, from birth through college and life, should be a top priority for every democratic country. Yet the exponential growth of the rich, at the expense of millions in poverty, has left large swaths of the country impoverished, drastically undereducated and isolated in what are frequently referred to as America's education deserts. Further, 99% of

---

69. "College" in the US generally means post-secondary education beyond high school; it may include two years at an American community college and/or up to four years at an American college or university.

new US jobs will require an education beyond high school. Yet labour economist Anthony Carnevale and colleagues report that the US has not supplied the talent pipeline prepared for America's workforce: on average only half of US undergraduates complete their tertiary studies in six years or less (Carnevale et al. 2016). The US has a long road ahead to build equitable access to quality college learning for all.

But even as the federal government stalls on making college affordable and equitable, many US communities and states are pointing the way towards new solutions. Today, the College Promise movement – often referred to as "free college" – is rapidly gaining ground, especially for students and communities that have long seen higher education as unattainable (Millett et al. 2020).

Until the Second World War, US colleges served only a privileged minority. In 1940, only 4.6% of Americans had earned a bachelor's degree (U.S. Census Bureau 2016). With the 1944 passage of the GI Bill (U.S. Department of Defense 2019), the Civil Rights Act of 1964 (Wilkins et al. 2014) and the authorisation (Johnson 1965) and subsequent reauthorisations of the Higher Education Act of 1965 (Public Law 89-329), the US made valiant efforts "to strengthen the educational resources of our colleges and universities and to provide financial assistance for students in postsecondary and higher education" (AACRAO 2020).

Nonetheless, college completion today remains highly stratified by race and income, with many students of colour and low-income learners remaining far behind their peers in degree attainment (Ma et al. 2019). Responding to this problem, a unique grassroots solution has emerged: the College Promise movement.

In 2009, US President Barack Obama set a North Star goal[70] for the nation to have "the best educated, most competitive workforce by the year 2020" (White House 2009). In 2015, President Obama announced America's College Promise to make the first two years of college free for students attending an American community college (White House 2015), followed by legislation to enact his proposal (Baldwin et al. 2015).

A divided government halted federal-level progress toward this College Promise goal. But communities and states moved forward to tackle the problem of putting college within reach. The College Promise Campaign, a new non-profit, non-partisan organisation independent of the federal government, was established and led by Dr Jill Biden, then Second Lady of the US and Northern Virginia Community College professor, and the Honourable James Geringer, former Governor of Wyoming, who led his state to ensure sustainable "Promise" scholarship funding (College Promise 2016).

At that time, 53 communities had already launched College Promise programmes to give hardworking students Promise scholarships, mentors and community service opportunities to pursue higher education (ibid.). In 2014, Governor William Haslam put the Tennessee Promise in place, providing a national example for state-wide action (ibid.: 6).

As often happens in the US, a diversity of programmes grew exponentially over the next five years. College Promise, the Washington DC organisation that serves

---

70. A big, lofty goal that requires great collective efforts.

as the national clearing house and systems integrator for these programmes, now supports 326 Promise programmes in 47 states, and 29 state-wide Promise programmes (College Promise 2019).

While there is no standard Promise, just as there is no standard US college or university, all share common goals and features. To put a College Promise in place, an institution, community and/or state adopts a public assurance (e.g. legislation, executive order, local policy or regulation) to make one to four years of college tuition-free for every eligible student advancing on the path to earn a college degree, a certificate and/or credits that transfer to a four-year university programme (ibid.: 5).

Beyond tuition, many College Promise programmes fund college fees and provide increased student support (e.g. mentors, advisers, community service and internship opportunities), making the first two or more years of college – at a minimum – as universal, free and accessible as public high school (Kanter and Venkatasen 2020). Most students meet a minimum Grade Point Average, complete an application for federal and state scholarship aid and remain in good standing each year while receiving Promise funds.

The majority of College Promise programmes share these characteristics:

- place-based: a college, city, region, or state;
- guaranteed financial support for college;
- wrap-around student supports;
- evidence- and performance-based;
- financially sustainable;
- cross-sector, sustainable leadership (Kanter 2019).

Led in many regions by America's colleges and universities in partnership with community leaders, residents and public and private organisations, the College Promise movement criss-crosses US cities and towns from west to east and from north to south (Miller-Adams 2019).

Today, the grassroots College Promise movement is ripe and ready for national policy leadership, girded with a wealth of research and policies to make its case for greater impact. Bipartisan leaders have recently proposed a federal–state partnership (Hoagland et al. 2020) to build a better educated, workforce-prepared America and to help reduce historical inequality and inequities in education.

PATHWAY 2: THE DEMOCRACY LEARNING MOVEMENT – PROVIDING ALL LEARNERS WITH A ROBUST, CIVIC-ENABLING AND PROBLEM-ENGAGED POST-SECONDARY EDUCATION

Making college affordable is necessary but insufficient for building US capacity to tackle democracy's "fierce urgencies". It is by no means a given that merely completing a US college degree (even with College Promise support) will in fact result in a generation ready to help create solutions to democracy's difficult and long-entrenched disparities (Finley 2012). Many students choose programmes of study that devote no time at all to any aspect of democracy inquiry, whether in the US context or in the larger context of global interdependence.

Indeed, in a series of 2004 focus groups conducted for the Association of American Colleges and Universities (AAC&U), college students and college-bound students ranked civic learning as one of their lowest priorities for higher education (Hart Research Associates 2004). Multiple surveys by the Annenberg Public Policy Center are consistent with these findings (Annenberg Public Policy Center 2019). In a recent analysis of needed college learning, former Harvard President Derek Bok synthesised a wealth of evidence showing young Americans' – including college-educated Americans' – political disengagement and even cynicism (Bok 2020: 23-4).

Most students' primary goal for college going is gaining access to good jobs. But it should not be an either/or choice between career preparation on the one hand and education for democracy learning and engagement on the other. As the leading American scholar of the connections between education and employment has found, the best preparation for career success combines broad general education (i.e. study across multiple disciplines) with specialised learning, not specialisation alone (Carnevale et al. 2020: 3). Broad multidisciplinary learning, as we explain below, is also a key to the democracy preparation and learning that students should acquire in college.

To play its part in the renewal of US democracy, American higher education needs to ensure that democracy-engaged studies become a core component of all students' college learning, rather than an option that many students readily avoid. The democracy learning we envision engages students directly with issues of democracy's principles and practices, with some of the "fierce urgencies" that Americans face as a multicultural society riven by deep inequities, and engages them with active experience in the hard work of collaborative civic problem solving.

This may seem a large agenda, but work on making democracy learning expected rather than optional in higher education has in fact already begun (Schneider 2017).

In what follows, we briefly review the resources the United States already has in hand for providing every college student with robust preparation for civic inquiry and democratic engagement. We then propose near-term and longer-term efforts to bring the College Promise and Democracy Learning movements together.

RESOURCES IN HAND FOR A REDEDICATION TO DEMOCRACY LEARNING

We can summarise the existing resources in five main areas.

1. US higher education's deep-rooted commitments to the civic mission, including:
   - ▶ A founding affirmation – promoted since the first decades of the US Republic – of the integral connections between higher education and the leadership needed to sustain a self-governing democracy;
   - ▶ A long history of re-affirming those integral connections at pivotal turning points in US history (see National Task Force 2012). To illustrate: after the searing destruction of the Second World War, President Truman's 1947 Commission on Higher Education issued a six-volume report which affirmed

"a fuller realisation of democracy" and the building of international co-operation as higher education's highest goals (President's Commission on Higher Education 1947, Vol. 1: 6).

2. US higher education's pervasive embrace of general education requirements intended – at least in theory – to provide the broad learning needed for informed citizenship:

- ▶ US higher education has long required general education studies to provide the big picture knowledge – of science, history, humanities, arts, social systems and global interdependence – that citizens need. The Truman Commission reaffirmed general education as the locus for democracy learning;
- ▶ In 2020, the seven major US accrediting associations for colleges, community colleges and universities include a purposeful general education programme in their required standards for quality learning (Council of Regional Accrediting Commissions 2016). Accreditation is mandatory for access to federal funding.

3. A 21st century do-over or restart for general education, now in the making and potentially poised for new democracy learning focus:

- ▶ A 21st century redesign of general education is underway across many colleges and universities (AAC&U 2015; Hart Research Associates 2016) and even in entire state systems of public universities such as that of Georgia (University System of Georgia 2019).
- ▶ The new designs typically emphasise three features, namely 21st century skills such as evidence-based analysis that are crucial to democratic problem solving (as well as career success); thematic pathways that feature cross-disciplinary examination of crucial societal questions such as race and health or global warming; and learning by doing, including service learning, community-based projects and other strategies for connecting knowledge to real-world problems (Wilson et al. 2017; Schneider 2017; Schneider 2020).
- ▶ If deliberately connected to civic engagement and democracy's "fierce urgencies", these general education redesigns are poised to update and revitalise the civic purposes long claimed as a primary rationale for US general education requirements.

4. Racial, ethnic, labour and social justice scholars and programmes well established across US higher education and in general education requirements:

- ▶ Since the 1960s, creative scholars and activists have established new fields of study to explore different groups' struggles for societal power and justice and to probe the deep fissures – such as structural racism and xenophobia, or the failure to provide workers with a living wage – that still impede societal efforts to create a fully inclusive multicultural democracy. These "new academy" programmes have pioneered civic problem-solving partnerships with the wider community. Undergraduate students engaged in these programmes help co-create solutions to a wide range of "fierce urgencies" (Minnich 1995).
- ▶ Early on, social justice educators recognised general education as a way to engage educated Americans with democracy's ongoing quests for inclusion and justice. By 2015, the majority of US higher education institutions already

required some version of diversity studies – often in general education (Hart Research Associates 2016).

▶ In July 2020 the nation's largest public higher education system, the California State University (CSU), added an ethnic studies/social justice requirement to its general education requirements (Los Angeles Times 2020). Diversity requirements established elsewhere in earlier eras will likely be updated soon to deal with Americans' "racial reckoning" and the nation's unfolding history as a multiracial democracy in which white people no longer are a majority.

5. *A crucible moment: college learning and democracy's future* (National Task Force 2012) is a 21st century framework for democracy learning developed and endorsed by civic-minded educators across the US.

▶ Federally commissioned and widely influential, the 2012 report *A crucible moment: college learning and democracy's future* called for civic learning in school and college to become expected rather than optional and provided a civic learning framework covering civic knowledge, civic skills, civic values and direct participation – i.e. learning by doing – in collective civic problem solving (see Appendix).

▶ Concurrent with publication of *A crucible moment*, a dozen major higher education organisations joined forces as the Civic Learning and Democratic Engagement network (CLDE) to help advance the key recommendations in the report (AAC&U 2019; AAC&U 2020).

▶ Collectively CLDE members already have developed civic learning curricula and co-curricula – in general education and many college majors – for community colleges, public and private colleges and universities and students from low-income communities. Many also have worked on advancing civic problem-solving partnerships between higher education and communities (AAC&U 2020).

The list above is necessarily abbreviated but our core point is simple. US higher education already is poised to help repair and renew US democracy by braiding democracy learning, including engagement with myriad "fierce urgencies", directly into the fabric of college degrees. Higher education's impact would be strengthened if the College Promise and the Democracy Learning movements were to make common cause.

CONNECTING THE PATHWAYS

We need to bring the College Promise and Democracy Learning pathways together – to increase societal equity and fuel civic problem solving.

Efforts to make higher education more equitably affordable have found a national megaphone. "Free College" became a rallying cry in the 2020 political campaigns, with media and students themselves further amplifying the call. America's College Promise legislation (U.S. House of Representatives 2019) was re-introduced in 2019 for a federal–state partnership with federal funding, creating incentives for states to enact their own Promise reforms.

As this legislation is considered, our top recommendation is that higher education leaders take bold steps to bring College Promise and Democracy Learning reforms together. We propose a new determination that everyone who benefits from College Promise support should devote part of their studies to democracy learning and civic problem solving.

Steps to take in the near term

In the near term, we ask educators and community partners promoting College Promise programmes to incorporate specific Democracy Learning expectations into their criteria for College Promise support.

As explained above, general education is already a requirement in most accredited two-year (community college) and four-year (college and university) institutions. Aligning with this well-established US educational practice, College Promise programmes can stipulate that, in meeting their institution's general education requirements, students should complete courses that engage them with:

- the workings and future of US democracy, including the ongoing efforts to create a more just and inclusive society;
- world cultures and global interdependence; and
- a significant experience in learning by doing, in partnership with an agency or organisation working to solve significant public problems.

Options for meeting these expectations are already available at virtually every two- and four-year institution. Advisers can help Promise students find them.

Some College Promise programmes already require students to engage in public service. But to our knowledge, none has yet asked College Promise beneficiaries to combine public service with intentional study concerning democracy's future in the US and abroad, or with active work on the "fierce urgencies" now roiling democracy both at home and in the wider world. The US can rededicate itself to its founding principles by asking students themselves to explore the meaning, application and future of these fierce urgencies.

Steps to take in the longer term

For the longer term, a more ambitious and ongoing alignment of College Promise and Democracy Learning reforms is needed. While higher education is in the midst of curriculum pathway redesigns, as discussed above, the reforms are moving forward too slowly and too unevenly. Concerted and ongoing leadership is needed to dramatically accelerate the pace and reach of these educational redesigns.

Concurrently, many policy leaders have already recognised the need for new funding models for US higher education. The pandemic, which has plunged both public and private higher education into fiscal crisis, now makes financing redesigns an immediate priority. It is critical that financing redesigns move forward in tandem with the ongoing curriculum pathway redesign. The last thing the US needs are new financial models for an old, outdated, democracy-optional college curriculum, or (worse) new financial models that foreground job-skills-only, democracy-discarded approaches to college learning.

US democracy needs new financing models for curriculum pathways that position graduates as inventive problem-solvers, ready to work on democracy's fierce urgencies and well prepared for a fast-changing economy. In the US, successful leadership for change always bubbles up from the grassroots, until what once was peripheral becomes a new frontier. The College Promise and the Democracy Learning movements exemplify this dynamic.

That said, the US now needs a catalytic agency that can distil the change energy rising from the grassroots and propel the new designs for college financing and democracy-engaged learning to become the reigning standard for good practice. This catalytic agency should be freed from the yin and yang of political infighting.

Our proposal for the longer term, therefore, is the creation of an independent and ongoing Democracy's Promise Trust to provide high-profile leadership for systemic educational redesign, new curriculum pathways and new financial models, including no-debt financing strategies for US learners.

The Trust would be charged with and funded for working in coalition with the full array of higher education influencers – institutional membership associations, faculty associations, accreditors, policy leaders at the federal and state levels, business and civic leaders, school leaders and students themselves. Sustainable financing for the Trust would come from government matched by civic-minded philanthropies, business and civic organisations committed to educational innovation and reform.

The Democracy's Promise Trust would first update and then help enact the Framework for Twenty-First Century Civic Learning and Democratic Engagement that was created in 2012 by the federally commissioned National Task Force that produced the report *A crucible moment: college learning and democracy's future* (see Appendix for framework).

The update would address learning related to US democracy's racial and inequity reckonings, and the rise of authoritarian movements across the world. The framework would be applied, as the authors of the report intended, at all levels, from school through higher education, including general education and college majors (National Task Force 2012: 26-30).

A second task would be a creative examination and redesign of how schooling at all levels should be financed in the US, undertaken with the goal of providing new resources to the nation's education deserts, new investments and guidelines for quality learning at all levels and new strategies for making access to quality and democracy-enabling learning affordable for all Americans, not just the fortunate few.

If higher education is to help create a more just and equitable democracy, its fiscal and educational practices must be reinvented. That re-invention should not be siloed but should facilitate equity and democracy-enabling reforms at all educational levels. The Democracy's Promise Trust we propose is intended to guide, align and urge those needed reinventions.

LIFTING AMERICA'S SOUL

In sum, we humbly and boldly offer a local–state–federal policy partnership that integrates the College Promise and Democracy Learning movements, spurred by a widespread call to action to advance the priorities and solution described in this chapter. We see this as one of several rescues for our democratic society, desiring a full recovery to inspire and sustain our nation's social, civic and economic prosperity, for all of which most Americans long.

Americans have long espoused equality in access to opportunity for all. This remains the essential first step for higher education in our rescue imperative for the 21st century. Getting students through high school and into college is only one step forward. The real question is what knowledge, skills and practical opportunities learners should gain to graduate as civic-minded, solution-oriented adults in a democratic society.

Before his passing in July 2020, Civil Rights icon The Honourable John Lewis told Americans:

> Ordinary people with extraordinary vision can redeem the soul of America … Continue to build union between movements stretching across the globe because we must put away our willingness to profit from the exploitation of others …. Now it is your turn to let freedom ring … When historians pick up their pens to write the story of the 21st century, let them say that it was your generation who laid down the heavy burdens of hate at last. (Lewis 2020)

Looking forward, we envision a new democratic policy partnership that will deliver on the priorities of the Civil Rights Act and the numerous Higher Education Reauthorisations, once and for all. This new partnership will connect, inspire and fund a sustainable College Promise for all who seek new access to opportunity through higher education. And it will provide an unparalleled, high-quality, civic-minded, solutions-oriented, problem-solving, inspiring education beyond high school that will prepare graduates with the conditions so aptly outlined by the Congress and Presidents from 1964 through 2008, by the European ministers in 2009, and by the authors of these chapters.

APPENDIX – FRAMEWORK FOR CIVIC LEARNING AND DEMOCRATIC ENGAGEMENT

Knowledge	
• Familiarity with key democratic texts and universal democratic principles, and with selected debates – in US and other societies – concerning their applications	• Knowledge of the diverse cultures, histories, values and contestations that have shaped US and other world societies
• Historical and sociological understanding of several democratic movements, in both the US and abroad	• Exposure to multiple religious traditions and to alternative views about the relation between religion and government
• Understanding one's sources of identity and their influence on civic values, assumptions and responsibilities to a wider public	• Knowledge of the political systems that frame constitutional democracies and of the political levers for influencing change

Skills	
• Critical inquiry, analysis and reasoning	• Quantitative reasoning
• Gathering and evaluating multiple sources of evidence	• Seeking, engaging with and being informed by multiple perspectives
• Written, oral and multi-media communication	• Deliberation and bridge building across differences
• Collaborative decision making	• Ability to communicate in multiple languages

Values	
• Respect for freedom and human dignity	• Empathy
• Open-mindedness	• Tolerance
• Justice	• Equality
• Ethical integrity	• Responsibility to a larger good

Collective Action	
• Integration of knowledge, skills and examined values to inform actions taken in concert with other people	• Navigation of political systems and processes, both formal and informal
• Moral discernment and behaviour	• Compromise, civility and mutual respect
• Public problem solving with diverse partners	

Source: The National Task Force on Civic Learning and Democratic Engagement (2012), *A crucible moment: college learning and democracy's future*, Washington, DC: AAC&U, p. 4. The report *A crucible moment* was commissioned by the U.S. Department of Education and developed in concert with K-16 educators, civic organisation leaders and research scholars from all parts of the United States.

REFERENCES

AAC&U (Association of American Colleges and Universities) (2015), *General education maps and markers: developing meaningful pathways to student achievement*, Washington, DC: AAC&U.

AAC&U (2019), National Civic Learning and Democratic Engagement Network [webpage], available at www.aacu.org/crucible/action-network, accessed 19 August 2020.

AAC&U (2020), "A crucible moment: college learning and democracy's future: how the National Report has spurred action 2012–2020", Washington, DC: AAC&U, available at www.aacu.org/sites/default/files/files/crucible/CrucibleUpdate2016_0.pdf, accessed 18 August 2020.

AACRAO (American Association of Collegiate Registrars and Admissions Officers) (2020), *Higher Education Act*, available at www.aacrao.org/advocacy/issues/higher-education-act, accessed 30 July 2020.

Annenberg Public Policy Center (2019), *Annenberg civic knowledge survey*, Philadelphia: University of Pennsylvania, available at www.annenbergpublicpolicycenter.org/political-communication/civics-knowledge-survey/, accessed 20 August 2020.

Baldwin T., Booker C. and Scott B. (2015), "Sens. Baldwin, Booker and Rep. Scott introduce America's College Promise Act to make higher education more accessible and affordable", Washington, DC: Office of Senator Baldwin, Press Release (8 July 2015).

Bok D. (2020), *Higher expectations: can colleges teach students what they need to know in the 21st century?*, Princeton, NJ: Princeton University Press.

Bologna Process (2009), "The Bologna Process 2020 – The European Higher Education Area in the new decade. Communiqué of the Conference of European Ministers responsible for Higher Education, Leuven and Louvain-la-Neuve, 28-29 April 2009", available at www.ehea.info/page-ministerial-declarations-and-communiques, accessed 19 August 2020.

Carnevale A. P. et al. (2020), *The overlooked value of certificates and associates' degrees*, Washington, DC: Georgetown University Center on Education and the Workforce, McCourt School of Public Policy.

Carnevale A. P., Jayasundera T. and Gulish A. (2016), *America's divided recovery: college haves and have-nots*, Washington, DC: Georgetown University Center on Education and the Workforce, McCourt School of Public Policy.

College Promise (2016), *2015-16 annual report*, Washington, DC: College Promise Campaign.

College Promise (2019), *2018-19 annual report*, Washington, DC: College Promise Campaign.

Council of Regional Accrediting Commissions (2016), *A statement from the Council of Regional Accrediting Commissions on student outcomes*, Alameda, CA: WASC Senior College and University Commission, available at www.wscuc.org/annoucements/statement-council-regional-accrediting-commissions-student-outcomes, accessed 18 August 2020.

Finley A. (2012), "A brief review of the evidence on civic learning in higher education", prepared for the National Task Force on Civic Learning and Democratic Engagement, available at www.cscc.edu/about/strategic-plan/pdf/CivicOutcomesBrief-A.Finley.pdf, accessed 18 August 2020.

Hart Research Associates (2004), "Qualitative research for the Association of American Colleges and Universities: key findings from [6] focus groups among college students and college-bound high school students", Washington, DC: AAC&U.

Hart Research Associates (2016), "Recent trends in general education design, learning outcomes, and teaching approaches", Washington, DC: AAC&U.

Hoagland G. W. et al. (2020), *A new course for higher education – strengthening access, affordability, and accountability*, Washington, DC: Bipartisan Policy Center.

Johnson L. B. (1965), "Remarks at Southwest Texas State College upon signing the Higher Education Act of 1965" (8 November 1965), Austin, TX: LBJ Library and Museum, available at www.lbjlibrary.net/collections/on-this-day-in-history/november.html, accessed 26 July 2020.

Kanter M. (2019), "The college promise landscape: a national perspective", College Promise Programs and Lower-Income Students: Design, Implementation, and Impact Conference of the Federal Reserve Bank of Philadelphia & University of Pennsylvania Alliance for Higher Education and Democracy, available at www.philadelphiafed.org/-/media/community-development/publications/special-reports/college-promise-programs/marthakanter_presentation.pdf?la=en, accessed 26 July 2020.

Kanter M. and Venkatasen A. (2020), "The promise of college: a campaign to open new pathways to the American dream", *Liberal Education*, Winter/Spring 106(1-2), available at www.aacu.org/liberaleducation/2020/winter-spring/kanter, accessed 26 July 2020.

Lewis J. (2020), "Together, you can redeem the soul of our nation", *New York Times*, Opinion (30 July 2020).

Liu M. (2017), "Why does democracy not make sense?", *Huffington Post* (6 December 2017), available at www.huffpost.com/entry/why-does-democracy-not-ma_b_12095334, accessed 18 July 2020.

Looney A., Wessel D. and Yilla K. (2020), *Who owes all that student debt? And who'd benefit if it were forgiven?*, Brookings, Policy 2020, available at www.brookings.edu/policy2020/, accessed 18 July 2020.

Los Angeles Times (2020), "CSU undergrads must take ethnic studies or social justice class starting in 2023", *Los Angeles Times* (22 July 2020), available at www.latimes.com/california/story/2020-07-22/cal-state-passes-ethnic-studies-social-justice-course-mandate, accessed 30 June 2020.

Ma J., Pender A. and Welch M. (2019), *Education pays: the benefits of higher education for individuals and society*, New York: The College Board, Trends in Higher Education Series, available at https://research.collegeboard.org/pdf/education-pays-2019-full-report.pdf, accessed 18 August 2020.

Miller-Adams M. (2019), *What can states learn from local College Promise programs?* College Promise Policy Brief No. 7, Washington, DC: College Promise Campaign.

Millett C. et al. (2020), "Setting the stage: a history and overview of the college promise movement", in Perna L. W. and Smith E. J. (eds), *Improving research-based knowledge of College Promise programs*, Washington, DC: American Education Research Association.

Minnich E. K. (1995), *Liberal learning and the arts of connection for the new academy*, Washington, DC: AAC&U.

National Task Force (National Task force on Civic Learning and Democratic Engagement) (2012), *A crucible moment: college learning and democracy's future*. Washington, DC: AAC&U.

President's Commission on Higher Education (1947), *Higher education for American democracy, Vol. 1: establishing the goals*, Washington, DC: Government Printing Office.

Schneider C. G. (2017), "The equity-minded civic learning all Americans need", *Inside Higher Ed* (25 September 2017), available at www.insidehighered.com/views/2017/09/25/light-charlottesville-colleges-must-teach-civic-learning-essay, accessed 18 August 2020.

Schneider C. G. (2020), "Equity, opportunity, and quality learning essentials (QLEs)", *Change: The Magazine of Higher Learning*, 52:3: 9-15.

University System of Georgia (2019), *Redesigning the Gen Ed curriculum*, video presentation, Atlanta, GA, available at www.youtube.com/watch?v=8E0x64jk8OE, accessed 18 August 2020.

U.S. Census Bureau (2016), *Educational attainment in the United States: 2015*, Washington, DC.

U.S. Department of Defense (2019), *75 years of the GI bill: how transformative it's been*, Washington, DC.

U.S. House of Representatives (2019), *H.R.4674: College Affordability Act*, Washington, DC.

The White House (2009), *Remarks by the President on higher education* (24 April), available at https://obamawhitehouse.archives.gov/the-press-office/remarks-president-higher-education, accessed 30 July 2020.

The White House (2015), *Remarks by the President on America's College Promise*, Pellissippi State Community College, Knoxville, TN (9 January 2015), available at https://obamawhitehouse.archives.gov/the-press-office/2015/01/09/remarks-president-americas-college-promise, accessed 30 July 2020.

Wilkins R. et al. (2014), *Civil rights era (1950–1963) – the Civil Rights Act of 1964: a long struggle for freedom*, available at www.loc.gov/exhibits/civil-rights-act/civil-rights-era.html, accessed 18 July 2020.

Wilson P., Reed S. and Wolfe K. (2017), *Rising to the LEAP challenge*, Washington, DC: AAC&U.

Chapter 20

Romanian higher education facing Covid-19: new challenges for the university–state partnership

Ligia Deca, Delia Gologan and Robert Santa

Higher education has a unique role in any societal or economic crisis. The global Covid-19 pandemic has also demonstrated the need to balance the traditional roles of higher education institutions with their pivotal mission to safeguard our democratic societies. In the spring and early summer of 2020, Romania saw its higher education sector rising to this challenge and providing needed resources and expertise in the fight to save lives and livelihoods. The state–university partnership was a key factor in enhancing the ability of public authorities to deal with the Covid-19 crisis. The article will outline the evolution of the pandemic in Romania and its impact on the higher education sector, detail the response of the academic community and consider the opportunities that public authorities have to support the higher education sector in maximising its potential in times of crisis.

THE COVID-19 PANDEMIC AND ITS IMPACT ON HIGHER EDUCATION

When news coming out of Italy pointed to a surge in the community transmission of Covid-19, the hitherto distant threat became a major topic in the Romanian media as well as among authorities at all levels. The existence of a large Romanian diaspora in Italy meant that the first cases – from Romanians returning home for holidays – were only a matter of time. Hâncean et al. (2020) documented in an article studying the patterns of early transmission of Covid-19 in Romania that this was indeed the case. However, Romania was not alone in this position; February and March saw an explosion in the number of Covid-19 cases across Europe. At this time, over two thirds of higher education institutions in countries surveyed by the International Association of Universities (IAU) replaced most or all of their contact teaching hours with distance learning, primarily using online instruments

(IAU 2020: 23). Romanian higher education institutions were no exception to the trend of replacing direct contact with online learning.

COVID-19 EVOLUTION IN ROMANIA

Romania registered its first Covid-19 case on 26 February 2020: a 20-year-old man who had been in contact with an Italian citizen who had visited Romania a week earlier. Nevertheless, Romanian authorities had started preparing for a potential epidemic as early as 22 January and intensified their efforts once six Romanian passengers from the *Diamond Princess* cruise ship returned home after the entire vessel had been quarantined. This was the first international liner to see intense Covid-19 transmission in a confined space, during its sea voyage and subsequent quarantine in a Japanese port. Over 700 passengers eventually contracted the coronavirus, becoming the first fully tracked population of sufferers. The Romanian passengers ultimately tested negative but were kept in preventive quarantine for an additional 14 days after their return home.

On 28 February, two new cases were confirmed, both persons who had returned from Italy. By that time, 8 231 persons were being monitored at home and 182 were already placed in institutionalised quarantine, after returning from Italy or countries with a similarly high risk of contamination.[71] During the next few days another nine cases were confirmed, and the numbers of those in quarantine and being monitored kept rising as many Romanians residing abroad started to return to Romania, some to seek shelter from rising Covid-19 transmission, others after being made redundant or as part of seasonal migrations (such as in preparation for the Easter holidays).

Restrictive measures were soon introduced. On 8 March, public and private gatherings with over 1 000 participants were forbidden, while smaller gatherings required approval from the Public Health Department.

On 10 March, the National Committee for Emergency Situations decided to suspend the educational process in pre-tertiary education from 11 to 22 March, with the possibility of expanding this measure for longer periods if necessary.

The number of infections started growing after this point: 11 March saw the first positive Covid-19 test for a medical professional, while the number of confirmed patients had reached 139 by 16 March, when the President of Romania announced the enforcement of a state of emergency for 30 days, which would later be prolonged for a further month. During all this period the suspension of face-to-face educational activities was prolonged, without a clear indication of whether pupils would return to school before the end of the school year.

While there was no centralised decision on the closure of higher education, between 10 and 16 March all universities – which were not initially bound by a centralised decision – announced the suspension of face-to-face activities and the switch to online education.

---

71. See www.mai.gov.ro/buletin-informativ-28-februarie-2020-ora-10-00/, last retrieved 28 July 2020.

The first three deaths from Covid-19 in Romania were on 22 March, with cases further climbing during the month of April. At the time of writing in mid-July, there has not yet been a slowdown in the pandemic in Romania, despite a short-lived dip in the average number of cases during May and June. The overall legal framework in place to combat the pandemic during the summer was that of a "state of alert", which was instituted in mid-May.

LEGISLATIVE REACTION TO THE COVID-19 PANDEMIC IN ROMANIA

The legislative response to the pandemic has been complex and gradual. On 26 February the Romanian Government issued a Ministry Ordinance establishing the quarantine conditions for all persons entering Romania from countries or regions with intensive community transmission of Covid-19, while the National Public Health Institute was constantly updating the list of countries considered as "high risk" for contamination.

The suspension of pre-tertiary contact education came on 10 March, and the next day there was a temporary suspension of the export of medicines, medical devices and sanitary materials. A state of emergency was decreed on 16 March, while a Military Ordinance issued on 17 March specified some of the restrictions associated with epidemiological control. Indoor events were severely restricted, while those occurring outdoors were limited. By 21 March limits were placed on travel, especially at night. On 24 March, the third Military Ordinance introducing restrictions was issued. This time, leaving home was restricted to specific activities, e.g. going to work, to a hospital, to the pharmacy or to the closest market for basic-needs shopping or to work. Persons over 65 were allowed to leave their homes only between 11a.m. and 1p.m.. A follow-up ordinance on 29 March clarified that citizens were allowed to leave the house to accompany their pets.

Further restrictions quickly followed, with flight restrictions reconfirmed by the fifth Military Ordinance and with another one instituting a quarantine for the entire city of Suceava and its surrounding area due to intense community transmission of the virus, including widespread contamination in the county hospital. Local lockdowns remained rare for the duration of the pandemic, though on 4 April quarantine was established for the small eastern town of Țăndărei.

While the state of emergency was prolonged beyond mid-April for the duration of one month, it was replaced by a "state of alert" in the middle of May. Some restrictions were gradually eased, with terraces able to open for example (while respecting social distancing norms) and citizens allowed to travel freely between towns. Declarations of intent were no longer needed. The major new public health measure introduced after 15 May was the compulsory use of masks in indoor spaces and public transport. Temperature scans were mandated for shops, though in practical terms (and unlike masks) enforcement of this rule was limited. Schools were opened only for two weeks in June for the students in final years (8th and 12th grade) to get some last-minute recap before their final exams. National-level examinations that facilitate progress to upper secondary and tertiary education were organised with special measures in place, aimed at limiting the risk of contagion. An additional exam date was set at two weeks following the first in order to make sure that students who were either suspected of having Covid-19 or rejected at triage were able to go through national examinations. No cases of Covid-19 were linked to the national examinations.

HIGHER EDUCATION DURING THE COVID-19 LOCKDOWN AND AFTERWARDS

As previously stated, in mid-March 2020 all universities switched to online learning and teaching, just a few days after primary and secondary schools had done the same. Most universities did not have dedicated or custom-made tools for online learning, and teachers often chose individually the specific method of delivery. A wide diversity of tools and platforms were ultimately used: classes were held via Facebook Live, Google Classroom and meetings, Zoom, Webex or other online platforms. WhatsApp and Facebook Messenger, widely popular messenger services for mobile devices in Romania, were often used for bidirectional communication between teaching staff and students as well as for groups of students to communicate with each other. This diversity of tools and instruments was not only evident in different universities, but often within them as well. Individual teachers could use different platforms, making access to online education needlessly complex for students. Practical activities and seminars were replaced by filmed experiments or online discussions, though most universities hoped that after the pandemic such activities would be rescheduled.

Initially, the legal basis for switching to online education was limited in scope, with the exception of the military ordinances enforcing the state of emergency. Within the first few weeks of the lockdown, however, the Ministry of Education facilitated the payment of regular wages for online work (until then, especially in pre-tertiary education, teachers could be paid only for contact hours) and gave the green light for online examinations (both periodic exams and final exams).

Later, as Romania failed to bring down community transmission, the number of activities that moved online increased. Admissions for the academic year 2020/21 were scheduled later than usual to correlate with the organisation of the national examination and moved online, while some universities waived requirements for additional testing.[72] This meant that admission was generally based on the applicants' secondary school average grades and baccalaureate results, plus occasional use of other tools that could be uploaded via the internet (e.g. essays). Exceptions to this norm were medicine and law programmes in some well-regarded universities, which organised examinations under very strict conditions, with the Medical University of Bucharest organising written examinations in the national expo centre, where social distancing could be guaranteed.[73] These moves were unprecedented for Romania, as only pre-admission had ever been organised online before, and entrance exams and testing had often been used as a status symbol by in-demand institutions. Bureaucracy was also reduced, with all necessary documents required for university admission accepted in scanned online versions.

---

72. See http://stiri.tvr.ro/multe-faculta--i-au-renun--at-la-admiterea-pe-baza-de-examen-in-contextul-pandemiei_863937.html#view, last retrieved 23 July 2020.
73. See www.mediafax.ro/social/admiterea-la-medicina-pe-bancile-de-la-romexpo-19441500, last retrieved 27 July 2020.

As of mid-July 2020, there is no comprehensive consensus on how higher education will be organised in the coming academic year. Hopes for a quick restart for face-to-face education have existed since early on in the pandemic but have yet to materialise. As of 27 July, the number of Covid-19 cases in Romania had hit an all-time high, with active cases in all counties.[74]

THE ROLE OF HIGHER EDUCATION IN SUPPORTING PUBLIC AUTHORITIES DURING THE COVID-19 PANDEMIC AND IN SHAPING THE POST-COVID-19 WORLD

Harkavy et al. (Chapter 1 in this volume) argue that the crisis associated with the Covid-19 pandemic opens up the opportunity for changes in society, while higher education institutions alone have the position and resources to shape the post-Covid-19 world due to their multifaceted role in society. As such, universities can and should contribute to developing skilled professionals (especially important in the medical field), sustaining a culture of democracy and fighting the fake-news pandemic. They are sources of new ideas and discoveries, they host cultural centres, foster creativity and "teach the teachers and the teachers' teachers", thus shaping the education system and indirectly the whole of society. Therefore, they have both the context and the instruments to shape the future of the world by educating "ethical, empathetic students for just and sustainable democratic societies".

But will they? This question may be especially pertinent in countries which link public funding of higher education with short-term economic conditions. The next sections of this chapter explore the ways in which higher education institutions were involved in fighting the pandemic, helping society cope with the consequences of Covid-19, and the degree to which they fulfilled their expected role as a bulwark for social progress.

PRACTICAL WAYS IN WHICH HIGHER EDUCATION INSTITUTIONS HAVE STEPPED IN DURING THE PANDEMIC TO HELP THE MEDICAL CRISES

While the education process itself largely observed existing institutional traditions, with the sole (but major) exception of moving teaching and learning online, universities became increasingly visible actors in the fight to keep the Covid-19 virus at bay. The University of Pitești, for example, drew up lists of over 100 volunteers (both students and teaching staff) who agreed to help in local efforts to fight the pandemic. A similar move was undertaken by the University of Brașov, which agreed to send 26 volunteers (medical students) to help in pandemic control efforts. The University of Sibiu also recruited 60 volunteers for activities at the local hospital.

Naturally, universities that encompassed a faculty of medicine or medical universities had a more hands-on approach. The George Emil Palade Medicine, Pharmacy,

---

74. Data on Covid-19 cases as listed on https://coronavirus.casajurnalistului.ro/, last retrieved 28 July 2020.

Science and Technology University of Târgu Mureș prepared a Covid-19 testing facility, offering important support to health authorities at a time when national testing capacity was still limited.[75] The Veterinary and Agriculture University of Cluj also provided three testing stations. Similarly, the Iuliu Hațieganu Medical and Pharmacy University of Cluj-Napoca helped the local Infectious Disease Hospital with five rtPCR machines (the real-time reverse transcription polymerase chain reaction test for the qualitative detection of nucleic acid is the dominant form of testing in Romania for Covid-19), and its staff helped boost local testing capacity and prepared and distributed hundreds of litres of disinfectant. It also helped house doctors and offered space for quarantine facilities, while even providing 200 volunteers for efforts to keep local transmission at bay.

At the same time, the universities of Iași and Suceava offered space for the housing of patients with suspected cases of coronavirus at the height of the outbreak in the city of Suceava, when there was a desperate need to ensure segregation between suspected and diagnosed patients. Furthermore, the local university was involved in research on diagnosis and testing for Covid-19, with some success in improving screening methods.[76]

The University of Alba Iulia and the Vasile Goldis University of Arad also offered support for quarantining suspects. The latter also organised groups of student volunteers to deliver food and medicine to vulnerable persons, notably the elderly. A similar activity was organised by students from the Technical University of Iași.[77]

Other universities used their research and even production capacities to offer resources to local hospitals or to offer information to public authorities. A group of researchers from the University of Bucharest statistically modelled the first 18 days of community transmission, for example, offering information on the path taken by infections. The University of Galați produced disinfectant substances, used within the institution but also available for use by the wider community. The University of Suceava deployed an automated testing line for Covid-19 using internal resources.[78] This was particularly important given that the height of the Suceava outbreak happened at a time when testing capacity was still severely limited.

All of these examples denoted a trend of significant local participation by universities in Covid-19 mitigation efforts. Universities were often well placed to help, having both space and – for those with medical faculties – laboratory equipment, which proved valuable in the fight against the pandemic.

---

75. Source: www.radiomures.ro/stiri/laboratorul-pentru-testele-covid-de-la-umfst-tg-mures-este-pregatit.html?fbclid=IwAR1K7iInhOzm-rY54DYywoiru0nA9i2OBX8t8MGi_iHYes2rKihg0_muBoE, last retrieved 23 July 2020.
76. Source: www.uaic.ro/cercetatorii-uaic-au-descoperit-o-metoda-de-detectie-rapida-a-diferitilor-patogeni-aplicabila-si-pentru-covid-19/?fbclid=IwAR1aQzKaVSF75-c67wshFsNWYNMh-TDcbE3j1vWrvHpEll1lQ5LGODxtS8M, accessed 23 July 2020.
77. Source: www.tuiasi.ro/…/studentii-universitatii-tehnice-or…/, last retrieved 23 July 2020.
78. Source: www.mediafax.ro/social/orasul-din-tara-care-a-implementat-o-linie-semi-automata-de-testare-pentru-coronavirus-pana-la-200-de-persoane-vor-putea-fi-testate-zilnic-19002096; last retrieved 23 July 2020.

HIGHER EDUCATION INSTITUTIONS' SUPPORT IN SAFEGUARDING DEMOCRACY AND FIGHTING THE FAKE-NEWS PANDEMIC DURING THE COVID-19 CRISIS

The previous section highlighted the efforts by higher education institutions to support the Romanian response to the Covid-19 pandemic. However, university involvement was not limited to sending volunteers, donating disinfectant and offering space or equipment to the health-care system. During the spring and summer of 2020, higher education institutions also made a unique contribution in countering the fake news pandemic. They did so by organising online debates on the phenomenon of fake news, on how to identify false or distorted information and on how to fight against the phenomenon, especially in such difficult times when emotionally driven responses tend to prevail. The University of Bucharest[79] and West University of Timișoara[80] were among the first to do so, while experts on this subject from the National School of Political and Administrative Studies (SNSPA)[81] were constantly active on national television explaining the phenomenon to the general public.

HOW CAN PUBLIC AUTHORITIES AID UNIVERSITIES IN ADAPTING TO THIS AND POTENTIAL FUTURE PANDEMICS?

As of July 2020, the immediate future of higher education in Romania is difficult to predict, as the number of positive Covid-19 cases is rising, and a second wave of the pandemic seems to be hitting the country. Therefore, preparing for several potential scenarios is the best thing higher education institutions can currently do. Some scenarios discuss blended learning, while others focus on continuing online education. The optimistic ones even envisage resuming face-to-face education. Regardless of how the situation develops, institutions need increased support from the Ministry of Education and other public authorities in order to operate effectively. Support could take the form of grants that will help universities invest in the infrastructure needed for a potential switch to online learning (e.g. for the acquisition of the necessary equipment for both academic staff and students), facilitated access to European funds for training academic staff in designing their teaching and learning processes to be adapted to online/distance/blended learning or changes in the legal framework to allow for online learning.

Developing mentoring schemes in order to enhance digital skills for both students and academics is also essential. In Romania, as a country where distance learning was the source of talk of "diploma mills" in the 1990s and early 2000s, moving back

---

79. Source: University of Bucharest debate on fake news, available at https://unibuc.ro/fakenews-rational-vs-emotional-cu-filosoful-sorin-costreie-si-psihologul-dragos-iliescu/; last retrieved 23 July 2020.
80. Source: West University of Timișoara debate on fake news, available at www.facebook.com/uvtromania/photos/a.295400520502774/2178480408861433/?type=1&theater; last retrieved 23 July 2020.
81. See www.mediafax.ro/marius-tuca-show/alina-bargaoanu-snspa-la-marius-tuca-show-despre-cum-ne-ferim-de-fake-news-trebuie-sa-fim-atenti-ce-prieteni-acceptam-pe-facebook-si-sa-dam-mai-putin-share-19185562; last retrieved 23 July 2020.

to distance education is not an easy proposition, not only due to legal impediments (as the legal framework purposely made distance learning difficult), but also due to lack of digital skills among both students and academic staff, as well as the preconceptions present in society. On 15 July 2020, Eurostat released the results of a 2019 survey of digital skills in the European Union. Romania ranks last, with only 56% of its young people (16-24 years old) having basic or above digital skills, compared to the 80% EU average (Eurostat 2020).

Moreover, there is a clear need for the government to move some administrative processes online. An example is the need to switch to online evaluation for accreditation purposes, so that the quality assurance processes can continue despite the need to ensure social distancing. Another example is the need to enable academics to advance in their careers without suffering penalties due to activity broadly moving online.

CONCLUSIONS

Despite the challenges that the Romanian higher education sector faces, in terms of adequate funding and autonomy, many universities have been instrumental in helping public authorities fight the Covid-19 outbreak. The relatively uniform response of the sector in providing help in facing the pandemic, switching to online education and quickly easing restrictions in their administrative processes, is an indication that academia retains its potential in both traditional roles, such as education delivery and scientific discovery, and in more diversified missions such as countering fake news, capacity building for public authorities and providing general support to local communities. This leads to the need to potentially redefine the balance of institutional autonomy and public responsibility, with a view to maximising the benefits of the partnership between universities and public authorities in times of crisis, but also reinforcing the role of academia in supporting democracies. Judging by the strain that these months of countering the pandemic put on the fabric of our societies, we need all the help we can get to make sure that no resources of any kind are wasted, in order to support our joint sustainable future.

However, the long-term impact of the current health-care emergency on universities and its implications have yet to be established. Was quality affected in a negative way? And if it was, to what extent? Will streamlined administrative processes remain in place after the pandemic? Will the current emergency push universities to digitalise further, for example by providing more online access to books and articles? Many of these questions will be answered in the coming months and years, but it is the opinion of the authors of this article that some of the transformations that have been kickstarted by the current pandemic were long overdue, and need to be retained in order to give Romania a higher education system fit for its multifaceted purpose.

REFERENCES

Eurostat (2020), "Do young people in the EU have digital skills?", available at https://ec.europa.eu/eurostat/web/products-eurostat-news/-/EDN-20200715-7, accessed 20 December 2020.

Hâncean M.-G., Perc M. and Lerner J. (2020), "Early spread of COVID-19 in Romania: imported cases from Italy and human-to-human transmission networks", *Royal Society Open Science*, 7(7): 7200780, available at http://doi.org/10.1098/rsos.200780, accessed 17 September 2020.

Harkavy I., Bergan S., Gallagher T. and van't Land H. (2020), "Universities must help shape the post-Covid-19 world", Chapter 1 in this volume.

IAU (International Association of Universities) (2020), *The impact of COVID-19 on higher education around the world – IAU Global Survey Report*, Paris, France: IAU, ISBN: 978-92-9002-212-1.

Part III

A DEMOCRATIC, SUSTAINABLE UNIVERSITY

Chapter 21

Academic freedom and institutional autonomy: victims of the Covid-19 pandemic?

Sjur Bergan

INTRODUCTION

While at least in a European context, and possibly also in the US context, academic freedom and institutional autonomy have long been taken for granted as part of the basic values of our higher education systems (Bologna Process 1999, 2004), this assumption has increasingly been questioned over the past few years (Bologna Process 2015a, 2015b, 2018; European Commission/EACEA/Eurydice 2018: 41-5). The basic statement on academic freedom and in particular institutional autonomy is more than three decades old (Magna Charta Universitatum 1988). It is also fairly general, and the debate has not halted since the basic text was adopted, including on a possible review of or supplement to the original text, originally foreseen for September 2020[82] but now very likely itself a victim of the Covid-19 crisis, at least in terms of timing.

At the same time, there have been attempts to nuance the understanding of academic freedom and institutional autonomy beyond the traditional focus on the legal relationship between public authorities and higher education institutions (Bergan, Egron-Polak and Noorda 2020) and to examine the importance of these fundamental values[83] of higher education to the development and well-being of democratic societies more broadly (Bergan, Gallagher and Harkavy 2020; Global Forum 2019). The 2018 ministerial communiqué on the European Higher Education Area (EHEA) indicates that

> Academic freedom and integrity, institutional autonomy, participation of students and staff in higher education governance, and public responsibility for and of higher education form the backbone of the EHEA. (Bologna Process 2018: 1)

---

82. See https://eua.eu/partners-news/344-a-new-magna-charta-universitatum-mcu-2020-consultation-open-until-2-august.html, accessed 27 July 2020.
83. For the latest Ministerial statement on fundamental values at the time of writing, see the Paris Communiqué (Bologna Process 2018), third paragraph.

The Covid-19 pandemic brought about major changes to public and institutional policies as well as, in some cases, legislation. For the most part, these changes had to be implemented very quickly, to deal with what was commonly perceived as the most serious global health emergency since the 1918 flu pandemic.[84]

Therefore, it is reasonable to ask what impact the Covid-19 crisis may have had on academic freedom and institutional autonomy. Such an impact could reasonably be expected in three different areas: as part of an overall clampdown on democracy; as a consequence of sweeping emergency measures applied to societies at large; and as a consequence of reprioritisation of learning, teaching and research. The question is not, however, only whether there has been or is likely to be such an impact. If the answer to that question is positive, the follow-up question, which is no less important, must be whether such an impact constitutes an unreasonable infringement.

The article is written from a European perspective, meaning "Europe" in the true sense of the word: the currently 48 countries engaged in the EHEA[85] and the 50 states parties to the European Cultural Convention.[86] To some extent, it takes account of developments in other parts of the world, in particular North America, but it does not pretend to offer a global perspective.

THE PANDEMIC AS A THREAT TO DEMOCRACY

The Council of Europe (2020) has stated clearly that the Covid-19 crisis must not be allowed to turn into a crisis of democracy. This aspiration is important and reflects the fact that some emergency legislation has gone beyond what can be considered reasonable. In at least one case – Hungary – the legislation introduced to increase the powers of the central government were not limited in time and drew criticism from the Secretary General of the Council of Europe.[87] In other cases, proposed emergency legislation was modified in response to criticism from civil society, including academia (see Gorntizka and Stølen, Chapter 9 in this volume). In some other parts of the world, attempts to reduce democratic space were a stronger feature of the overall Covid-19 response of public authorities. In some cases, such as Hong Kong, legislation introduced during the pandemic drastically curtailed democratic rights, but it is questionable whether the legislation was a direct consequence of the Covid-19 crisis.[88] It can, however, have implications for higher education (Altbach

---

84. The seriousness of the situation was not understood immediately but, when it was understood, public authorities generally acted quickly and with broad public support. The United States, with Belarus and Brazil, was an exception in that there was political disagreement about the reality of Covid-19, with the Trump Administration and many Republican-led states seeking to downplay the crisis and the measures needed to address it. The Swedish authorities chose a different course of action and suffered higher infection rates than most European countries, but this was a deliberate policy choice and not a consequence of downplaying the seriousness of the situation.
85. See www.ehea.info/page-members, accessed 5 October 2020.
86. See www.coe.int/en/web/conventions/full-list/-/conventions/treaty/018, accessed 27 July 2020.
87. For the Secretary General's letter, see www.coe.int/en/web/portal/-/secretary-general-writes-to-victor-orban-regarding-covid-19-state-of-emergency-in-hungary, accessed 27 July 2020.
88. For the changes in Hong Kong, see https://edition.cnn.com/2020/07/01/china/hong-kong-national-security-law-july-1-intl-hnk/index.html, accessed 27 July 2020.

and Postiglione 2020), as already seen with the dismissal of the opposition activist Benny Tai from his position as a professor of law at the University of Hong Kong.[89]

Academic freedom and institutional autonomy are hallmarks of democratic societies (Global Forum 2019), in addition to being essential conditions for high-quality education and research. Societies cannot be considered fully democratic if they do not honour academic freedom and institutional autonomy. Conversely, these fundamental values of higher education cannot be fully operational except in societies imbued with a culture of democracy. The latter designates a set of attitudes and behaviours that enables laws, institutions and elections to function democratically in practice; that accepts that, while majorities decide, minorities have certain inalienable rights; that holds that conflicts should be resolved through dialogue; and that sees diversity as a source of richness rather than as a threat (Council of Europe 2018a, b, c).

This implies that governmental measures weakening academic freedom and institutional autonomy are more likely to be part of measures weakening democracy in a broader sense than aimed specifically at higher education. At least in Europe, this has been the case during the Covid-19 crisis so far (mid-July 2020). Emergency legislation and other measures threatening democracy have not focused solely or even mainly on the fundamental values of higher education. As an example, the emergency legislation criticised by the Secretary General of the Council of Europe, referred to above, had a broad scope and was instituted in a country that had already been singled out for criticism because of its new higher education legislation of 2017, for its attempts to curtail the operation of a specific university and because of its banning of programmes in gender studies (European Commission/EACEA/Eurydice 2018: 42).

It is therefore clear that some measures taken by governments in response to the Covid-19 pandemic have weakened democracy. However, contrary to the situation in the media, for example,[90] it is not easy to identify measures that have aimed to weaken academic freedom and institutional autonomy without attacking other aspects of democracy. This is not to say that the Covid-19 pandemic has not had a political impact on higher education and on the role of universities in broader society, as is the case, for example, in Brazil (Knobel 2020; Leal 2020).

ACADEMIC FREEDOM AND INSTITUTIONAL AUTONOMY UNDER EMERGENCY MEASURES

Higher education institutions operate within a framework established by public authorities (Council of Europe 2007: §7) and are regulated not only through specific higher education laws but also through general legislation (Bergan, Egron-Polak and Noorda 2020; Farrington, Chapter 27 in this volume). General measures as well as specific education measures taken to counter the Covid-19 pandemic can therefore have an impact on academic freedom and institutional autonomy.

---

89. For more on Benny Tai, see www.bbc.com/news/world-asia-china-53567333, accessed 29 July 2020.
90. On media freedom, see for example www.bbc.com/news/world-europe-53531948, accessed 27 July 2020.

As shown in the case of Romania (Deca, Gologan and Santa, Chapter 20 in this volume), higher education institutions shifted from face-to-face to online teaching and learning almost as rapidly as primary and secondary education in response to an overall decision by public authorities to move most sectors of society into lockdown. These measures met with the support of higher education institutions and their leaders, so they were not imposed on unwilling or resisting institutions. Had higher education institutions wished to keep lecture rooms, libraries and other facilities open, however, it is doubtful they would have been able to do so in the face of general public policy – and they would not have acted responsibly had they tried. The example is one of co-operation between public authorities and higher education, but it also illustrates that institutional autonomy does not imply irresponsibility. Autonomous higher education institutions can no more disregard public safety measures than they can disregard general rules and regulations on public accounting or safety regulations for laboratories.

Covid-19 measures have a very considerable impact on the operation of higher education institutions. Whereas, at least as at late July 2020, many countries expect to open primary and secondary schools for the autumn semester, few higher education institutions seem to envisage providing all education face to face. Even more importantly, higher education is highly international, with many more students and staff from other countries than one would find in other areas of education. The travel restrictions imposed by most national authorities in response to the Covid-19 pandemic may limit the possibility of institutions to receive new international students and staff, even if EU guidelines now exempt "third-country" students starting or continuing their studies in the EU in the academic year 2020/21 from the general travel restrictions.[91] At the time of writing, Germany, for example, accepts students from other countries, subject to the quarantine regulations in force for the students' countries of origin, as long as the studies in question are not conducted fully online.[92] The Association of Norwegian Students Abroad provides advice to students whose exchange programmes have been cancelled,[93] which is the case of the majority of Norwegian universities.

Even where students may be legally able to enter a country, they would be faced with considerable practical difficulties, including finding transportation. Air traffic was reduced by up to 95% at the height of the pandemic in Europe and is resuming

---

91. See https://ec.europa.eu/info/live-work-travel-eu/health/coronavirus-response/travel-and-transportation-during-coronavirus-pandemic/travel-and-eu-during-pandemic_en#exemptions-from-travel-restrictions, accessed 27 July 2020. "Third country" is an unfortunate EU term designating a "country that is not a member of the European Union as well as a country or territory whose citizens do not enjoy the European Union right to free movement, as defined in Art. 2(5) of the Regulation (EU) 2016/399", cf. https://ec.europa.eu/home-affairs/what-we-do/networks/european_migration_network/glossary_search/third-country_en, accessed 27 July 2020.
92. See information on the DAD (Deutsches Akademisches Austauschdienst/German Academic Exchange Service) website www.daad.de/de/coronavirus/#2, accessed 27 July 2020.
93. See www.aftenposten.no/norge/i/op4xrV/oeyvind-haugan-skulle-til-usa-for-aa-studere-og-gaa-paa-ski-naa-er-alt-usi, accessed 27 July 2020. See also the overview in the higher education online paper *Khrono* (10 June 2020) at https://khrono.no/slik-forbereder-europeiske-universiteter-seg-pa-hosten/494733, accessed 27 July 2020.

only very gradually.[94] Many prospective international students may also be reluctant to run what they see as an undue risk by undertaking international travel at a time when the Covid-19 pandemic is still not under control and no vaccine is yet available. Even if the risk may be no higher in their intended country of study than in their home country, facing a pandemic in an unknown environment far from their family, and not knowing when and how they may be able to return home, could reduce the pool of potential students.

It therefore seems well established that the restrictions arising from public policy to combat the Covid-19 crisis do limit the ability of higher education institutions to decide freely on key issues like the organisation of teaching and learning or the admission of foreign students. However, it does not follow that these restrictions are unreasonable or disproportionate, in light of the seriousness of the Covid-19 crisis, nor are strong limits on internal and international movement and travel or the right of assembly specific to higher education. All sectors of society face similar restrictions; at least in Europe, higher education is not targeted for political or other reasons. Some adaptations have actually been made to ease restrictions for higher education somewhat, such as the exemption for foreign students from the broader travel ban referred to above.

While face-to-face teaching was discontinued in spring 2020 in almost all European countries, and while it is uncertain at the time of writing when and to what extent it will resume, higher education institutions in Europe were generally free to organise their teaching and learning within the limits on physical presence imposed by Covid-19 restrictions. There was no ban on online classes (even if there may in some cases have been capacity problems), nor were there attempts by public authorities to influence or modify the content of teaching in any specific direction, whereas occasional attempts had been made prior to the Covid-19 pandemic, as seen in the example of gender studies being banned by public authorities in an EHEA member country. Where Covid-19 restrictions made holding exams requiring physical presence impossible, public authorities did not seek to prevent alternative forms of assessment or impose specific forms of assessment.

Overall, therefore, the Covid-19 pandemic undoubtedly limited the ability of higher education institutions to decide key aspects of their mission, including the organisation of teaching and learning and the admission of students. It is, however, difficult to argue that these restrictions were disproportionate in view of the seriousness of the health crisis or that they targeted higher education while exempting most other areas of society.

REPRIORITISING EDUCATION AND RESEARCH IN THE TIME OF COVID-19

Responding to the Covid-19 crisis requires research-based knowledge and understanding, as well as competent staff in many sectors with an education enabling them to understand complex issues and make use of relevant research findings. In

---

94. A daily update on the effects on air traffic will be found at www.eurocontrol.int/publication/eurocontrol-comprehensive-assessment-covid-19s-impact-european-air-traffic, accessed 27 July 2020.

a word, higher education and research are key to the ability of our societies to face this crisis, as they are to our ability to face most other crises.

If higher education is central to our collective Covid-19 measures, what does this mean for the ability of higher education institutions and individual academics to set their own agendas and pursue their own research interests?

Even in normal times, academic freedom and institutional autonomy are not absolute. To some extent, they are a question of finding the right balance between the concerns of the academic community and its members on the one hand and other stakeholders on the other hand. In Europe, it is generally accepted that public authorities have a responsibility for the overall design of the higher education system, including ensuring higher education provision in peripheral areas of the country and ensuring that there is education and research capacity in academic disciplines which the public authorities consider of national importance (Bergan, Egron-Polak and Noorda 2020). Non-public actors will also set priorities for the funding they provide. In the United States, the relative weight of public and non-public stakeholders is different than in Europe, but in both cases the balance between the concerns and priorities of the academic community and those of external stakeholders is a difficult issue that does not lend itself easily to broad generalisation. The issue is compounded by the fact that neither the academic community nor external stakeholders, whether public or non-public, are monolithic groups.

Some broad guidelines can nevertheless be identified. It may be legitimate for public authorities to fund and initiate higher education provision and/or research capacity in specific academic or geographical areas. If a peripheral area of the country has no higher education provision, or if the country lacks competence in a discipline of key importance to its society or economy, the competent public authorities would be acting within their prerogatives if they establish such provision. They would, however, overstep their prerogatives if they sought to dictate the details of study programmes or stipulate desired research results. Public authorities may decide that an outlying area needs a study programme in economics or medicine or that the country needs academic competence in its minority languages and cultures. They would overstep their authority if – in a slightly caricatured example – they were to stipulate that medical research needs to demonstrate that the population in an outlying area suffers no particular consequences of hitherto insufficient health care or that the relationship between minority groups and the majority population has always been harmonious, even if these contentions are not borne out by the research evidence.[95]

Facing the Covid-19 crisis requires not only solutions based on current research results but also considerable new research efforts. All disciplines will not be equally concerned, nor will all institutions be in a position to provide the research. It would be legitimate for public authorities and other stakeholders to encourage and fund

---

95. One example of political concerns over-riding research evidence, albeit not in a democratic society, is the power wielded by Soviet agronomist Trofim Lysenko, who insisted that theoretical biology must be fused with Soviet agricultural practice and was supported in this contention by the Soviet authorities to the extent that scientific debate was muted, see www.britannica.com/biography/Trofim-Lysenko, accessed 27 July 2020.

research projects considered of particular importance in the effort to overcome the Covid-19 pandemic, and to provide funding for research groups that have developed the required competence.

This seemingly obvious statement nevertheless needs to be nuanced. The first nuance is how to balance the need for short-term results and the imperative of ensuring broad competence in the longer term. The short-term concern may dictate concentrating funding and efforts, whereas meeting the longer-term needs may require developing research capacity and study programmes at all levels in several institutions spread around the country.

The second nuance is that of focus: a concerted effort to overcome the Covid-19 crisis and its consequences cannot be too narrowly focused. Epidemiology is an obvious but not sufficient priority. Reconstructing and reorienting our societies in the wake of the Covid-19 crisis will require academic competence in a broad range of academic disciplines, ranging from medicine and natural science through economics and social sciences to humanities and theology. Public authorities, other stakeholders and the academic community and its leaders share the responsibility to ensure that our Covid-19 response is adequate and based on research results.

CONCLUSION

Academic freedom and institutional autonomy are essential to complex democratic societies, yet the finer aspects of both concepts may seem elusive even in the best of times. Defining the basic principles is reasonably straightforward, but spelling out the detailed consequences of these principles is so complex that no definitive answer has yet been provided.

These challenges are compounded by the Covid-19 pandemic and the need for societies to react to it forcefully, rapidly and on the basis of knowledge and understanding of both a hitherto unknown virus and the complex societal phenomena the crisis has unleashed. One of the challenges is the need to base decisions on imperfect information and to make them without anything resembling a firm understanding of what even the immediate future is likely to bring. The contribution of higher education and research is essential to the success of this endeavour, and the quality of education and research – as well as the quality of our societies – will depend on academic freedom and institutional autonomy.

While the Covid-19 crisis has entailed severe restrictions on the activities and decisions of higher education institutions and their members, it is encouraging to see that there have so far been few signs of public authorities seeking to impose undue restrictions on higher education or to single out higher education for greater restrictions than those placed on other sectors of society.

This does not mean there is no reason for concern. In some countries, governments have taken advantage of the Covid-19 crisis to seek to limit democracy. If the Covid-19 crisis were to persist, new ways would need to be found to ensure the free circulation of ideas and, as far as possible, the international movement of students and staff. Not least, devising an adequate Covid-19 response in the medium to longer term requires that all academic disciplines contribute. Public authorities and the academic community share a responsibility for ensuring that the Covid-19 response is strong and broad. As former UK Prime Minister Gordon Brown[96] and many others have said, education and research are no less important to our success in beating the Covid-19 virus than is medicine. If we take this contention seriously, it means we need to continue to be vigilant that academic freedom and institutional autonomy underpin our Covid-19 response in the months and years to come.

REFERENCES

Altbach P. and Postiglione G. A. (2020), "Will new security law prove a turning point for HE?", *University World News* (24 July 2020), available at www.universityworldnews.com/post.php?story=20200724110105165, accessed 27 July 2020.

Bergan S., Egron-Polak E. and Noorda S. (2020), "Academic freedom and institutional autonomy – What role in and for the EHEA?", in Bergan S., Gallagher T. and Harkavy I. (eds), *Academic freedom, institutional autonomy and the future of democracy*, Higher Education series No. 24, Strasbourg: Council of Europe, pp. 41-55.

Bergan S., Gallagher T. and Harkavy I. (eds) (2020), *Academic freedom, institutional autonomy and the future of democracy*, Higher Education series No. 24, Strasbourg: Council of Europe.

Bologna Process (1999), "The Bologna Declaration of 19 June 1999. Joint declaration of the European Ministers of Education", available at www.ehea.info/page-ministerial-declarations-and-communiques, accessed 27 July 2020.

Bologna Process (2004), "Further accession to the Bologna Process: procedures for evaluation of applications and reports from potential new members", Document BFUG B3 7 dated 4 October 2004, available at https://media.ehea.info/file/20041012-13_Noordwijk/79/9/BFUG3_7_further_accessions_579799.pdf, accessed 27 July 2020.

Bologna Process (2015a), "Yerevan communiqué", available at www.ehea.info/page-ministerial-declarations-and-communiques, accessed 27 July 2020.

Bologna Process (2015b), "Belarus roadmap for higher education reform", available at www.ehea.info/page-ministerial-conference-yerevan-2015, accessed 27 July 2020.

Bologna Process (2018), "Paris communiqué 25th May 2018", available at www.ehea.info/page-ministerial-declarations-and-communiques, accessed 27 July 2020.

Council of Europe (2007), Recommendation Rec(2007)6 by the Committee of Ministers to member states on the public responsibility for higher education and research, available at https://search.coe.int/cm/Pages/result_details.aspx?ObjectId=09000016805d5dae, accessed 27 July 2020.

Council of Europe (2018a), *Reference framework of competences for democratic culture. Volume A: Context, concepts and model*, Strasbourg: Council of Europe, available at www.coe.int/en/web/reference-framework-of-competences-for-democratic-culture/context-concepts-and-model, accessed 27 July 2020.

---

96. Gordon Brown was speaking in his capacity as UN Envoy for Education at a webinar organised by UNESCO for the Steering Group for Sustainable Development Goal 4, on 4 June 2020, in which the author participated.

Council of Europe (2018b), *Reference framework of competences for democratic culture. Volume B: Descriptors of competences*, Strasbourg: Council of Europe, available at www.coe.int/en/web/reference-framework-of-competences-for-democratic-culture/descriptors-of-competences, accessed 27 July 2020.

Council of Europe (2018c), *Reference framework of competences for democratic culture. Volume C: Guidance for implementation*, Strasbourg: Council of Europe, available at www.coe.int/en/web/reference-framework-of-competences-for-democratic-culture/guidance-for-implementation, accessed 27 July 2020.

Council of Europe (2020), *Making the right to education real in times of crisis*, a report on the education response to COVID-19, available at www.coe.int/en/web/education/making-the-right-to-education-real-in-times-of-crisis, accessed 19 September 2020.

Deca L.; Gologan D. and Santa R. (2020), "Romanian higher education facing Covid-19: new challenges for the university–state partnership", Chapter 20 in this volume.

European Commission/EACEA/Eurydice (2018), *The European Higher Education Area in 2018: Bologna Process implementation report*, Luxembourg: Publications Office of the EU, available at https://op.europa.eu/en/publication-detail/-/publication/2fe152b6-5efe-11e8-ab9c-01aa75ed71a1/language-en?WT.mc_id=Selectedpublications&WT.ria_c=677&WT.ria_f=706&WT.ria_ev=search, accessed 27 July 2020.

Farrington D. (2020), "The challenges of the Covid-19 pandemic for higher education legislation in Europe", Chapter 27 in this volume.

Global Forum (2019), "Global Forum on academic freedom, institutional autonomy and the future of democracy. Declaration", available at https://rm.coe.int/global-forum-declaration-global-forum-final-21-06-19-003-/16809523e5, accessed 27 July 2020.

Gorntizka Å. and Stølen S. (2020), "University challenge – the role of research-intensive universities in crisis management", Chapter 9 in this volume.

Knobel M. (2020), "Universities have a vital role in fighting coronavirus", *University World News* (30 May 2020), available at www.universityworldnews.com/post.php?story=20200529085010849, accessed 27 July 2020.

Leal F. (2020), "COVID-19 is a wake-up call for Brazil's universities", *University World News* (24 July 2020), available at www.universityworldnews.com/post.php?story=20200724100221821, accessed 27 July 2020.

Magna Charta Universitatum (1988), Bologna: The Observatory, available at www.magna-charta.org/magna-charta-universitatum/read-the-magna-charta/the-magna-charta, accessed 27 July 2020.

Chapter 22

The impact of Covid-19 on internationalisation and student mobility: an opportunity for innovation and inclusion?

Dorothy Kelly

The Covid-19 pandemic will no doubt be remembered worldwide for the enormous impact it has had on numerous spheres of human activity, and higher education is of course no exception.

The pandemic has reminded us all in a very cruel way just how interdependent, interconnected and globalised a world we live in, and just how vulnerable we are. It has also shown that we lack the robust global governance structures and mechanisms we need if we are to face up to extremely threatening global crises such as this. Solutions to this truly global problem have been sought (and sadly often not found) at national level. Much narrative of the pandemic seeks to lay guilt outside national borders, on the Other, once again fanning a xenophobic discourse which we as universities must reject outright and combat. All of this serves to underline how important it is for universities to ensure the development of international and intercultural competences in our students and staff, fully assuming our mission as educators of active, critical citizens, who are aware of the huge challenges of our globalised, interdependent and interconnected society, precisely one of the major aims of internationalisation processes in higher education.

REACTING FAST TO THE PANDEMIC

In the month of March 2020, on-campus universities the world over had to switch practically overnight from face-to-face to fully online learning and teaching. Researchers turned their attention to contributing urgently to the fight against the virus; medical faculties supported overstretched health professionals; student volunteers offered their solidarity in helping vulnerable groups of the elderly or homeless. International mobility programmes were suspended, many international students were repatriated, and international collaboration activities of all kinds were interrupted, modified or cancelled altogether.

In this emergency response, alongside the deep concern for the health and safety of our communities, huge professional challenges have had to be faced: insufficient digital competences, insufficient digital infrastructure and resources for institutions and for individuals, issues of equity in access to technology and through it to higher education, issues of ethics in respecting personal data and privacy, or of reconciling professional and family responsibilities while working from home, among others. But huge opportunities have also been detected: renewed reflection on learning and teaching practices and spaces, reaching distant student populations and thus promoting inclusion, simplifying procedures, introducing more flexible working times and practices, reducing pollution and lowering our carbon footprint, to name but a few. All of this in a disquieting political context prioritising national responses, despite the global nature of the crisis and the need for global co-operation to help resolve it.

UNIVERSITIES HAVE NOT BEEN CLOSED, BUT MORE OPEN THAN EVER

One of the main threads of the media narrative of the pandemic has centred on the concept of "lockdown" or "closure", and now centres on the "road to (new) normalcy" and on "re-opening". While of course it is true that universities around the world have suspended their on-campus activities, in the vast majority of cases the idea that universities have been closed during these months could not be further from the truth, as any student, academic or administrator will testify.

Arguably, universities have been more open than ever, through intense remote activity in teaching and learning, in tutorial, psychological, logistical and administrative support, through research into the coronavirus, through production of necessary hospital supplies, carrying out diagnostic tests and through volunteer contributions to local communities.

Universities have been open also in their approaches to their mission. In many cases, academics have devoted seemingly limitless hours to reworking teaching and learning materials, to recording classes, to learning the intricacies of learning management systems normally seen as back-up support for on-campus teaching but suddenly converted into the only means able to provide learning activities for their students, and to designing viable and reliable remote assessment activities. Students have devoted the same long hours to attending synchronous teaching activities, to asynchronous learning activities, to adapting to new digital tools and the huge variety of ways their teachers use them, to previously un-tried forms of assessment exercises, all without the ease of in-class and on-campus contact with their peers and their teachers. Administrative staff have moved into remote working, logging into their universities' digital administration systems from their living rooms, adapting procedures and work routines designed for on-campus settings to new environments in hugely diverse conditions. Senior management teams have spent long hours urgently adapting internal regulations, ensuring – as far as possible – adequate digital resources for all, with a close eye on the evolution of the pandemic and the safety of their communities, and facing the steep learning curve required to enable them to produce the robust contingency planning needed for an extremely uncertain immediate and medium-term future.

Universities and their staff and students the world over have been grappling with this decision-making and planning process, in a context of high uncertainty. In this process, universities have on the whole also been open to sharing experiences, concerns, best practices and solutions with neighbouring and partner institutions at both national and international level, as part of the large and complex interconnected interdependent network they form at both European and global levels. It makes great sense for decisions of this kind to be taken collectively, and heavily internationalised universities have beyond a doubt found greater strength and coherence in that close collaboration with their strategic partners. This is confirmed by the survey carried out by the European Commission into the impact of the pandemic on the new European University Alliances (European Commission 2020), where the vast majority of respondents indicated the positive impact of belonging to an alliance on their response to the crisis. This is undoubtedly also the case of longer-standing networks such as the Coimbra Group,[97] which published in June a report into its universities' and the network's responses (Gatti et al. 2020).

INTERNATIONALISATION OFFERS IMPORTANT ADDED VALUE FOR THE FUTURE

Thus, in this deep crisis, belonging to international networks and alliances of different kinds seems to have served as a "vaccination" against the strong temptation to look only inwards, to devote all attention to immediate local problems and to relegate others. If we add to this the fact that one of the major aims of internationalisation as a process is precisely the education of active, critical citizens who are aware of the huge challenges of our globalised interdependent and interconnected society, challenges which the pandemic has so crudely put on all our agendas, then the added value for university policies and practices is clear.

Internationalisation is more often than not associated with student mobility, both for short periods (credit mobility) and for full degree programmes (degree-seeking mobility), as reported once again by the IAU 5th Global Survey on the Internationalization of Higher Education (Marinoni 2019). And the pandemic has of course had a hugely negative impact on international mobility in all its forms, as confirmed in numerous surveys such as Gatti et al. 2020 or Marinoni et al. 2020. Over the past few months, mobility programmes have been suspended or modified, starting in Asia and finally affecting the whole planet. New mobilities have not commenced, many students and staff interrupted their periods in their different destinations and returned to their places of origin, while others remained in the destinations under varying degrees of confinement or lockdown. Many potential international degree-seeking students and their families have opted to stay in their home countries or nearby until the health situation is safer, causing serious concern at those institutions which are financially dependent on income from this source. Indeed, some analysts, amongst them Simon

---

97. See www.coimbra-group.eu/, accessed 15 July 2020.

Marginson of the Centre for Global Higher Education at Oxford, foresee that 2019 levels of this kind of physical international mobility will not be recovered until 2024 or 2025 (Bothwell 2020).

At the same time, large-scale mobility programmes such as the Erasmus+ programme have been adapted to make emergency response (*force majeure*) provision for virtual teaching and learning, a matter which this chapter will return to below. Many study-abroad programmes have been cancelled until spring of 2021, as universities across Europe have gradually been announcing whether or not they are able and open to receive incoming physical credit mobility students in the autumn of 2020, with contingency plans for the event of fresh outbreaks of Covid-19 in place.

However, beyond the immediate crisis management and support for internationally mobile students, the negative financial impact or the potential health risks, this crisis has also offered us a huge opportunity to re-think many of the usually unquestioned givens with which we work in international mobility. When analysts foresee that the impact of the pandemic will last for three to four years before we "recover" 2019 levels of mobility, they are taking for granted that the ideal solution is a return to business as usual. But do we really need/want to recover those levels of mobility with the same traditional models used for the past 30-odd years?

Let us remember why universities and education authorities have set so much store by international mobility, its impact and its added value. International mobility is not an end in itself but a means to internationalise our universities, as a means of enhancing the quality of our educational provision, enriching our research activity and increasing the societal impact of our activity. Without forgetting the pros and cons of current models of mobility, we should consider how this emergency can help us to design a new mobility or, even better, a new internationalisation able to maintain and enhance the positive impact of existing models. We should at the same time aim to reduce or eliminate as far as possible the difficulties and inequities detected from experience, using the tools at our disposal, especially information and communication technologies.

The added value brought by mobility at personal, institutional, systemic and societal levels has, unsurprisingly, been confirmed by impact studies over the years (see, for example, Souto-Otero 2019), and there is little doubt that the Erasmus programme, as the largest student mobility programme in the world, has been a major driver of internationalisation in Europe and beyond, opening minds and enriching lives, as its slogan says. The standards it set for planning, support and academic recognition have become a benchmark for mobility schemes around the world. It has contributed to a profound transformation of the European higher education system, as the origin of the European Credit Transfer System,[98] a shared measure of academic value in order to facilitate full recognition of study abroad, and hence the Bologna Process and the European Higher Education Area (EHEA),[99] inspired by the principles of mobility, transparency and mutual recognition, among others.

---

98. See https://ec.europa.eu/education/resources-and-tools/european-credit-transfer-and-accumulation-system-ects_en, accessed 15 July 2020.
99. See www.ehea.info/, accessed 15 July 2020.

Yet, for some time now, internationalisation based solely on mobility has been criticised for benefiting only a minority of the university community, and thus for being elitist. Within the EHEA, the target set for 2020 of 20% of students graduating each year having had a significant study or work placement experience abroad during their studies has not yet been met in many institutions or countries. And even if it had been met, it should not be forgotten that the figure necessarily implies that up to 80% of students graduating would not have had access to that opportunity.

Since the late 1990s, authors like Jane Knight (2011), Betty Leask (2015), Fiona Hunter, Eva Egron-Polak, Laura Howard, Hans de Wit (de Wit et al. 2015), Jos Beelen (Beelen and Leask 2011; Beelen and Jones 2015) to name but a few, have advocated a more inclusive, more transversal, more comprehensive approach to internationalisation, coining for that a series of terms in different contexts and with different nuances: "internationalisation at home", "internationalisation of the curriculum", "internationalisation of the campus" or "comprehensive internationalisation", with a view to ensuring that our universities truly ensure international and intercultural competences for all.

Such an approach requires an explicit strategy which implies the inclusion of international approaches in teaching and learning content (case studies, comparative approaches, international bibliography and sources, and more), but also in teaching methodology. Strategies could include the development of methodologies based on intercultural interaction, for example by forming multinational, multilingual and multicultural student teams; careful planning of teaching by incoming mobile staff from partner universities or the use of authentic multilingual situations in the classroom, to name but a few. But above all, it requires awareness of the benefits, which should be included explicitly among the learning outcomes of our degree programmes at all levels. In de Wit et al. (2015), the authors point to how the classroom thus becomes a lower-level instance of the globalised, interconnected and interdependent world for which our students are preparing.

VIRTUAL MOBILITY

That said, let us turn to virtual mobility, or rather "digitally enhanced mobility" or "virtual exchange", which also constitutes an instrument to progress towards a more inclusive and more sustainable model. Following the experience of these past months, there are predictable voices directly advocating virtual mobility as a replacement for physical mobility. While it is true that we have learned a great deal over this period, and we have learned first-hand some of the benefits of virtual exchange, we must never forget that the online teaching and learning set up so rapidly in 2019/20 has been a tool to allow us to successfully complete teaching and learning this academic year, to complete mobility in an emergency situation, and in most cases, following an on-campus start to teaching and physical presence at the host university (in some cases of up to six months).

A well-planned and well-designed virtual exchange is a completely different kettle of fish. Just as the emergency virtual teaching which has taken place during the pandemic does not constitute fully-fledged, good-quality remote education provision, in the same way online teaching should not be confused with fully-fledged quality online mobility. This in no way questions the value of sharing academic offers between or among trusted partners. On the contrary, this is a form of collaboration which has considerable potential for enriching the academic offer of an individual university, but it should always be built on careful planning, mutual knowledge and trust and good-quality provision, and it must bring added value.

Thus, while taking courses online "at" another university brings value through the academic experience, the concept of "virtual exchange" goes much further in order to ensure the added value of cultural immersion and intercultural learning, for the development of interpersonal and personal competences, such as autonomy, initiative, adaptability, all of which together constitute the nucleus of the positive impact of physical mobility for the development of international and intercultural competences. See, for example, Helm (2018) or O'Dowd (2018) for overviews of the history of the concept and its implementation.

Thus that added value can only be ensured by developing specific explicit actions to convert online teaching into online or digitally enhanced exchange. One interesting example is the COIL (collaborative online international learning) approach designed at the State University of New York (SUNY).[100] This approach necessarily implies the collaborative design of specific academic provision by academics from at least two universities in at least two countries, with the participation of joint teaching teams and mixed student groups, using a multitude of active learning formats, including multicultural teamwork.

ACTING ON LESSONS LEARNED

As we plan for the immediate and medium-term future, for what has been called the "new normal", the time is ripe to take stock of the lessons learned so far from the emergency experience of these three or four months, to ensure that universities act as learning institutions. We need to seize the huge opportunities which this unprecedented and unexpected experience has opened up for us, building on the steep learning curve we have all (students, academics, researchers, administrators) been subject to. If we are to make optimal use of the silver lining, we must seek behind the dark cloud of the pandemic. This necessarily includes a critical look at the "old normal", examining just how normal it actually was and to what extent a return to it is or is not desirable.

Today, as we look to the future, at a time of considerable vulnerability for the European Union, more broadly for the whole of Europe, for our globalised society, of crisis for the sustainability of the planet, and as we set out on the tough path towards recovery from the Covid-19 pandemic, it is a good time for us as universities to reaffirm the values on which comprehensive internationalisation is based: the European values of democratic culture, solidarity, inclusion and respect for the other. Internationality and interculturality form part of the DNA of universities, and in the design of the "new normal", new mobility and new internationalisation, universities will prove once again that they know how to take advantage of the enormous capacity to evolve, to face up to challenges, and to adapt to changing scenarios, which they as institutions

---

100. See http://coil.suny.edu/, accessed 15 July 2020.

have demonstrated over their nine centuries of existence. Universities will show that they know how to undertake the necessary dialogue of innovation with tradition, of the present and the future with the past, combining the strengths of the traditional with new forms of teaching and learning, mobility, academic exchange and internationalisation, in order to fulfil their basic missions of education, research and service to society in the face of enormous shared global challenges.

REFERENCES

Beelen J. and Jones E. (2015), "Redefining internationalisation at home", in A. Curaj et al. (eds), *The European Higher Education Area between critical reflections and future policies*, Heidelberg: Springer, pp. 59-72.

Beelen J. and Leask B. (2011), "Internationalisation at home on the move", *Internationalisation of higher education handbook*, Berlin: Raabe Academic.

Bothwell E. (2020), "Coronavirus: global student flows to suffer 'massive hit' for years", *Times Higher Education* (26 March 2020).

European Commission (2020), "Survey on the impact of Covid-19 on European Universities", available at https://ec.europa.eu/programmes/erasmus-plus/resources/documents/coronavirus-european-universities-initiative-impact-survey-results_en, accessed 5 August 2020.

Gatti T. et al. (2020), *Practices at Coimbra Group universities in response to the Covid-19: a collective reflection on the present and future of higher education in Europe*, available at www.coimbra-group.eu/wp-content/uploads/Final-Report-Practices-at-CG-Universities-in-response-to-the-COVID-19.pdf, accessed 14 July 2020.

Helm F. (2018), "The long and winding road…", *Journal of Virtual Exchange*, Vol. 1: 41-63.

Knight J. (2011), "Five myths about internationalisation", *International Higher Education*, 2011(62): 14-15.

Leask B. (2015), *Internationalising the curriculum*, Abingdon: Routledge.

Marinoni G. (2019), *IAU 5th Global Survey on the internationalization of higher education: executive summary*, available at https://iau-aiu.net/Global-survey-on-Internationalization, accessed 5 August 2020.

Marinoni G., van't Land H. and Jensen T. (2020), *The impact of Covid-19 on higher education around the world: IAU global survey report*, available at www.iau-aiu.net/IMG/pdf/iau_covid19_and_he_survey_report_final_may_2020.pdf, accessed 5 August 2020.

O'Dowd R. (2018), "From telecollaboration to virtual exchanges: state-of-the-art and the role of UNICollaboration in moving forward", *Journal of Virtual Exchange*, Vol. 1: 1-23.

Souto-Otero M. (2019), *Erasmus+ higher education impact study*, Brussels: European Commission, available at https://op.europa.eu/en/publication-detail/-/publication/94d97f5c-7ae2-11e9-9f05-01aa75ed71a1, accessed 19 September 2020.

de Wit H. et al. (2015), *Internationalisation of higher education*, Brussels: European Parliament, available at www.europarl.europa.eu/RegData/etudes/STUD/2015/540370/IPOL_STU(2015)540370_EN.pdf, accessed 19 September 2020.

Chapter 23

Internationalisation of higher education in a post-Covid-19 world: overcoming challenges and maximising opportunities

Hans de Wit and Giorgio Marinoni

The Covid-19 pandemic is causing enormous disruption in higher education all over the world. The first and most evident impact of the pandemic has been the physical closure of campuses and the slowdown of all academic activities. Internationalisation has probably been one of the activities most affected, and in all its aspects: student and staff mobility, internationalisation of the curriculum/at home, internationalisation of research and internationalisation for the local community. Altbach and de Wit (2020) state that the Covid-19 pandemic is upending higher education and ask themselves, as we will in this chapter, what the medium- and longer-term implications for international higher education will be:

> Will online education take over or will it be more integrated in a hybrid form of education .... Will this crisis be indeed both an end of internationalisation as tradeable commodity and its revival as internationalisation at home? (ibid.: 5)

STUDENT AND STAFF MOBILITY

Border closures and travel limitations in spring 2020 brought all academic mobility, especially student mobility, to an end, often abruptly, leaving international students and staff in very complicated situations.

Almost 90% of the respondents to a global survey by the International Association of Universities (IAU), conducted during the first half of April 2020, reported that student mobility had been affected (IAU 2020). About half of them mentioned degree-seeking and exchange students blocked on their campuses, and a third reported that all student exchanges had been cancelled. The same trend is visible from the perspective of students. A survey conducted by the Erasmus Student

Network (ESN) during the second half of March 2020 shows that one fourth of the 21 930 student respondents reported that their student exchange programme had been cancelled (ESN AISBL 2020). The ESN survey also shows that 37.5% of the respondents experienced at least one major problem related to their exchange. The most common one was the cancellation of their travel home, followed by problems with accommodation and with access to basic commodities such as food and sanitary products.

While these challenges are short-term and maybe temporary, the Covid-19 pandemic is also causing more long-term and long-lasting impacts. One of the main effects of the drastic drop in student mobility is the related financial impact for higher education institutions that rely heavily on fees from international students. A survey of senior leadership at US higher education institutions, conducted in early April on the financial impact of Covid-19 on the field of international education, indicates that US higher education overall has potentially lost nearly US$1 billion due to shortened or cancelled study-abroad programmes, and that it will lose at least US$3 billion due to anticipated international student enrolment declines for autumn 2020 (NAFSA: Association of International Educators 2020). It is easy to understand that this financial loss could imply cuts in salaries and staff dismissals, and in the most extreme cases even closures of higher education institutions.

Similar impacts are noted in Australia and the United Kingdom, where higher education is even more dependent on international student tuition fees. In that respect, the impact in continental Europe will be less severe, as in the majority of European countries more than half of international students are from within the region and pay local fees (Eurostat 2020). The drop in the group of non-European students paying full-cost fees does not have such a severe impact on the income of most institutions since, in general, continental European institutions do not have such high percentages of international fee-paying students as in Australia, the United Kingdom and the United States.

Most credit mobility in Europe is funded through the Erasmus+ programme, so a decline does not have direct financial implications for the institutions. The impact, for both students and institutions, is on the quality of education: a drastic decline in the international classroom environment at home and in study-abroad opportunities for students.

Although some countries have now lifted their travel restrictions, the current development of the pandemic around the world leaves little hope of a quick recovery of student mobility. The development of the pandemic globally is uneven in terms of both peak times and impact, so travel restrictions are likely to remain in place for quite a while. Most institutions in the United States have cancelled their autumn 2020 study-abroad programmes, and it is still uncertain if these programmes will be offered in spring 2021. Although most US institutions intend to welcome international students in the academic year 2020/21, federal limitations, in particular visa regulations, will have a serious impact. Although in July the announced visa restrictions for international students taught entirely online as a result of the pandemic were retracted, the damage is done, due to the uncertainty caused by the announced measures. Australia and the United Kingdom also face serious challenges, in combination with national and geopolitical factors, in particular their complicated relationship with the top sending country, China. As mentioned above, continental Europe will also be impacted by the pandemic and related geopolitical and economic factors, but less significantly.

Other factors are likely to prevent international student mobility from recovering in the short term. One is a sensation of fear. Students may now think twice before deciding to go to study and live in another country, unsure about the health situation in their potential host country or concerned about a resurgence of the virus during their stay abroad. More recently, concerns about racism in the wake of the Black Lives Matter movement may also have had a negative impact on mobility to the United States and other Western countries.

Another barrier in the future may be the cost of studies abroad. As a result of the global financial crisis caused by Covid-19, students and their families may not have sufficient funding at their disposal to cover a period of study abroad, and governments that in pre-crisis times were providing financial support for student mobility might decide to cut back on those programmes and dedicate resources to other more pressing priorities.

On the other hand, greater numbers of students deciding to stay home, particularly in the main sending countries, could create a problem of capacity of the higher education sector in those countries, as these students will now seek admission at national institutions. At the same time, this is an opportunity for these countries to retain their most talented students – the category that tends to study abroad most frequently.

For all these reasons, the enrolment of international students worldwide is expected to drop in the next academic year and in years to come, with severe financial consequences for higher education institutions in receiving countries (less so in continental Europe). At the same time, short-term student mobility for credits, such as Erasmus+ mobility, may be affected as well.

Academic staff mobility, both in terms of short-term stays and full appointments, has also been affected by the pandemic. The lockdown is affecting them in many ways: conferences are being cancelled or postponed and, as a result, the opportunity to present their research in person; guest lectures, visiting professorships and research collaborations have moved online, possibly with a drop in quality; and visas for visits and appointments are delayed – often indefinitely.

INTERNATIONALISATION AT HOME

Loss of revenue is the most obvious challenge for higher education institutions, but it is not the only one. Fewer international students on campus means a loss of cultural diversity and reduced internationalisation at home, with limited opportunities for local, non-mobile students to receive some international and intercultural exposure during their studies.

At the same time, there are new opportunities. The forced reduction – even complete interruption – of international student mobility gives higher education institutions a chance to move away from it, particularly from the recruitment of international students for financial reasons, and adopt a more holistic approach focusing on the benefit of a better quality of education and research for all students and staff.

The problems of perceiving internationalisation mainly in terms of international student mobility are well known. First of all, the process leads inherently to inequality. Mobility fluxes are not balanced. Globally, degree-seeking students move from east to west and from south to north, causing brain drain in some countries, while exchange opportunities mainly benefit students from high-income families. Second, the very low percentage of students able to experience mobility compared to the overall student population (around 2% globally) makes student mobility intrinsically unequal. In continental Europe, in particular thanks to Erasmus+, the percentage of mobile, credit-seeking students is much higher, with an effort to reach 20% of all students. Even there, however, one notices an imbalance between east and west, and insufficient participation of students from low-income and immigrant backgrounds.

In the past several years, different voices in the higher education community, including the authors of this chapter, have been aware of this issue and advocated a more inclusive process, for instance through internationalising the curriculum (by including different perspectives) and the campus (by creating an international environment: internationalisation at home). The Covid-19 crisis offers higher education institutions the opportunity to focus on improving their curricula, for the benefit of all their students.

To compensate for the relative lack of international students in the classroom and the absence of visiting professors, technology can bring valid solutions. According to the IAU survey on the impact of Covid-19 (IAU 2020), virtual mobility and/or collaborative online learning has lately increased at 60% of the higher education institutions that responded to the survey. Both virtual mobility and collaborative online learning are useful tools to offer intercultural perspectives to a larger number of students.

However, technology cannot be the only solution. First, access to technology is uneven. In some parts of the world, for instance in South Africa, and elsewhere in Africa, as noted by Professor Chika Sehoole (in Waruru 2020), the pandemic has exposed "fault lines of inequalities" both in society and in higher education institutions. Some students could not take part in online learning due to a lack of devices and electricity, and a lack of access to the internet. In some other countries, such as Brazil, some higher education institutions have decided to discontinue all their teaching activities instead of moving them online, because they realised that only a very limited percentage of their student population would have access to infrastructure allowing good-quality online learning (Globo 2020; Knobel 2020). In addition, teachers must receive appropriate training, as pedagogy needs to be entirely thought through again, which implies allocations of considerable time and resources.

Undoubtedly, technology cannot provide all the benefits of physical mobility. The non-academic experience of a period of study abroad, by immersion in the society and culture of another country, cannot be replicated online. Anyone who has lived in another country knows that adapting to a different climate, dealing with a foreign language, eating different food and dealing with different societal norms and behaviours can often be more formative than sitting in a classroom. Human contact is, and will remain, fundamental in creating a truly international experience.

Instead of treating the issue of virtual or physical mobility as an either/or choice, finding the right balance between physical mobility and online teaching and learning is an opportunity to address Sustainable Development Goal 13 to combat climate change, by encouraging a more carbon-neutral interaction between international students and staff. According to UNESCO data provided in Rumbley 2020, the greenhouse gas emissions generated by student mobility in 2014 were already equivalent to those of some entire countries, such as Croatia and Tunisia. These are now, for sure, even greater.

INTERNATIONALISATION OF RESEARCH

With the pandemic, international research has also been put under pressure, as well as being presented with unprecedented opportunities. The very first impact was of course negative. More than 80% of the higher education institutions in the IAU survey reported that cancelling international travel and scientific conferences had become commonplace. At half of the respondent higher education institutions, scientific projects were put at risk of not being completed, and at 20% of them scientific research, in particular international research, had come to a complete halt.

However, at the same time, the pandemic has highlighted the crucial importance of research, and of international collaboration in research. The results of the IAU survey show that almost all higher education institutions conducting Covid-19 research are recognised by their governments as sources of relevant expertise and are therefore consulted for national policy making.

The pandemic gives an opportunity to strengthen the collaboration between researchers in academia and the private sector, to join forces in the search for a vaccine. Having said that, there is a considerable risk of competition between countries and pharmaceutical companies in the race to develop the vaccine and to secure exclusive rights over it. Earlier this year, a claim (later retracted) from the head of a big pharmaceutical company in France that the US Government had "the right to the largest pre-order [of Covid-19 vaccines] because it [had] invested in taking the risk" made the headlines in the news (BBC 2020). In the case of a global health threat such as Covid-19, international competition in research is deleterious: instead of pooling resources and sharing knowledge among different research groups around the world, research efforts end up being unnecessarily duplicated, increasing the delay in finding a vaccine and causing a waste of resources.

Higher education institutions in different countries are subject to different kinds of pressure from their governments. Some governments follow a nationalist approach and provide incentives for research on Covid-19, but only at the national level, hindering international collaboration, while others foster international co-operation. A good example here is the "European initiative for the Covid-19 vaccine" (French Government 2020), a memorandum signed by four European countries (France, Germany, Italy and the Netherlands) announcing the creation of an "inclusive vaccine alliance" against the coronavirus. The interesting part of the memorandum is that "the countries wish to ensure a fair price for the vaccines, enabling global distribution for the benefit of the poorest nations too, including in Africa". This shows an inclusive approach, putting global health above national interests.

This example shows that the Covid-19 pandemic is an opportunity for the global higher education sector to reaffirm its relevance to society. But, in some countries, there is a risk that higher education institutions will have to demonstrate the relevance of their research to national interests and will have to fight against their governments to be allowed to continue participating in global research co-operation.

The current crisis demonstrates the synergy between international education and international research. To overcome the global Covid-19 threat, international research collaboration will be more effective when done by researchers who have received an international education, who have intercultural skills and competences as well as an international network of contacts and are able to operate within a global frame of reference. This is particularly true and urgent in the case of medical education (Wu et al. 2020).

INTERNATIONALISATION AND THE LOCAL MISSION OF HIGHER EDUCATION INSTITUTIONS

The impact of the pandemic on community engagement has been mixed. Some higher education institutions have had to reduce their community engagement while attending to more urgent tasks, such as ensuring the continuity of education by moving teaching online, providing support to students and staff or reorganising the institution to comply with health-related measures. Other institutions, especially those with medical and nursing schools, have responded actively to the emergency call of their local communities to help fight the epidemic.

This crisis has given higher education institutions an opportunity to demonstrate, or restate, their importance for local communities. However, in a context of reduced resources due to the economic crisis following the health crisis, the dichotomy of local relevance/global engagement of higher education institutions could resurface, bringing several risks. The first one might be the global disengagement of some higher education institutions narrowly focused on local issues, no longer considering internationalisation a priority. This might be particularly true for less-resourced higher education institutions and could lead to a situation where internationalisation is pursued only at a few higher education institutions, those that have more resources and are already in a privileged position. This would increase inequalities among higher education institutions and among countries. The risk of growing inequality was already present before the crisis, as demonstrated, for instance, by the results of the IAU Global Survey on Internationalisation (Marinoni 2019), but the Covid-19 crisis might exacerbate it.

The solution to this problem lies in breaking the false dichotomy between local relevance and global engagement. Many problems regarding local relevance may already have been solved in other parts of the world and, by sharing experiences, higher education institutions could benefit from existing good practices. Likewise, local solutions may have a global relevance. The report for the German Academic

Exchange Service (DAAD) on *Internationalization in higher education for society* (Brandenburg et al. 2020) provides valuable examples and insights in this respect.

CONCLUSION

The Covid-19 crisis is not only a health crisis: it is also an economic, social and educational crisis. Its impact on higher education and internationalisation is considerable. At the same time, the crisis is offering new opportunities and showing the potential of already existing solutions that had not been implemented before on a large scale, such as online education. Higher education institutions are demonstrating reactiveness and inventiveness in spite of the crisis, which may contribute to a rise in reputation and status.

The main risks for internationalisation are the two extremes of trying as soon as possible to go back to the pre-Covid-19 situation, forgetting lessons learned and perpetuating the inequalities and dysfunctions of the past, and of wanting to change everything, forgetting the achievements and best practices of the past, while underestimating the challenges of the future. Instead, a wiser strategy is to learn from the crisis and re-think internationalisation in order to correct existing malfunctions and open up new opportunities that will lead to benefits for all. Although severely impacted, European higher education is in a better position than counterparts elsewhere to take the lead in innovation and reform for a more sustainable and inclusive internationalisation. This implies that professional international educators (higher education institutions' teaching, managerial and administrative staff, their professional associations – such as the European Association for International Education – and the international industry that has developed over the past decades) have to look for new ways of interacting and quality assuring their work.

Altbach and de Wit are not optimistic:

> The inclination of national governments and institutional leaders will be to push the reset button and return as quickly as possible to the glorious days of international trade before Covid-19. ... Also a number of surveys spread optimism that international students are still interested in studying abroad in the main English speaking countries. (Altbach and de Wit 2020: 15)

They argue that such optimism is naïve, as is the expectation that institutions will opt for a more inclusive policy of internationalisation at home. Yet, this may be the only constructive way forward, given the assets and opportunities for positive change revealed by the serious crisis we are living through.

REFERENCES

Altbach P. G. and de Wit H. (2020), "The impact of COVID-19 on the internationalisation of higher education, revolutionary or not?", *Internationalisation of Higher Education – Policy and Practice*, (2): 5-18, available at www.handbook-internationalisation.com/en/handbuch/gliederung/?articleID=2935#/Beitragsdetailansicht/190/2935/The-Impact-of-COVID-19-on-the-Internationalisation-of-Higher-Education%252C-Revolutionary-or-not%253F, accessed 20 September 2020.

BBC (2020), "Coronavirus Sanofi: French drug giant rows back after vaccine storm" (14 May 2020), available at www.bbc.com/news/world-europe-52659510, accessed 24 June 2020.

Brandenburg U. et al. (2020), *Internationalization in higher education for society (IHES): concept, current research and examples of good practice* (DAAD Studies), Bonn: DAAD.

ESN (Erasmus Student Network) AISBL (2020), "Student exchanges in times of crisis", Brussels: Erasmus Student Network AISBL.

Eurostat (2020), "Origin of students from abroad", available at https://ec.europa.eu/eurostat/statistics-explained/index.php/Learning_mobility_statistics#Origin_of_students_from_abroad, accessed 22 July 2020.

French Government (2020), "European initiative for the Covid-19 vaccine", available at www.gouvernement.fr/en/european-initiative-for-the-covid-19-vaccine, accessed 24 June 2020.

Globo (2020), available at https://g1.globo.com/educacao/noticia/2020/05/14/so-6-das-69-universidades-federais-adotaram-ensino-a-distancia-apos-paralisacao-por-causa-da-covid-19.html, accessed 24 June 2020.

IAU (International Association of Universities) (2020), *The impact of COVID-19 on higher education around the world*, Paris: International Association of Universities.

Knobel M. (2020) in webinar "The future of higher education: short, medium and long-term perspectives in mid- and low-income countries", available at https://iau-aiu.net/IAU-Webinar-Series-on-the-Future-of-Higher-Education-929, accessed 24 June 2020.

Marinoni G. (2019), *Internationalization of higher education: an evolving landscape, locally and globally*, IAU 5th Global Survey, Berlin: International Association of Universities/DUZ Medienhaus.

NAFSA: Association of International Educators (2020), *Financial impact of COVID-19 on international education*, Washington DC: NAFSA: Association of International Educators.

Rumbley L. E. (2020), "Internationalization and the future of the planet", *International Higher Education*, No. 100 (Winter 2020): 32-4.

Waruru M. (2020), "Internationalisation and COVID-19 – challenges and lessons", *University World News*, available at www.universityworldnews.com/post.php?story=20200715110850412, accessed 24 June 2020.

Wu A. et al. (2020), "Internationalisation of medical education is now vital", *University World News*, available at www.universityworldnews.com/post.php?story=2020062007182132, accessed 24 June 2020.

Chapter 24

Recognition of foreign qualifications in the time of Covid-19

Stig Arne Skjerven

The Covid-19 pandemic has created challenges with disrupted learning – and learners – in Europe and beyond. This disruption creates challenges to academic mobility, in which recognition of qualifications is highly relevant. This chapter describes some of the challenges to mobility caused by Covid-19. We also consider how recognition authorities and higher education institutions are meeting these challenges. First, however, we have to see why recognition is so relevant in this respect.

WHY IS RECOGNITION RELEVANT?

Recognition is defined as formal acknowledgement of qualifications by a competent recognition authority, with a view to access to educational and/or employment activities, as described in the Lisbon Recognition Convention, Article I (Council of Europe and UNESCO 1997). Recognition – of the validity and academic level of a foreign education qualification, of partial studies or of prior learning – can be granted by either a higher education institution or a recognition authority such as an ENIC-NARIC centre.[101]

Recognition is a powerful tool to facilitate mobility from one country to another for purposes of study, research, teaching or work. Through recognition, a qualification from one education system is given value in another education system. By their use of this powerful tool, recognition authorities serve as door openers and gatekeepers. These roles have to be balanced carefully. Recognition authorities can open the door to mobility and inclusion in the academic world or labour market of another country. They can also provide a service enhancing public trust by protecting national education and labour markets from fake diplomas and substandard qualifications. A relevant question for this article is: during and after the Covid-19 pandemic, how will the role of recognition as both a door opener and a gatekeeper be challenged?

---

101. The European Network of National Information Centres (ENIC Network) was established in 1994, in close collaboration between the Council of Europe and UNESCO as co-secretariats. The National Academic Recognition Information Centres (NARICs) were established in 1984 with the European Commission as secretariat.

THE CRUCIAL ROLE OF THE LISBON RECOGNITION CONVENTION

The Convention on the Recognition of Qualifications concerning Higher Education in the European Region, known as the Lisbon Recognition Convention, or Lisbon Convention (Council of Europe and UNESCO 1997), sets the framework for recognition of foreign qualifications among member states of the Council of Europe and of UNESCO's Europe and North America region. With Canada ratifying the Lisbon Recognition Convention in 2018, 54 countries have joined the convention[102] (Bergan and Skjerven 2018). The key concept of the convention is the term "substantial differences", meaning that, as a starting point, a foreign qualification should be recognised unless there are substantial differences between the foreign qualification and a comparable qualification in the country in which recognition is sought. Non-recognition is the exception and needs to be duly explained and justified. Applicants no longer need to prove that their qualifications are "good enough"; it is up to the recognition body to demonstrate that they are not (Bergan and Skjerven 2017).

The implementation mechanisms of the convention include the Lisbon Recognition Convention Committee, with a Bureau elected to work between meetings of the committee, and the ENIC Network. The Lisbon Convention Committee and the ENIC Network are open to all states parties to the convention, and in addition the European Commission has established the NARIC Network. One way of explaining the similarity and the difference between the ENIC and the NARIC networks is that all NARICs are ENICs, while not all ENICs are NARICs.[103] The governing mechanisms of the two networks (often referred to jointly as the ENIC-NARIC networks) are the ENIC Bureau and the NARIC Advisory Board, respectively.

As the Covid-19 pandemic developed during the spring of 2020, the Lisbon Recognition Convention Committee Bureau, the ENIC Bureau and the NARIC Advisory Board, with the support of the co-secretariats of the Council of Europe, UNESCO and the European Commission, started working on a reflection document on the effects on recognition and admission, and the implications for ENIC-NARIC centres (LRC 2020). In the work leading up to the reflection document, the national ENIC-NARIC centres were consulted.

The effects identified in the document include those on mobility and admissions, recognition of disrupted learning and its impact on policies/procedures, and possible long-term effects. The document also aims to give an overview of the state of the ENIC-NARIC centres in the time of Covid-19. Finally, the document provides input on the response of the ENIC and NARIC networks, including possible actions for the Lisbon Recognition Convention Committee Bureau, the ENIC Bureau and the NARIC Advisory Board.

In the following sections, key findings of the reflection document are presented.

---

102. A constantly updated list of signatures and ratifications may be found at www.coe.int/en/web/conventions/full-list/-/conventions/treaty/165/signatures, accessed on 23 June 2020.
103. For further information, see www.enic-naric.net/, accessed 23 June 2020.

COVID-19 AND THE RECOGNITION OF FOREIGN QUALIFICATIONS AND ADMISSIONS

Based on existing and expected trends in student mobility and education delivery, which can be considered as the two main "drivers" for change in recognition, the following negative effects are to be highlighted.

Admissions for the next academic semester are disrupted in different ways: exams are delayed, admissions deadlines postponed and the start of the academic year may also be postponed. In addition, there are increasing reports that international students (who may have applied for admission already) may decide to remain in their country of origin due to uncertainties of higher education operations at the start of the next academic year.

More generally, international student mobility is currently halted because of border closures and measures restricting movement. A scenario where this continues into the autumn semester of the 2020/21 academic year, or even longer, is currently leading to a significant drop in the enrolment of international students. At the same time, we may see a growth in off-campus digitally based education provision for many new international students for the autumn semester and following semesters, during which they may have to stay in their country of origin until the situation normalises.

RECOGNISING DISRUPTED LEARNING AND ITS IMPACT ON POLICIES AND PROCEDURES

Covid-19 has disrupted learning worldwide. This disruption has occurred despite an unprecedented shift from classrooms to an online learning environment in order to continue delivering (at least part of) the curriculum.

While going online offers a solution to delivering education to many, it is not a solution for all. Some students have had to quit their studies because they cannot afford to continue. Those who continue may see a delay in their studies because exams are postponed. This may also lead to a gap between those learners who are able to complete studies and those who cannot. Moreover, there are also education sectors – i.e. TVET (technical and vocational education and training) and VET (vocational education and training) – that, due to their applied and practical nature, are not able to provide virtual learning for the full curriculum, and it is still very unclear how this will play out. In addition, and this has relevance to the recognition of qualifications, one may also in some instances raise questions relating to quality and adaptation in the longer term.

The applications that will land on the desks of credential evaluators in higher education institutions and recognition offices may re-open old debates and may create more unique cases shaped by the Covid-19 context. In line with the role of the ENIC-NARIC networks, and the principle of fair recognition enshrined in the Lisbon Recognition Convention, the networks may wish to seek to anticipate some of these issues now to ensure fair recognition, especially to protect the learning of vulnerable or at-risk students. Examples of such cases, as presented in the reflection document, are:

- ▶ How to assess the quality of a qualification if the accreditation of the institution or programme has expired?
- ▶ If an examination was postponed, cancelled or altered, will this challenge the learning outcomes of the course and programmes provided during the 2019/20 academic year?
- ▶ What will happen to the learning of students if their higher education institutions do not survive financially through the crisis before the students graduate?
- ▶ How are we to deal with applications which are incomplete because the applicant could not retrieve documents due to the closure of education institutions?
- ▶ Would a situation occur where a qualification obtained in spring 2020 is perceived as having less value because traditional exams were cancelled and alternative forms of assessments were used?

Entities responsible for evaluating and recognising qualifications may need to adopt alternative policies and procedures. Especially during the pandemic, some authorities may temporarily not be able to issue paper copies of a student's academic documents and send them by post. Based on the survey findings of ENIC-NARIC centres' current situation, policies and procedures favourable to the use of digital student data may be a promising route to secure continuation of services. The survey findings show a strong link between the extent of centres' digitisation and the extent to which centres can continue their operations.

THE PARTICULAR CASE OF REFUGEES

Moreover, could we expect a new type of vulnerable student, ending up in a refugee-like situation in the sense of Article VII of the Lisbon Recognition Convention? Article VII of the convention requires each party to develop recognition procedures for refugees, displaced persons and persons in a refugee-like situation, even in cases in which the qualifications obtained in one of the parties cannot be proven through documentary evidence (Council of Europe and UNESCO 1997). For the persons covered by Article VII, the use of tools such as the European Qualifications Passport for Refugees (EQPR) by the Council of Europe may become even more relevant during and after the Covid-19 crises (Council of Europe 2020a).

Already during the second quarter of 2020, we have seen examples of how the EQPR scheme can be expanded to include refugees and persons in a refugee-like situation with health or health-related qualifications (Bergan and Skjerven 2020; TIME 2020). In co-operation with the UNHCR, the Council of Europe has organised new specific rounds of assessments for refugees with health-related qualifications, in the first instance in France, the United Kingdom and Italy, aiming to cover all relevant qualifications. The scheme may expand to include other countries as well.

The methodology of the Qualifications Passport was developed by NOKUT (the Norwegian Agency for Quality Assurance in Education), which is also the Norwegian ENIC-NARIC centre and plays a key role as assessment co-ordinator (NOKUT 2020). The EQPR provides a tested methodology for assessing such qualifications and a format for describing the qualification in an understandable and comparable format. It aims to have value in cases when EQPR holders move to a new country. The last point is important as it provides a potential cross-border solution to a cross-border challenge, providing EQPR holders with a document that has potential usage and validity across borders.

POSSIBLE LONG-TERM EFFECTS ON RECOGNITION AND ADMISSIONS

The reflection note stresses that while it is too early to say how this crisis will play out, some compare the Covid-19 crisis with a catalyst or pressure cooker, accelerating existing trends and developments, such as a future of more online education delivery and online education exchanges. Also, geographic mobility trends may accelerate, including less east–west student mobility due to strengthened education capacity in Asia.

Covid-19 has had significant economic repercussions worldwide that are already affecting the economic position of students, education institutions, governments and even ENIC-NARIC offices.

It is too early to tell, but these developments need to be monitored, as they may transform recognition in the states parties to the Lisbon Recognition Convention in terms of methodology and volume. In a similar way, Covid-19 could also affect developments in other regions, including with regard to the UNESCO Global Recognition Convention (UNESCO 2019).

ENIC-NARIC CENTRES IN THE TIME OF COVID-19

The Council of Europe, in co-operation with the Lisbon Recognition Convention Committee Bureau, ENIC Bureau and NARIC Advisory Board, carried out a survey in March 2020 among the ENIC-NARIC centres. The summary was made available in April 2020 (Council of Europe, 2020b), and the results indicated the following.

In many countries, the recognition of qualifications is regarded as a public service. The continuity of the public service has therefore been a priority, and almost all ENIC-NARIC centres have switched to teleworking. Mostly, this shift took place relatively smoothly in cases where there was already a legislative framework for teleworking and IT services were already fully or partly equipped for this mode of work. In one case, however, a centre had to close for 15 days, re-opening in early April 2020, in order to make teleworking technically possible. Where a centre's switchover to digitalisation was made or was in progress, this made teleworking possible. In one extreme case, a centre had to stop its action completely owing to no teleworking legislation and no digitalisation.

However, even in cases where the transition to teleworking ran relatively smoothly, some centres found themselves legally obliged to provide certificates of recognition in hard copy, and these had to be signed, stamped and sent. This led to some employees having to travel to their workplace – albeit in compliance with the protection rules – to carry out this obligation.

In addition, recognition was in some cases delayed for one of three reasons: lack of access to records of similar decisions already taken; records not being digitised; or difficulty contacting higher education institutions in which services regarding verification and other relevant provisions for recognition were suspended. For some centres, the Covid-19 pandemic has resulted in a drop in the number of applications, with the concomitant fear that this number will soar after the crisis.

For the future, it seems clear that the emphasis will be on digitalisation for ENIC-NARIC centres in order to be more prepared for further potential challenges, and one can expect substantial investments in this field in the years to come.

THE RESPONSE OF THE ENIC-NARIC NETWORKS

The ENIC Bureau, the NARIC Advisory Board and the Lisbon Recognition Convention Committee Bureau, along with the three co-secretariats of the Council of Europe, UNESCO and the European Commission, have been strongly committed to supporting a dialogue in the ENIC-NARIC networks that ensures that learning is recognised according to the Lisbon Recognition Convention, and to organising peer support for specific challenges caused by Covid-19.

One concrete step has been to organise the annual ENIC-NARIC meeting online, as a first meeting point for sharing information and building competence, on 15 June 2020, with the sole focus on recognition in the time of Covid-19. It is important, however, to keep in mind that the strategy aims to respect the limited resources within the bureaus as well as in the ENIC-NARIC centres. In addition, the strategy needs to respect the diversity of types of centre in the networks and take account of the fact that the Covid-19 pandemic's impact and resulting actions may vary from one country to another. Moreover, as the Covid-19 pandemic progresses, the Lisbon Recognition Convention Committee Bureau, the ENIC Bureau, the NARIC Advisory Board and the three secretariats will have to enlarge their actions, as new issues and challenges surface.

HOW TO BALANCE RECOGNITION IN THE FUTURE?

In this chapter, we have seen that the Covid-19 pandemic will have a significant impact on educational provision in 2020 and that it may pose challenges to admission and recognition. It also raises other key questions. Will it have a longer and more lasting impact on mobility? Will it challenge today's equilibrium established nationally in recognition between the roles of door opener and gatekeeper? For example, will we have to seek out new criteria in assessing online provisions? Will we have to look differently at aspects of quality assurance of provisions than we do today?

It is hoped that the Covid-19 pandemic and its aftermath may strengthen international co-operation in recognition, but one would need resources to develop this further. Outside Europe, the challenges that Covid-19 poses to higher education might be greater than on this continent. Relevant in this respect is the UNESCO Global Recognition Convention, which was adopted by UNESCO's General Conference in November 2019, and which has so far been ratified by one state, Norway (Mørland,

Snildal and Skjerven 2020). It is now more important than ever that the required 20 states ratify this convention for it to enter into force as the first global legal UN agreement on higher education.

The pandemic affects the learning of nearly every international student and creates new, unforeseen challenges for faculty, admissions officers and credentials evaluators. Disrupted learning and admission make it more important than ever to secure fair, non-discriminatory and transparent recognition, and for national authorities to adopt flexible and quality-assured practices that are adapted to the post-crisis situation. The Lisbon Recognition Convention, other regional conventions and the UNESCO Global Recognition Convention provide the most important platforms for national authorities to join forces and collaborate on recognition of foreign qualifications. This will be to the benefit of the centres and higher education institutions – and most importantly, this will be to the benefit of the mobile learner of the future.

REFERENCES

Bergan S. and Skjerven S. A. (2017), "Recognition is a moral duty", *University World News* (1 September 2017), available at www.universityworldnews.com/post.php?story=20170829115603253, accessed 11 June 2020.

Bergan S. and Skjerven S. A. (2018), "Lisbon Recognition Convention moves to North America", *University World News* (31 August 2018), available at www.universityworldnews.com/post.php?story=20180829090940936, accessed 11 June 2020.

Bergan S. and Skjerven S. A. (2020), "A way to enable refugees to help in the COVID-19 crises", *University World News* (2 May 2020), available at www.universityworldnews.com/post.php?story=2020050114282238, accessed 11 June 2020.

Council of Europe (2020a), *European Qualifications Passport for Refugees*, available at www.coe.int/en/web/education/recognition-of-refugees-qualifications, accessed 11 June 2020.

Council of Europe (2020b), *Recognition of qualifications in this time of coronavirus*, available at www.coe.int/en/web/education/recognition-of-qualifications-in-this-time-of-coronavirus, accessed 11 June 2020.

Council of Europe and UNESCO (1997), *Convention on the Recognition of Qualifications concerning Higher Education in the European Region*, available at www.coe.int/en/web/conventions/full-list/-/conventions/treaty/165, accessed 11 June 2020.

LRC (Lisbon Recognition Convention Committee Bureau, ENIC Bureau and NARIC Advisory Board, with the support of the co-secretariats of Council of Europe, UNESCO and the European Commission) (2020), *Recognition of foreign qualifications in times of COVID-19: a reflection document for the ENIC NARIC networks and their stakeholders*, available at www.enic-naric.net/reflection-documentrecognition-of-foreign-qualifications-in-times-of-covid-19.aspx, accessed 11 June 2020.

Mørland T., Snildal A. and Skjerven S. A. (2020), "Norway is first to join the new Global Recognition Convention", *University World News* (14 May 2020), available at www.

universityworldnews.com/post.php?story=20200514140938511, accessed 11 June 2020.

NOKUT (Norwegian Agency for Quality Assurance in Education) (2020), *Qualifications Passport for Refugees*, available at www.nokut.no/om-nokut/internasjonalt-samarbeid/qualifications-passport-for-refugees/, accessed 11 June 2020.

TIME (2020), "Healthcare workers from refugee backgrounds want to help fight COVID-19: one man's journey shows how that might be possible" (18 April 2020), available at https://time.com/5826166/refugees-coronavirus-healthcare/, accessed 11 June 2020.

UNESCO (2019), *Global Convention on the Recognition of Qualifications concerning Higher Education 2019*, available at http://portal.unesco.org/en/ev.php-URL_ID=49557&URL_DO=DO_TOPIC&URL_SECTION=201.html, accessed 22 June 2020.

Chapter 25

From fire-fighting to re-thinking external quality assurance: European quality assurance agencies' response to the challenges of the Covid-19 pandemic

Maria Kelo

INTRODUCTION

ENQA is the European Association for Quality Assurance in Higher Education and represents over 50 quality assurance agencies across the European Higher Education Area (EHEA).[104] Its member agencies have demonstrated through an external review that their activities, processes and criteria are aligned with the Standards and Guidelines for Quality Assurance in the European Higher Education Area (ESG 2015). The ESG standards were adopted as an official document of the Bologna Process, have become the backbone of the European quality assurance framework and have since 2005 guided the development of external and internal quality assurance across the EHEA.

The ESG standards are in three parts, with a total of 24 standards. The first part is related to internal quality assurance, the second to external quality assurance processes, and the third to the operation of quality assurance agencies. An agency that wishes to be a member of ENQA, or to be registered in the European Quality Assurance Register (EQAR),[105] needs to go through an independent external review every five years to demonstrate its compliance with the ESG. An external agency review addresses directly the standards of parts 2 and 3 and ensures that the standards that the agency uses to evaluate institutions and/or programmes encompass the requirements of the standards in part 1.

---

104. For ENQA see https://enqa.eu/, accessed 20 July 2020; for EHEA see www.ehea.info/, accessed 20 July 2020.
105. For the European Quality Assurance Register (EQAR), see www.eqar.eu/, accessed 20 July 2020.

The ESG standards have been designed to provide a substantial common basis to support trust in higher education systems across Europe, while being sufficiently flexible to be applicable to different higher education systems, different types of institution and different quality assurance approaches. They can be used for the evaluation of all education, independently of the place or mode of delivery, including e-learning. The document describes also the commonly accepted quality assurance process with its four components: a self-assessment, a site visit, a published report and a follow-up (ESG 2015: 18). Specific standards describe the role of peer reviewers and stakeholders in the process, and underline the importance of transparency of information, from criteria and processes used, to quality assurance reports and accreditation decisions.

When the global Covid-19 pandemic brought several European countries to lockdown and significantly restricted the movement of people within and between countries, higher education institutions needed to close their campuses and move education provision online. For many, this raised concerns related to the status of the institutions' accreditation in the national context, and questions on ESG compliance with the emergency measures applied, both within institutions and in quality assurance agencies.

This chapter provides an overview of some first experiences of European quality assurance agencies in these exceptional circumstances. It is based on information collected through a number of webinars organised by ENQA from April to June 2020 and on a number of brief written updates shared by its members (ENQA 2020). While it by no means offers a comprehensive picture of the reaction of the quality assurance community across the EHEA, and nor do its findings apply equally to each country, it gives an idea of the main direction that quality assurance agencies have taken in this period and how the ESG standards factor into the picture. It provides a first impression of the impact these experiences may have on how we see external quality assurance in the future.

INITIAL RESPONSE FROM AGENCIES: SUPPORT AND FLEXIBILITY

As the Covid-19 pandemic forced a large part of Europe into lockdown in spring 2020, simultaneously quality assurance agencies needed to confront a situation they had never faced before. The institutions they were tasked to review could no longer be physically accessed, with no staff or students on campus. Travelling between countries, as well as within countries, was severely restricted. Keeping review processes running as usual was naturally not possible under these circumstances.

Higher education institutions needed to react quickly and decide how to best address the needs of their students and support their staff in a fast transition to move activities online. In this first phase of the crisis, institutions turned to quality assurance agencies for support and advice. At the same time, agencies realised that institutions needed to free resources from non-urgent administrative tasks to focus on addressing the emergency, and – subsequently – to focus on planning for the 2020/21 academic year, expected to require extraordinary arrangements. Agencies often extended the validity of accreditation and reassured institutions that the exceptional measures undertaken during the crisis would not have a negative impact on the institution's or programme's accreditation status.

In many quality assurance systems, the reviewed entity (institution, programme or agency) needs to submit a change report when significant changes are made during the validity of an accreditation or evaluation period. The details vary but a report would typically be required if the mode of education delivery changed from face-to-face to online. To reduce the immediate administrative burden on institutions, many agencies announced that no formal change reports would be required for programmes that had been moved temporarily online, at least not in the short term. The trust that had been established over the years between institutions, agencies and stakeholders could be strongly relied on in this initial "fire-fighting stage".

In addition to accreditation-related concerns, agencies responded to requests from institutions for online training sessions on topics such as e-assessment, students' rights and the organisation and quality of online learning. Specific guidelines on these have emerged in several systems where they did not exist yet. The ENQA paper on "Considerations for quality assurance of e-learning provision" has proved to be useful to agencies and institutions (Huertas et al. 2018). Agencies have also played an important role as facilitators of dialogue between different higher education stakeholders in their respective national contexts and as providers of reliable information on how the situation may impact quality and quality assurance.

While the European context does not pose immediate concerns about agencies or institutions in respect to the status of their accreditation, national regulations may in some cases be more difficult to manage. In many countries, agencies have been facilitators and drivers of a dialogue between stakeholders and the national authorities, in order to evaluate to what extent national regulations and laws may need to be changed to enable continuity in the quality work of institutions and agencies. Such changes relate principally to lengths of evaluation cycles and their extension, and to physical meeting requirements for evaluation panels as well as agencies' decision-making bodies, such as accreditation council or commissions.

EXTERNAL QUALITY ASSURANCE: FROM POSTPONEMENT TO ONLINE PROCEDURES

In terms of the execution of external reviews, agencies have opted for postponement of the reviews or – increasingly – for online reviews. Postponement was initially the option preferred by agencies, as it was hoped that the period of lockdown would be limited to only a few months. The ESG standards do not determine the duration of the evaluation cycle, which can be decided freely in each national context, as long as it is "cyclical" (ESG 2015: 15). However, in some countries, regulations are strict in this respect and allow only limited possibilities for prolongation of accreditation periods, which therefore cannot be a long-term solution. Even where regulations allow for larger flexibility, the widely shared thinking in the sector is that quality assurance procedures cannot and should not be postponed indefinitely.

While several agencies have postponed all current reviews to late 2020 or to 2021 (e.g. by prolonging accreditation validity by a year), many had already started to carry out online quality assurance procedures systematically in the summer of 2020. Practical considerations related to the workload, staffing and – in some cases – financing of the agencies have played a role in these decisions. The key motivator for the move online is, however, the need to re-establish a normal rhythm of reviews as soon as possible, and to the extent possible. Keeping quality assurance activities going is important also to ensure continued trust in the quality of education provision within and between systems because emergency solutions, such as programme delivery online, may need to be prolonged well into the academic year 2020/21.

Moving quality assurance processes online is thus slowly becoming a norm, although many agencies have opted – at least for the moment – for a combination of postponement and online procedures. Several agencies consider online reviews apt for smaller or lighter procedures such as initial accreditation, follow-up procedures and – eventually – programme reviews. On the other hand, more complex reviews, such as institutional evaluations or other full reviews, are less suited to being completed fully online. For medical and lab-based programmes, where visiting the facilities is considered crucial, video tours and photos of facilities and equipment have been used in some cases to replace a physical visit, if postponement of the review has been impossible. However, a physical site visit remains the preferred option for such programmes.

The overall picture is naturally not uniform: while many agencies have moved all their activities online, with some having completed hundreds of online procedures between March and June 2020, some are only starting with the first pilot procedures (ENQA 2020). In addition to different strategic choices, the move to online quality assurance has understandably been easier for agencies that had already started to experiment with (partly) online visits before the crisis or those with better developed online support structures and tools, such as robust databases, document depositories and well-established, already used online meeting tools.

CONSIDERATIONS FOR ONLINE VISITS

Overall, the higher education sector has reacted well to the fast move online, and it has been surprising to see how well the work of institutions and agencies has continued in these exceptional circumstances. However, it is also clear that teaching, training, meeting and reviewing online is not the same as face to face. In order to achieve the best balance between the benefits and challenges of online education, online training, online meetings and online quality assurance, specific issues need to be addressed.

As explained above, the ESG standards stipulate an external quality assurance process "normally including a site visit" (ESG 2015: 18), which should be carried out by a team of external experts, including a student member (ibid.: 19). While the site visit is not the only part of the process, it has a pivotal role in involving all relevant stakeholders (in person) and creating a connection point between the internal self-assessment process and the external expert evaluation report. While the ESG standards do not explicitly determine that the "site visit" needs to be a physical one, this has been always the assumption and understanding of the authors and users of the ESG. How and in what circumstances could a "virtual visit" count as a "site visit"?

In order to ensure that an online visit meets as closely as possible the purpose and expectations of a (physical) site visit, most of the established good practices contained in the ESG and in national and agency regulations remain valid and should be safeguarded. These include, for example, requirements related to the number, profile and expertise of the peer reviewers. In addition, as online site visits have been proven to require even more careful preparation than physical visits, the experts' dedication and professionalism are crucial for the success of the procedure. While the basic concept of a review process and the role of the experts within it remain unaltered, specific information and (re-)training sessions for experts are needed as reviews move online. Many agencies are also working on guidelines for experts, institutions and staff that can help all participants to take part effectively in an often unfamiliar setting.

The same interviewee groups should take part in the online sessions as would have participated in the face-to-face visits, including academic and non-academic staff, students, institutional leadership and a wide range of stakeholders within and outside the institution. Confidentiality, professionalism and non-conflict of interest need to be ensured at least as rigorously as for physical visits, while acknowledging the specific challenges posed by the online environment. It is crucial that existing criteria and procedures are honoured to the maximum, so as to ensure similar quality, reliability and validity in the online process, including the site visit. Institutions and programmes that need to go through an online review in this period should not be disadvantaged.

While respecting all key features of the site visit, it must be recognised that organising an online site visit is not simply a question of transferring – *mutatis mutandis* – all its elements into a virtual environment. Several practical and methodological considerations related to the when, who and how of the review quickly emerge and need to be addressed.

When travelling is involved, it is natural that all meetings are concentrated in a few consecutive days, to maximise the use of time and funds. Online visits both demand and allow for a different set-up and the distribution of meetings across a longer time span. Different planning may also be needed for the structure of individual interview sessions, including careful consideration of the number of people attending each session. Some people have found it important to build in an informal pre-review meeting for the experts, to allow them to get to know each other: when sharing a meal and a drink is no longer an option, other ways of informal interaction need to be designed.

Naturally, all sessions – including the internal discussions of the review panel – need to be organised to guarantee the confidentiality of all participants. Agencies are experimenting with different online tools to assess their suitability for the review process, including safety and user friendliness. Simple measures, such as creating distinct meeting rooms with different passwords for each interviewee group, will help to protect the confidentiality of the process, and the use of the camera function will help to identify the interviewees throughout the session, as well as to create a more collegial atmosphere. Recording of sessions is by and large considered inappropriate as well as unnecessary: recording is not usual practice for face-to-face visits, and as the only reason to record online meetings would be to ensure completeness of notes in case a person falls offline due to technical issues, this is better solved by simply appointing double note-takers. Recording would raise issues related to the EU General Data Protection Regulation (GDPR)[106] and could lead to lower degrees of openness and honesty in responses.

The cost of an online site visit may be reduced compared to a physical site visit, as costs related to travel and stay are cut. However, it is clear that the workload of a process with an online site visit is not lower than the workload of a process including a physical site visit. Rather, in this initial phase, when experience and routines still need to be built, tested and evaluated, the workload has increased rather than decreased. It seems thus unreasonable to reduce the expert fee (where applicable) or the agency co-ordination fee beyond the possible deduction of travel costs. A reduced fee could also give the wrong impression that an online review is a "discount review" and as such not as thorough or serious as a normal procedure including a physical site visit.

Initial feedback from agencies has shown that sometimes review experts and the institutions have been sceptical about the online quality assurance processes and even reluctant to take part in them. However, for those who have participated, the experience has proved to be amply positive. Indeed, online site visits can work very well, as long as they are properly prepared and carried out by highly motivated and engaged experts. Based on the cases that have been observed so far, the willingness of experts to take part in online site visits does not depend on their level of expertise or the composition of the review team but is rather a highly individual matter. Although teams in which the members know each other well and have worked together in the past adjusted to the online mode more swiftly, the personal disposition and dedication of the experts were the most important criteria for a successful move to online reviews.

Admittedly, online visits bring a number of challenges, but also a range of additional benefits such as the possibility to engage experts from abroad without additional cost, or to engage certain stakeholder groups, such as employers and alumni, which has often been a challenge for physical meetings. As agencies are becoming more concerned about the ecological impact of their activities, particularly those involving (international) travel, a lower carbon footprint has been mentioned as an important positive consequence of moving quality assurance procedures online. Going online has also forced agencies, experts and institutions to reflect on the best possible use of time during a site visit, increasing desk-based preparation to allow the panel to focus on what really matters during the online meetings. Participants in such procedures have evaluated online visits as being at least as efficient as face-to-face visits or, if time used for travelling and making practical arrangements is factored in, even more so.

THE WAY FORWARD

Have we changed the way to do external quality assurance forever? Is there no going back? While the move online in these times of crisis has been forced and fast, and

---

106. General Data Protection Regulation 2016/679 is an EU law on data protection and privacy in the European Union and the European Economic Area and the transfer of personal data outside the EU and EEA.

many agencies and institutions have had to proceed without significant planning, testing or specific expertise, in order to implement changes at a fast pace, it has allowed agencies to keep activities running reliably and to a high standard. However, it is important to make a clear difference between emergency measures and longer-term strategies. In the long term, institutions and agencies need to carefully gather, analyse and consider the lessons learned, so that when their situation normalises, the sector can move forward to a "new normal" that has been carefully thought through, rather than automatically revert to the ways of the past. A crisis that nobody would have wished for has provided us with an opportunity to pause and consider alternatives to our usual ways of doing things, and to re-think carefully the review processes used, including the purpose and structure of the site visits. The experience of the agencies that have had to experiment with alternatives should not be wasted.

When reconsidering the elements of the external review processes, and in particular the purpose of the site visit, questions such as "what should it be used for and what should it achieve that cannot be done by desk and online meetings?" will be important. Agencies in the ENQA community are by and large convinced that the future will be different and that it will see a blended or hybrid external review process. It can be expected that some types of external quality assurance procedures continue to use an online visit (e.g. initial accreditation or follow-up procedures) while others revert to face-to-face visits; or that some attendees of each procedure take part online and others in person (to allow greater international involvement and/or the participation of hard-to-reach groups such as employers and alumni in the interviews); or that some parts of each process are covered through online meetings, such as initial fact collection and confirmation, allowing the physical visit to focus on verification, enhancement-oriented dialogue and feedback from stakeholders. In other words, future quality assurance approaches will likely use online methods where they can bring added value, be more efficient or be more sustainable in financial and ecological terms, and retain face-to-face meetings for activities where an online replacement will be only a second best, to be reserved for situations where nothing else is possible.

In the current exceptional circumstances, the European framework for quality assurance (ESG, EQAR, ENQA) does not pose obstacles to the implementation of online site visits. In the longer term, it will, however, be necessary to achieve consensus among the relevant stakeholders (the Bologna Follow-up Group and the key European-level stakeholder organisations) on a correct understanding of what a "site visit" means and to what extent, and in what circumstances, this could be adequately understood as being sufficiently – if not better – addressed by an online visit.

REFERENCES

ENQA (2020), "External quality assurance in the time of COVID-19 – case examples from ENQA member agencies", available at https://enqa.eu/wp-content/uploads/2020/06/External-QA-in-times-of-COVID-19_case-examples.pdf, accessed 29 July 2020.

ESG (2015), *Standards and guidelines for quality assurance in the European Higher Education Area (ESG) (2015)*, Brussels: ESG, available at https://enqa.eu/index.php/home/esg/, accessed 29 July 2020.

Huertas E. et al. (2018), *Considerations for quality assurance of e-learning provision*, Brussels: ENQA, available at https://enqa.eu/indirme/papers-and-reports/occasional-papers/Considerations%20for%20QA%20of%20e-learning%20provision.pdf, accessed 29 July 2020.

Chapter 26

Sustainable financing of higher education after the pandemic

Jamil Salmi

INTRODUCTION

After triggering a health crisis of unprecedented scale, the Covid-19 pandemic has quickly evolved into a deep financial crisis threatening national economies worldwide. The higher education sector has been particularly hit by both the health emergency and the economic recession, as universities, their students and most households have suffered substantial income loss. The outlook for the next academic year is highly worrisome.

Even before the pandemic, very few countries, rich or poor, had managed to define and implement a sustainable financing strategy for higher education. With the exception of some of the richest nations in the world – the Nordic countries, the Gulf states, Singapore and Scotland (United Kingdom) – that rely almost exclusively on public funding (more than 1.5% of GDP) and public provision (more than 90% of enrolment), and another small group of predominantly public systems that are relatively well funded through a combination of public resources and substantial cost sharing with appropriate student aid – Australia, Canada, England, Hong Kong (China), Iceland, the Netherlands, New Zealand and Switzerland – most higher education systems in the world tend to be insufficiently funded, highly inequitable or both (Salmi 2017). What was true before Covid-19 is likely to be even more accurate in the aftermath of the health and economic crisis.

Against this background, this chapter examines the financial challenges faced by universities as a result of the Covid-19 crisis and explores what putting in place sustainable financing strategies would entail. After analysing the short-term effects of the pandemic, especially through the equity prism, the chapter analyses the longer-term implications of the crisis and outlines the main features of sustainable funding strategies.

SHORT-TERM EFFECTS

As country after country decreed partial or total lockdown in March 2020 to deal with the Covid-19 pandemic, the number of universities and colleges closing their campus and switching to e-learning soared. However, few of these institutions were well prepared for such a sudden and disruptive move. A lot of scrambling and improvisation occurred as administrators, instructors and students struggled to implement broad-based online learning in the space of just a few days.

In looking at the consequences of the Covid-19 crisis, it is easy to fall into the trap of the equaliser myth. After all, are we not all equal before the virus? The truth is that, in the same way as the disease has been found to affect more severely low-income minorities – African Americans and Latinx in the United States, immigrant groups in Europe, for example – there is a great danger that the pandemic could amplify disparities in higher education (Gavi 2020; NPR 2020). Interestingly, the majority of African countries have been less affected health-wise during the first phase of the pandemic. While the disruptions caused by the pandemic affect both rich and poor countries, and upend the lives of every societal group, students from vulnerable groups are hit especially hard.

In wealthy societies, where most residence halls were shut down, often abruptly, many students from low-income families faced major difficulties. They had problems finding off-campus housing at short notice when they could not travel back home, they lost access to campus-based health care, struggled to pay unexpected living expenses and felt unprepared for a sudden shift to online studies. In North America, community college students, who are more likely to be people of colour, or older, to have lower family incomes and to care for dependents, are much more vulnerable than those attending four-year institutions. These challenges could lead to large numbers of dropouts by the end of the academic year and far fewer students enrolled in autumn 2020. International students stranded far from home have also faced severe economic and emotional hardships. In the United States, in early July 2020, the federal government took the cruel decision – since rescinded – of denying a visa to all foreign students enrolled in online programmes.[107]

In developing nations, students from disadvantaged groups are facing tremendous difficulties (Malee Bassett and Arnhold 2020). Limited internet access and low broadband capacity have severely constrained opportunities for online learning, especially in rural areas. Many students from low-income households – sometimes even faculty members – do not own a laptop or a tablet. In addition to digital-divide challenges, colleges and universities in poor nations have struggled to rapidly launch quality distance learning programmes. The majority of institutions lack experienced instructional designers, sufficient educational resources, an adequate grasp of the specifics and nuances of online education, and strong institutional capacity to deliver it.

The African University Association has already signalled that, among the 700 universities operating in sub-Saharan Africa, very few are well prepared and sufficiently equipped to deliver their programmes online (Brown and Salmi 2020). Connectivity remains an intractable issue and, in some instances, governments have had difficulties guaranteeing continuity in power supply, another major challenge faced by the higher education sector in several sub-Saharan African countries. Furthermore,

---

107. See e.g. https://edition.cnn.com/2020/07/06/politics/international-college-students-ice-online-learning/index.html, accessed 11 July 2020.

universities in the developing world have scrambled to arrange for alternative learning assessments and exams, which in turn will likely disrupt preparations for next year's admissions. Students from disadvantaged groups, who often have less access to relevant information, may be affected even more by these developments.

CHANGING LANDSCAPE IN THE LONGER TERM

Some OECD countries have been able to partly alleviate the immediate shock through financial measures in support of universities and/or students. Australia, Denmark, Finland, Germany, Taiwan and the United States were among the first countries that approved economic rescue packages that included assistance to higher education institutions. This assistance will help public colleges and universities weather the crisis by protecting the employment of most administrative and academic staff, boosting student welfare and helping to pay for the technology that can enable a rapid transition to online education. France and Germany have provided emergency financial aid, targeting students who have lost their part-time job and/or access to subsidised residence halls. Many governments also are providing universities with targeted research funding to help identify effective medicines to treat Covid-19 patients and develop a vaccine. The Nordic countries are also funding research in the social sciences to study and mitigate the social consequences of the pandemic.

Unlike those of some high-income countries, by and large the governments of developing nations have not been able to provide a stimulus package to support the higher education sector during the pandemic. On the contrary, more often than not they have been compelled to hastily reallocate resources away from the education budget to fund the soaring health expenses. In Kenya, for example, the Commission on University Education shifted the equivalent of US$2.5 million of its development fund to the Covid-19 emergency fund. The Kenyan Treasury has already announced a US$460 million cut for next year (Nganga 2020). In Nigeria, the federal government has indicated its intention to take about US$130 million from the education sector in support of its pandemic response (Fatunde 2020). In Pakistan, the governing body of the Higher Education Commission warned in June 2020 that the sudden cut in the higher education budget by the equivalent of another US$36 million could result in "dismantling the country's higher education system by forcing the shutdown of universities".[108] And even within education, many governments might be inclined to move funds away from the university sector towards lower levels, as the needs of younger students are considered to be more pressing.

Indonesia stands out as one of the few developing countries that have managed to free up resources in support of higher education. The Minister of Education recently announced a US$70 million grant to prevent low-income students from dropping out. Eligible students in both public and private universities are allowed to defer tuition fee payments or can use the subsidy to pay their tuition fees. Fees have been reduced for last-year students (Yamin 2020). The Colombian Government also announced a US$270 million programme to help needy students directly or through the national

---

108. See www.thenews.com.pk/print/672533-hec-denounces-cut-in-higher-education-budget, accessed 11 July 2020.

student loan agency (ICETEX).[109] In the Philippines, the public Land Bank is offering loans of up to the equivalent of US$6 000 (300 000 pesos) under its "study-now-pay-later" programme meant to cover students' tuition and assist parents whose income has been severely affected by the pandemic.[110]

While there are still many uncertainties about the prospects for universities re-opening next academic year, the medium-term outlook is definitely grim in many countries, forcing them to ask themselves difficult questions and contemplate substantial changes. In Europe, a number of countries are going back on the principle of free movement of students. For instance, as a result of Brexit, the United Kingdom will be imposing international fees on European students as of September 2021. Belgium is planning to restrict the number of French students enrolling in its universities; in some cases they represent more than 20% of the student population.

The crisis has revealed structural weaknesses in the existing financing models of higher education systems and institutions. In OECD countries with substantial cost sharing, universities and colleges will be facing diminished resource envelopes, especially if students are successful in their demands for lower fees as long as online education remains in place. Students have signed petitions or gone to court to obtain reduced fees in countries as diverse as Chile, England, South Korea and the United States (Anderson 2020). For private higher education institutions that are fully dependent on tuition fees and/or on international students, financial survival will be seriously tested during the deep recession that many economists predict. Large numbers of students with limited resources could drop out of higher education altogether, or at least shift to more affordable public institutions. It would not be unrealistic to see a wave of mergers in the public and private sub-sectors and expect significant numbers of private colleges and universities to close their doors for good.

In many countries, students graduating this academic year are likely to encounter huge employment challenges as a result of the economic recession. Similarly, working students who lose their job may not have the resources to continue studying. As a general principle, the lower the share of public funding and public provision in a higher education system, the more vulnerable it is likely to be. In the United Kingdom, for instance, where half of higher education funding comes from private sources, a £2.5 billion shortfall is expected next academic year.

Student aid is equally at risk in many countries, especially when it takes the form of student loans rather than grants and scholarships. Unlike Australia, New Zealand and the United Kingdom (except Scotland), which have income-contingent loans that protect their graduates in time of financial difficulty, all the countries that rely on mortgage-type student loans are likely to see soaring rates of non-payment as long as the economic crisis endures. The Canadian and US governments announced a halt to all student loan repayments for the next six months. While this manoeuvre will

---

109. See www.universidad.edu.co/por-la-pandemia-gobierno-anuncia-apoyos-a-estudiantes-y-creditos-para-ies/?ct=t(Noticias_abril_8_21_COPY_01)&mc_cid=071dc3d0fe&mc_eid=eca4cdf437, accessed 20 July 2020.
110. See https://news.abs-cbn.com/business/07/09/20/study-now-pay-later-landbank-offers-new-loan-for-education-support, accessed 11 July 2020.

provide welcome relief to unemployed graduates and those with limited incomes, it will not address the in-built design defect of all mortgage-type student loan schemes. This is a structural change that countries ought to consider seriously in their quest for more sustainable funding approaches.

In the many developing nations that have traditionally allocated insufficient public funding for higher education, usually less than 0.5% of GDP, the consequences could be dire. The prospects for both quantitative expansion and improved quality would be very poor. Reduced public budgets and limited room for increased private funding could translate into many students opting out of higher education and institutions unable to sustain the quality of teaching and research.

FINANCIAL SUSTAINABILITY FOR SYSTEM RESILIENCE

Based on the lessons of experience arising from the evolution of funding mechanisms in OECD countries in the past decade, a sustainable funding model for higher education in the post-pandemic world would be well served by the following guiding principles (Salmi 2017).

- ▶ Link to national priorities
  It is important to achieve full consistency between the national policy goals set by governments to achieve their vision of the future of higher education in the post-pandemic era and the funding instruments in place to attain high performance and financial sustainability. Funding without a national strategic orientation serves no useful purpose. Conversely, a higher education development vision or plan that does not have appropriate financial resources and incentives is unlikely to come to fruition.
- ▶ Performance orientation
  The level of funding that governments allocate to higher education institutions should reflect their performance. International experience reveals that tying the distribution of funds for institutions and/or students to performance measures can make a real difference in the ability of higher education systems to achieve key policy goals. The main dimensions of performance should be defined by indicators reflecting their contribution to access and equity, quality and relevance, research production, knowledge transfer and efficiency in the use of public resources. For instance, the proportion of female students in STEM programmes can be used to measure progress towards gender equity. To promote internal efficiency, graduation rates can be used as an indicator.
- ▶ Equity in resource allocation
  The distribution of public resources should reflect the principle of equal opportunities for all population groups: income groups, females and males, minorities and youth with special needs. This implies, in particular, that funding should respect the principle of universalism and provide all citizens with the same benefits when it comes to access to public funding.
- ▶ Objectivity and transparency
  The rules and criteria for the allocation of public funds to the higher education sector should be objectively defined and fully transparent. The results of each round of funding allocation should be publicly available at all times.

- ▶ Multiplicity of instruments
  No funding mechanism can satisfy all the policy objectives of any country at the same time. It is therefore essential to rely on a combination of instruments that are complementary, consistent and mutually reinforcing. For example, a country can complement its funding formula with an innovation fund that universities can access on a voluntary basis to finance new initiatives included in their strategic plan.
- ▶ Stability over time
  Multi-year funding allows higher education institutions to plan their reform programmes and investment over the medium to longer term in accordance with their strategic plan. University leaders must have a long-term perspective to design and implement the development strategy of their institution, whether investing in new infrastructure (facilities and labs) or recruiting academic staff. Thus, it is important that governments maintain a reasonable degree of funding stability from one year to the next. This is better achieved with a multi-year budgeting process, as is the case in Denmark, Hong Kong or in the University of California system, for example.
- ▶ Institutional autonomy and accountability
  International experience shows that universities that are fully autonomous are better positioned to become innovative and be responsive to rapidly changing external conditions and evolving labour market needs. At the same time, higher education institutions and students that receive government subsidies should be fully accountable for the appropriate use of public resources through independent audit mechanisms and clear measures of performance.
- ▶ Block grant allocation
  Rather than organising the budget into line items, it is good practice to allocate and transfer each university's funding as a single sum, instead of rigidly predetermining the use of resources by category of expenses. This gives the universities more flexibility in planning and deploying their resources in the spirit of institutional autonomy mentioned above.

With these principles in mind, a sustainable financing strategy would involve two complementary dimensions. First, countries need to mobilise adequate levels of public and private resources in a balanced way. Second, they must rely on transparent and objective mechanisms to allocate public resources reflecting each institution's performance with respect to access and equity, quality, relevance and efficiency in the use of resources – and research production and knowledge transfer in the case of research-intensive universities.

CONCLUSION

It is not the first time that countries in the industrial and developing world have faced major crises. Wars, natural catastrophes and financial downturns are alas too frequent. But the strength of universities, from low- to high-income countries, may never have been tested as thoroughly as during the current pandemic. Over the past months, policy makers and institutional leaders have come to realise that the crisis was not just a short parenthesis from the traditional academic routine. In many parts of the planet, things are unlikely to get back to normal anytime soon.

The main issue, therefore, is not to find ways of coping with the short-term effects of the Covid-19 pandemic, but to reshape higher education for resilience. This unprecedented crisis portends drastic structural changes in the higher education landscape and in funding strategies.

Hopefully, the Covid-19 crisis will serve as a wake-up call to reassess the vulnerabilities of the higher education sector and the challenge of living in a global and interdependent world. The emergency support and goodwill of spring 2020 must now give way to a more systematic approach when it comes to the organisation of higher education in the medium term (the next two academic years) and the definition of a longer-term funding approach based on more innovative educational approaches and more resilient business models at the institutional level.

Now more than ever, countries need to design sustainable financing strategies along the lines set out above. This is a high-order priority, considering that the long-term prosperity of any nation is dependent on its ability to train the qualified professionals, scientists and technicians needed to run the economy and conduct relevant research to spearhead innovations, including in the health sector. This was adequately captured in a recent letter of the general secretary of the Association of African Universities, urging the African Ministers of Higher Education to

> use this as an opportunity to strengthen our educational institutions by making them much more resilient to unforeseen crises. This is a great opportunity to communicate clear messages to our African governments on the urgent need to strengthen our educational institutions and systems by making them future-ready and able to survive and thrive in a world of uncertainty.[111]

Finally, it is essential that the new financing strategies give priority to achieving fairness in higher learning for racial and ethnic minorities and those from low-income families, especially girls, who might be left out when household resources are scarce. These students are likely to suffer most because of the Covid-19 crisis. The next 12 months will therefore be a critical test of the capacity of the international community, national governments and higher education institutions to act swiftly and effectively in order to avoid a growing gap between rich and poor countries, between well-endowed and resource-limited institutions, and among the students themselves. It will be crucial to avoid choices that reinforce or deepen existing disparities. Instead, governments and higher education institutions must search together for solutions that create opportunity for all, especially people who have faced barriers to the economic success and social mobility that higher learning can bring.

REFERENCES

Anderson G. (2020), "Feeling shortchanged", *Inside Higher Ed* (13 April 2020), available at www.insidehighered.com/news/2020/04/13/students-say-online-classes-arent-what-they-paid, accessed 11 July 2020.

---

111. See www.aau.org/wp-content/uploads/sites/9/2020/03/Final_Letter-to-Ministries-of-Education-in-Africa-COVID-19.pdf, accessed 11 July 2020.

Brown C. and Salmi J. (2020), "Putting fairness at the heart of higher education", *University World News* (18 April 2020), available at www.universityworldnews.com/post.php?story=20200417094523729, accessed 20 July 2020.

Fatunde T. (2020), "Outcry over health, education capital projects budget cuts", *University World News* (28 April 2020), available at www.universityworldnews.com/post.php?story=2020042806512836, accessed 20 July 2020.

Gavi (2020), "Why are BAME groups experiencing high rates of death from COVID-19?", *The Global Alliance for Vaccines and Immunizations* (29 May 2020), available at www.gavi.org/vaccineswork/why-are-bame-groups-experiencing-high-rates-death-covid-19, accessed 20 July 2020.

Malee Bassett R. and N. Arnhold (2020), "COVID-19's immense impact on equity in tertiary education", *World Bank Blogs*, available at https://blogs.worldbank.org/education/covid-19s-immense-impact-equity-tertiary-education, accessed 11 July 2020.

Nganga G. (2020), "Government cuts universities budget by 26%", *University World News* (11 June 2020), available at www.universityworldnews.com/post.php?story=20200610144752328, accessed 20 July 2020.

NPR (2020), "What do coronavirus racial disparities look like state by state?", National Public Radio (20 May 2020), available at www.npr.org/sections/health-shots/2020/05/30/865413079/what-do-coronavirus-racial-disparities-look-like-state-by-state?t=1595249117871, accessed 20 July 2020.

Salmi J. (2017), *The tertiary education imperative: knowledge, skills and values for development*, Boston and Rotterdam: Sense Publishers.

Yamin K. (2020), "Government allows fee concessions but students protest", *University World News* (3 July 2020), available at www.universityworldnews.com/post.php?story=20200703101555310, accessed 11 July 2020.

Chapter 27

The challenges of the Covid-19 pandemic for higher education legislation in Europe

Dennis Farrington

INTRODUCTION

When plagues, smallpox and other diseases hit the medieval European universities, resulting as now in quarantines and lockdowns – for example in Oxford (Chance et al. 1979) and Bologna (Wray 2009) – the Holy See as the principal source of degree-awarding powers invented dispensations to award degrees to men (*sic*) who had not fulfilled university requirements for residence (Cox 2003). Now, like the medieval pandemics, Covid-19 presents new and unexpected challenges and requires an inventive response.

From mid-March 2020 many countries adopted measures to avoid the spread of the highly infectious virus, which could lead to an initially projected global death rate not experienced since the "Spanish" flu pandemic of 1918. In 2020, using existing public health legislation or emergency powers, governments closed the premises of the majority of higher education institutions in Europe to staff and students. Depending on the extent of their autonomy, institutions were more or less free to adopt alternative methods of online teaching and assessment and to dispense, as in earlier times, with residence requirements.

The question now is how to ensure that institutions can continue to adopt innovative responses and plan for the possibility of further lockdowns, and what this means for higher education legislation.

HIGHER EDUCATION – "LEGISLATION" OR "LAW"

Examining the challenges of the Covid-19 pandemic for higher education legislation requires an understanding of what we mean by "higher education legislation". Until fairly recently, charters, statutes and other rules originating in the 11th to 14th centuries, as for example at Cambridge (Hackett 1970), largely regulated the work of the universities, which enjoyed a high level of autonomy. Today, "higher education legislation" is a generic term for how substantive areas of the law in a given country affect higher education institutions, their staff and students, and define the extent of institutional autonomy, critical to the way in which institutions can respond to the challenges ahead. With the co-operation of legislators, they can take advantage of the unanticipated opportunities which the Covid-19 crisis presents.

Any interested party can undertake a multilingual internet search for the "higher education law" of countries in the European Higher Education Area (EHEA): if the search produces any results, and if the information is reasonably up to date, the search will show that most laws, decrees and regulations are officially published only in national languages. The available sources in English or French may only be summaries prepared by Euridyce,[112] other EU agencies or the European Universities Association (EUA),[113] or when specific international projects have published advice on draft legislation. Even if technically accurate translations of primary legislation are available, it is far from easy to compare national provisions and so make generic proposals for change or to try to identify some common features which might make the task easier and the recommendations more fruitful.

With relatively little direct impact on higher education of international treaties and agreements, apart from the Council of Europe/UNESCO Lisbon Recognition Convention (LRC)[114] and the EHEA/Bologna Process,[115] and to a degree the International Covenant on Economic, Social and Cultural Rights,[116] member states have been free to structure their legal framework in accordance with national priorities and domestic politics. It remains the case that some laws on higher education in Europe are highly regulatory, despite the advantages of a flexible framework law long advocated by Council of Europe experts, where the state would be responsible only for fundamental principles.

No law on higher education as such has directly contemplated a situation arising like Covid-19, although there may be reference to health and other emergencies affecting the otherwise inviolability of university premises as autonomous bodies, as for example in the higher education legislation of Bulgaria, Croatia, Serbia and the Slovak Republic. The law in Finland obliges universities to prepare contingency plans, and most institutions in Europe will or should have initiated specific risk assessments in preparation for the new academic year, or as part of regular internal audits prescribed as a condition of public funding.

To add to the complexity of the task, national legislation governing higher education in a particular country is usually not just a specific law, which in most countries is a relatively recent development, but is part of a complex array of constitutional provisions on autonomy, freedom of speech and expression – in Europe derived from the European Convention for the Protection of Human Rights and Fundamental

---

112. For Eurydice, see https://eacea.ec.europa.eu/national-policies/eurydice/home_en, accessed 21 July 2020.
113. For the European Universities Association, see https://eua.eu/, accessed 21 July 2020.
114. For the Lisbon Recognition Convention, see www.coe.int/en/web/conventions/full-list/-/conventions/treaty/165, accessed 14 July 2020.
115. For the EHEA and Bologna Process, see www.ehea.info/, accessed 14 July 2020.
116. For the International Covenant on Economic, Social and Cultural Rights, see www.ohchr.org/en/professionalinterest/pages/cescr.aspx, accessed 14 July 2020.

Freedoms (the Convention)[117] – accompanied by detailed laws, codes and regulations dealing with: education as such; property and intellectual property; accreditation, quality assurance and inspection; data protection; protection against discrimination; research generally and in specific fields; and, of particular significance in the current difficult climate, laws dealing with public finance, employment, and health and safety. So this is a complex and highly specialised area of law in all countries. Even in the United Kingdom, where universities enjoy a relatively high level of autonomy, the principal textbook on higher education law is some 800 pages long (Farrington and Palfreyman 2020a), albeit dwarfed by its 2 200-page two-volume equivalent in the United States (Kaplin et al. 2019).

In Europe, legislation specific to higher education, which may stand alone or may be subordinate to a general law on education, normally concentrates on autonomy, academic freedom, quality assurance and finance (which may include student finance), protection of university titles, protecting staff and students from arbitrary sanctions and ensuring participation of both staff and students in governance. It may also prescribe in detail the governance and management structures of institutions, with terminology (rector, senate, dean, faculty, etc.) recognisable from the medieval statutes; it usually defines higher education within a national qualifications framework, and implements at least some of the outcomes of the Bologna Process. Naturally, there are also topics specific to the country concerned, notably issues of language of instruction or regulation of particular institutions. All of this makes governing and managing a higher education institution a challenging task, particularly in countries where a low level of trust mandates frequent and intrusive inspections to ensure compliance.

IMPACT OF COVID-19 ON "HIGHER EDUCATION LAW"

In most countries, the impact of Covid-19 has seen an unprecedented intervention in the public interest in different aspects of the traditional autonomy of higher education institutions: organisational (closure of premises and furloughing of non-essential staff), financial (state support, accompanied by conditions) or academic (from admission procedures to awarding of grades and graduation). Normal processes of accreditation, assurance and evaluation, which are now key to maintaining and enhancing the quality of higher education, have been put on hold or severely attenuated. Although by July 2020 some restrictions were being eased, the Covid-19 pandemic presents unprecedented challenges and opportunities for higher education legislation. There are challenges because, as already observed, legislation specific to higher education in a particular country may be overly detailed and inflexible, preventing institutions from readily adapting to the inevitable new methods of working that differ from long-standing teaching methods, and to moves away from traditional diplomas to new forms of internationally-recognised certification including micro-credentials, which could be delivered by non-institutional providers. There are also opportunities because, having identified where problems lie, member states are now in a

---

117. See www.coe.int/en/web/conventions/full-list/-/conventions/treaty/005, accessed 14 July 2020.

good position to modernise their legislation, preferably through a transparent and consultative process involving risk assessment, contingency and strategic planning, and committing to international co-operation to maintain essential mobility and quality assurance.

The extent to which publicly funded institutions are able to act independently depends on the extent of their autonomy, detailed in 2017 for 29 systems by the EUA Autonomy Scorecard (EUA 2017). Among other positive legal obligations placed on institutions as part of an educational standard or otherwise may be the minimum and maximum number of hours of lectures, a requirement for a specific amount of practical (or clinical) training, complex *ex ante* accreditation requirements and state attestation of higher education awards. Article 79 of Croatia's Higher Education Law, for example, goes into considerable detail about the requirements of the curriculum, allowing for "distance education" only with the approval of the National Council of Higher Education. Arguably, where there is a trusted relationship between government and higher education institutions, underpinned by transparency and accountability, such matters should be delegated for internal regulation, rather than being regulated by, and possibly suspended by, ministries under emergency conditions. The emergency conditions have brought into focus the need for member states to review the entirety of their laws affecting higher education so that they are flexible enough to allow higher education institutions to cope adequately with any future pandemic or similar event. A post-Covid-19 review is recommended in all jurisdictions.

EFFECTS ON STUDENTS

Most laws on higher education have something to say about the wider objectives of higher education to promote equal opportunities for citizens and to achieve certain state goals. For example, the Law on Higher Education of Ukraine defines higher education as

> a collection of systematized knowledge, skills and practical aptitudes, manners of thought, professional, worldview and social qualities, moral and ethical values, and other competences, acquired in a higher education institution in an appropriate field, in a certain qualification, at higher education levels that are more complex than the full secondary education level. (Ukraine Law Blog 2015)

So institutions, following such objectives expressed in the applicable law, normally provide opportunities for students coming from a restricted school environment to develop their personalities, independence of thought and responsibilities as citizens of democratic societies, to work together with peers from different cultural and socio-economic backgrounds and so to develop tolerance and understanding, apart from simply having a good time with their peer group. Without direct exposure to debate and discussion in an organised way, higher education becomes simply transmission of knowledge. Where institutions have a sufficient degree of autonomy within the law, finding innovative ways to overcome the social limitations will be a very important issue. So, it is critical that institutions have freedom of operation in that area.

Obviously, the effects on potential students preparing for disrupted state examinations for entry to higher education, and on those already studying at all cycles, are unprecedented in modern peacetime. Some member states, including the United Kingdom, have issued regulations or guidance (Office for Students 2020)[118] to protect students from any detriment or harm due to the pandemic, arranging new forms of assessment at the point of transition from secondary to higher education, and adapting to new ways of working. For those leaving school and due to enter higher education in 2020, admissions procedures have been disrupted; some leading institutions – for example, the University of Cambridge – have stated that, subject to the latest public health advice, traditional lectures may be delivered only or mainly online in the academic year 2020/21 (University of Cambridge 2020), with limited safe physical interaction in small groups, of particular significance in laboratory-based subjects, and requiring specific attention to be given to ensure that all students, particularly those from low-income backgrounds, have equal access to technology.

The UK House of Commons Petitions Committee (House of Commons 2020) conducted a survey which received over 25 000 responses and revealed that "the vast majority of students" were "dissatisfied or very dissatisfied" with their experience of online/virtual teaching. Regardless of the mode of teaching, higher education students in the academic year 2020/21 will almost certainly miss out on some extracurricular social interaction, which has always been a crucial part of the traditional experience. Distance-learning universities that already deliver all or most programmes online, such as the Open University (UK and Ireland) dating from 1969, and the more recently established Università Telematiche (Italy), may be distinguished from those which before March 2020 were offering a traditional experience but also using services such as Google Classroom as an integral element of teaching. This switch in mode of delivery may provide an important model for future development, and higher education law should allow for it.

The existence of a contractual relationship between institutions and students gives rise to the question of how the contract is affected by events constituting *force majeure*. These events can include prolonged periods of industrial action affecting teaching and research, or in this case the impact of Covid-19. Potentially the unavailability of services in the academic year 2019/20 through the impact of the emergency measures may produce a situation of *force majeure* rendering the original contract undeliverable, so undermining the basis for charging full fees where these are charged, even if teaching has continued uninterrupted but online. The legal position depends on the law of domicile of the contract, which is normally the national law of the country concerned, where professional advice is essential (Eversheds Sutherland 2020), and it also depends on the precise nature of the student–institution contract, whether in a single document or drawn from a variety of sources.

Further, where countries accept that the student is legally a consumer, while *force majeure* may be accepted as allowing institutions to default in 2019/20 on contractual obligations, it may not be accepted in 2020/21 if an institution is unable to deliver its promised services and has not taken adequate steps to minimise disruption caused

---

118. For England only: the four nations of the UK each have their own regulator for higher education.

by the pandemic. The Consumer Rights Directive 2011/83/EU has been implemented in EU member states, for example in the UK in the Consumer Rights Act 2015, and there is no doubt that this applies to the institution–student contract (Farrington and Palfreyman 2020b). These rights may be independent of whatever may be included in "higher education law" but that law has to recognise them. Therefore, all institutions should define in accordance with national legislation the precise legal nature of their relationship with students.

EFFECTS ON FINANCE AND CONTRACTS

In the publicly financed higher education institutions, the effect of reduced participation will be seen in income streams, affecting institutions in different ways, through reduced state subsidies, tuition fees, accommodation charges and commercial income. Institutions which have sufficient financial autonomy and operate on an essentially commercial basis will adopt strategies to save costs, deferring non-critical purchases, reducing non-academic expenses, reducing capital and recurrent expenditure, and limiting staff recruitment with potential redundancies, to avoid or reduce any call on reserves.

As in any business, issues arise in contractual relationships with suppliers and in possibilities of breaching covenants in commercial borrowing. One damaging effect on higher education institutions, at least for 2020/21, will be seen in member states where there are significant tuition fees, both for domestic students and "overseas students" who may not attend. The impact of reduced participation on non-public institutions will be even more severe, since the great majority of their income is from tuition fees. Freedom to diversify income streams will be essential.

USE OF DIGITAL PLATFORMS

The impact of the use of digital platforms on students includes:
- ▶ a requirement to ensure equality of access to the necessary technology, which may be difficult in some countries, even the relatively rich western European economies, where high-speed internet access is not universal or families cannot afford the subscription;
- ▶ the educational institution's general or legal duty of care for the safeguarding and mental health of those who may be isolated from peer contact, particularly those with special educational needs;
- ▶ how those using online services are protected from cybercriminals, who may also seek to hack institutional systems;
- ▶ how online assessment can be secured against academic misconduct while protecting the Convention's right to privacy of individuals.

The Council of Europe ETINED platform[119] is preparing recommendations to tackle all forms of education fraud. The opportunities for perpetrators of such fraud, and for students to cheat individually or collectively, are enhanced when assessments

---

119. For ETINED, see www.coe.int/en/web/ethics-transparency-integrity-in-education, accessed 14 July 2020.

are online. While member states and institutions have developed mechanisms for detecting education fraud in submitted work, until now these have rarely been tested in an examination environment. So employers, professional bodies and other stakeholders in higher education are concerned that the value of qualifications awarded under emergency conditions may be questionable, an issue addressed for higher education institutions in the UK by the Quality Assurance Agency (Quality Assurance Agency 2020) and by other agencies in Europe. As noted in a report of May 2020 by the Lisbon Recognition Convention (LRC) Committee Bureau, ENIC Bureau and the NARIC Advisory Board:

> For the countries that ratified the LRC, the treaty provides an internationally binding legal framework and principles on which solutions should be based. The operational framework is offered by the 57 centres of the ENIC (in close co-operation with NARIC) which are tasked by the LRC to promote the treaty's implementation. (ENIC-NARIC 2020)

The report addresses the question of recognition, among other recommendations to identify action(s) to support fair recognition of "disrupted learning" due to Covid-19, in collaboration with the LRC Committee Bureau and external stakeholders including EUA, EURASHE, ESU, ENQA, EQAR, IAU, BFUG and others. There may be a need to review whether some traditional examinations can be replaced indefinitely by secure forms of assessment, and whether this requires changes in legislation.

INTERNATIONALISATION AND MOBILITY

There is also an impact on the internationalisation of higher education through mobility programmes, notably Erasmus+, European Solidarity Corps and bilateral agreements. While borders remain fully or partly closed, participation in programmes is suspended because Covid-19 is considered to be *force majeure* in respect of project contracts, and appropriate arrangements have been put in place by the European Commission. Once borders are re-opened, potential participants may still be reluctant to travel, and public authorities when opening borders may also decide to suspend or limit student and staff exchanges in the 2020/21 academic year.

RESEARCH

Higher education in most countries is closely connected to fundamental and applied research. Closure of premises – except for research and development related to the development of relevant tests, treatments and vaccines for Covid-19 – has had a serious impact on scientific research requiring laboratories or technical equipment, with legal consequences for funding and human resources, and generally on academic progression based on conference attendance and related issues. The last of these is important when considering higher education legislation, since some recent laws, adopted or amended to deal with the proliferation of "fake" journals and conferences, have introduced stringent regulations about academic progression. Arguably this is a matter to be regulated within institutional autonomy, or as a compromise regulated by national rectors' conferences or independent quality assurance agencies.

CONCLUSION: CHALLENGES AND OPPORTUNITIES

Once the immediate crisis is over, the Covid-19 pandemic presents a unique opportunity for all countries to:

- review their legislation governing higher education to ensure that maximum autonomy is granted to institutions to respond quickly and effectively to public emergencies,
- remove unnecessary obstacles in legal provisions relating to licensing, accreditation, human resources and other areas, and
- define the precise nature of their legal relationship with students.

This last item is not an easy task, but fortunately the Council of Europe is well positioned to offer relevant advice.

REFERENCES

Chance E. et al. (1979), "Early modern Oxford", in Crossley A. and Elrington C. R. (eds), *A history of the County of Oxford: Volume 4, the City of Oxford*, pp. 74-180, *British History Online*, available at www.british-history.ac.uk/vch/oxon/vol4/pp74-180, accessed 14 June 2020.

Cox N. (2003), "Dispensations, privileges, and the conferment of graduate status: with special reference to Lambeth degrees", *Journal of Law and Religion*, 18: 101-26.

ENIC-NARIC (2020), *Reflection document on recognition of foreign qualifications in times of Covid-19*, available at www.enic-naric.net/reflection-documentrecognition-of-foreign-qualifications-in-times-of-covid-19.aspx, accessed 16 June 2020.

EUA (European Universities Association) (2017), *University autonomy in Europe*, available at www.university-autonomy.eu/, accessed 11 June 2020.

Eversheds Sutherland (2020), *Force majeure global guide*, available at https://ezine.eversheds-sutherland.com/force-majeure-global-guide/home/, accessed 12 June 2020.

Farrington D. J. and Palfreyman D. (2020a), *The law of higher education*, 3rd edn, Oxford: Oxford University Press.

Farrington D. J. and Palfreyman D. (2020b), "Student consumers, refunds, discounts and the law", available at https://wonkhe.com/blogs/student-consumers-refunds-discounts-and-the-law/, accessed 24 July 2020.

Hackett M. B. (1970), *The original statutes of Cambridge University – the text and history*, Cambridge: Cambridge University Press.

House of Commons (2020), *Report from the Petitions Committee* (13 July), "The impact of Covid-19 on university students", available at https://publications.parliament.uk/pa/cm5801/cmselect/cmpetitions/527/52702.htm, accessed 13 July 2020.

Kaplin W. A. et al. (2019), *The law of higher education*, 6th edn, San Francisco: Jossey-Bass.

Office for Students (2020), *Student guide to coronavirus*, available at www.officeforstudents.org.uk/for-students/student-guide-to-coronavirus/, accessed 12 June 2020.

Quality Assurance Agency (2020), *Covid-19 support and guidance*, available at www.qaa.ac.uk/news-events/support-and-guidance-covid-19#, accessed 12 June 2020.

Ukraine Law Blog (2015), *Law of Ukraine "on higher education"*, available at https://ukrainianlaw.blogspot.com/2015/05/law-of-ukraine-on-higher-education.html, accessed 11 June 2020.

University of Cambridge (2020), *Update from the senior pro-vice-chancellor*, available at www.cam.ac.uk/coronavirus/news/update-from-the-senior-pro-vice-chancellor-education-regarding-the-academic-year-2020-21, accessed 12 June 2020.

Wray S. K. (2009), "Communities and crisis: Bologna during the Black Death", Volume 83 in Kennedy H. et al. (eds), *The Medieval Mediterranean*, Leiden: Brill.

Chapter 28

The challenges of the Covid-19 crisis for students

Robert Napier

The Covid-19 pandemic has not been easy on anybody, but the education sector at large, and students in higher education in particular, have been affected in a way that requires long analysis, discussion and a long recovery period. The challenge is that, in the field of education, we do not have the luxury of waiting until the situation improves, particularly because everyone deserves an equal chance at accessing and achieving high-quality education in a timely manner. Throughout this article, the main challenges of the pandemic for students will be touched upon. Needless to say, this is not an exhaustive list, and possibly not even a list of the most pressing issues, but rather a take on what evidently has made students' lives more challenging during these months.

THE OBVIOUS AND NOT-SO-OBVIOUS CHALLENGES OF THE PANDEMIC

Before delving into the matter at hand, reference should be made to a collective study which was led by a team of researchers at the University of Zadar in collaboration with the Institute for Development of Education and the European Students' Union (ESU), with the support of the Ministry of Science and Education in Croatia (Doolan et al. 2020). This study sought to understand the impact of the Covid-19 pandemic on students' lives and gathered more than 17 000 responses from all across the European Higher Education Area (EHEA). One result that deserves significant attention relates to the mental health of students. The report states that "Among questionnaire respondents, 80.7% of the respondents did not indicate any difficulty in that [health] respect. It is worth noting that 12.9% reported some sort of mental health problem" (ibid.: 8). This percentage is surprisingly high, and while we are not certain whether this percentage is due to the effects of the lockdown or not, we can definitely not ignore the impact of the pandemic on mental health, and how that in turn affects students' ability to perform well in education.

Another major challenge is the impact on freedom of movement, and more specifically on mobility programmes of higher education, along with the impact on international students. Starting with the latter, the pandemic has put huge strain on the performance of international students, particularly as they were faced with considerable uncertainties about their studies in their host universities, with many struggling to decide what was best for them: reuniting with their families at home or waiting for the situation to improve to be able to complete their studies successfully. Many students from outside the EU also faced increased challenges when it came to obtaining their visas or residency permits, as many offices that deal with such requests had closed their doors.

This issue reminded us of the importance of the freedom of movement that the Schengen area has afforded the general public and students over the years. The problems that Covid-19 has caused for international students surely serve as an eye opener for the future, highlighting the role of educational institutions in working hand in hand with the relevant national authorities to facilitate the processing of visa applications. Furthermore, mobility programmes are under threat, with some actors in the field of education trying to use the current circumstances as a justification for making virtual mobility the norm. The issue of mobility rather needs to be seen through two separate lenses: the first is the challenge of ensuring that physical mobility returns as the norm and is not displaced by a shift towards virtual mobility; and the second is the opportunity to establish more sustainable mobility as we emerge from the pandemic and people are allowed to be mobile again.

The recognition and validation of the distance learning that followed the closure of higher education institutions is also a pressing matter that goes hand in hand with other repercussions of the pandemic on students' well-being. According to the research (Doolan et al. 2020), students, mostly those in their first and final years of studies, felt that their academic performance had worsened. It is crucial to learn from this experience and make sure that there is proper communication between higher education institutions and the ENIC/NARICs[120] to remove barriers that might prevent students' access to the right information. It is very important that there is constant communication and collaboration between higher education institutions, national authorities, recognition agencies, student representatives and other stakeholders in order to design and implement suitable and efficient solutions. Staff working in this area need to be supported with the necessary training and knowledge to ensure the transparency and fairness of these processes.

Furthermore, this pandemic should serve as an eye opener to the need to develop clear guidelines for digitising recognition processes while ensuring that all relevant stakeholders, including students, are involved throughout the process. In the field of recognition, we also need to foster a more personal, flexible approach and this should be the case even beyond the pandemic. Improved recognition procedures would provide additional support for refugees, displaced persons and people in refugee-like situations in higher education, who will undoubtedly face bigger challenges as a result of the past few months (ESU 2019).

---

120. National information centres on recognition, see www.enic-naric.net/, accessed 16 July 2020.

EMERGENCY V. DIGITAL EDUCATION

This also brings me to make the point that effective digital education is much more than simply transferring traditional education to online platforms. In the same vein, what we have experienced during the Covid-19 pandemic has been emergency education, not sustainable and effective digital education. Therefore, we now need to make significant investment to ensure that the transition to digital education maintains or enhances the efforts that have been put into achieving high-quality, inclusive education. Furthermore, it is important that our education systems are not only prepared for similar emergencies, but that they also empower students to contribute to the preparedness and recovery of our society.

In this regard, the aforementioned survey (Doolan et al. 2020) sought to analyse the impact on academic life as well as the skills and infrastructure needed for studying at home. Most respondents felt that a larger workload had been imposed on them, highlighting the importance of effective pedagogical training for lecturers. A majority of students felt comfortable using digital platforms, but felt less confident about the context in which they had to use them. Such basic conditions as a quiet area to study, a suitable desk to work on or a stable internet connection were their top priorities to successfully follow the online lectures. All this disruption has definitely been a challenge but it needs to be seen from the "half-full glass" perspective. This is an opportunity for ministries, agencies and institutions to work towards truly inclusive education, ensuring that marginalised, vulnerable and disadvantaged students in particular have equitable access to the resources necessary to be able to successfully finish their studies. Equity and not equality is emphasised on purpose, because those individuals who fall into the categories above will not succeed or have access to resources simply by applying the principle of equality.

Special consideration also needs to be given to students with physical disabilities, who are often considered as a minority and are the first to suffer through the introduction of tools dealing with this emergency education situation. One example has been students with impaired sight or hearing, who found it difficult if not impossible to follow mass lectures online, especially when the platforms were not suited to dealing with these situations. Also, lecturers had little or no pedagogical training on how to safeguard these individuals within a class. Another issue that may have been forgotten is the digital gap that exists among those enrolled in tertiary education and the impact this might have on being able to cope with an emergency education situation. This in itself has proved the lack of preparedness for emergency situations in the education sector, for which ongoing training and consultation should have been in place.

Institutions have a particular challenge ahead of them for the 2020/21 academic year in ensuring that the platforms introduced are accompanied by relevant instructions and training to support and equip all members of the academic community with sufficient digital competencies and skills. All in all, we need to understand that, although studying from home might seem an easier option, the survey results show that this setting can be more distracting. Particularly,

> [c]oncentrating on studying in a family setting is demanding. Moreover, continued online presence and day-long working on the computer, as well as

more challenging teacher–student interaction[,] brings out some additional risks to the study experience. (ibid.: 14)

One answer might be Student Centred Learning (SCL), which represents both a mindset and a culture broadly related to, and supported by, constructivist theories of learning. In higher education institutions, this learning approach has become increasingly difficult to uphold, especially with the suspension of seminars, tutorship and practical classes which are usually better suited to safeguarding this principle. Many students simply became one audience in an online class, with very little time for follow-up or questions. This is in no way meant to underestimate the role of lecturers or their efforts. On the contrary, it is remarkable and highly appreciated how academic staff adjusted to the unprecedented emergency situation, at a very fast rate, while seeking to keep students at the centre of their work.

Obviously, the digital platforms that were introduced in many institutions, alongside the interruption to seminars and practical classes, had an impact on the delivery of lectures, and this challenge now needs to be addressed in order to ensure that this situation does not recur. A strong connection between SCL and the social dimension of higher education[121] should be reflected in the creation of flexible learning pathways, as well as curricular design and innovative pedagogical methods, especially as many institutions prepare themselves for a new academic year (ESU 2019), which might take place entirely through digital or blended learning.

THE *PRINCIPLES AND GUIDELINES* AS A TOOL FOR RECOVERY

The *Principles and guidelines to strengthen the social dimension of higher education in the European Higher Education Area* (Bologna Process 2020) could actually not have been prepared at a better time, and the Bologna Process and the Bologna Follow-Up Group (BFUG) have an important opportunity to prove their relevance. The focus on the "social dimension", a term that combines the principles of accessibility, inclusiveness and equity in higher education, needs to become a policy and practical priority. The proposed principles and guidelines put the social dimension at the core of higher education institutions' policies and strategies at all levels, in an effort to ensure sufficient support for all current and future students. More so amid the current pandemic, emphasis is put on how policy makers and administrators of higher education systems can maintain a level playing field for all students – those who have already started and those who are yet to start their higher education studies – to succeed.

The issue of funding will be a huge challenge for public authorities, institutions and student organisations in particular. It is understandable that public health has cost many governments more than was predicted due to this pandemic and this will necessarily have an impact on other budget sectors. Both the education and civil society sectors (including student organisations) had already been suffering from cuts and a major lack of funding in many countries before the pandemic, and the situation is getting worse. Public authorities, institutions and civil society organisations need to work together to ensure sustainable funding. It is imperative that the

---

121. See www.ehea.info/page-social-dimension, accessed 16 July 2020.

crisis is not used to take advantage of students by increasing tuition fees or reducing student grants. This would be totally unacceptable, not least as it would add to the existing stress that students face.

We must also address the challenge of those who do paid work alongside their studies to be able to sustain themselves, and more specifically those who have lost their jobs due to the Covid-19 pandemic. It comes as no surprise that many student jobs were lost during this period, resulting in fewer students being able to both afford their studies and sustain an acceptable level of living. As highlighted in ESU's policy paper,

> States have an obligation to actively ensure that enough affordable and accessible housing is available. When considering availability, the variety of housing should also be kept in mind, to ensure access to Higher Education for people with varying needs regarding housing. (ESU 2019: 9)

Student housing needs to be prioritised as part of the impact that the pandemic has had on students. It was saddening to read how students lost their jobs when the pandemic hit, and tried to move back home in order to avoid becoming bankrupt from the situation, only to be faced with massive charges for terminating their contracts early or, even worse, fined for breaching the clauses of their original contracts.

These situations are the challenges that lie ahead, and they are also an opportunity: to put things right for the current student generation; to be compassionate and understanding; to treat them honestly; and to allow them to get through their studies in a dignified way. Numerous governments have now started promoting measures aimed at alleviating the situation for businesses and employees in an effort to restart the economy. It is absolutely crucial that, amid these measures, governments take account of the needs of students, most especially of the most vulnerable and marginalised, to ensure the fulfilment of basic needs such as housing, food, utilities and transport, and beyond that the possibility of obtaining grants in cases where students cannot afford to start or complete their tertiary education either in the current semester or in the next academic year.

CONCLUSION

Reference has to be made to the infringement of human rights, including of students, that has been occurring over the first part of 2020 across the continent and the globe. Many governments and political actors used the emergency situation to aggrandise their political authority, to fuel racism and xenophobia, to infringe on the freedoms and dignity of vulnerable people, to bypass the independent press, public authorities, public institutions and civil society in the name of "public health" (see ESU 2020). Such behaviour is unacceptable, and civil society organisations, public authorities and institutions should work hand in hand to challenge it, and demand political accountability, more transparency and involvement in taking the next steps to overcoming the pandemic.

In conclusion, one of the biggest challenges facing higher education in the near future is to ensure that the concerns outlined above do not become impassable obstacles, but rather are turned into opportunities for meaningful and progressive change. Solidarity needs to be embedded at the core of our actions for the foreseeable future if we want to promote inclusion and equity. The right to quality education is universal. We have a collective role to unite, at all levels, and use this as an opportunity to make higher education more accessible, inclusive and equitable. The pandemic has undoubtedly had a negative impact on education, but the ball is now in our court to change the narrative and use it to create a new era, in which everyone, regardless of background or socio-economic standing, has the possibility of successfully completing their studies.

REFERENCES

Bologna Process (2020), *Draft principles and guidelines to strengthen the social dimension of higher education in the EHEA*, available at http://ehea.info/Upload/BFUG_HR_UA_71_6_1_AG1_Annex_Communique.pdf, accessed 10 July 2020.

Doolan K. et al. (2020), *Student life during the COVID-19 pandemic: Europe-wide insights*, University of Zadar, available at http://ehea.info/Upload/BFUG_HR_UA_71_8_1_Survey_results.pdf, accessed 10 July 2020.

ESU (European Students' Union) (2019), *2019 Social dimension policy paper*, Malta: ESU.

ESU (2020), *Review of human rights violations during the COVID-19 Pandemic* (June 2020), available at www.esu-online.org/?policy=european-students-union-review-of-human-rights-violations-during-the-covid-19-pandemic, accessed 10 July 2020.

International Commission on the Futures of Education (2020), *Protecting and transforming education for shared futures and common humanity: a joint statement on the COVID-19 crisis*, available at https://reliefweb.int/sites/reliefweb.int/files/resources/373207eng.pdf, accessed 9 July 2020.

UNESCO (2020), *Safe to learn during COVID-19: new recommendations released*, available at https://en.unesco.org/news/safe-learn-during-covid-19-new-recommendations-released, accessed 9 July 2020.

World Bank (2020), *The COVID-19 crisis response: supporting tertiary education for continuity, adaptation, and innovation*, available at http://pubdocs.worldbank.org/en/621991586463915490/WB-Tertiary-Ed-and-Covid-19-Crisis-for-public-use-April-9.pdf, accessed 7 July 2020.

Chapter 29

Addressing the challenges of the Covid-19 pandemic: a view from higher education staff

Rob Copeland

The impact of Covid-19 on higher education systems in Europe has been profound. They have closed their campuses, shifted academic staff to "emergency remote teaching" and been forced to put their research projects on hold. International academic mobility has been adversely affected by the closure of borders and the suspension of overseas travel. This chapter identifies the main challenges faced by higher education staff, especially in their working conditions, and explores the potential impact of the crisis on fundamental values such as academic freedom and public responsibility for higher education, including funding. In developing a response to the crisis, public authorities and higher education institutions should work with staff and student organisations to improve the funding, functioning and sustainability of higher education systems in Europe.

"EMERGENCY REMOTE TEACHING" AND THE FUTURE OF ONLINE LEARNING

As Hodges and colleagues (2020) have suggested, the terminology used to describe recent experiments in learning and teaching is important:

> Well-planned online learning experiences are meaningfully different from courses offered online in response to a crisis or disaster. Colleges and universities working to maintain instruction during the COVID-19 pandemic should understand those differences when evaluating this emergency remote teaching. (Hodges et al. 2020)

The immediate challenge facing higher education staff in the Covid-19 pandemic has been the shift to homeworking and emergency remote teaching as a result of the closure of campuses in spring 2020. According to a survey published in May 2020, 85% of European higher education institutions were able to speedily move teaching and learning online (IAU 2020: 24).

Academic staff showed considerable professionalism, creativity and hard work in moving quickly to remote teaching. Many of them undertook these tasks while juggling caring responsibilities and home schooling, a process which has exacerbated existing gender inequalities (Donald 2020). In addition, staff and students struggled with poor infrastructure such as inadequate broadband, IT equipment and "office" space and a lack of prior training in digital pedagogies. Staff have also reported increased work intensification and diminished well-being as a result of adapting learning to online instruction (Watermeyer et al. 2020) and this situation is likely to worsen following proposed cuts to thousands of fixed-term and casualised teaching posts (Staton 2020).

At the time of writing (July 2020) most universities in Europe will be offering a form of "blended learning" for the 2020/21 academic year, with large-scale lectures shifting online and smaller group teaching such as seminars being conducted either in person or remotely. For staff and their organisations, the primary challenge is how to guarantee a safe return to on-site working, including measures to support physical and emotional well-being and recovery (Education International 2020a). Pressures to return to face-to-face provision in the autumn are common to all European higher education systems, but are particularly acute in systems that are based on institutional competition for fee-paying students (Marginson 2020). Whatever the financial or political context, health and safety considerations must remain paramount in determining the return to on-site working and that will depend, in part, on the proper involvement of staff and student representatives. Another key challenge is to support academic staff in the transition to online teaching and assessment for the 2020/21 academic year. In many jurisdictions, universities are currently providing specialist training to assist staff in online learning but there is arguably insufficient time, expertise and resources to do this in a way which mirrors "best practice" in established distance education providers.

A key strategic issue is whether the online pivot will become a more permanent feature of European higher education in the period ahead. To some extent this will depend upon the scale of the disruption caused by Covid-19 but also on the strategic decisions of individual higher education institutions, for example, whether an institution is teaching- or research-focused and/or its disciplinary focus. What is clear is that rushed attempts to use private education companies to shift teaching and learning permanently online (and without proper engagement with staff and students) are unworkable and also risk damaging a university's reputation (Hall and Batty 2020). Moreover, institutional plans to scale up online provision not only require investment in staff skills and buy-in from colleagues, but very careful consideration as to whether partnerships with private education companies are in the interests of staff, students and the wider public (Morris 2020).

The Covid-19 crisis has led to an enhanced role for private providers – the so-called Edtech industry – in delivering online learning within schools (Williamson and Hogan 2020) and in intensifying the processes of automation and datafication within universities (Williamson 2020). And while this has occurred during an emergency, the Edtech industry has a clear objective of ensuring it becomes a permanent actor in education systems in the future. This, in turn, raises major concerns around data ownership and control, privacy and surveillance, but also has the potential to negatively affect the overall funding and purposes of higher education (for example, in allowing governments to justify longer-term budget cuts to higher education and/or encouraging a shift towards narrower, employer-focused curricula).

IMPACT ON RESEARCH AND RESEARCHERS

While the primary focus has been on the challenges facing teaching and learning, it is important to recognise the impact of Covid-19 on research and researchers. First, university staff have played a direct role in supporting medical research efforts to combat the virus, most notably in the search for a vaccine. In a number of European countries, there has also been increased research funding for Covid-19 related research. This is to be welcomed, though additional public funding should also be made available for the arts, humanities and social sciences, which will play a key role in ensuring a just and sustainable social, economic and cultural recovery (Cannadine and Black 2020).

At the same time, there has been significant disruption to many research programmes, with fixed-term researchers and PhD students being particularly badly affected (Eurodoc 2020). The response from governments and funders has been mixed, with many bodies, including the European Union, failing to provide funded extensions for its researchers (Pola 2020). This points to a long-standing problem affecting the global higher education workforce: namely, that fixed-term and casualised staff are always the hardest hit by cuts to university budgets and research income. As the editors of *Nature* point out:

> Yet again, the academic precariat finds itself at a disadvantage. Governments, research managers and senior colleagues have a duty to help so that universities can keep these essential and valuable employees. (Nature 2020: 314)

These problems are particularly acute in marketised, fee-paying systems such as in Australia, the United States and the United Kingdom (UK) but, even within publicly funded systems in Europe, early career academics are likely to face a difficult period ahead in their search for stable forms of employment (Matthews 2020a). Thus, we need a more systematic review of the academic career structure in higher education, which should involve public authorities and universities working with the trade unions to ensure greater job security for early career staff (ETUCE 2020).

As highlighted above, the Covid-19 crisis has disproportionately affected women's working lives, and in the higher education sector we have already seen a decline in submissions from female researchers during the pandemic lockdown (Matthews 2020b). The cuts to fixed-term and casualised posts have also disproportionately affected women and black, Asian and ethnic minority (BAME) staff (McKie 2020b). In the context of existing inequalities in higher education, particularly for working-class, BAME and disabled students, universities and public authorities need to ensure that the Covid-19 crisis does not lead to further increases in educational inequality.

Finally, it is possible to identify a number of positive developments for staff in relation to research policy during the pandemic. These include a further shift towards open access publishing (Grove 2020) and a temporary suspension of performance-based funding schemes such as in the UK and Italy (Macintyre 2020; Turone 2020). While these pandemic-induced shifts are welcome, we must ensure they become lasting changes that usher in more ethical, sustainable and co-operative models of research funding and assessment.

PUBLIC FUNDING AND PUBLIC RESPONSIBILITY FOR HIGHER EDUCATION

One of the big challenges facing higher education institutions, including staff, is funding. As the European University Association (EUA) has argued, "The overall impact of the current crisis will be large and long-lasting, and universities must prepare for operational and financial difficulties in the coming few years" (EUA 2020: 11).

In Europe, some universities are facing immediate financial difficulties due to the loss of international student fees and commercial income, for example, as in Ireland (McGuire 2020). The financial crisis, however, is particularly acute in the UK, with its relatively high tuition fees and large numbers of international students at research-intensive universities, while the greater market competition for domestic students is likely to disrupt financially weaker teaching-intensive institutions (London Economics 2020; Drayton and Waltmann 2020). One of the consequences is that the UK is one of the few higher education systems in Europe contemplating major redundancies, including of permanent staff, as well as pay and increment freezes, and other reductions to terms and conditions (Matthews 2020a).

In a number of publicly funded systems, there is a different concern, namely, that budget cuts will kick in from 2021 as a result of a conservative fiscal response to the economic crisis (EUA 2020). Countries such as Italy and Spain that have been badly affected by the pandemic but also suffered severe education cuts after the 2008 financial crisis may be particularly vulnerable to further austerity measures. In addition, higher education systems where institutional income depends significantly on domestic tuition fees (for example, Spain and Romania), and where student participation often depends on the availability of part-time jobs to supplement low levels of student support, may also suffer badly as a result of the economic downturn (ibid.). After the 2008 crisis, many education workers in Europe, particularly in southern and eastern Europe endured cuts in pay, pensions and working conditions (ETUCE 2013) and it is vital that this process does not repeat itself, particularly in light of the major role played by key workers such as teachers in ensuring the continuity of learning during the pandemic.

At the same time, systems that are based on high levels of public funding and public responsibility for higher education and research, such as in the Nordic countries, are likely to be more resilient in coping with the crisis. These are also the education systems that are based on positive traditions of social dialogue, stakeholder engagement and consultation and collaboration between governments, higher education institutions, trade unions and student organisations. For example, one of the reasons why an organised return to schooling in Denmark has been more successful than in England[122] is that the teacher unions have been closely and routinely consulted throughout the process (Orange 2020).

---

122. Education is a devolved matter in the UK and decisions on how and when to re-open schools in Scotland, Wales and Northern Ireland are the responsibility of the Scottish Parliament and the Assemblies of Wales and Northern Ireland rather than the UK Government in London. In England, the consultation on the re-opening of schools between the Department for Education and the education trade unions has been particularly acrimonious.

One of the lessons of the current crisis, therefore, is that governments should commit to boosting public investment in quality higher education for all and to enabling institutions to provide staff with the appropriate resources, working conditions and academic autonomy that they need to undertake excellent teaching and research (ETUCE 2020). In addition, there is a need to strengthen social dialogue and collective bargaining between education trade unions and education employer organisations on all matters relating to working conditions and professional issues, including digitalisation (ETUCE/EFEE 2020).

COVID-19 AND THE IMPACT ON FUNDAMENTAL VALUES

In recent years, there has been renewed interest in fundamental values such as academic freedom, institutional autonomy and public responsibility for and of higher education (Bologna Process 2018b). Academic freedom and institutional autonomy – as in the case of press freedom – are also integral to democratic societies and therefore are particularly in need of promotion and protection (Global Forum 2019). How do the issues of fundamental values relate to the challenges posed by the Covid-19 crisis?

First, there are concerns that governments, including some in Europe, have adopted unrestricted emergency measures to manage the Covid-19 health crisis. For example, the Hungarian Government's original "emergency decree" was heavily criticised for having no set time limit and for undermining the rule of law. As the Council of Europe has argued, the emergency measures taken by member states during the pandemic must remain proportional to the threat posed by the spread of the virus and be of limited duration (Council of Europe 2020).

Second, these principles should apply to any extraordinary measures introduced for the higher education sector. Hence, in terms of safeguarding the autonomy of higher education institutions, the implementation of special regulatory powers – for example, as proposed by the Office for Students in England to address the financial stability of the sector – should also include time limits (McKie 2020a).

Compared to many other parts of the world, academic freedom is better protected in Europe, although this is not the case for all member states of the Council of Europe and in recent years there has been a major deterioration in countries such as Turkey (Kinzelbach et al. 2020: 15) as well as violations against individual universities in Hungary and Russia (Bologna Process 2018a: 41). At the same time, we need to be alert to subtle erosions of academic freedom within liberal democracies and the potential role that the pandemic may play in this process. For example, the shift to emergency remote teaching is already generating concerns about how to ensure the academic freedom of staff and students in situations where students are studying remotely in jurisdictions where there are severe forms of internet censorship and surveillance (Coughlan 2020; Li et al. 2020). This reinforces the case for the Bologna Follow-Up Group (BFUG) to continue its work on developing an effective monitoring framework on fundamental values, especially on academic freedom, within the European Higher Education Area.[123] There is also a potential key role for the Council

---

123. For a brief article on the work of the BFUG task force on the future monitoring of values and the development of a common understanding of academic freedom, see Upton (2020).

of Europe, particularly through its education programmes, in ensuring that academic freedom and institutional autonomy are safeguarded in the "new normal".

Staff and student participation is another fundamental value of European higher education (Bologna Process 2018b). In the current emergency, university managements must resist the temptation to bypass their traditional governance structures in the interests of speed and efficiency. On the contrary, during these difficult times, it would be better to open up university governance – based on the principles of collegiality and democratic decision making – and to ensure transparency of financial accounts and scenario planning with the campus trade unions.

The Covid-19 pandemic has also highlighted the significance of the civic role played by higher education institutions and the staff who work in them. One of the positive developments in recent months has been an upsurge in university public engagement during the pandemic (Sursock 2020; IAU 2020: 5, 9). This has included direct contributions to national health systems in the form of staffing (e.g. the secondment of clinical academic staff) and resources (e.g. the production of coronavirus test kits and the donation of ventilators and personal protective equipment). More indirectly, it has involved staff and students supporting the local community in dealing with the effects of Covid-19, for example, on mental health and food poverty (Universities UK 2020). The objective going forward will be to ensure that these practices are embedded in the day-to-day operations of higher education institutions; for staff, that will mean proper recognition of public engagement activities in workload allocation and career progression.

Finally, it is important to recognise the challenges to internationalisation as a result of Covid-19. International students and staff have been the most affected by the closure of borders and restrictions on travel, and international education is likely to suffer a "massive hit" for years (Bothwell 2020). First of all, while recognising the environmental benefits of reduced international travel, we need to restate the case for international mobility and exchange as a fundamental part of European higher education. That means resisting the neo-nationalist tendencies that have gained currency in recent months (DeLaquil 2020) and boosting the funding for flagship mobility schemes such as Erasmus+. Second, the current crisis in countries such as Australia and the UK should prompt a re-evaluation of a funding model based on sky-high international student fees. Instead, we should look to more financially progressive and ethically sustainable approaches to international student participation that exist in countries such as Germany and Norway.

A POST-COVID OPPORTUNITY FOR STRUCTURAL REFORM OF HIGHER EDUCATION?

As with many other sectors, the Covid-19 pandemic has hit higher education staff and students hard. For staff, the key challenges include the shift to emergency remote teaching and further pressure to work with private providers to move their classes online; the disruption to research programmes; cuts to fixed-term and casualised teaching and research posts; and increased financial uncertainties facing higher education institutions as a result of student volatility, particularly from international students. Many of these processes have increased inequalities between different groups of staff and students.

At the same time, the emergency situation has opened up new possibilities to expand open educational resources and open science, to recognise the public engagement work undertaken by universities and to reassert the notion of higher education as a public good (Harvaky et al. 2020; International Commission on the Futures of Education 2020). Moreover, the situation may provide an opportunity to improve the funding, functioning and sustainability of education systems, particularly as the wider public now has a greater appreciation of the complexity and value of the work done by teachers and scientists. Education unions have a key role to play in persuading public authorities and education institutions to ensure that "recognition of the profession and for the status of those who exercise it should be a priority to advance education in the post-pandemic era" (Education International 2020b). It is an opportunity we must seize in the months and years ahead.

REFERENCES

Bologna Process (2018a), *The European Higher Education Area in 2018: Bologna Process implementation report*, p. 41, available at https://eacea.ec.europa.eu/national-policies/eurydice/sites/eurydice/files/bologna_internet_chapter_1_0.pdf, accessed 29 July 2020.

Bologna Process (2018b), *Paris communiqué* (25 May 2018), available at www.ehea.info/Upload/document/ministerial_declarations/EHEAParis2018_Communique_final_952771.pdf, accessed 12 July 2020.

Bothwell E. (2020), "Coronavirus: global student flows to suffer 'massive hit' for years", *Times Higher Education* (26 March 2020), available at www.timeshighereducation.com/news/coronavirus-global-student-flows-suffer-massive-hit-years, accessed 14 July 2020.

Cannadine D. and Black J. (2020), "All subjects have a role to play in rebuilding post-Covid. Let's SHAPE the future together", *Wonkhe* (21 June 2020), available at https://wonkhe.com/blogs/all-subjects-have-a-role-to-play-in-rebuilding-post-covid-lets-shape-the-future-together/, accessed 8 July 2020.

Coughlan C. (2020), "UK universities comply with China's internet restrictions", *BBC News* (9 July 2020), available at www.bbc.co.uk/news/education-53341217, accessed 12 July 2020.

Council of Europe (2020), *Respecting democracy, rule of law and human rights in the framework of the COVID-19 sanitary crisis: a toolkit for member states*, Strasbourg: Council of Europe (7 April 2020), available at https://rm.coe.int/sg-inf-2020-11-respecting-democracy-rule-of-law-and-human-rights-in-th/16809e1f40, accessed 6 July 2020.

DeLaquil T. (2020), "Neo-nationalism is a threat to academic cooperation", *University World News* (4 July 2020), available at www.universityworldnews.com/post.php?story=20200630104920899, accessed 6 July 2020.

Donald A. (2020), "The disproportionate effect of Covid-19 on women must be addressed", *Times Higher Education* (25 June 2020), available at www.timeshighereducation.com/opinion/disproportionate-effect-covid-19-women-must-be-addressed, accessed 23 June 2020.

Drayton E. and Waltmann B. (2020), *Will universities need a bailout to survive the COVID-19 crisis?*, London: Institute for Fiscal Studies, available at www.ifs.org.uk/uploads/BN300-Will-universities-need-bailout-survive-COVID-19-crisis-1.pdf, accessed 12 July 2020.

Education International (2020a), *International guidance on reopening schools and education institutions*, Brussels: Education International (30 April 2020), available at www.ei-ie.org/en/detail/16760/education-international-guidance-to-reopening-schools-and-education-institutions, accessed 12 July 2020.

Education International (2020b), *Forward to school: guidance, considerations and resources for and from education unions to inform decision-making in times of Covid-19*, available at www.ei-ie.org/en/detail/16862/learning-from-one-another-ei-publishes-forward-to-school, accessed 14 July 2020.

Eurodoc (2020), *The aftermath of the pandemic for early career researchers in Europe*, Brussels: Eurodoc (6 July 2020), available at www.eurodoc.net/news/2020/the-aftermath-of-the-pandemic-for-early-career-researchers-in-europe, accessed 7 July 2020.

ETUCE (European Trade Union Committee for Education) (2013), *The continued impact of the crisis on teachers in Europe*, Brussels: ETUCE, available at www.csee-etuce.org/en/campaigns/education-in-crisis/271-impact-of-the-crisis-on-teachers, accessed 12 July 2020.

ETUCE (2020), *ETUCE Statement on the road to recovery from the COVID-19 crisis*, Brussels: ETUCE, available at www.csee-etuce.org/en/resources/statements/3885-etuce-statement-on-the-road-to-recovery-from-the-covid-19-crisis-june-2020, accessed 26 June 2020.

ETUCE/ EFEE (European Federation of Education Employers) (2020), *Joint ETUCE/EFEE Statement on the impact of the COVID-19 crisis on sustainable education systems at times of crisis and beyond*, Brussels: ETUCE/EFEE, available at www.csee-etuce.org/en/news/etuce/3902-education-trade-unions-and-employers-commit-to-a-comprehensive-vision-to-support-education-systems-in-the-covid-19-recovery, accessed 27 June 2020.

EUA (European University Association) (2020), *The impact of the Covid-19 crisis on university funding in Europe: lessons learnt from the 2008 global financial crisis*, Brussels: EUA (May 2020), available at https://eua.eu/resources/publications/927:the-impact-of-the-covid-19-crisis-on-university-funding-in-europe.html, accessed 10 June 2020.

Global Forum (Global Forum on Academic Freedom, Institutional Autonomy, and the Future of Democracy) (2019), Declaration (21 June 2019), available at https://rm.coe.int/global-forum-declaration-global-forum-final-21-06-19-003-/16809523e5, accessed 12 July 2020.

Grove J. (2020), "Open-access publishing and the coronavirus", *Inside Higher Education* (15 May 2020), available at www.insidehighered.com/news/2020/05/15/coronavirus-may-be-encouraging-publishers-pursue-open-access, accessed 6 July 2020.

Hall R. and Batty D. (2020), "Durham University retracts controversial plan to provide online-only degrees", *The Guardian* (25 April 2020), available at www.theguardian.com/education/2020/apr/25/durham-university-retracts-controversial-plan-to-provide-online-only-degrees, accessed 25 May 2020.

Harkavy I., Bergan S., Gallagher T. and van't Land H. (2020), "Universities must help shape the post-COVID-19 world", *University World News* (18 April 2020), available at www.universityworldnews.com/post.php?story=20200413152542750, accessed 6 May 2020.

Hodges C. et al. (2020), "The difference between emergency remote teaching and online learning", *EDUCAUSE Review* (27 March 2020), available at https://er.educause.edu/articles/2020/3/the-difference-between-emergency-remote-teaching-and-online-learning, accessed 6 July 2020.

IAU (International Association of Universities) (2020), *The impact of Covid-19 on higher education around the world: IAU global survey report* (May 2020), Paris: IAU, available at www.iau-aiu.net/IMG/pdf/iau_covid19_and_he_survey_report_final_may_2020.pdf, accessed 20 June 2020.

International Commission on the Futures of Education (2020), *Education in a post-COVID world: nine ideas for public action*, Paris: UNESCO, available at https://unesdoc.unesco.org/ark:/48223/pf0000373717/PDF/373717eng.pdf.multi, accessed 14 July 2020.

Kinzelbach K. et al. (2020), *Free universities: putting the academic freedom index into action* (March 2020), Berlin: GPPI, available at www.gppi.net/2020/03/26/free-universities, accessed 12 July 2020.

Li H., Arnsperger L. and Cerny M. (2020), "Censorship fears and vampire hours: Chinese international students, Zoom, and remote learning", *SupChina* (30 June 2020), available at https://supchina.com/2020/06/30/chinese-international-students-zoom-and-remote-learning/, accessed 6 July 2020.

London Economics (2020), *Impact of the Covid-19 pandemic on university finances. Report for the University and College Union*, London: UCU, available at www.ucu.org.uk/media/10871/LE_report_on_covid19_and_university_finances/pdf/LEreportoncovid19anduniversityfinances, accessed 23 April 2020.

Macintyre F. (2020), "REF 2021 'put on hold' because of coronavirus outbreak", *Research Professional News* (24 March 2020), available at www.researchprofessionalnews.com/rr-news-uk-ref-2014-2020-3-ref-2021-put-on-hold-because-of-coronavirus-outbreak/, accessed 6 June 2020.

Marginson S. (2020), "Pandemic shows need for HE for the global common good", *University World News* (25 July 2020), available at www.universityworldnews.com/post.php?story=20200724114218359, accessed 27 July 2020.

Matthews D. (2020a), "European universities spared coronavirus cuts – for now", *Times Higher Education* (28 May 2020), available at www.timeshighereducation.com/news/european-universities-spared-coronavirus-cuts-fornow, accessed 28 May 2020.

Matthews D. (2020b), "Pandemic lockdown holding back female academics, data show", *Times Higher Education* (25 June 2020), available at www.timeshighereducation.com/news/pandemic-lockdown-holding-back-female-academics-data-show, accessed 28 June 2020.

McGuire P. (2020), "Colleges face crisis as funding in freefall", *Irish Times* (9 June 2020), available at www.irishtimes.com/news/education/colleges-face-crisis-as-funding-in-freefall-1.4269546, accessed 12 July 2020.

McKie A. (2020a), "Fears raised over scope of OfS' crisis regulatory powers", *Times Higher Education* (19 May 2020), available at www.timeshighereducation.com/news/fears-raised-over-scope-ofs-crisis-regulatory-powers, accessed 12 July 2020.

McKie A. (2020b), "Bonfire of casual contracts 'a huge setback' for racial equality", *Times Higher Education* (9 July 2020), available at www.timeshighereducation.com/news/bonfire-casual-contracts-huge-setback-racial-equality, accessed 7 October 2020.

Morris N. (2020), "Scaling up online education? More haste less speed", *Higher Education Policy Institute* (29 April 2020), available at www.hepi.ac.uk/2020/04/29/scaling-up-online-education-more-haste-less-speed/, accessed 28 May 2020.

Nature (2020), "Boosting research without supporting universities is wrong-headed", *Nature*, 582: 313-14, available at doi: 10.1038/d41586-020-01788-6, accessed 20 June 2020.

Orange R. (2020), "Split classes, outdoor lessons: what Denmark can teach England about reopening schools after Covid-19", *The Observer* (17 May 2020), available at www.theguardian.com/education/2020/may/17/denmark-can-teach-england-safe-reopening-of-schools-covid-19, accessed 12 July 2020.

Pola L. (2020), "Marie Curie fellows fear Covid-19 crisis will lead to career devastation", *Research Professional News* (18 June 2020), available at www.researchprofessionalnews.com/rr-news-europe-horizon-2020-2020-6-marie-curie-fellows-fear-covid-19-crisis-will-lead-to-career-devastation/, accessed 7 July 2020.

Staton B. (2020), "Universities to cut thousands of academics on short contracts", *Financial Times* (20 July 2020), available at www.ft.com/content/67f89a9e-ac30-47d0-83e7-eba4d1284847, accessed 29 July 2020.

Sursock A. (2020), "The vital role of civic engagement for universities", *University World News* (16 May 2020), available at www.universityworldnews.com/post.php?story=20200515072822480, accessed 12 July 2020.

Turone F. (2020), "Extra time for exercise to measure research quality", *Research Professional News* (23 April 2020), available at www.researchprofessionalnews.com/rr-news-europe-italy-2020-4-extra-time-for-exercise-to-measure-research-quality/, accessed 6 June 2020.

Universities UK (2020), *How universities are helping fight Covid-19*, London: UUK. www.universitiesuk.ac.uk/covid19/supporting-national-effort/Documents/we-are-together-case-studies-covid-19.pdf, accessed 7 October 2020.

Upton B. (2020), "Seeking independence", *Research Europe*, 518 (7 May): 8-9.

Watermeyer R. et al. (2020), "COVID-19 and digital disruption in UK universities: afflictions and affordances of emergency online migration", *Higher Education*, available (Open Access) at https://link.springer.com/article/10.1007/s10734-020-00561-y, accessed 28 June 2020.

Williamson B. (2020), "Datafication and automation in higher education during and after the Covid-19 crisis" (6 May 2020), available at https://codeactsineducation.wordpress.com/2020/05/06/datafication-automation-he-covid19-crisis/, accessed 6 July 2020.

Williamson B. and Hogan A. (2020), *Commercialisation and privatisation in/of education in the context of Covid-19*, Brussels: Education International, available at https://issuu.com/educationinternational/docs/2020_eiresearch_gr_commercialisation_privatisation, accessed 10 July 2020.

Chapter 30

Universities as catalysts of post-Covid recovery and renewal in communities

John Gardner

INTRODUCTION

Universities, globally, have been cast as key actors in dealing with the many effects of the Covid-19 pandemic. As centres of excellence in research, education and innovation, their warrant for this role is long established and it is a reasonable expectation, post-Covid-19, that the higher education sector will indeed step up in these areas of strength. But we should ask more of our universities, requiring contributions from them that are more deeply embedded in their social responsibilities as "anchor" institutions. This local, regional and even national community dimension for an anchor institution is captured in Wilson's characterisation as

> an important presence in the community; a key cultural centre; a major impact on employment; a gatherer and spender of significant revenue; a role as a major employer; a purchaser of goods and services; an attractor of businesses and talented individuals. (Wilson 2012: 73)

Reaching out and reaching into the community are not wholly unfamiliar activities for most universities. However, post-Covid-19 financial stringencies may tempt them into disproportionate efforts to try to recoup lost revenue – to the detriment of existing or new community-focused activities. There is a certain inevitability about this type of reaction if cash-strapped universities do not reflect sufficiently on the challenges and opportunities for change that the post-Covid-19 period will present. They may elect to engage partly or not at all in tackling social challenges that attract smaller revenue rewards.

One such challenge is the need to improve social cohesion and trust in the system, for example by improving access to higher education for disadvantaged groups, and to move away from the perceived sole purpose of enabling "the individual accrual of cultural capital which can be traded up into wealth for an elite, and instead seek to understand and challenge inequality, injustice, exclusion and othering" (Maginess 2020). Universities, post-Covid-19, must also do more to improve community health and well-being, address digital deficits in their host communities, and counter community ignorance that is sustained by inadequate education. It is not unreasonable to argue that, over the past decade or so, inadequate education has contributed to enabling populist movements to manipulate whole sections of society and undermine the very core of democratic society.

THE CONSEQUENCES OF THE PANDEMIC FOR UNIVERSITIES

The early stages of the Covid-19 pandemic literally brought the world to a standstill, giving pause to reflect on all aspects of modern society. Rapidly affecting over 200 states and dependent territories in the first half of 2020 (Worldometer 2020), many developed countries have experienced this catastrophe from the level of the individual citizen to the very roots and structures of their governance. Personal hardships have included lockdown restrictions such as prohibitions on travel, communal activity, schooling and even funereal customs – and many have endured the debilitating ill-health and tragic death of loved ones. National economies have nose-dived into recession attended by huge increases in unemployment, food poverty and demands on welfare and health services that are unprecedented in modern times. In the least developed nations at the other end of the GDP spectrum, these pandemic effects are less well documented, but it is reasonable to assume that low economic resilience, less established systems of communication, education, welfare and health and potentially less stable governance will contribute to even more tragic human, social and economic circumstances.

Facing such catastrophic challenges to society, governments have had different levels of success in bringing the situation under some semblance of control. In the UK, the neoliberal notion of allowing matters to take their course – for example, to breed "herd immunity" (Guardian 2020), to continue with open border travel in spite of at least 130 countries operating travel restrictions (Financial Times 2020), to allow huge gatherings of people (for example, the four-day Cheltenham racing festival attracting 250 000 people; see Jockey Club 2020) – finally gave way to a grudging adoption of some of the WHO advice on containment strategies that had begun to see success in Asia and Europe. The corporate voice has unsurprisingly focused more on rallying the business and manufacturing communities to tackle adversity head on, characterised by simple messaging such as the Gartner soundbite: Response-Recovery-Renewal (Gartner 2020). Entwined in all aspects of these sectors' activities lies the reaction of the world's universities. The pandemic has arguably cast them as key actors in the current and future dramas.

This should come as no surprise, of course. Universities have high concentrations of experts that can advise governments and lead on crucial activities such as vaccine development. They have huge wells of innovation to be tapped for new approaches to economic and social challenges that have been exacerbated by the pandemic. And, arguably, they have long-established reserves of integrity and objectivity, sustained by academic freedom, to enable dependable monitoring and analysis of the multivariate impacts that Covid-19 is having on today's society. In no short measure, therefore, society can justifiably expect that "THE TASK [sic] of a university is the creation of the future" (Whitehead 1938: 233). Horizon-scanning, blue-sky research and innovation are all tools for securing the future, but I would suggest that universities must also contribute significantly to repairing the present.

And the present is broken. Many communities throughout the world live hand-to-mouth, so to speak. Poverty, economic disadvantage, inadequate health care and education provision are just some of the many challenges that can curtail life chances and indeed life expectancy, especially when these are combined with pernicious internal conflicts and the erosion or absence of human rights. In most developed nations, democracy offers a voice to contest and to varying degrees ameliorate these inequities and inequalities. However, even in the most advanced of democratic nations the legacy of the "selfish amoralism" (Judt 2010: 236) of such leaders as Margaret Thatcher and Ronald Reagan has over time prompted the rise of populist movements that revel in sustaining inequalities, disadvantage and outrageous levels of personal wealth for the few. The pandemic has raised these and other new challenges (in sustaining health-care capacity, for example) to catastrophic levels of concern and it may be tempting for some universities to wring their hands and wait for the storm to blow over.

Unfortunately, however, the Covid-19 storm is already taking its toll on universities. Robinson and Maitra (2020), for example, recount a litany of financial difficulties for colleges and universities across North America. These difficulties include up to 20% decreases in enrolments, reduced state and private funding, and the prospect of students suing for refunds for interrupted or inadequate tuition. In order to protect core academic functions they recommend a higher education version of slash-and-burn that calls for the elimination of low-performing departments, reduction in administrative "bloat" (the proportion of non-academic staff), pay cuts and freezes, and cuts in spending on what they patronisingly term "grievance studies" (exemplified as race, ethnic, gender and women's studies). The latter recommendation signals that in some institutions, post-Covid-19 financial exigencies might threaten academic freedoms and the capacity to address social issues.

The financial situation for many UK universities is also critical, especially those institutions that usually recruit large numbers of international students or that had been struggling financially before the crisis. The representative body, Universities UK, suggests that there could be a loss of £3.2 billion in the 2020/21 academic year for universities in England alone, owing to potential reductions in fee income of 50% and 15% respectively from international student recruitment and home students who elect to defer entry for a year (UUK 2020a). Scottish and Northern Irish universities will be relatively even worse off because chronic underfunding of home student tuition over many years has meant that they have subsidised their research and other activities through international student fee income. Concerns about the indirect impact of the loss of this income on research activity, estimated by the Scottish Funding Council as £450 to 500 million for the 18 Scottish institutions (Scottish Government 2020: 58), has prompted the central UK Government to offer mitigation funds of up to 80% of these losses for all UK universities. Independent assessments of the wider Covid-19 impacts on UK universities (DBEIS 2020), by the Institute of Fiscal Studies (Drayton and Waltman 2020), suggest that almost 10% of the UK's universities (13 institutions) may not be viable in the long term, needing government bailouts or debt restructuring to stave off insolvency.

UNIVERSITIES CATALYSING RECOVERY AND RENEWAL

In addition to finding ways to cope with the financial fall-out from the pandemic, most UK universities are, to their credit, taking a longer view of their role in local and national recovery. As an anchor institution, a university typically provides "economic, environmental and cultural benefits to its community and, critically, should play a central role in rebalancing the economy of a community under stress and promoting growth in one that is prosperous" (Wilson 2012: 73). Contributing to growth and prosperity are already success stories for the UK university sector. For example, in 2014-15 universities contributed £95 billion to the UK economy and provided employment for 944 000 people (Oxford Economics 2017). And Holland et al. (2013) have calculated that 20% of economic growth in the UK from 1982 to 2005 was a direct result of graduate skills accumulation from higher education. Just as importantly, graduating students are considered to have significant impact on society through creating greater social cohesion, trust and tolerance, and political stability (BIS 2013), including the communities around their alma mater.

Although post-Covid-19 circumstances will have an impact on all communities, those with higher levels of affluence will enjoy some cushioning of the harshest effects. However, most universities will have some degree of interface with communities that, even before the pandemic struck, suffered from a toxic cocktail of challenging social circumstances and disadvantage, which inevitably affects the quality of life of everyone and especially the life chances of young people. These social disadvantages include below-norm levels of educational achievement, household income, employment, digital literacy and access, and of physical and mental well-being. In the latter case, research (e.g. Kessler et al. 2005, 2007) suggests that 75% of mental disorders will have occurred in young people before age 24 – making it crucial that universities, in consort with the appropriate local bodies, should remain alert to any challenging social circumstances that could contribute to the mental ill-health of their staff, students and young people in their host communities.

Universities UK, in a Covid-prompted refresh of its 2017 mental health advice framework (UUK 2020b), exhorts all of its member institutions to address mental health openly and systematically for staff and students and also emphasises collaboration with local communities and bodies (NHS, schools, colleges, parents) to mitigate any risks involved in transition to university. Institutions can seek to address community-based problems in various ways but I cannot argue that they can easily repair the effects of decades of government neglect and austerity, certainly not alone or without the government taking effective measures to address the many inequities and disadvantages that have become entrenched in low-income communities. However, I will argue that universities' role as anchor institutions implies a greater imperative, post-Covid-19, to increase their efforts to ensure all sections – young and old – of their host communities are empowered to improve their resilience and capacity to recover from Covid-exacerbated social problems.

In a bid to win intervention funding from government, Universities UK has pitched a case (UUK 2020c) that bluntly outlines the risks that post-Covid-19 reductions in income would have on all the key areas of research and innovation. Importantly, however, UUK also signals how the impending financial consequences of the pandemic could reduce the capacity of its member institutions to improve life chances for people of all backgrounds, through driving social mobility, improving quality of life through social and cultural impact, and reskilling people for the post-Covid-19 context through increased part-time provision and flexible adult learning.

Clearly, no single response could be designed for all institutions, but the overarching aims should be the active promotion of appropriate course offerings, equitable access to all courses and the embedding in every course of such democratic underpinnings as academic freedom, collaborative working, lifelong learning skills, critical thinking, ethical decision making and the various forms of digital communication and productivity.

Some universities have already shown broad intent in this regard. For example, the 18 higher education institutions in Scotland have collectively committed to a strategy of "collaborative recovery" to enable Scotland and its regions and cities to recover (Universities Scotland 2020: 3). Support for business is unsurprisingly prominent in the institutions' intentions, with strong resolutions to support a re-invention and recovery of the Scottish economy through entrepreneurship education, internships and increased facilities for incubating small businesses. Importantly, though, this relatively brief strategic declaration is also strong on community and environment-related action. Recognising that "the recession will have the hardest impact on the socio-economically disadvantaged and the digitally excluded" (ibid.: 2), the universities assert their "relentless commitment to widening access to higher education for those from disadvantaged backgrounds" (ibid.). This resolve is complemented by community-focused intentions to increase access to cultural opportunities, to promote digital inclusion and to make more of their resources digitally accessible to communities. On the education front they focus on skills, with commitments to strengthen links with the college sector and to create responsive pathways and flexible courses that address the post-Covid-19 need for reskilling and upskilling.

Undoubtedly, there will be similar pledge-type publications from universities across the world in the year ahead, but the rate and extent of effective progress will be moderated by a variety of hindering factors, not least of which will likely be restricted access to resources and finance. However, key to improving the odds of a successful response-recovery-renewal campaign will be the need for collaboration, a must-have condition emphasised in the Universities Scotland approach. Universities have long-established routes and vehicles for collaboration with the government and with key sectors such as manufacturing, engineering, science, technology, construction and health, and indeed with other universities, and their engagement with local authorities, communities and employers around them has improved immensely in recent years. However, the predicted post-Covid-19 recession is set to exaggerate to unprecedented levels the already inequitable wealth gaps in society as unemployment rises and household incomes fall.

Low income levels and high unemployment within communities have predictable associations with above-norm levels of debt difficulties, food poverty, health and nutrition problems, mental ill-health, alcohol and substance abuse, suicide, domestic violence, dysfunctional family life, crime and teenage pregnancy. Poor educational attainment and low levels of literacy in these communities compound these problems and are also major threats to democracy. As Sen (2017) has said: "Illiteracy muffles the political voice of people and leads to insecurity". Young people from these communities are under-represented in higher education, particularly in some sectors of higher education in the United States (New York Times 2017) but both the UK Government and the university sector have long-standing polices of widening access to attract them in, and once there to try to ensure they progress and complete their courses.

Arguably, however, widening access as a strategy, complete with inducements of all kinds, has not lived up to its promise. Aside from a reluctance in some academic quarters to acknowledge that talent and the ability to benefit from a university education are not determined by background, there is no overt resistance in UK universities to increasing and widening access for all, young and old. However, many people out in the surrounding communities still perceive universities as august, sombre and essentially remote places, full of clever, aloof people and maintaining an "ivory tower" elite. Much more needs to be done to lower the drawbridge and make all comers welcome! One clear avenue of development, however, is systematically to analyse appropriate datasets on existing and former students to identify inequalities in the inputs (such as admissions and subject choices) and outcomes (such as achievements and completion) of students from disadvantaged groups, making any problems visible and enabling steps to be taken to address them.

The relatively low numbers of young and older adults from disadvantaged backgrounds applying for courses in higher education may in some part be related to universities' ignorance of their desires, dispositions and circumstances. Echoing Bernstein's (1970) exhortation to teachers to better understand the factors causing disaffection and underachievement in schools, and not to patronise students, denigrate their backgrounds or harbour low expectations for their progress, Pennacchia et al. (2018) argue that it is imperative that universities should seek to understand the motivations of adults to learn, and the often multiple barriers and competing priorities that frustrate that final step into the university. University staff need to be sensitive to the fact that, in addition to the circumstantial community problems above (such as low-income and high-unemployment contexts) many potential learners may have poor prior experiences of education that ingrain a fear of learning or a lack of confidence, and may have competing priorities such as care responsibilities.

One partial remedy to the circumstantial barriers faced by prospective adult learners is the development of flexible pathways and courses, mentioned as a stratagem by Universities Scotland (2020). And perhaps paradoxically, the pandemic-related lockdown of campuses has given the development of online and blended teaching and assessment approaches a major fillip. Though given very little advance warning, hundreds of thousands of academics around the world worked rapidly and assiduously to deliver the final semester of their academic year – "a semester unlike any other" (Sciences Po 2020) – and the scale of individual university provision is worthy of mention. In France, for example, Sciences Po, Paris (a private university of approximately 14 000 students), chalked up 217 new Moodle-based courses and recorded 6 659 online assessments (Sciences Po 2020) while, in Northern Ireland,

Queen's University (a public university with about 25 000 students) recorded 86 804 participants in 1 317 video-conferences and 19 000+ submitted online assessments (Fee and Morgan 2020).

The level of effort from university academic and professional staff bodes well for any potential programme of flexible learning development that is designed to reach non-conventional student groups, including those from disadvantaged backgrounds, older adults, carers with limited capacity to attend campus and learners in remote locations. In the UK, this type of provision is guided by the Quality Assurance Agency's principles (QAA 2020), which require the quality and standards of conventional approaches to be maintained online. Importantly, given the potential anxiety and stress for students in such a radical and unforeseen change to their learning, one of the QAA principles is that universities should engage with students (and staff) in planning the changes, and that these should remain flexible and responsive to students' changing needs.

This latter point – being responsive to students' needs – introduces a hugely important next-generation move in university curriculum design, namely co-construction of curricula. With a full understanding of their potential students' motivations, needs, dispositions and circumstances, whether from disadvantaged backgrounds or not, academics have a wealth of information to enable them to co-construct courses that are attractive to prospective students. I should emphasise that co-construction is not new to universities – it features in many professional and vocational courses in which the design and content, in social work and journalism for example, are co-constructed with employers, practitioners and prospective students. Broadening the reach of such strategies to the wider curriculum is the next-generation move to which I refer. There will always be a need for curricula (and pedagogy) to impart the basics of a discipline, but co-constructive design could prove of significant benefit in improving student engagement, retention and completion due to the perceived increase in relevance of the courses, a better match with students' needs and aspirations, a greater sense of belonging and ownership and the prospect of closer alignment with employers and employment opportunities.

CONCLUDING REMARKS

A recession visits many ills on a nation and the "perfect storm" of Covid-related sickness, restricted movement, locked-down social venues and increased unemployment, among other things, is predictably taking its toll on health and well-being more generally, and mental health specifically. The Office for National Statistics, ONS, estimates that the people with the poorest levels of personal well-being (around 1% of the population) will have at least one of the following characteristics: be in bad health, middle-aged, economically inactive, have a disability, be single, have no basic education and live in rented accommodation (ONS 2018). Before the pandemic, inequality and its various effects was continually fomenting discontent, with government neglect in economic investment undermining the capacity of whole communities, cities and even regions to aspire to reasonable levels of prosperity, employment and life chances for their citizens. Little wonder that the ONS (2020) estimates that trust in government fell by 11 percentage points in the year to autumn 2019.

Insidious inequality grows over time and the attendant long-term frustration, arising from various deprivations and lack of opportunity, slowly begins to fracture social cohesion, leaving people at best unhappy and at worst in conflict with the law of the land. Universities must step up and help to reinvigorate social democracy and communal well-being. They can do this in the time-honoured way of ensuring that their graduating students are imbued with the democratic values of fairness and equity, and equipped with the skills of ethical decision making, critical thinking, collaborative working, lifelong learning and digital literacy. But more to the point, universities can and should engage more purposefully with their host communities – educationally, culturally and collaboratively – to involve the young and old in higher education that can reduce the democratic deficit of recent decades by instilling a sense of purpose, enabling access to opportunity and driving up confidence, well-being and autonomy.

> Much of what is amiss in our world can best be captured in the language of classical political thought: we are intuitively familiar with issues of injustice, unfairness, inequality and immorality – we have just forgotten how to talk about them. (Judt 2010: 234)

Over the years, the discourse within universities on supporting purposeful community engagement has never quite been forgotten but it has certainly waxed and waned as financial imperatives variously grabbed the attention of managers and staff. In the post-Covid-19 world, however, our anchor institutions must talk much more openly about reaching out and putting community engagement high on the agenda – to raise education levels (including digital literacy), break the cycles of disadvantage, drive growth in community well-being and prosperity, and reinvigorate social democracy.

REFERENCES

Bernstein B. (1970), "Critique of compensatory education", in Rubenstein D. and Stoneman C. (eds), *Education for democracy*, London: Penguin, pp. 111-21.

BIS (Department for Business Innovation and Skills) (2013), *The benefits of higher education participation for individuals and society: key findings and reports: "the quadrants"*, BIS Research Report 146. Department for Business, Innovation and Skills, available at https://assets.publishing.service.gov.uk/government/uploads/system/uploads/attachment_data/file/254101/bis-13-1268-benefits-of-higher-education-participation-the-quadrants.pdf, accessed 26 July 2020.

DBEIS (2020), *Press release: government to protect UK research jobs with major support package*, UK Government Department for Business, Energy and Industrial Strategy, available at www.gov.uk/government/news/government-to-protect-uk-research-jobs-with-major-support-package, accessed 26 July 2020.

Drayton E. and Waltman B. (2020), *Will universities need a bailout to survive the COVID-19 crisis?*, London: Institute of Fiscal Studies, available at www.ifs.org.uk/publications/14919, accessed 26 July 2020.

Fee W. and Morgan P. (2020), Personal communication.

Financial Times (2020), "Britain's open borders make it a global outlier in coronavirus fight", *Financial Times* (16 April 2020), available at www.ft.com/content/91dea18f-ad0e-4dcb-98c3-de836b1ba79b, accessed 26 July 2020.

Gartner (2020), *Reset your business strategy in COVID-19 recovery*, Smarter with Gartner, available at www.gartner.com/smarterwithgartner/reset-your-business-strategy-in-covid-19-recovery/, accessed 26 July 2020.

Guardian (2020), "Documents contradict UK government stance on Covid-19 'herd immunity'", *The Guardian* (12 April 2020), available at www.theguardian.com/world/2020/apr/12/documents-contradict-uk-government-stance-on-covid-19-herd-immunity, accessed 26 July 2020.

Holland D. et al. (2013), *The relationship between graduates and growth across countries*, BIS Research Report 110, Department for Business Innovation and Skills / National Institute of Economic and Social Research, available at www.gov.uk/government/publications/graduates-and-economic-growth-across-countries, accessed 26 July 2020.

Jockey Club (2020), Press release (13 March 2020), The Jockey Club, available at www.thejockeyclub.co.uk/cheltenham/media/press-releases/2020/03/crowd-of-68859-for-fourth-day-in-2020/, accessed 26 July 2020.

Judt T. (2010), *Ill fares the land*, London: Allen Lane.

Kessler R. C. et al. (2005), "Lifetime prevalence and age-of-onset distributions of DSM-IV disorders in the national comorbidity survey replication", *Archives of General Psychiatry*, 62(6): 593-602.

Kessler R. C. et al. (2007), "Lifetime prevalence and age-of-onset distributions of mental disorders in the World Health Organization's world mental health survey initiative", *World Psychiatry*, 6: 168-76.

Maginess T. (2020), Personal communication.

New York Times (2017), "Some colleges have more students from the top 1 percent than the bottom 60: find yours", *New York Times* (18 January 2017), available at www.nytimes.com/interactive/2017/01/18/upshot/some-colleges-have-more-students-from-the-top-1-percent-than-the-bottom-60.html?searchResultPosition=1, accessed 26 July 2020.

ONS (2018), *Understanding well-being inequalities: who has the poorest personal well-being?* [analysis covers period 2014-16], UK Office for National Statistics, available at www.ons.gov.uk/peoplepopulationandcommunity/wellbeing/articles/understandingwellbeinginequalitieswhohasthepoorestpersonalwellbeing/2018-07-11, accessed 26 July 2020.

ONS (2020), *Social capital in the UK: 2020*, UK Office for National Statistics, available at www.ons.gov.uk/peoplepopulationandcommunity/wellbeing/bulletins/socialcapitalintheuk/2020, accessed 26 July 2020.

Oxford Economics (2017), *The economic impact of UK universities*, 2014-15, Oxford Economics Ltd, available at www.universitiesuk.ac.uk/policy-and-analysis/reports/Documents/2017/the-economic-impact-of-universities.pdf, accessed 26 July 2020.

Pennacchia J., Jones E. and Aldridge F. (2018), *Barriers to learning for disadvantaged groups*, UK Government Department for Education, available at https://assets.publishing.service.gov.uk/government/uploads/system/uploads/attachment_data/file/735453/Barriers_to_learning_-_Qualitative_report.pdf, accessed 26 July 2020.

QAA (2020), *Preserving quality and standards through a time of rapid change: UK higher education in 2020-21*. The Quality Assurance Agency for Higher Education (2 June 2020), available at www.qaa.ac.uk/docs/qaa/guidance/preserving-quality-and-standards-through-a-time-of-rapid-change.pdf?sfvrsn=6a1dcc81_10, accessed 26 July 2020.

Robinson J. and Maitra S. (2020), "Higher education after COVID-19 – policy brief", Rochester, NY: SSRN, available at https://ssrn.com/abstract=3604670, accessed 26 July 2020.

Sciences Po (2020), *Key takeaways from a semester unlike any other*, Paris: Sciences Po, available at www.sciencespo.fr/en/news/news/key-takeaways-from-a-semester-unlike-any-other/5000, accessed 26 July 2020.

Scottish Government (2020), *Towards a robust, resilient wellbeing economy for Scotland: Report of the Advisory Group on Economic Recovery*, Edinburgh: Scottish Government, available at www.gov.scot/publications/towards-robust-resilient-wellbeing-economy-scotland-report-advisory-group-economic-recovery/, accessed 26 July 2020.

Sen A. (2017), *What is the use of education?* [keynote lecture], launch of the Centre for Education and International Development, University College London (15 June 2017), available at https://mediacentral.ucl.ac.uk/Player/7200, accessed 26 July 2020.

Universities Scotland (2020), "Scotland's recovery – universities' role", available at www.universities-scotland.ac.uk/wp-content/uploads/2020/06/Scotlands-Recovery-Universities-Role-v-1.0.pdf, accessed 26 July 2020.

UUK (2020a), *Letter to Chair of the Education Committee, Westminster* (28 April 2020), Universities UK, available at www.universitiesuk.ac.uk/news/Documents/UUK-letter-to-Rt-Hon-Robert-Halfon-COVID19.pdf, accessed 26 July 2020.

UUK (2020b), *Stepchange: mentally healthy universities*, Universities UK, available at www.universitiesuk.ac.uk/policy-and-analysis/reports/Documents/2020/uuk-step-change-mhu.pdf, accessed 26 July 2020.

UUK (2020c), *Achieving stability in the higher education sector following COVID-19*, Universities UK, available at https://universitiesuk.ac.uk/news/Documents/uuk_achieving-stability-higher-education-april-2020.pdf, accessed 26 July 2020.

Whitehead A. N. (1938), *Modes of thought*, New York: Macmillan.

Wilson T. (2012), *A review of business–university collaboration*, UK Government Department for Business, Innovation and Skills, available at https://assets.publishing.service.gov.uk/government/uploads/system/uploads/attachment_data/file/32383/12-610-wilson-review-business-university-collaboration.pdf, accessed 26 July 2020.

Worldometer (2020), *COVID-19 coronavirus pandemic*, Worldometers.Info, available at www.worldometers.info/coronavirus/, accessed 26 July 2020.

Chapter 31

The local university mission after Covid-19: two Irish case studies

Tony Gallagher and Ronaldo Munck

CONTEXT

In Ireland the universities north and south of the border were already reeling from another external shock before Covid-19 came on the scene at the start of 2020. The Brexit process – the United Kingdom's exit from the European Union – had already unsettled the universities in both jurisdictions as long-standing research collaborations across Europe were jeopardised. The very economic survival of Northern Ireland was at stake and the threat of political instability became a real and present danger. It is remarkable how the universities north and south of the border worked together to seek some degree of protection from the coming storm – now (in mid-July 2020) predicted for the start of 2021 – not least Queen's University Belfast (Northern Ireland) and Dublin City University (Republic of Ireland).

In this chapter we seek to illustrate the history of these two Irish universities in terms of their early leadership in the area of commitment to the local community. In both cases they were set in areas of high deprivation where there was a perceived divide between society and the local university. We examine their place-making drive over the past 10 years or so to see what lessons we might learn. We also turn our attention to the situation in 2020 and the way in which these two Irish universities have responded to the Covid-19 crisis. Like other universities across the world they have responded very quickly, not only in the area of medical research, but also in terms of local engagement.

We believe the local should not be seen as in some way inferior to the global, and anyway the two are interlinked in practice. Globalisation is only constructed through local "globalisations", as it were. The local mission represents a great opportunity for the university to have a very real and direct impact on society. The leverage of place is a powerful means to enhance the reputation of a university, as many university leaders are now realising. Above all, it fulfils a social obligation; it is part of the democratic mission of the university that needs to go side by side with the knowledge project. It is the only way we will reach out to wider layers of students and build the educational capacity of our universities (see Bergan, Harkavy and Munck 2019).

DUBLIN

Dublin City University (DCU), situated in the high-unemployment northern part of the capital city of the Republic of Ireland, was the first Irish university to launch a civic and community engagement strategy back in 2006. While some higher education institutions might just accept as a given the geographical location they inhabit, DCU has recognised the importance of its immediate surrounding area and has made concerted efforts to engage with local stakeholders by creating mutually beneficial partnerships and links. Its surrounding communities (Ballymun, Finglas, Kilmore, Darndale and Coolock) have been characterised by complex interlocking forms of deprivation that have remained a constant despite urban regeneration efforts in recent decades (Munck 2009). In 2010 the university decided to make a concerted effort to address these issues through an outreach centre located in Ballymun with support from Dublin City Council (Munck 2012).

The mission of the "DCU in the Community" initiative[124] is to provide educational and lifelong learning opportunities to local residents in order to promote equality in third-level education and to broaden access to higher education among under-represented groups – "second chance" learners, mature students and learners from socio-economically disadvantaged areas. In the years since the Ballymun centre opened, the spectrum of civic engagement activities offered through DCU in the Community has broadened significantly, and currently also includes student volunteering, community-based learning and community-engaged research, as well as a range of ad hoc local community–university projects (Ozarowska 2019).

Two other, more recent initiatives complement the work of DCU in the Community in terms of student engagement and community-based research respectively. A student volunteering initiative was set up in 2015, greatly empowering the work done by the students' union, and it led to a new strategy. It was focused on engaging with civic society organisations (CSOs) to provide nourishing and rewarding volunteering opportunities in local, national and international communities for all students and CSOs so they are mutually beneficial. The strategy also sought to enable access to civic activity for all students at DCU, through a grounded, guided approach in collaboration with our community partners and stakeholders. It committed to continue to develop and roll out unique, grassroots events which focus on hands-on voluntary action which feeds into our community-driven and approachable attitude. Above all it is about building on collaborative partnerships within the university and beyond to continue to deliver innovative voluntary activity models.

This strategy builds on the DCU co-led initiative for the national engagement platform Campus Engage to set up a dedicated website[125] to act as a national management system for higher education student volunteering. Between 2010 and today, close to a thousand DCU students from across all schools and faculties have been linked with volunteering and service-learning opportunities in the local community. Many of the students have led the development of new volunteering opportunities in consultation with community partners and based on community needs. Student engagement,

---
124. See www.dcu.ie/community, accessed 28 July 2020.
125. See www.studentvolunteer.ie, accessed 24 July 2020.

leadership and volunteering activities promoted by DCU in the Community have provided DCU students with an opportunity to develop graduate attributes, such as creativity and enterprise, problem solving, communication skills, community and global awareness and leadership.

In 2020 DCU moved to set up a Centre for Engaged Research[126] to bring under one roof all the various initiatives around community-based research in the humanities and social sciences but also in the science and technology areas. This new centre is part of the broader move towards engaged research, which promotes research approaches and methodologies implying collaborative engagement with the community and other stakeholders to address societal challenges in a responsive manner, and promotes public engagement with science and technology. It explores the potential for increased collaborative activities, participation and knowledge dissemination, facilitated through new technologies, shared governance structures and partnerships. This brings greater public ownership of, and connection with, policy making and responses to societal issues such as climate change, pandemics and social marginalisation. It also embodies the DCU mission to transform lives and transform societies through education, research, engagement and innovation, and reflects the social responsibility mission of the university. Finally, it reflects the need to rebuild societies towards a new sustainable, collaborative resilience after the current health crisis and to harness and communicate the knowledge of the university to address social needs directly, understanding the transformative power of university–community partnerships.

BELFAST

Queen's University Belfast has a long history, having originally been founded as part of the federal Queen's University of Ireland, with campuses in Cork and Galway, as well as Belfast. It became an independent university, in its own right, in 1909 and took on some of the features of the civic universities then being established in industrial centres in the United Kingdom. Thereafter, and especially after the partition of Ireland in 1922, Queen's University became a core institution of the new political establishment in Northern Ireland. Higher education expanded in the UK in the 1960s and Queen's saw a growth in the number of students from the Catholic minority, many of whom were inspired by the US Civil Rights campaign to support an eponymous campaign in Northern Ireland. This contrast between Queen's as an institution at the heart of the social, economic and political establishment in Northern Ireland, and at the same time the location for a campaign for radical change in Northern Irish society, was thrown into sharp relief by the onset of political violence in the period from 1969 to 1998 commonly known as "the troubles" (Gallagher 2019).

For some time the university authorities discouraged research on the conflict, a sentiment confirmed by the University Vice Chancellor in 1977 when he suggested that direct involvement in society would "negate professional independence" and put at risk "the *contract social* that gives autonomy to the university in return for its institutional neutrality" (Froggatt 1977, quoted in Taylor 1988: 29). This position

---

126. See www.dcu.ie/engagedresearch, accessed 24 July 2020.

became unsustainable when a series of legal challenges to the hiring practices of the university highlighted a highly differential pattern of recruitment. This in turn led to a complete reform of hiring policy and, over the next two decades, a marked shift in recruitment profiles (Gallagher 2019).

It also prompted a revision of the claim to neutrality and the start of more active engagement in societal issues. Queen's is now a signatory of the NCCPE Manifesto for Public Engagement[127] and its work in this area has steadily grown over time (Gallagher 2012; Gallagher and Harrison 2016; McDonald et al. 2016). Currently this involves active support for research which has a positive impact on society; long-term community partnerships in distressed parts of Belfast to co-create strategies for renewal; a Science Shop, which acts as a broker between community organisations and the university to support community-based research projects which benefit both students, by giving them an opportunity to research real-world issues, and communities, by giving them access to material they can use in their own campaigns; and an extensive programme of student and staff volunteering, highlighted by a student-led system of Homework Clubs across Belfast.

In 2017 the university moved to institutionalise this work by establishing a Social Charter[128] with three main commitments based on: providing leadership, locally and globally; making a positive impact on society through research and teaching; and promoting equality and social justice. The charter identifies seven key areas of work focused on research, teaching, innovation, equality, civic culture and intercultural dialogue, sustainability, and recognition and reward for staff.

There are a number of lessons from the Queen's experience in relation to the local mission of universities. The first of these is that the local mission can take various forms and at times might locate the institution as part of a local social, economic and political elite. But the second lesson is that this can change. In the case of Queen's, the process of change in the university towards a form of local engagement founded on principles of inclusion and social justice began as a bottom-up process, initially led by students and later adopted by academic staff, who were prepared to set aside the institutional preference not to engage with difficult and controversial political issues and actually deal with these issues through their teaching and research. The example of Queen's also shows that the institutional ethos itself can change, but that this change is most likely to be sustainable if it can be formally incorporated into the policy and practice of the university. The development of a Social Charter, as an explicit statement of values and principles, is one way in which this can be achieved.

COVID-19 RESPONSES

As in other Irish universities, DCU quickly put in place a dedicated Covid-19 research group with substantial funding (see Keogh, Chapter 10 in this volume, for more

---

127. National Co-ordinating Centre for Public Engagement (NCCPE) at www.publicengagement.ac.uk/support-engagement/strategy-and-planning/manifesto-public-engagement, accessed 13 July 2020.
128. For the Queen's University Social Charter, see www.qub.ac.uk/social-charter/, accessed 13 July 2020.

detail). It also set up a fully staffed Contact Tracing Centre to assist the Health Service Executive in its efforts to trace and contact those who had come into contact with Covid-19-infected people. Other academics worked with campaigns, around older people in particular, to combat misinformation and scams. Data analytics and health staff created a series of resources on Facebook on how people could stay active during lockdown. The Corona Citizen's Science Project,[129] in collaboration with Galway University, conducted a large-scale survey on how the coronavirus pandemic affected people's work, school and childcare, to identify barriers and coping mechanisms. DCU staff delivered substantial supplies of personal protective equipment (PPE) and 3D printers to make masks to local hospitals and other care facilities. Most of this work has been conducted by individual staff members on their own initiative and is testimony to the extent to which civic engagement has become embedded in the culture of the university.

DCU students have also responded to local social challenges during the Covid-19 pandemic by engaging in virtual volunteering – voluntary activities, with a similar commitment and training process as physical opportunities, that took place remotely over the internet.

Both local and national charities experienced an "unprecedented social and economic crisis in the wake of Covid-19".[130] According to the Charities Regulator survey[131] over two thirds of charities in Ireland reported that their activities were restricted as a consequence of the Covid-19 lockdown, while at the same time the need for services in areas such as mental health, poverty relief, homelessness support and disability support increased significantly.

DCU student volunteers took steps to address some of these challenges, for example through fundraising initiatives for the sector, with online campaigns such as Clear Your Head in aid of Darkness into Light, and Climb Every Mountain and Busk for Barretstown in aid of Barretstown (DCU official charity partner).[132] Another example of DCU students' virtual civic engagement was the Pen Pal Project organised jointly with Silver Thread and Carechoice Homes, whereby DCU student volunteers were paired up with residents at the care homes, who were under strict lockdown restrictions, had little access to the outside world and had seen all regular activities and visits halted. The exchange of letters was conducted via email, with the DCU students and residents making contact weekly to fill each other in on their news, share stories and get to know one another.

On a more local level, DCU in the Community rapidly transferred its teaching online when the lockdown came in March 2020, and successfully completed its courses and remained in touch with its students in the community. However, this exercise

---

129. See www.dcu.ie/news/news/2020/Apr/Corona-Citizens%E2%80%99-survey-will-ask-public-which-social-restrictions-should-be, accessed 27 July 2020.
130. See www.wheel.ie/news/2020/05/charities-face-unprecedented-social-and-economic-crisis-wake-covid-19, accessed 17 July 2020.
131. See www.charitiesregulator.ie/media/1924/report-impact-of-coronavirus-covid-19-on-charities-survey.pdf, accessed 17 July 2020.
132. See www.dcu.ie/news/news/2019/Sep/DCU-announces-three-year-partnership-Barretstown-Children%E2%80%99s-Charity.shtml, accessed 27 July 2020.

highlighted the extent of the digital divide in socially disadvantaged areas, with approximately one third of students unable to access online learning. This deficit will need to be addressed.

When the Covid-19 crisis hit and the government in Northern Ireland implemented lockdown, many staff and students at Queen's had already "voted with their feet" and were staying away from the campus. This was true also for many schools across Northern Ireland. De facto this meant that lockdown came into place about a week before it was officially imposed which, in the longer term, may have contributed to the fact that Northern Ireland has been somewhat less severely impacted by Covid-19 in comparison with other parts of the UK. In part this "popular" decision to lock down early was influenced by the decision of the government in the Republic of Ireland, in common with most EU countries, to enter lockdown before the UK.

Once this was put in place there was an immediate priority given to identify ways in which the university could make the most positive impact on the efforts to tackle the health crisis. Since lockdown was predicated in part on a concern that the health system might become overwhelmed by patients affected by Covid-19, an early decision was made, in co-operation with the appropriate accreditation authorities, to fast-track final-year students in health-related professions to graduation so they could take up roles in the health service and free up more experienced staff to deal with Covid-19 cases. This fast-track process was put in place for doctors, nurses and social workers. Medical and pharmaceutical research facilities were also re-prioritised to support the health service, with the establishment of systems to support population testing for the virus, and engagement with local and international efforts to develop vaccines and treatments. Engineers repurposed some of their facilities to design and produce personal protective equipment as this was in short supply at the start of the crisis.

As in DCU, some of these initiatives emanated from the personal initiatives of staff, which served as an indication of the extent to which the commitment to making a difference locally is being embedded in the culture and ethos of the institution. The decision to fast-track key student groups to graduation was an institutional decision, predicated on recognition of the way Queen's could, and should, contribute to the emergency preparations that were being put in place across society to deal with the impending health crisis. Again, the fact that this decision was taken and implemented so quickly is a powerful indication of the ethos of local support which is embedded in the university.

LESSONS

The World Health Organization has constantly stressed throughout the pandemic that the level of social engagement has been a critical factor in whether countries deal successfully with its impact. The universities are, or should be, part of that active social engagement.

It is sometimes suggested that there is a contradiction between the priorities of a local mission and a commitment to global excellence. In our view, this is a tension but one that can be almost entirely positive. A commitment to global excellence in research and teaching can bring significant local benefit if there is joined-up thinking within the system. In the same way, engagement with local communities can help universities to refine and sharpen research and teaching agendas. The way both Irish institutions have responded to the Covid-19 crisis, with a combination of local action and involvement in research programmes at national and international scales, serves to reinforce this sense of the connectedness of the local and global in promoting the university's mission. In consequence we will be moving forward after the Covid-19 crisis subsides, with more social and community engagement, greater local commitment and socially embedded teaching, research and student volunteering.

The Covid-19 crisis has also shown up the weaknesses in our university system and the need to build in much more resilience. It has brought into sharp relief some of the consequences of inequality in our societies and heightened the need for our institutions to address this more effectively in future. In Ireland a juridical border between north and south has hampered efforts for an all-island strategy to combat Covid-19, but the universities have continued to collaborate. More engagement between the two university systems will make sense post-Covid-19 and, of course, post-Brexit. In the troubled times ahead, deep local-to-local collaboration across the board is the only way forward.

REFERENCES

Bergan S., Harkavy I. and Munck R. (eds) (2019), *The local mission of higher education: principles and practice*, Dublin: Glasnevin Publishing.

Gallagher T. (2019), "Embedding engagement: the example of Queen's University Belfast", in Bergan S., Harkavy I. and Munck R. (eds), *The local mission of higher education: principles and practice*, Dublin: Glasnevin Publishing.

Gallagher, T. (2012), "Student-community engagement at Queen's University Belfast" in S. Bergan, I. Harkavy and H. van't Land (eds), *Reimagining democratic societies: a new era of personal and social responsibility*, Council of Europe Publishing, Strasbourg.

Gallagher T. and Harrison J. (2016), "Civic engagement in a divided society: the role of Queen's University Belfast in Northern Ireland", in Bergan S., Gallagher T. and Harkavy I. (eds), *Higher education for democratic innovation*, Higher Education series No. 21, Strasbourg: Council of Europe, pp. 51-62.

Keogh D., "*Maireann na daoine ar scath a chéile*: Dublin City University, Covid-19, and the creation of the 'next normal'", Chapter 10 in this volume.

McDonald J., Johnston N. and Busby G., with Gallagher T. (2016), "Community engagement in Belfast: Queen's University and the Sandy Row community", in Bergan S., Gallagher T. and Harkavy I. (eds), *Higher education for democratic innovation*, Higher Education series No. 21, Strasbourg: Council of Europe, pp. 63-70.

Munck R. (2009), "Bridging the 'town and gown' divide" (with D. O'Broin) in McCrann A. (ed.), *Memories, milestones and new horizons: reflection on the regeneration of Ballymun*, Belfast: Blackstaff Press.

Munck R. (2012), "Civic engagement in a cold climate: a glocal perspective" (with McQuillan H. and Ozarowska J.) in McIlrath L., Lyons A. and Munck R. (eds), *Higher education and civic engagement: new perspectives*, New York: Palgrave, available at www4.dcu.ie/sites/default/files/community/docs/Chapter1.pdf, accessed 20 September 2020.

Ozarowska J. (2019), "The university and local civic engagement: an Irish case study", in Bergan S., Harkavy I. and Munck R. (eds) (2019), *The local mission of higher education: principles and practice*, Dublin: Glasnevin Publishing.

Taylor R. (1988), "The Queen's University of Belfast: the liberal university in a divided society", *Higher Education Review*, 20(2): 27-45.

Biographical notes

EDITORS

Sjur Bergan

Sjur Bergan is Head of the Education Department of the Council of Europe and leads the current Council of Europe projects on Competences for Democratic Culture and the European Qualifications Passport for Refugees. He has represented the Council of Europe in the Bologna Follow-Up Group and Board since 2000 and chaired three successive working groups on structural reforms in 2007-15. Sjur was a member of the editorial group for the Council's White Paper on Intercultural Dialogue and a main author of the Lisbon Recognition Convention and recommendations on the public responsibility for higher education; academic freedom and institutional autonomy; and ensuring quality education. He is series editor of the Council of Europe Higher Education Series and the author of *Qualifications: introduction to a concept*; *Not by bread alone*; and numerous book chapters and articles on education and higher education policy. Sjur was also one of the editors of the *Raabe handbook on leadership and governance in higher education* (2009-15) and one of the session co-ordinators at the Bologna Process Researchers' Conferences in 2015, 2018 and 2020. He is the recipient of the 2019 European Association for International Education Award for Vision and Leadership.

Tony Gallagher

Tony Gallagher is an elected Fellow of the Academy of Social Science and a Professor of Education at Queen's University Belfast. He has previously held a number of leadership roles at Queen's, including Head of the School of Education (2005-10), Pro Vice Chancellor (2010-15) and Faculty Dean of Research (2018-19). He is a member of the Advisory Group on Higher Education Policy of the Council of Europe's Steering Committee on Education Policy and Practice (CDPPE); a deputy board member of the European Wergeland Centre; a member of the Steering Group of the International Consortium for Higher Education, Civic Responsibility and Democracy; and a board member of the Maze Long Kesh Development Corporation. He has published extensively on the role of education in divided societies and on the civic and democratic role of higher education.

Ira Harkavy

Ira Harkavy is Associate Vice President and Founding Director of the Barbara and Edward Netter Center for Community Partnerships at the University of Pennsylvania. Harkavy teaches in the departments of history, urban studies and Africana studies and in the Graduate School of Education. He is Chair of the International Consortium for Higher Education, Civic Responsibility and Democracy as well as Chair of the Anchor Institutions Task Force. Harkavy has written and lectured widely on the history and current practice of urban university–community–school partnerships and the democratic and civic missions of higher education. His recent books include *Knowledge for social change: Bacon, Dewey, and the revolutionary transformation of research universities in the twenty-first century* (2017, co-authored with Rita A. Hodges) and *The local mission of higher education: principles and practice* (2019, co-edited with Sjur Bergan and Ronaldo Munck). Among other honours, Harkavy is the recipient of the New American Colleges and Universities' Ernest L. Boyer Award; Campus Compact's Thomas Ehrlich Faculty Award for Service Learning; the University of Pennsylvania's Alumni Award of Merit; and two honorary degrees. Harkavy received his bachelor's, master's and PhD in history from the University of Pennsylvania.

Ronaldo Munck

Ronaldo Munck is Head of Civic Engagement at Dublin City University, Director of the national Centre for Engaged Research, and visiting professor in international development at universities in Liverpool, Halifax and Buenos Aires. He has written widely on globalisation, the changing patterns of work and social movements. He is on the international editorial boards of a number of journals including *Globalizations*; *Global Social Policy*; *Global Discourse*; *Labor History*; *Global Labour Journal*; *Labour, Capital and Society*; *Latin American Perspectives*; *Kaleidoscope: Alternative Media and Social Movements*; *Review: A Journal of the Fernand Braudel Center*; and the *Canadian Journal of Development Studies*. His work in the area of higher education includes *Higher education and civic engagement: comparative perspectives* (2012) and *Higher education and community-based research: creating a global vision* (2014) for which he was lead contributing editor. Professor Munck represents the Irish national platform for civic engagement, Campus Engage, on the International Consortium for Higher Education.

Hilligje van't Land

Dr Hilligje van't Land serves the global higher education community as Secretary General of the International Association of Universities (IAU), a global NGO with UNESCO Associate Status. For the past two decades, she has fostered the key role of higher education in societal transformation. She supervises the overall programme activities of the IAU, develops the Association's strategic plans and oversees the everyday work of the secretariat. She positioned the IAU as partner in UNESCO's work on Education for Sustainable Development and in the UNESCO Futures of Education initiative, and in higher education as a key stakeholder for the UN Agenda 2030 – Transforming our world. Hilligje van't Land strongly believes in the importance of international co-operation and intercultural understanding and has developed projects to promote related higher education initiatives. She represents the IAU in various working groups and expert committees, including at the Council of Europe, where she contributed to intercultural understanding initiatives, the development of the Council of Europe Framework for Competences for Democratic Culture and the development of an international reflection on the role of higher education for society.

Hilligje van't Land holds a PhD in comparative francophone literature, speaks six languages and publishes on a number of higher education issues.

EDITORIAL ASSISTANT

Irina Geantă

Irina Geantă has been involved in higher education policy since 2010. She is a former member of the Romanian BFUG Secretariat (2010-12), contributing to policy support, including the drafting of the Bucharest Ministerial Communiqué. She has been involved as a policy expert in several national and EU higher education projects focusing on internationalisation, the social dimension and quality assurance and has recently co-authored the *Study on the impact of admission systems on higher education outcomes* commissioned by the DG-EAC. She is currently co-ordinating the internationalisation activities in a large-scale national project focused on evidence-based policy recommendations, focusing on the StudyinRomania website and related promotional efforts. She was also involved in the co-ordination of the Bologna Process Researchers' Conference in 2011, 2014, 2017 and 2020 and contributed to the subsequent Springer publications.

AUTHORS

Santiago Acosta

Santiago Acosta-Aide earned his Doctorate in Philology at the Universidad de La Laguna (Spain) with the Extraordinary Doctorate Prize and is a full professor of Spanish-American Literature at the Private Technical University of Loja – UTPL (Ecuador). He has been a professor at universities in Peru (1987-93), Russia (1993-06), Bolivia (1996-07) and Ecuador (1997 to the present). He has served in university management positions at the Pontifical Catholic University of Ecuador, Ibarra Campus; as Director of the Institutional Project and as Acting Rector at the UTPL (Ecuador), where he has been Academic Vice Rector and, since February 2020, the Rector. His current areas of teaching and research, with a number of publications, are Latin American literature, philosophical anthropology and ethics. He has lectured on his specialist areas at universities in the Russian Federation, Colombia, Spain, Lithuania and Ecuador, in addition to representing the UTPL at events by major world networks of distance education, such as the European Association of Distance Teaching Universities (EADTU) and the International Council for Open and Distance Education (ICDE). Santiago Acosta is the Executive Secretary of the Latin American and Caribbean Institute for Quality in Distance Higher Education (CALED), Director of the Fernando Rielo Chair for Philosophy and Metaphysics at UTPL and a member of the Idente School of Thought.

Nancy Cantor

Nancy Cantor is Chancellor of Rutgers University – Newark. A distinguished leader in higher education, she is recognised internationally as an advocate for leveraging diversity in all its dimensions, re-emphasising the public mission of colleges and universities, and achieving the fullest potential of universities as anchor institutions. As a social psychologist, she has focused on understanding how individuals perceive and think about their social worlds, pursue personal goals and regulate their behaviour to adapt to life's most challenging social environments. A fellow of the American Academy of Arts and Sciences and member of the National Academy of Medicine, she previously led Syracuse University and the University of Illinois at Urbana-Champaign and was provost at the University of Michigan, where she was closely involved in the defence of affirmative action in the 2003 Supreme Court cases *Grutter* and *Gratz*. She is co-editor with Earl Lewis of the book series Our Compelling Interests, published by Princeton University Press. Among her recognitions for higher education leadership are the Ernest L. Boyer Award from New American Colleges and Universities; the Anchor Institutions Task Force Community Engagement Award; the Robert Zemsky Medal for Innovation in Higher Education; the American Council on Education Reginald Wilson Diversity Leadership Award; and the 2008 Carnegie Corporation Academic Leadership Award, one of higher education's highest honours.

Elena Consolini

Elena Consolini is Head of the International Relations Strategy Support Unit at the University of Bologna. The goals of the unit are to support the implementation of the internationalisation strategy, in particular by co-ordinating activities, projects and initiatives of various university departments and structures and by encouraging co-ordination between them. This includes the development of specific international projects concerning the organisational structure and the institutional role of the university. Elena Consolini is engaged in improving the visibility of international relations and the most successful research co-operation at international level, also encouraging systematisation at the level of countries and geographical areas, and giving visibility to the relevance of policy making on global challenges.

Rob Copeland

Rob Copeland is a policy officer with the University and College Union (UCU) in the United Kingdom. His areas of responsibility include international affairs and UK higher education policy issues, such as teaching, research, academic freedom and governance.

Rob is currently the Chair of the Higher Education and Research Standing Committee for the European Trade Union Committee for Education (ETUCE) and an Observer on the Council of Europe's Steering Committee for Education Policy and Practice (CDPPE).

Ligia Deca

Ligia Deca is currently the Presidential Adviser for Education and Research within the Romanian Presidential Administration. In this capacity, she also co-ordinates the Educated Romania national project.

She graduated with a PhD in Political Sciences and Educational Policies at the University of Luxembourg and was a research fellow at the New Europe College, with a focus on the internationalisation of higher education. The author of several papers and studies in the field of educational policies, Ligia Deca also worked as an expert for the Council of Europe, the European Commission, EQAR, DAAD and other bodies. In 2014 she was a member of the Science in Education Expert Group set up by the European Commission and in 2019 she was chosen as an evaluating expert for the European Universities pilot project. Ligia Deca is also a member of the board of directors at Fulbright in Romania, since 2017.

Mirko Degli Esposti

Mirko Degli Esposti is Full Professor of Mathematical Physics at the Department of Computer Science and Engineering of the University of Bologna. He is currently Deputy Rector and Vice Rector for Digital Technologies and Dean of the Unibo Centre for the protection and promotion of health and safety, both in the workplace and protecting animal welfare in the university's educational and scientific facilities. He has been Head of the Department of Mathematics and a member of the Academic Senate.

Mirko Degli Esposti's research was initially devoted to mathematical aspects of quantum mechanics and of the theory of complex systems. Lately he has turned his attention to applications of the theory of dynamic systems, and of information theory, to life science and human science. He is visiting Professor at the Georgia Institute of Technology. He collaborates with the Sony Computer Science Laboratory in Paris on the relations between art and technology.

Peter Englot

As Senior Vice Chancellor for Public Affairs and Chief of Staff at Rutgers University – Newark, Peter Englot both serves as the university's Chief Rhetorical Officer and supports Chancellor Nancy Cantor and her leadership team in advancing the institution's mission collaboratively across divisions. A higher education professional for more than 30 years, he has deep and broad experience in organisational leadership and communications spanning from vision setting and strategic planning to marketing and crisis management. As a writer and presenter on revitalising the public mission of universities, who has co-authored numerous journal articles and book chapters, Peter Englot is known as an advocate for diversity in higher education and for universities to embrace their roles as anchor institutions by forging sustainable cross-sector partnerships in their communities. He has an MA in linguistics from Syracuse and a BA in the same discipline from Binghamton University.

Dennis Farrington

Dennis Farrington PhD has been a consultant to the Council of Europe in higher education reform since 1994, initially within the Legislative Reform Programme for Higher Education and Research, and has advised in 17 European countries, with major projects in Kosovo,[133] Ukraine, Bosnia-Herzegovina and Armenia. After nine years as a UK civil servant, including roles in ministerial private offices, he returned to higher education in 1981, working at the universities of Hull and Stirling. He joined the South East European University Foundation in 2000, and thereafter held several university positions, retiring after 12 years as President of the university board in 2020. In 2020, the third edition of *The law of higher education*, jointly authored by Dennis Farrington and David Palfreyman OBE, of New College, Oxford, will be published by Oxford University Press.

John Gardner

John Gardner is a professor of Education at the University of Stirling and is the former Senior Deputy Vice-Chancellor of the university. In 2012 he completed a four-year term as President and Vice President of the British Educational Research Association. He has been a visiting professor at the University of Oxford, Department of Education (2009-17) and is currently a visiting professor at Queen's University Belfast and Dublin City University. He was elected to fellowship of the UK Academy of Social Sciences in 2007, the British Computer Society in 2004 and the Chartered Institute of Educational Assessors in 2007. Since 2018, he has been chair of the Welsh Government's Teacher Recruitment and Retention Advisory Board.

Delia Gologan

Delia Gologan is an educational policy expert who has collaborated with the Executive Agency for Higher Education, Research, Development and Innovation Funding (UEFISCDI) and is now working in the Education and Research Department of the Romanian Presidential Administration. She is a programme and project evaluator within the National Agency for Community Programmes in the Field of Education and Vocational Training (ANPCDEFP) and external evaluator for higher education institutions and study programmes for the Quality Assurance Agency of Kosovo. She was a Councillor within the team of the Secretary of State responsible for quality assurance in education (September to December 2016) and Vice President of the National Alliance of Students Organisations in Romania (2011-13). Delia's main fields of expertise are in equity policies and policy for quality assurance of education, areas in which she has facilitated training programmes and workshops for the NGOs and institutions that she has collaborated with.

---

133. All references to Kosovo, whether to the territory, institutions or population, in this text shall be understood in full compliance with United Nations Security Council Resolution 1244 and without prejudice to the status of Kosovo.

Åse Gornitzka

Åse Gornitzka is professor at the Department of Political Science and, since 2017, Vice Rector for Research and Internationalisation at the University of Oslo. Gornitzka holds a doctoral degree in Public Administration from the University of Twente. She has studied reform and change in higher education, organisational change within universities and the interface between expertise, public administration and governance in the EU and at the national level. Gornitzka's most recent contributions deal with reputation management in public sector organisations, such as *Universities as agencies: reputation and professionalization* (Palgrave Macmillan, 2019), a book she edited together with Tom Christensen and Francisco O. Ramirez.

James T. Harris

Dr James T. Harris is the President of the University of San Diego, a Roman Catholic institution ranked among the top 100 United States universities. Over the past 27 years, he has served as the president of three universities. He has also served on multiple global, local and national boards. Most recently he served as the board chair for the Council for Advancement and Support of Education (CASE).

In 2019, Dr Harris was honoured by the Urban League of San Diego with the Diversity and Equity Award for his work in civic engagement. In June 2020, he was recognised by the *San Diego Business Journal* in its "SD 50", spotlighting the Top 50 business leaders and organisations who have made an impact during the Covid-19 pandemic.

Earlier in Dr Harris' career, the National Association for the Advancement of Colored People recognised him with a leadership award for his work defending civil rights; he was named one of the Top 50 Character-Building Presidents in America by the John Templeton Foundation and received the CASE Chief Executive Leadership Award. Dr Harris remains an active scholar and teacher.

Ellen Hazelkorn

Ellen Hazelkorn is joint Managing Partner, BH Associates education consultants. She is Professor Emerita, Technological University Dublin (Ireland) and Joint Editor, *Policy Reviews in Higher Education*.

Ellen is a member of the Quality Board for Higher Education in Iceland. She was Policy Advisor, and board member, of the Higher Education Authority of Ireland (2011-17) and Vice President, Dublin Institute of Technology (now TU Dublin) for 20 years. She has written numerous reports and/or led evaluations and reviews for governments/government agencies, universities, OECD, EU and UNESCO. She has been a member of various university and government boards. Ellen has published extensively on higher education policy and global rankings: *Research handbook on quality, performance and accountability in higher education* (2018); *The civic university: meeting the leadership and management challenges* (2016); and *Rankings and the reshaping of higher education: the battle for world-class excellence*, 2nd edn (2015). Forthcoming are *Research handbook on university rankings: history, methodology, influence and impact* (2021) and *Global governance of international higher education and global science: re-thinking multilateralism* (2022).

Ellen was awarded a BA and PhD from the University of Wisconsin, Madison, and the University of Kent, UK, respectively.

Rita A. Hodges

Rita A. Hodges is Assistant Director of the Barbara and Edward Netter Center for Community Partnerships at the University of Pennsylvania. She oversees the Center's development and alumni relations activity and helps advance the Center's regional, national and global outreach activities. Her research focuses on the democratic engagement of colleges and universities as anchor institutions. Hodges has co-authored two books: *The road half traveled: university engagement at a crossroads* (2012, with Steve Dubb); and *Knowledge for social change: Bacon, Dewey and the revolutionary transformation of research universities in the twenty-first century* (2017, with Lee Benson, Ira Harkavy, John Puckett, Matthew Hartley, Francis E. Johnston and Joann Weeks). Hodges received her bachelor's degree in psychology and master's degree in education from the University of Pennsylvania and is pursuing a doctor of education (EdD) degree in higher education management at Penn's Graduate School of Education.

Martha J. Kanter

Martha J. Kanter leads the College Promise Campaign, a national nonpartisan initiative in the United States to increase college access, affordability, quality and completion. She specialises in policy efforts to identify and apply evidence-based education interventions, financing models and behavioural incentives to raise US high school and college graduation rates. Dr Kanter also serves as a Distinguished Senior Fellow at New York University's Steinhardt Institute for Higher Education Policy. From 2009 to 2013, Dr Kanter served President Obama as the U.S. Under Secretary of Education and from 1993 to 2009, she was President of De Anza College and then Chancellor of the Foothill-De Anza Community College District in Silicon Valley, California, after serving as the state's Community College Vice Chancellor for Policy and Research.

Dorothy Kelly

Dorothy Kelly is a professor of Translation at the University of Granada (Spain), where she has also been Vice Rector for Internationalization since 2008. She obtained her BA in Translating and Interpreting at Heriot-Watt University, Edinburgh (Scotland) with First Class Honours, and her doctoral degree from the University of Granada. Her main research interests are translator training, directionality in translation and intercultural competence, all areas in which she has published extensively.

She has combined this research activity over the years with intense international involvement, co-ordinating international mobility and joint degree programmes, as well as studies into the impact of mobility on intercultural competence and the learning environment. She is founding editor – and until January 2020 was co-editor with María González Davies – of Routledge's *Interpreter and Translator Trainer*, the only indexed journal devoted specifically to translator education; she has also been editor of the Translation Practices Explained series at St Jerome Publishing. She was a member of the European Master's in Translation Expert Group appointed by the Directorate General for Translation at the European Commission between 2006 and 2009.

In the field of the internationalisation of higher education, she was Chair of the Executive Board of the Coimbra Group of Universities from 2010 to 2017 and was a member of Spain's national Bologna Experts Team from 2010 to 2013. She has participated intensely in Spanish, European and international advisory boards and events in the field of higher education and in particular its internationalisation. She was a member of the board of the Committee for Internationalization and Development Cooperation at the Spanish Rectors' Conference between 2008 and 2012, and again between 2014 and 2020; from 2018 to 2020 she was executive secretary of the board and is currently a special adviser. She is a member of the Advisory Group on Higher Education to the Steering Committee for Education Policy and Practice (CDPPE) of the Council of Europe.

Currently, she is the co-ordinator of Arqus, one of the first 17 European University Alliances to be approved by the European Commission and composed of the universities of Bergen, Graz, Leipzig, Lyon, Padova and Vilnius, along with Granada.

Maria Kelo

Maria Kelo has been the Director of ENQA, the European Association for Quality Assurance in Higher Education, since 2011. In this capacity, she is in charge of the strategic management of the Association. She represents ENQA in European higher education policy-making processes and internationally. Maria was a member of the executive board of the European Quality Assurance Register 2012-20.

Prior to joining ENQA in 2011, Maria worked for nine years in the field of international higher education, including as a senior officer at the Academic Cooperation Association (2003-09), programme manager at the European University Association (2010) and an independent consultant (2010-11). During these years Maria carried out a number of projects and studies on international higher education in the fields of transnational education, student mobility, student services, promotion of European higher education and human resource management in higher education.

Maria is a graduate of University College London (2000) and the London School of Economics (2002).

Daire Keogh

Daire Keogh is President of Dublin City University, Ireland. He has published widely on the history of popular politics, religion and education in Ireland. He was a founder member of the European Quality Assurance Register (EQAR) and is a Fellow of the University Design Institute at Arizona State University.

Giorgio Marinoni

Giorgio Marinoni has been Manager of Higher Education and Internationalization at the International Association of Universities (IAU), since February 2015. He oversees Internationalisation as one of the four strategic priorities of the association.

Among his responsibilities at IAU are research projects, advisory services and external representation of the Association as concerns internationalisation. He is the co-ordinator of the ISAS (2.0) programme of advisory services for advancing internationalisation and the co-ordinator of the Network of International Education Associations, a global network of non-profit, non-government associations whose main stated purpose is to advance international higher education.

Giorgio Marinoni has recently published the report of the 5th Global Survey on Internationalization of Higher Education and of the 1st Global Survey on the impact of Covid-19 on Higher Education.

Before his current position at IAU, Giorgio Marinoni worked for UNICA, the Network of Universities from the Capitals of Europe, in the field of internationalisation and higher education policy and reform at the European level and beyond. He has been an active member of the Erasmus Student Network (ESN) at local, national and international level, and served as its President in 2007-08.

Liviu Matei

Liviu Matei is the Provost of the Central European University (CEU) and a Professor of Higher Education Policy at CEU's School of Public Policy. He directs the Yehuda Elkana Centre for Higher Education. He has taught at universities in Europe and the US, consulted extensively in the area of higher education policy and conducted applied policy research projects for the World Bank, UNESCO, OSCE, the Council of Europe, European Commission and other international intergovernmental and non-governmental organisations, national authorities and universities from Europe, Asia and the US.

David Maurrasse

Dr David Maurrasse is the founder and President of Marga Incorporated, which has been providing strategic advice and research to philanthropic initiatives and community partnerships since 2000. Marga co-ordinates the work of the Anchor Institutions Task Force (AITF), and Dr Maurrasse serves as AITF's Director.

Since 2000, Dr Maurrasse has been affiliated with Columbia University, where he currently serves as adjunct associate professor and adjunct research scholar. From 1995 to 2000 Dr Maurrasse was an assistant professor at Yale University, and from 1998 to 2000 a senior program advisor at the Rockefeller Foundation.

Dr Maurrasse's books include: *Philanthropy and society* (2020), *Strategic public private partnerships: innovation and development* (2013), *Listening to Harlem* (2006), *A future for everyone: innovative social responsibility and community partnerships* (2004), and *Beyond the campus: how colleges and universities form partnerships with their communities* (2001). *Strategic community partnerships, philanthropy, and nongovernmental organizations* (2021) is his latest book project, now underway.

Brian Murphy

Brian Murphy is the President Emeritus of De Anza College in Cupertino, California. He served as president from 2004 to 2018 and is now Senior Scholar at the Vasconcellos Institute for Democracy in Action at De Anza. He is also an Associate at the Center for Studies in Higher Education at the University of California, Berkeley. Prior to his appointment at De Anza, Murphy was the Executive Director of the San Francisco Urban Institute at San Francisco State University (SFSU), where he also held a tenured faculty position in Political Science. He has taught political theory, urban and American politics at SFSU, Santa Clara University and the University of California, Santa Cruz.

Murphy served as the Chief Consultant for the California State Legislature's review of the state Master Plan for Higher Education in the mid-1980s and was the principal negotiator of the Legislature's community college reform legislation in 1987. He has served on multiple non-profit and education boards and was a mayoral appointee to the Human Services Commission in San Francisco. He holds a BA from Williams College and master's and doctoral degrees from the University of California, Berkeley, all in Political Science.

Koji Nakamura

Koji Nakamura is Director of the Office for Global Initiatives, and in charge of international co-operation and campus internationalisation, at Tokai University, Japan. He holds a PhD in International Studies from Kwansei Gakuin University, Japan and an MA in Economics from Kyoto Sangyo University, Japan. In 2009-16, he worked at Hawaii Tokai International College as Executive Manager. His research areas include economic policy, university–industry–government co-operation, anchor institution strategy for regional economic development and international education.

Robert Napier

Robert Napier is a passionate human rights and student activist from Malta and is the President of the European Students' Union (ESU) for the mandate 2019-20. Before moving to Brussels, he obtained his Bachelor of Laws (Hons) and Master of Advocacy degrees from the University of Malta. He has also been elected as a member of the Advisory Council on Youth of the Council of Europe, where he follows the education, artificial intelligence and space for civil society portfolios, while also serving as a member of the programming committee of the European Youth Foundation. Within his time in ESU, he has been mostly responsible for the Social Dimension portfolio, and served as a co-chair of the Advisory Group on Social Dimension of the Bologna Follow-Up Group in 2018-20.

Barnabas Nawangwe

Professor Barnabas Nawangwe has been the Vice Chancellor of Makerere University, one of the oldest and premier universities in Africa, since August 2017. Prior to that, he was Deputy Vice Chancellor, Dean and Principal of the College of Engineering, and Head of the Department of Architecture, all at Makerere University. Prof. Nawangwe is a member of several international professional organisations and has overseen the academic and administrative transformation of Makerere University, including its transformation from a faculty-based institution to a collegiate university. His research interests are in the areas of vernacular architecture and sustainable human settlements. Prof. Nawangwe has published more than 50 journal articles and is a co-author of the *Encyclopedia of vernacular architecture of the world* and several other books on architecture. He has also co-authored several publications on higher education in Africa.

Paul C. Pribbenow

Paul C. Pribbenow, PhD, the 10th President of Augsburg University, a private liberal arts university located in Minneapolis, Minnesota (USA), is recognised as one of the country's most engaging commentators and teachers on ethics, philanthropy and American public life. Since joining Augsburg in 2006, Pribbenow has enhanced the university's role as an active community partner in its urban setting. By identifying and embracing initiatives that mutually benefit Augsburg and its neighbours, the university has achieved national recognition for its excellence in service learning and experiential education, including the 2010 Presidential Award for Community Service, the highest honour possible for service work.

Pribbenow serves on the national boards of the Coalition for Urban and Metropolitan Universities (CUMU) and the Council of Independent Colleges (CIC). He is also active in the Anchor Institutions Task Force. Pribbenow holds a BA degree from Luther College (Iowa), and a master's degree and doctorate in social ethics from the University of Chicago.

Jamil Salmi

Jamil Salmi is a global tertiary education expert providing policy advice to governments, universities, professional associations, multilateral development banks and bilateral co-operation agencies. Until January 2012, he was the World Bank's tertiary education co-ordinator. In the past 25 years, Dr Salmi has provided advice on tertiary education development, financing reforms and strategic planning to governments and university leaders in more than 100 countries.

Dr Salmi is Emeritus Professor of Higher Education Policy at Diego Portales University in Chile and Research Fellow at Boston College's Center for Higher Education. He is also a member of the International Quality Assurance Advisory Group, Emeritus Advisor on the President's Council at Olin College of Engineering, and chair of the board of the Chilean EdTech start-up u-planner.

Dr Salmi's 2009 book addressed *The challenge of establishing world-class universities*. His 2011 book, co-edited with Professor Phil Altbach, was entitled *The road to academic excellence: the making of world-class research universities*. His latest book, *Tertiary education and the sustainable development goals*, was published in August 2017.

He holds a master's degree in Public and International Affairs from the University of Pittsburgh and a PhD in development studies from the University of Sussex.

Robert Santa

Currently a PhD candidate at the National University of Political Studies and Public Administration of Bucharest, a graduate of University College London's Institute of Education and Deusto University in Bilbao, Robert Santa has been active in the student movement at local, national and European level. He has previously been employed in the private sector on graduate employability issues and has conducted research work on a variety of education-related topics. He is currently an adviser within the Education and Research Department of the Romanian Presidency.

Nicholas R. Santilli

Nicholas R. Santilli, PhD, serves as Senior Director for Learning Strategy for the Society for College and University Planning (SCUP). In this role, he drives the development of learning content for individual practitioners and institutions looking to build the professional competencies of their faculty and staff. He also leads the SCUP Planning Institute, the premier professional development programme for integrated planning in higher education. Prior to joining the SCUP staff, Dr Santilli co-chaired two SCUP annual conferences; served on the SCUP board of directors for three years, two of which as chair, and served as a Planning Institute facilitator.

Dr Santilli is also Professor Emeritus of Psychology at John Carroll University and held several positions in academic administration, including Interim Provost and Academic Vice President and Associate Provost for Accreditation, Planning and Institutional Effectiveness. He was also Vice President for Academic and Student Affairs at Notre Dame College of Ohio.

In 2003, Dr Santilli completed the prestigious American Council on Education Fellowship. The ACE Fellowship is the signature higher education leadership programme. He spent a year working with senior administrators on topics that included strategic planning and assessment, government relations, admissions, and financial aid and advancement. He was recently appointed to the board of directors for the ACE Fellows program of the American Council on Education.

Alessandra Scagliarini

Alessandra Scagliarini is full professor of Infectious Diseases and currently Vice Rector for International Relations at the University of Bologna. She is an international expert in veterinary virology with a particular interest in epitheliotropic viruses infecting animals and humans, antivirals and innovative diagnostic tools. In these areas, Alessandra Scagliarini has carried out research projects at international, European and national level. She has been visiting scholar at Moredun Research Institute, Edinburgh; the Department of Microbiology, Otago University, New Zealand; Rega-Instituut, Virologie en Chemoterapie Unit, Leuven; and the Department of Paraclinical Sciences University of Pretoria, South Africa. She trained in Epidemiology at Imperial College, London and is a member of the board of the International Society of Infectious Diseases.

Carol Geary Schneider

Carol Geary Schneider is the former President of the Association of American Colleges and Universities (AAC&U), which she led from 1998 to 2016. She is now a consultant with the Lumina Foundation on equity-minded approaches to quality learning and on ways to embed quality learning outcomes across all students' college studies. While at AAC&U, she designed and led the organisation's long-term initiative on Liberal Education and America's Promise (LEAP) and served as a member of the National Task Force on Civic Learning and Democratic Engagement. She continues to write and speak about liberal learning as a necessity in a globally connected democracy.

Stig Arne Skjerven

Stig Arne Skjerven is Director of Foreign Education in NOKUT (the Norwegian Agency for Quality Assurance in Education). He is thus Head of the Norwegian ENIC-NARIC office, which is in charge of the recognition of foreign qualifications and information provision in accordance with the Lisbon Recognition Convention. He has been strongly involved in establishing and developing recognition schemes in Norway. Together with his team in NOKUT, he has been crucial in developing the methodology behind the European Qualifications Passport for Refugees, which has been established by both the Council of Europe and UNESCO as the Global Qualifications Passport for Refugees and Vulnerable Migrants.

Skjerven is in his second term as President of the ENIC Network. He has also held elected office in the European Association for International Education. He has been a member of various international working groups, most notably the Drafting Committee for the UNESCO Global Convention for Recognition of Higher Education Qualifications. Previously, Skjerven has held positions as Director of Academic Affairs at a Norwegian higher education institution and Project Manager in Quality Assurance of Higher Education, and has worked as a Political Advisor in the field of International Higher Education. He has published extensively on topics related to mobility and recognition in publications like *University World News*.

Svein Stølen

Svein Stølen is professor at the Department of Chemistry and, since 2017, Rector, of the University of Oslo. Stølen's scientific work focuses on functional materials for renewable energy. Stølen has held numerous leadership positions at different levels at the University of Oslo, is vice-chair of the board of The Guild of European Research-Intensive Universities, and has led the development of the European University initiative, Circle U.

Henry Louis Taylor, Jr

Henry Louis Taylor, Jr, PhD, is a full professor in the Department of Urban and Regional Planning, founding director of the Center for Urban Studies and associate director of the UB Community Health Equity Research Institute at the University at Buffalo. He is an urban historian and has in particular worked on urban planning that focuses on city-building, under-developed neighbourhoods, health and the built environment, and Black social movements. Taylor has written and/or edited five books, along with many articles and technical reports. He has been cited in numerous national publications, including the *New York Times*, the *Washington Post*, *CNN*, *The Atlantic*, the *Huffington Post* and *Time Magazine*. Taylor is the recipient of numerous awards, including the 2018 Marilyn J. Gittell Activist Scholar Award by the Urban Affairs Association. He is currently completing a book, *From Harlem to Havana: the Nehanda Isoke Abiodun Story* (SUNY Press).

Francesco Ubertini

Francesco Ubertini is currently the Rector of the University of Bologna (2015-21). He is full professor of Mechanics of Solids and Structures and a member of the Academy of Sciences of Bologna Institute. He is member of the Board of Rectors of the UnaEuropa–European University Alliance and a member of the board of the European University Association. Moreover, he chairs several foundations, and is a member of the board of the Confucius Institute at the University of Bologna, of the Italian University Rectors' Conference and of the Magna Charta Universitatum Observatory. In 2016, he was awarded the Thomas Hart Benton Mural Medallion by the President of Indiana University, celebrating the 50th anniversary of the partnership between Indiana University and the University of Bologna. In 2018-19 he received many awards, including Commendatore, Order of Merit, Italian Republic; Grand Officer, Ordem de Rio Branco, Brazil; and Cavaliere di Gran Croce, Ordine di Sant'Agata, Republic of San Marino.

Hans de Wit

Hans de Wit is Director of the Center for International Higher Education at Boston College and professor of the practice at the same institution. He is a leading expert on the internationalisation of higher education and has published many books, chapters and articles on the topic. He has advised the European Commission and Parliament, the OECD, the World Bank, national governments and higher education institutions on internationalisation policies. He is Founding Editor of the *Journal of Studies in International Education*, Consulting Editor of *Policy Reviews in Higher Education*, and Associate Editor of *International Higher Education*. Hans de Wit writes a regular blog for *University World News*. He is Senior Fellow of the International Association of Universities, and President of the Board of Directors of World Education Services.

Kiyoshi Yamada

Professor Kiyoshi Yamada currently serves as Chancellor of Tokai University, Japan, and Chair of the Board of the Hawaii Tokai International College, USA, a US-accredited junior college. He is an experienced educator as well as a highly accomplished global school administrator. He graduated from the School of Law, Waseda University. He received an honorary PhD in Business Administration from King Mongkut's Institute of Technology Ladkrabang (Thailand) in 2010 and the title of Professor Emeritus from Moscow State University (Russia) in 2011. His research areas include economic and administrative law, intellectual property law, policy study on university–industry collaborations and international education.

Sales agents for publications of the Council of Europe
Agents de vente des publications du Conseil de l'Europe

BELGIUM/BELGIQUE
La Librairie Européenne -
The European Bookshop
Rue de l'Orme, 1
BE-1040 BRUXELLES
Tel.: + 32 (0)2 231 04 35
Fax: + 32 (0)2 735 08 60
E-mail: info@libeurop.eu
http://www.libeurop.be

Jean De Lannoy/DL Services
c/o Michot Warehouses
Bergense steenweg 77
Chaussée de Mons
BE-1600 SINT PIETERS LEEUW
Fax: + 32 (0)2 706 52 27
E-mail: jean.de.lannoy@dl-servi.com
http://www.jean-de-lannoy.be

CANADA
Renouf Publishing Co. Ltd.
22-1010 Polytek Street
CDN-OTTAWA, ONT K1J 9J1
Tel.: + 1 613 745 2665
Fax: + 1 613 745 7660
Toll-Free Tel.: (866) 767-6766
E-mail: order.dept@renoufbooks.com
http://www.renoufbooks.com

CROATIA/CROATIE
Robert's Plus d.o.o.
Marasoviçeva 67
HR-21000 SPLIT
Tel.: + 385 21 315 800, 801, 802, 803
Fax: + 385 21 315 804
E-mail: robertsplus@robertsplus.hr

**CZECH REPUBLIC/
RÉPUBLIQUE TCHÈQUE**
Suweco CZ, s.r.o.
Klecakova 347
CZ-180 21 PRAHA 9
Tel.: + 420 2 424 59 204
Fax: + 420 2 848 21 646
E-mail: import@suweco.cz
http://www.suweco.cz

DENMARK/DANEMARK
GAD
Vimmelskaftet 32
DK-1161 KØBENHAVN K
Tel.: + 45 77 66 60 00
Fax: + 45 77 66 60 01
E-mail: reception@gad.dk
http://www.gad.dk

FINLAND/FINLANDE
Akateeminen Kirjakauppa
PO Box 128
Keskuskatu 1
FI-00100 HELSINKI
Tel.: + 358 (0)9 121 4430
Fax: + 358 (0)9 121 4242
E-mail: akatilaus@akateeminen.com
http://www.akateeminen.com

FRANCE
Please contact directly /
Merci de contacter directement
Council of Europe Publishing
Éditions du Conseil de l'Europe
F-67075 STRASBOURG Cedex
Tel.: + 33 (0)3 88 41 25 81
Fax: + 33 (0)3 88 41 39 10
E-mail: publishing@coe.int
http://book.coe.int

Librairie Kléber
1, rue des Francs-Bourgeois
F-67000 STRASBOURG
Tel.: + 33 (0)3 88 15 78 88
Fax: + 33 (0)3 88 15 78 80
E-mail: librairie-kleber@coe.int
http://www.librairie-kleber.com

NORWAY/NORVÈGE
Akademika
Postboks 84 Blindern
NO-0314 OSLO
Tel.: + 47 2 218 8100
Fax: + 47 2 218 8103
E-mail: support@akademika.no
http://www.akademika.no

POLAND/POLOGNE
Ars Polona JSC
25 Obroncow Street
PL-03-933 WARSZAWA
Tel.: + 48 (0)22 509 86 00
Fax: + 48 (0)22 509 86 10
E-mail: arspolona@arspolona.com.pl
http://www.arspolona.com.pl

PORTUGAL
Marka Lda
Rua dos Correeiros 61-3
PT-1100-162 LISBOA
Tel: 351 21 3224040
Fax: 351 21 3224044
E mail: apoio.clientes@marka.pt
www.marka.pt

**RUSSIAN FEDERATION/
FÉDÉRATION DE RUSSIE**
Ves Mir
17b, Butlerova ul. - Office 338
RU-117342 MOSCOW
Tel.: + 7 495 739 0971
Fax: + 7 495 739 0971
E-mail: orders@vesmirbooks.ru
http://www.vesmirbooks.ru

SWITZERLAND/SUISSE
Planetis Sàrl
16, chemin des Pins
CH-1273 ARZIER
Tel.: + 41 22 366 51 77
Fax: + 41 22 366 51 78
E-mail: info@planetis.ch

TAIWAN
Tycoon Information Inc.
5th Floor, No. 500, Chang-Chun Road
Taipei, Taiwan
Tel.: 886-2-8712 8886
Fax: 886-2-8712 4747, 8712 4777
E-mail: info@tycoon-info.com.tw
orders@tycoon-info.com.tw

UNITED KINGDOM/ROYAUME-UNI
The Stationery Office Ltd
PO Box 29
GB-NORWICH NR3 1GN
Tel.: + 44 (0)870 600 5522
Fax: + 44 (0)870 600 5533
E-mail: book.enquiries@tso.co.uk
http://www.tsoshop.co.uk

**UNITED STATES and CANADA/
ÉTATS-UNIS et CANADA**
Manhattan Publishing Co
670 White Plains Road
USA-10583 SCARSDALE, NY
Tel: + 1 914 472 4650
Fax: + 1 914 472 4316
E-mail: coe@manhattanpublishing.com
http://www.manhattanpublishing.com

Council of Europe Publishing/Éditions du Conseil de l'Europe
F-67075 STRASBOURG Cedex
Tel.: + 33 (0)3 88 41 25 81 – Fax: + 33 (0)3 88 41 39 10 – E-mail: publishing@coe.int – Website: http://book.coe.int